Forensics in America

Forensics in America

A History

Michael D. Bartanen and Robert S. Littlefield

ROWMAN & LITTLEFIELD
Lanham • Boulder • New York • Toronto • Plymouth, UK

Published by Rowman & Littlefield
4501 Forbes Boulevard, Suite 200, Lanham, Maryland 20706
www.rowman.com

10 Thornbury Road, Plymouth PL6 7PP, United Kingdom

British Library Cataloguing in Publication Information Available

Library of Congress Cataloging-in-Publication Data
Bartanen, Michael D.
  Forensics in America : a history / Michael D. Bartanen and Robert S. Littlefield.
    pages cm
  Includes index.
  ISBN 978-1-4422-2620-3 (cloth : alk. paper) — ISBN 978-1-4422-2621-0 (electronic)
  1. Forensics (Public speaking) 2. Debates and debating—United States. I. Littlefield,
Robert, 1952– II. Title.
  PN4181.B338 2014
  808.5'1—dc38   2013029784

Printed in the United States of America

Contents

Tables

Preface

A century is a very long time and a very short time. The twentieth century witnessed an incredible array of political, social, economic, scientific, and technological changes transforming an American nation from that of a largely rural and agrarian-based economic entity into an urbanized, highly developed military and economic power. There was so much change that it can be difficult to attend to those innovations whose impact, while significant, paled with the vast tides of history. The creation, nurturance, and maturity of competitive speech and debate, commonly labeled forensics, is one such innovation whose importance is worthy of examination.

A major intellectual paradigm of the century is general systems theory. Systems theory invites us to understand the whole by looking at the interrelationship of its parts. A change in one subsystem affects the whole, in ways not always visible but nevertheless significant. The reverse is also true. Systems evolve through reacting to internal and external forces. They exist within a complicated environment. They need inputs to function and in turn produce throughputs and outputs influencing other systems. We easily understand our natural world by applying general systems theory. We understand ecosystems and why even the existence of microscopic organisms can affect the entire planet. We continually react to changes in our families and understand that when something happens to one, it will affect us all. We instinctively react to human triumph and tragedy, whether it is landing astronauts on the moon or watching the horror of terrorist-caused violence.

This book addresses higher and secondary education as a system and describes an important, if not always well-understood, subsystem: competitive forensics. While the antecedents of argumentation and rhetoric are ancient, their nature in the twentieth century was far different from how those elegant models were used in Athens, Rome, or Renaissance Europe. Students, before there was any particular theory to guide them, discovered that infusing competition with rhetorical principles could yield a product that was far more than just the sum of the two parts: a practical preparation for daily life, a chance to interact with interesting and like-minded people, and an essential tool in addressing complex problems in an increasingly complicated and difficult world.

We stress that forensics, as practiced from its modest roots in the 1880s to its global presence at the end of the twentieth century and beyond, is epistemic. Each person who chooses to engage in any of its varied competitive forms uniquely understands its value. Generations of forensics alumni have testified to the life-changing qualities of forensics competition. It would almost obscure the point to list the substantial number of prominent figures in all walks of life who include forensics participation as a part of what contributed to their vocation and success. The enduring legacy of forensics lies in both the personal benefits participation has provided to millions of students, one by one, and the role the activity played in helping to shape the educational philosophy and practices of high schools and colleges during the century.

We begin, in chapter 1, with an introduction laying out the importance of historical-critical research as a way to understand the study of American forensics. Guided by the assumptions that forensics is epistemic and rhetorical, we outline five themes: the need to understand the history of American forensics, the relationship between collegiate and high school forensics, the identification of forensics as a promise and consequence of American education, the resiliency and enduring nature of forensics, and the relationship between forensics and the communication discipline. Within each of these themes, the inherent tensions are revealed in order to explain how and why forensics evolved the way it did.

The book is then divided into three major parts. Part I provides the historical context of forensics practice by examining it in greater detail in three chapters. Chapter 2 details forensics in the precompetitive era, forces that shaped American life and education in the early twentieth century, characteristics of the public oratory era, and the nature of forensics practice as identified through the emergence of forensics models and the consolidation of forensics practices. In chapter 3, the technical era is revealed as a more complex time when the impact of science, technology, and governmental intervention changed the nature of higher education. The uneasy relationship between practicality and intellectualism altered forensics practices in several ways. The role of the honorary organizations and the development of organizational structures within the forensics community provide the focus for chapter 4. The importance of the social and fraternal organizations in organizing forensics and influencing forensics scholarship cannot be overstated.

Three underlying tensions within the forensics community are revealed through the chapters that comprise part II of our book. These tensions stemmed from how much competition should influence forensics, where forensics should be placed within academic units, and whether debate as it was evolving was the best educational preparation for civic engagement. Chapter 5 examines how tensions associated with competition shaped the evolution of forensics through an investigation of competitive targets identified by anti-competition forces within the growing field. In chapter 6, we first trace the foundation of the speech discipline and the influence of student interest on developing curricula supporting forensics practice. Then we provide an explanation of how the controversy over debate versus discussion served to weaken the place of competitive forensics within the academic community. Chapter 7 shifts to the tensions between the high school and collegiate communities. The emergence of a large high school forensics community and the challenges it faced, which were similar to, yet uniquely different from, those of the collegiate community, frame a century of growth.

Part III of this book takes a look at sociocultural dimensions of forensics, particularly why forensics appealed to its participants and how the dominant paradigm, established by and for white men, shaped the development of forensics among historically black colleges/universities and mounted significant challenges for women seeking to compete as equals in forensics activities. Chapter 8 provides rationale explaining why forensics educators overemphasized forensics for its intellectual benefits instead of for the enjoyment it provided to those who participated in its various forms. In chapters 9 and 10, we reveal how the forensics community dealt with the "Other" through an examination of the African American experience and that of women through the public oratory and technical eras.

We conclude our work in chapter 11 with reflections on the evolution of forensics during the twentieth century. Using the social constructivist paradigm, we provide a broad analysis illustrating how the forensics community established its structures, practices, and communication, mixing knowledge and social interaction in order to sustain itself. We speculate that forensics may be entering a postmodern era and conclude with a hypothesis about why forensics will continue to evolve and thrive in the twenty-first century.

As forensics evolved, not every choice was sound. The unmistakably clear role of forensics as an educational tool in the first half of the century became less well understood and agreed upon after World War II. There has always been controversy regarding the costs and benefits of competition, or whether one rhetorical canon should be emphasized over another, and whether the activity eventually morphed into the modern version of sophistry: an emphasis on form rather than content. But to confront these issues is to peek behind the curtain into the great issues of the century confronting American society and its educational institutions. That forensics never found a consensus about its role and practices is no different from any other aspect of education about which similar doubts are consistently raised. It is from an understanding of how systems evolve that we gain insight into how they will work in the future.

Acknowledgments

We acknowledge the assistance of the many organizations, individuals, archives, and libraries enabling this project to be completed:

The American Forensic Association for providing us with a Wayne Brockriede Research Award to conduct archival research supporting this project.

Butler University staff in Indianapolis, Indiana, for providing access to the Delta Sigma Rho–Tau Kappa Alpha Archives and the university archives.

James M. Copeland, immediate past executive director of the National Forensic League (NFL) in Ripon, Wisconsin, for his institutional memory and for granting the researchers access to the NFL Archives.

Harvard University staff in Cambridge, Massachusetts, for access to the university archives and Widener Library.

LeMoyne-Owen College staff in Memphis, Tennessee, for access to the university archives.

Allan Louden, director emeritus and historian for the Wake Forest Debate Team in Winston-Salem, North Carolina, for his insight, notes, and access to materials gathered from the Robert W. Woodruff Library Archives/Special Collection, Atlanta University Center, Atlanta, Georgia.

North Dakota State University administrators for providing funding to support travel and release time to conduct archival research.

Ripon College library staff in Wisconsin for access to the Pi Kappa Delta Archives.

Donus D. Roberts, past president of the NFL.

The University of Iowa Libraries staff in Iowa City for access to the special collections and university archives.

Robert O. Weiss, professor emeritus, DePauw University, Greencastle, Indiana.
The University of Texas Libraries and the Center for American History staff at the University of Texas, Austin, for access to the E. D. Shurter papers.
The University of Utah Archives staff in Salt Lake City for access to the American Forensic Association Records and Malcolm O. Sillars Collection.

We would also like to thank Kris, Peter, Julie, and Brendan Bartanen; Larry S. and Marilyn Richardson; David Frank; Kathy Littlefield; Brady Littlefield, Lindsay Littlefield and Thomas Allen; and Timothy L. and Deanna D. Sellnow.
Finally, to all of our forensics colleagues not named here who inspired and supported our efforts to complete this book, we extend our sincere appreciation.

1

❖ ❖

An Introduction to the Study of American Forensics in the Twentieth Century

Evolving from literary societies, political spectacles, and town meetings, forensics education in the United States during the twentieth century reflects the promise and turmoil of the so-called American century. While debating unions existed for centuries in Great Britain and elsewhere, the fusion of argumentation with competition is an American innovation. For better or worse, forensics has been a major and sometimes overriding influence on the study of argumentation and communication in the twentieth century.

The demand for forensics training and competitive opportunities inspired the creation of independent speech departments and later was a factor in the establishment of the National Association of Teachers of Speech, which remains (under its current title, the National Communication Association) the major professional organization for communication professionals. Growing interest in competitive debate created a demand for new argumentation theories grounded in the social sciences, with a substantial influence on public policy discussions in the United States. American society perceived participation in competitive speech and debate as appropriate and necessary training for political leaders, and now even candidates for minor political offices are expected to master basic debate and speaking skills.

In recent years, interest in competitive speech and debate has emerged in nations on every continent. Competitive forensics truly has become global, with speech and debate tournaments regularly held in Asia, Europe, Australia, and North America. The formats used for competitive activities vary across the globe, but American practices dominate competitive speech and debate activities no matter where they are conducted. Tournaments, multiple rounds of events, decision rules, and even such arcane notions as power matching are just a few of the practices found virtually everywhere. Given the ongoing influence of American practices, an examination of the process by which competitive speech and debate evolved in the United States is appropriate.

Such analysis, while intrinsically valuable as part of a comprehensive understanding of the history of higher education in the United States, is also significant in providing a context for understanding the role forensics may play elsewhere in the twenty-first century. This opening chapter introduces the history of twentieth-century American forensics. We place our study in the context of historical studies generally and as a historical examination of the communication discipline particularly. We also identify the themes and methodological assumptions guiding our examination of this important educational experiment.

Historically, the use of the term "forensic" or "forensics" to describe competitive speech and debate activities stems from Aristotle's classification of speech types: deliberative, epideictic, and forensic. According to Aristotle, forensic or legal oratory provoked a judgment from a third party to determine the superior position. In other words, the presentation of arguments or disputations—for and against a particular position—resulted in a winner being declared by a third-party judge or audience. Ancient Greek sophists used disputations to teach forensic oratory, a practice that continued in universities across Western Europe well into the nineteenth century. In the early American colonial period, colleges and universities viewed the mastery of argumentation through debates and disputations as a hallmark of a sound education (Potter, 1944).

When secondary schools and colleges began interscholastic and interstate debating, the format called for two teams to present their arguments for the benefit of a third party—judges or an audience—to decide the winner of the debate. As debate grew in popularity, organizations emerged to recognize the achievements of debaters and to provide leadership in the organization of additional opportunities for competition. Based on a wide sample of documents drawn from Nichols (1936a, 1936b, 1937), use of the term "forensic" as it relates to competitive speech and debate activities emerged at about the same time as the national forensic honor societies (e.g., Delta Sigma Rho, Tau Kappa Alpha, Pi Kappa Delta, and later Phi Rho Pi were described as national forensic honor societies or, as they were more commonly known, forensic honoraries). By association, forensics activities or forensics became the competitive activities of these organizations.

We use the term "forensics" to refer to competition in debate and various public speaking and oral interpretation contests. As our findings reveal, the types of debate and forensic speaking events encompassed a wide variety of activities and competitive rules. Unlike athletic events such as basketball, whose structure and rules remain relatively static, debate and forensic speaking contest structures and rules are extremely fluid. While the general nature of a debate or an oration is the same today as in the earliest contests, the specifics of these events have changed dramatically over the years. Thus, the use of "forensics" or "forensic speaking" carries certain risks when discussing the wide variety of speech and debate formats and contests. In fact, the elasticity of the competitive forms provides one important clue to the vitality of an educational form that has survived more than its share of critics and challenges over the years.

The primary claim that we offer in this text is that forensics, as practiced in the United States, remains an uneasy fusion of contradictory premises. Forensics fuses the need to prepare students to participate in democratic governance with the conflict created by a student's need to express personal and competitive impulses. There is a tension between free expression inherent in the creation of arguments and in the choice of style and the necessity that those chosen arguments and styles be grounded in the expectations of a real-world audience.

Forensics represents a push and pull between an activity simultaneously considered to be both a public and a private good. Intercollegiate and interscholastic forensics began the twentieth century as a public spectacle, drawing crowds that often dwarfed those attending sports contests. It ended the century as an activity confined to closed classrooms, where audiences, if present at all, most likely consisted of a small group of insiders well versed in the rules and norms of an increasingly closed system. Yet forensics endures as an educational force inspiring student passion and public support regardless of general understanding or appreciation of the nuances of its practice. Forensics represents the best and the worst of secondary and higher education in the twentieth century. The next section explains the methodological choice of historical-critical research for analyzing the events and development of this activity.

THE IMPORTANCE OF HISTORICAL-CRITICAL RESEARCH IN FORENSICS

Public address has a long and established historical-critical research tradition in the study of communication in America. Historical-critical research focuses primarily on reporting the nature and chronology of events and analyzes their significance or meaning. Dovre (1965), borrowing from J. Jeffrey Auer, identified the nature of historical research as differing from critical research. Auer (1959) described the historical method as "the study of a period, person, or phenomena in human development in order to record discovered facts in an accurate, coherent, and critical narrative that posits causations and probabilities" (p. 28). The study of public address flourished in the mid-twentieth century, notably as the study of American and British public address. However, the primary emphasis of public address studies has been on the influence of single individuals and social movements rather than on broader and less directed areas such as competitive forensics.

There is an extremely rich vein of public address studies grouped under the general heading of studies of public argument. These studies of public argument often examine controversies (e.g., abortion rights, slavery, and nuclear policies) and apply a wide range of tools to critically analyzing actors, events, and impacts. These critical studies applying argumentation-related constructs to understanding the social and political effects of discourse and justifying the significance of argumentation as a means of analysis are invaluable.

Oliver (1965) identified a rationale for the historical study of public speaking: First, "what matters principally in history is what relates to the minds, the emotions, and the behavior of people" (p. xv). Included within this view was the "Great Man" theory, a major influence in early public address studies, suggesting that historical events were primarily shaped by the actions of individuals who, for all practical purposes, altered historical events through the force of their personality, actions, and, in this context, rhetoric. Second, Oliver (1965) observed that "what people do or what they reject doing is ultimately decided or at least declared by those who speak for and to the people" (p. xv). Here, Oliver justified the study of public discourse through its ability to influence the cultural values important to society, particularly political and social changes. Unfortunately, as the emphasis on public address focused on individuals and discrete moments of rhetorical influence, a significant area of study was neglected: the study of the history of competitive forensics in the United States and its relationship to the general study of argumentation and communication, as well its unique status as a tool for teaching students necessary skills for being active participants in democratic societies.

Despite a tradition dating back to at least 1870, little historical research has materialized focusing on modern American forensics, particularly as an educational movement. What information exists constitutes a well-chronicled history of colonial literary societies and the development of argumentation and debate as educational forms (Potter, 1944). The most comprehensive analysis of the history of American forensics was published in the 1930s in a series of three definitive articles written by one of the seminal figures in the nascence of American forensics, Egbert Ray Nichols (1936a, 1936b, 1937), an active forensics educator for nearly half a century.

Other studies focusing on specific aspects of forensics history exist and can be classified into several reasonably discrete categories: organizational studies, critical studies, and anecdotal studies. Organizational studies trace the development of forensics organizations. Critical studies analyze the strengths and weaknesses of the forensic activity by using methods grounded in historiography. Anecdotal studies generally present stories supporting the value of forensic training grounded in the personal reflections of participants.

Organizational studies have the goal of tracing the development of forensics organizations at local, state, or national levels. At the local level, program directors compiled their own histories, often in sketchy, underdeveloped ways, but occasionally in more elaborate forms (Sillars, 1949). Elaboration was often the product of both archival record keeping and the interests of someone to record and report a school's history. Often, local histories are piecemeal, found in various books and monographs but not treated as a distinct entity.

There also are regional and national organizational studies. As American forensics organizations reached longevity milestones, organizational histories emerged. The most comprehensive and complete were organizational histories connected with the various honoraries, formerly called fraternities, that were particularly important in the founding and nurturing of forensics in the twentieth century. Several examples typify these organizational studies. Norton (1987) compiled a history of Pi Kappa Delta to celebrate that organization's seventy-fifth anniversary. His book relied on earlier monographs describing the history of the organization as well as archival data. Norton's work emphasized organizational politics (e.g., presidents and officers, significant national decisions, and so forth) and provided insight into some of the systemic factors influencing the development of forensics during the twentieth century. For example, Norton analyzed Pi Kappa Delta's role in the development of the debate tournament and the emergence of a national debate proposition. Similarly, historians have provided brief chronologies of the history of forensics organizations (Burnett, 1996), the National Forensic League (Jacob, 1928), the American Forensic Association (Klumpp, 2000), the National Forensics Association (Fryar, 1984), and Phi Rho Pi (Mariner, 1969).

Critical studies comprise the second category of forensics historical analysis. Critical studies do more than describe as they delve into more complex explanations and critiques of practices or historical events. Critical studies of forensics, especially debate practices, have been by far the most common form of historical-critical research. The explanation for this focus is reasonably straightforward. After its origin as a formal educational tool in American education, debate was perceived, in both the communication disciplines and the popular press, as a public good rather than a technical skill. Critics assumed there to be an ideal method of debate that was nearly mythological in nature. In a significant sense, critics of debate employed John Winthrop's city on the hill metaphor in creating possibly insurmountable standards as to what debate should be.

The city on a hill is a particularly important American metaphor, invoked countless times by politicians and social critics alike. Applying it to debate training, critics throughout the century created standards and expectations that bore little relationship to actuality. They asserted that academic debate should train students to engage in serious and mannerly disputes, ignoring the fact that American history is replete with rowdy debate with a decided penchant for ad hominem arguments, sometimes punctuated with fistfights and even duels. Nonetheless, critics consistently lamented the failure of academic debate training to create a genuine class of citizen-scholars who could use debate to actively participate in civic deliberations.

From its emergence as an educational form near the turn of the twentieth century, critical analysis began. While the topic is developed more fully in chapter 6, a few examples illustrate the critical attention focused on forensics: the practice of debating both sides of the resolution, the preference for particular delivery styles, and the use of coaches to prepare for debate competition. After World War II, critics began to idealize the good old days of debate. This line of criticism reached its peak in the 1960s, as speech communication scholars began to criticize debate training as "emasculated rhetoric" (Stelzner, 1961).

At about this time, forensics educators began a vigorous and at times heated discussion in the literature about what constituted appropriate debate training. This discourse emerging from a vigorous critical discussion of debate practices also produced a number of new practices: cross-examination, the Lincoln-Douglas format, counterplan theory, and value propositions. This critical analysis paralleled similar discussions occurring in the communication discipline at large: rhetoric, as the dominant paradigm of communication study, began to give way to the scientific empiricism model embodied in the emerging area of communication theory; standards for political campaign debate, initiated through the resurrection of the practice by John Kennedy and Richard Nixon in 1960, were contested; and in recent years, there has been renewed criticism that debate is too technical, too rhetorically flawed, and even too informal.

The third form of historical-critical forensics research is represented by anecdotal studies. Anecdotal studies have been used to justify the value of forensics training, predicated on the testimony of former participants as to the usefulness of their training in preparing them for productive lives (Hellman, 1942). Anecdotal studies appeared as early as the 1920s, as former debaters claimed that debate training was useful for preparation in law, politics, broadcasting, and business.

In summary, a rich tradition of various historical-critical approaches focusing on aspects of American forensics exists. Unfortunately, missing is a comprehensive study of forensics' evolution that synthesizes the various historical strands into a unified explanation of how forensics contributed to the academic training of its participants. By themselves, organizational, critical, or anecdotal studies are sufficient to interpret the role, if any, of competitive forensics on the social, intellectual, and educational life of Americans. Why, then, would such a comprehensive examination of forensics be justified?

American inventor and manufacturer Henry Ford observed in a 1916 *Chicago Tribune* column, "History is more or less bunk. . . . We want to live in the present, and the only history that is worth a tinker's damn is the history we make today" (Martin, 2012). In contrast, George Santayana (1905) suggested that "those who cannot remember the past are condemned to repeat it" (p. 284). Whose perspective is correct? The reality is, of course, found somewhere between these two extremes. On the one hand, prior events are as much the product of their particular milieus as they represent lessons that can be applied to changing contexts. On the other, history plays a crucial role in providing meaning and context to prior events that can be productively applied to understanding similar events regardless of their different contexts. The eminent American historian Allan Nevins (1962) observed,

> History enables bewildered bodies of human beings to grasp their relationship with their past, and helps them chart on general lines their immediate forward course. And it does more than this. By giving peoples a sense of continuity in all their efforts, red-flagging error, and chronicling immortal worth, it confers on them a consciousness of unity, a realization of the value of individual achievement, and a comprehension of the importance of planned effort as contrasted with aimless drifting. (p. 14)

Nevins's notion of the "consciousness of unity" is particularly significant in that, while some historical contexts seem unrelated other than through broad social connections, in the case of forensics, the intentional choices ("planned effort") of the practitioners consciously built upon the choices of earlier practitioners. From our perspective, the history of forensics is progressive rather than revolutionary because its record mirrors tradition-bound educational practices in the United States. In many ways, just as students sitting in today's classroom would not feel totally out of place in a similar classroom at the turn of the twentieth century, so, too, would someone watching an academic debate find its basic premises, structures, and practices virtually unchanged in the last century. These assumptions were intentionally grounded in Western rhetorical practice as that practice emerged after the time of the Greeks.

Nevins's notion of "aimless drifting" provides additional support for studying the history of American forensics because "aimless drifting" characterized much of the history of the activity. Many of the changes that occurred throughout the twentieth century seem not to be the result of deliberate planning. For example, beginning in the 1950s, the gradually increasing influence of science and technology on academic debate practice was not as much a deliberate systemic choice as it was an incidental, microcosmic product of larger social change.

Understanding both the consciousness of unity and the differences between aimless drifting and planned effort provides the primary justification for this in-depth historical study. In a sense, of course, it might not even be considered necessary to justify this analysis. After all, the aesthetic dimension embodied in studying the history of forensics for its own sake may suffice because American forensics has thrived for more than one hundred years. The activity was one of the direct causes leading to the creation of the National Association of Teachers of Speech, which remains the primary national professional organization in the field. That said, more concrete justifications exist, including expanding the study of American public address, focusing on the pedagogy of forensics training, and exploring the cultural dimensions of forensics.

From the perspective of historical study, competitive speech and debate form a significant part of the tradition of American public address. Thus, tracing that history is an important and underexamined subfield of American public address. Nichols clearly established this rationale by grounding the study of speech and debate in the very fiber of American life. Since the beginning of the migration to the New World, New England town meetings, literary societies consisting of individuals debating important ideas, and declamation and oratory in public schools have all spoken to the powerful role played by speech and debate pedagogy in the creation and sustenance of democratic institutions. As late as the 1920s, people regularly gathered in public forums to hear skilled public debaters dispute critical issues of public concern. While recent attention has focused on political campaign debating, such studies often seem to assume that Kennedy and Nixon or Abraham Lincoln and Stephen Douglas somehow invented the format. A more nuanced study is needed to unpack how debates should be understood, independent of the social context that fostered the teaching of students (even in the proverbial one-room schoolhouse of American cultural lore) how to debate, and that provided the appropriate cues for how audiences should interpret debates.

Closely connected with the first justification, identifying and analyzing the pedagogy of forensics training provides a second reason for this study. It seems apparent, even without in-depth analysis, that forensics pedagogy has been the product of a relatively gradual evolution rather than a revolution. Debate, in particular, is clearly grounded in Western rhetorical practices that emerged from Greece and Rome and were refined in Western Europe, particularly Great Britain. At the same time, a rather deliberate decision was made to formalize competitive debate in American schools and universities in the late nineteenth century. Thus began a process whereby competitive speech and debate developed unique practices that, in numerous ways, maintained some forms of debate practice while creating entirely new ones. For example, literary societies rarely discussed policy propositions; yet the emerging competitive debate system moved largely to use that form of resolution as a basis for debate. A historical analysis of this evolution enhances our ability to distinguish intentional choice from aimless drifting.

The third justification for this study stems from the need to explore the cultural dimensions of forensics in order to provide a framework for understanding the likely similarities and differences (e.g., "consciousness of unity") of particular forensics practices. This framework is even more essential as competitive speech and debate activities continue to become more popular in Europe and elsewhere. Inherently, there is little doubt that public address is culturally bound. Although it was once believed that rhetorical study was primarily a Western concept, with only minor and insignificant traces elsewhere in the world, scholars have now broadened their understanding to acknowledge that rhetorical impulses have existed rather significantly in non-Western societies. Our understanding of the level at which culture uniquely shapes public address is limited at this time. Complicating what would be a straightforward analysis are, of course, the confounding variables created by speakers training in universities outside the United States, being influenced by political and social practices and borrowing American pedagogical techniques, such as academic debate.

THE BROAD OUTLINE OF A HISTORICAL
STUDY OF AMERICAN FORENSICS

In order to illustrate the utility of an in-depth analysis of the history of American forensics as an important area of research in American public address, some recurring themes and key outcomes should be identified. The framing of these developments provides a touchstone for assessing the role that competitive forensics activities may take as they continue to be practiced in other cultures.

First, any analysis must pay as much attention to themes and trends as to chronological events. The rationale for this position is probably self-evident: it would not be an especially onerous task to trace the chronology of major events in forensics history since many of the extant articles and books already perform that function. What is needed is an extension of the original research Nichols began in the 1930s. Nichols used chronology (dividing history into discrete decades) both to trace and to contextualize actual events. Based on his example, the key to creating a relevant history of forensics is to identify and signify the "big picture" and consider such questions as the following: How and why did competition overcome the earlier public debate model? Why did it become important to identify a single national debate question? Why did argumentation and debate theory borrow so heavily from legal models as opposed to parliamentary models used in Great Britain?

Second, an analysis of American forensics must identify the larger impact on the communication discipline and America's social and educational systems. The relationship between forensics and the communication discipline is an important one. Forensics predates the communication discipline and in the early years was the dominant organizational focus. That focus gradually, during the pre–World War II era, gave way to other emphases, much in the same way that the focus of public speaking training moved from "eloquence" in the nineteenth century to "competence" in the twentieth century (Cerling, 1995).

Similarly, a historical analysis must account for the uneasy fusion between democracy and forensics competition. Competition has been a controversial aspect of forensics in the United States since the field's inception. Because forensics was considered a form of citizenship training for participants and societal leaders, the activities associated with forensics experienced a level of scrutiny that may have been unique in the history of education in the United States. As noted earlier, the basis for this critical focus on forensics was the disconnect between the romantic belief in the power of speech and debate training and the reality of how that training was accomplished by our educational institutions.

Third, while our analysis will necessarily concentrate on traditional areas such as organizations, leadership, and politics, the elements of social history worthy of study must not be ignored. For example, forensics always depended on the ability of teams to travel, sometimes to the next town but often great distances, to tournaments. Thus, the tournament format became popular simultaneously with the increased availability of automobiles and improved highway systems. Travel also created a unique situation in which unmarried men and women traveled together with the debate teacher as chaperone. Similarly, the challenges of travel, whether by plane, train, or automobile, influenced the structure of early tournaments.

These tournaments were more "grand events" than the Spartan competitions typical of twenty-first-century American forensic tournaments. The early tournaments held dances, dinners, and skits, published informal newspapers complete with team gossip, and involved many members of the college, high school, or local community. This extended tournament format also led to the emergence and popularity of individual events speaking competitions. Any historical study of forensics should address the implications of how social models changed as travel became easier, tournaments became more frequent and shorter, and students became more sophisticated in their social interactions.

Finally, the influences of both American culture in particular and Western culture in general must be studied in order to provide a baseline for cross-cultural comparison of both processes and effects of forensics as a form of education. How much of the practice of competitive forensics was driven by American cultural forces? Why was American forensics typified by more of a competitive drive, while forensics elsewhere in the world enjoyed a larger social dimension? Could this explain why forensics became less popular than in previous generations? Could this be a mistake that other cultures should avoid as they embrace the activity?

THE FOCUS OF THIS TEXT AND ASSUMPTIONS GUIDING OUR ANALYSIS

As discussed in chapter 2, competitive speech and debate emerged with the decline of the literary societies and became a significant educational force in secondary and postsecondary education in the United States in the twentieth century. Before moving to our analysis of the nature and significance of forensics, we set the stage by identifying the principal themes that emerge in subsequent chapters. Our main claim is that forensics is inherently epistemic and rhetorical in nature.

Forensics Is Epistemic

The history of forensics is characterized by upheaval, conflict, and significant internal dissonance about philosophy and practices. That it survived and prospered is due to in no small part to its ability, in whatever forms it was practiced, to inspire learning and passion among its participants. Clearly, the birth and subsequent growth of forensics testified to the belief that the activity inspired student passion and public support regardless of any understanding or appreciation individuals outside the activity may have had for what actually was occurring. However, for the participants, the knowledge gained through involvement—at whatever level and to whatever extent—drew them into the activity, kept them involved, and left them changed and better able to meet the challenges they faced in other aspects of their personal and professional lives.

We argue that forensics is epistemic in that participation in the activity, in and of itself, created a knowledge that could not be gained without engagement. Littlefield (2006) initially developed this perspective: "The experience of forensics provides knowledge that is unique to the nature of the activities involved; and from forensic activities comes truth, or certainty, about the nature of the experience for the individuals involved" (p. 7). While some might have suggested that particular forensics practices were or were not educational, forensics undeniably provided firsthand knowledge—even knowledge that would help the participant to identify bad practices in future contexts—that could not be gained otherwise. We will return to confirm our argument in chapter 11 as we bring our examination of forensics in the twentieth century to a close.

Forensics Is Rhetorical

One may argue that forensics is significant simply because it is epistemic in nature, and this quality has served as an organizing principle for many people as they have sought to make sense of their world. As a result, the epistemic nature of forensics participation has inspired passionate disagreement about its rhetorical properties, both actual and desired. Forensics has been understood to represent assumptions about education and society that are by their very nature rhetorical.

This view that forensics is a rhetorical form created crucial tensions that constantly threatened to tear the activity apart while simultaneously holding it together. Unable or unwilling simply to accept forensics for what it is, a rhetorical form that is fun and engaging for participants in ways that are inscrutable to those who have not experienced it, supporters of forensics activities have sought to justify forensics through a variety of explanations grounded in the belief that for a rhetorical form to be worthy of time and attention, it must have a greater meaning. That meaning has taken various forms: that engaging in organized argument and speech is valuable for training citizens, that understanding rhetorical forms helps individual students become more effective thinkers and arguers, or that forensics provides a supplementary means of improving the act of education itself.

The fact that forensics has never achieved consensus regarding why it exists and what its value is beyond the epistemic is simultaneously both its greatest strength and most profound weakness. As a strength, the context of forensics has allowed for multiple interpretations of what constitutes best practices to constantly mutate into new forms, responding to changes in social, political, and educational forces that have possessed the force of ocean tides on the shore, constantly changing the landscape even as it seems as if nothing at all has changed. As a weakness, the lack of consensus about rhetorical purposes has created constant dissociative pressures, causing deep fissures within the activity itself and between the activity and other constituencies, as there has been a constant push and pull between whether forensics, at any given moment, should be assessed in terms of its impact on a universal or particular audience.

Forensics, as an educational form, has been held to unachievable standards when its critics have expected it to be a rhetorical form aimed at a universal audience. Just as Burke (1961) observed that humans are "rotten with perfection," forensics, it is claimed, must be perfection as measured by achieving the properties of teaching students how to reach a balance between all the rhetorical canons. Simultaneously, forensics practitioners have found similar shortcomings even when understanding the activity as a rhetorical form aimed at particular audiences. Who should make up those audiences? Which canon should be prioritized?

The work of Perelman and Olbrechts-Tyteca (1969) addressed these questions of argument form and audience and provided a useful framework for analyzing the rhetorical properties of forensics history—specifically, the nature of universal and particular audiences, the analysis of argumentation regarding the nature of reality, and the relationships between the parts and the whole in argument. These three theoretical concepts characterize the argumentative properties illustrating the history of forensics. In addition to the fundamental dispute as to the appropriate construction of the audience stemming from the nature of the audience being a psychological and sociological construction of the speaker (Perelman and Olbrechts-Tyteca, 1969, pp. 19–35), their analysis of the relationships between the whole and the parts (pp. 231–41) is also useful.

Much of intellectual conflict about forensics can be understood as resulting from the distinct ways those making arguments aggregated and separated parts from the whole. Perelman and Olbrechts-Tyteca (1969) observed, "The relation of inclusion gives rise to two groups of arguments between which it will be important to differentiate: those restricted to dealing with this inclusion of the parts in the whole, and those dealing with the division of the whole into its parts and with the relations between the parts which result from this division" (p. 231).

As discussed later, forensics practitioners and critics tended to construct forensics in two ways: (1) as a vehicle in which all parts constituted the whole, and because not all parts could be perfect (e.g., a debate format emphasizing rhetorically pleasing delivery), the activity itself was not perfect, or (2) as an entity that could be divided into parts (e.g., into different forensics organizations or into debate and discussion or debate and individual speaking events), allowing for the practitioners and critics to prefer their individual parts and experience perfection while simultaneously dissociating themselves from other parts with which they found fault.

Combining the Epistemic and Rhetorical

We can interpret forensics chronologically and thematically, simultaneously assessing changes in the activity's epistemic and rhetorical properties. Chronologically, we suggest four distinct eras of intercollegiate competitive forensics, with two of these being distinct in the twentieth century (see table 1.1). Each of the eras can be differentiated by the changes in how the activity was practiced and understood.

Table 1.1. Eras and Periods in Twentieth-Century Forensics History

Eras of American Forensics	Periods of Change within Eras
Precompetitive/literary society era (before 1880)	
Public oratory era (1880–1945)	
Technical era (1945–1995)	Crossroads (1945–1970)
	Divergence (1970–1995)
Postmodern era (1995–present)	

Our analysis primarily centers on the public oratory and technical (crossroads and divergence periods) eras and focuses on how the teachers and practitioners responded to four critical tensions grounded in the activity's epistemic and rhetorical properties. These critical tensions revolved around the following questions:

- Was the preferred audience the universal or the particular?
- Should forensics emphasize style over delivery or vice versa, and to what extent should the canons associated with these areas be emphasized in the context of forensics competition?
- How should the balance be struck between competition and education?
- Should the activity be organized using tightly or loosely coupled organizational structures?

It should be noted that some have suggested that beginning in the late 1990s, the postmodern era began reflecting an acceptance within the forensics community of the dissociation of its unified parts and the tacit agreement that consensus about theory and practice was impossible. In addition, acknowledging the epistemic nature of forensics permitted multiple forms to be equally valued and to flourish in an increasingly diverse universe in which the activity seemed to grow internationally and be accessed by more diverse groups. Table 1.2 anticipates the distinctions between the two twentieth-century eras to be developed later in our analysis.

ASSUMPTIONS AND THEMES OF THIS ANALYSIS

The theoretical assumption underlying this history is described by Berger and Luckmann (1966) in *The Social Construction of Reality*. According to their view, reality or truth is constructed from social systems and not on an individual basis. As Allen (2005) suggested, "Social constructionists maintain that humans construct the world through social practices" (p. 36). Thus, the application of social constructionism (or social constructivism) to the development of forensics as an educational movement provides a way for us to explain how this uniquely American innovation came to exist and evolve throughout a century of activity.

Social constructivism is a way of viewing the world that describes how social systems or realities are created. Spiering (2008) identified several key characteristics that explained social constructivism: critical perspective, the influence of history and culture, the act of communication, and the interaction of knowledge and practice. First, social constructivism takes "a critical stance toward our taken-for-granted ways of understanding the world" (Burr, 1995, p. 3). Individuals following this principle tend to be suspicious of traditional views of how the world is structured and question established ways of thinking and acting. A

Table 1.2. General Distinctions between Twentieth-Century Eras

Public oratory era	The universal audience was preferred; forensics was seen as a public good. Delivery was devalued as a reaction to the excess of literary society. Competition was nascent and seen as subsidiary to education. Organizational structures emerged that were loosely coupled, as each emerging organization had a different objective. Breakdown from a universal to a particular audience began as the tournament model emerged. Fractures emerged with fears about dominance of style over delivery. Education was still perceived as the central focus, although fears of competitive excess revealed themselves. Demands for standardization of topics, judging criteria, and so forth, created conflict in a loosely coupled organizational framework.
Technical era	***Crossroads period***
	The particular audience was preferred; forensics was seen as a private good. Style, as dictated by national competitive norms, devalued delivery. Competition was central to the educational process. Outside forces begin to force tighter coupling, leading to organizational fracturing.
	Divergence period
	Particular audience emphasis dominated, although disparate organizations had widely divergent views. Style and delivery were perceived to be at odds and the source of a tug-of-war between forensics organizations. Forensics was generally accepted as a private good resulting from competition. Virtually complete loose coupling emerged as forensics fractured into many different groups.

second assumption of social constructivism suggests that knowledge is specific to history and culture (Allen, 2005; Burr, 1995; Gergen, 1985). Based upon this assumption, labels or classifications used to identify things, practices, individuals, or groups at one point in time may later be abandoned because of events that influence the system. A third aspect of social constructivism is that knowledge is constructed collaboratively through social processes (Burr, 1995; Gergen, 1985). In other words, the daily interaction of people involved in the system shapes how the world is viewed and understood. This organic process evolves as people come together to communicate. Finally, social constructivism is built on the assumption that knowledge and social interaction are interrelated (Burr, 1995; Gergen, 1985). In the broader system, what we know affects what and how we do something. There are multiple social constructions that affect the way people respond to their environments.

Communication plays a key role in the formation of beliefs and views of social reality and is determined by our relationship to others. Allen (2005) explained, "We learn communication styles and rules based upon our membership in certain groups, and we communicate with other people based upon how we have been socialized about ourselves and about them [the other]" (p. 15). Because communication is central to the creation and sustainability of socially constructed views, language itself is a key component (Allen, 2005). As people interact with others, they participate and share their views because they use a common language. Buzzanell (1995) supported this position by suggesting that language and discourse practices reinforce social structures and allow certain practices to continue. Language is an important component of culture; thus, language impacts the construction processes and affects identity development (Leeds-Hurwitz, 1995).

For example, the norm in forensics competition for many years was to separate men and women into different competitive events, effectively constructing a way of viewing male and female speaking styles, how contestants of different sexes were valued, and the orientation of the activity toward segregation rather than integration. An illustration of social constructivism might reveal how communication within the forensic honoraries created and sustained the social reality within those organizations, including power relations that impacted people's identities (Deetz, 1992). Another application stems from the racial-ethnic backgrounds of the participants. Interaction between white, male judges and African American male debaters may have been affected by stereotypes and expectations based on racial-ethnic identity. Spiering (2008) has suggested that "different perceived cultural norms or cultural backgrounds can influence someone's attitudes, expectations, and perceptions of another person" (p. 24). Finally, behavioral confirmation can affect the expectations that people hold when engaged in social interactions. Snyder and Klein (2005) described behavioral confirmation as the process when an individual's "belief about another person may, in the course of social interaction, come to be confirmed by the behavior of the other person" (p. 54). These authors believed that behavioral confirmation has a significant impact on how people construct their social realities. People act upon their beliefs and expectations, thereby reinforcing them: "The reality of how people behave is not only a reflection of who they are, but also of who others believe them to be" (Snyder and Klein, 2005, p. 64). Both the perceiver and the receiver hold expectations, and this can lead to the confirmation of those beliefs and expectations.

Our claim that forensics in the twentieth century emerged organically from the simultaneous interactions of people, educational and other institutions, and society makes it necessary to locate forensics in a much broader context of how both secondary and postsecondary education developed as a response to the nearly constant tumult of a century in which the United States was transformed into a dominant military, economic, and social force that forever changed the world. While there is an almost mythological belief that educational institutions are static and firmly grounded in the past (e.g., the Ivory Tower), such is hardly the reality. Instead, a society depending on higher education to both train and socially liberate encouraged the emergence and almost constant reinvention of innovations such as competitive forensics while never really finding consensus as to what precisely should be the role of such an innovation. Was forensics training to be understood as an essential means of improving civic discourse or a means of teaching critical thinking skills? Was the ancient canon of invention to be preferred over that of delivery? Was forensics a necessary ingredient of the curriculum or an extracurricular pastime? These questions and others are illustrative of a wider disagreement about the role of higher education in general in the last century. In the following chapters, we develop five primary themes, introduced here as a preview to their further development.

Theme One: The History of American Forensics

We divided twentieth-century competitive forensics history into distinct eras, with the technical era divided into periods with very different sets of assumptions and practices, reflecting pedagogical, cultural, and organizational demands. Understanding the history of forensics involves examining both intentional and unintentional forces influencing its development, as well as the systemic forces that, not unlike the influence of celestial bodies on ocean tides, worked to push and pull forensics in various directions. These gravitational forces were not linear.

Forensics did not evolve in a singular direction at an easily referenced rate of speed. The shift from the long-standing literary society model to the competitive one in the public oratory era was extremely abrupt, while the movement toward what we call the technical era was more gradual. Further, it is important to understand that the periodic transitions were not exclusively replacements of one set of assumptions with another but involved an assimilation and shift of emphasis. Thus, if a literary society participant from 1760 were transported into a debating or speaking forum in 1860 or 1960, some aspects of forensics training would seem very familiar and others completely new and unanticipated. The oral communication aspect of forensics has masked some of the more fundamental philosophical changes occurring through the centuries of its practice.

Prior to the introduction of interscholastic competition, the precompetition/ literary society era encompassed the time beginning with the introduction of argumentation and debate pedagogy into colonial schools and colleges. This era is well understood through the work of Potter (1944). Debating is not new, but the essential difference between the literary society period and the two or three that followed involved the simultaneous "curricular and extracurricular" foci. While teachers were using argumentation techniques in the classrooms, their students were pursuing a parallel track through the distinctly extracurricular forums of the literary societies that were deliberately controlled by students without faculty or administrative control or influence. In many ways, these literary societies were much more the precursors of the modern residential and social sorority and fraternity systems of the twentieth century than the ancestors of competitive speech and debate as practiced during the century.

As noted earlier, interest in debate and speech competition arose directly from dissatisfaction with literary society practices. But to ignore the importance of the precompetition period is to miss a key theoretical issue in understanding the challenges that forensics faced in the twentieth century in maintaining status in an increasingly elitist academic world. The view of the debate in the academy has inherently been influenced by an almost romanticized view of argumentation practiced in colonial classrooms and the social chambers of literary societies. The failure of modern forensics to live up to idealized expectations is due at least in part to this romanticizing of its roots.

The public oratory era began with the sudden growth of interest in competition after 1880, gradually spread in popularity up to 1900, and lasted until the end of World War II and the resulting upheaval in the nature of higher education. The public oratory era saw the introduction of organizational structures, theories, and pedagogical practices that largely defined the broad outline of forensics during the century even as new practices later came into vogue. The underlying assumption of the public oratory era affirmed that forensics competition was primarily aimed at citizenship training and that standards of argument construction and performance were measured against public audiences and their expectations. Important building blocks emerged during this time, including key ideas such as professional debate and speech coaching, the tournament model, and the honoraries as the arbiters of rules and processes.

The technical era that began after World War II and lasted at least until 1995 introduced systemic changes that directly affected the forensic organizational structures and practices. The periods within the technical era resulted directly from the demands on higher education imposed by a massive influx of new students, the need for highly scientific and technical training for the substantial number of new career opportunities available to students, and the exponential growth in graduate education. The focus of forensics shifted from existing for the public good (e.g., arriving at the best decisions for solving societal problems) to offering private benefits (e.g., personal success) for the individuals who engaged in the activity.

For example, practices were introduced that students adopted (e.g., reading evidence faster so that more could be introduced into the debate, preparing blocks and briefs in advance against specific arguments to increase efficiency and enhance organization), and their personal success was measured based upon their ability to master those practices. Debates became very technical, and the creation of national competition and interest in public speaking and oral interpretation caused those forms to become very technical as well. Much of the consensus about the values and goals of forensics fractured, and new organizational structures arose to challenge the role of the forensic honoraries in governing practices. In many research universities forensics became marginalized, while the activity flourished at smaller institutions. The technical era is thus best understood as having two distinct periods, the first being when the activity reached a crossroads in addressing its aims and identity, and the second when the philosophical fissures caused significant organizational changes.

While our analysis does not go beyond the technical era, we speculate that a postmodern era began as the twentieth century came to a close and is playing an increasingly significant role in influencing forensics theory and practice. Chapters 2 and 3 describe the public oratory and technical eras, which were the principal demarcations in the twentieth century.

Theme Two: The Relationship between Collegiate and High School Forensics

High school forensics began at about the same time as college competition and in fact may have predated it. The activities of the two educational entities developed along parallel tracks in the early years, but the relationship between the two groups was complex. High school programs depended on colleges to provide resources such as summer workshops and training materials to facilitate high school competitive success. They also depended on colleges to supply a steady stream of trained practitioners to teach, coach, and judge at tournaments. While high school programs adopted many of the theories and practices of college debate, the relationship was hardly one-sided. College programs looked to high school programs and competitors as sources of important revenue streams in the form of tournament entry fees, summer workshop tuition, and the sale of research handbooks. College programs also looked to the high schools to provide a steady stream of trained competitors, ready to step in and succeed immediately in the highly technical world of collegiate forensics competition. Organizationally, the National Forensic League for high school forensics was founded by a collegiate alumnus of Pi Kappa Delta to serve as a coordinating entity for high school forensics activities.

There has always been uneasiness and even occasional resentment between the two levels. High school forensics appeared disempowered at times by the effects of changes in college practices, especially in the late days of the technical divergence period. Collegiate forensics participants felt constrained by conventions used by high school programs and tournaments (e.g., no disclosure of decision or in-round critiques) and undercut by many high school program directors' practice of discouraging participants from continuing their own competitive careers after graduation in order to retain them as assistant coaches for their own high school programs.

Theme Three: Forensics as a Promise and Consequences for American Education

The distinctions between the four eras of forensics (i.e., precompetition, public oratory, technical, postmodern) are largely the result of responses by forensics educators to changes in American education. This is likely true of virtually every discipline, program, and activity, especially at the collegiate level. But the changes most definitely buffeted forensics and caused the need for significant adaptations.

The introduction of the residential college pounded the final nail into the coffin of the literary society. Student demand for training in debate and public speaking influenced the creation of speech departments employing teaching methods that were very different from the preceding emphasis on elocution and were a significant factor in the creation of a new speech discipline, separate from English. The perception that the new speech discipline needed to identify a distinct theory and research tradition caused a devaluation of forensics because of that activity's emphasis on experiential learning, which was out of step with an academy favoring lectures, strict laboratories, and faculty churning out research publications. The significant shifts in the educational landscape during the Cold War further caused forensics to shift toward emphasizing its personal value to students as preparation for a highly technical career. At the high school level, increased demand for accountability through standardized testing and college preparation needs marginalized speech courses and led to an increasing belief that forensics was best seen as an extracurricular rather than a cocurricular activity—as a club and not a vocation.

Theme Four: Forensics as a Resilient and Enduring Educational Form

That forensics prospered and overcame organizational infighting, a dramatic shift in emphasis from the public to the private, changing demands from educational institutions, and even the hangover of a society possessing a highly romanticized view of the activity is testimony to the very important core values underlying forensics, regardless of time or format. Forensics is, first and foremost, fun. Students enjoy participating, and teachers enjoy teaching and coaching. The significance of the enjoyment aspect of forensics typically has not been emphasized in the haste to find serious and sober justifications for its inclusion in college and high school contexts.

Forensics also has more than a century of anecdotal evidence and some empirical findings demonstrating its value in improving the personal lives of its practitioners. Regardless of the type of forensics competition, on reflection after concluding their forensics careers, students regularly reported evidence of their own self-improvement in critical thinking, research, public speaking, and personal confidence. That students consistently were attracted to forensics despite the challenges they faced in finding viable programs is analogous to the primordial need of the salmon to swim upstream, outwitting predators and man-made obstacles like dams and spillways to fulfill their biological needs.

Theme Five: The Relationship between Forensics and the Communication Discipline

Forensics emerged as an educational method due in part to changes created by the residential college innovation of the latter nineteenth century. Students attending residential colleges sought intellectual, physical, and social activities to buttress their classroom educations. Students dismissed the long-standing literary societies as lacking the intellectual depth evident in even the earliest debate contests. Students then pushed colleges to provide more systematic training in debate and public speaking at a time when faculty teaching public speaking in existing English departments were chafing against the limits of elocution and elitism within the English discipline and seeking to establish their own discipline and achieve the hoped-for academic respect.

Initially at the heart of the new speech discipline, forensics was fairly quickly shunted to the side, as the new departments branched out into other areas of study. When competitive debate failed a rather arbitrary and capricious set of criteria for providing citizenship training established by those devaluing experiential learning and cocurricular activities, and did not fit neatly into a rapidly changing set of curricular assumptions drawn from the influence of the social sciences, those involved with forensics found themselves struggling to remain viable within the larger academic community. Higher education generally resisted the educational values of cocurricular activities such as debate. But despite these pressures, the constant student demand for competitive outlets kept forensics programs very visible, particularly as a source of pride for schools, which could point to the successes of the programs as evidence of their academic standing as an alternative to measurement solely by the achievements of their athletic teams.

THE PLAN OF THE BOOK

The remaining chapters develop these five themes through three general parts. Part I provides the broad historical context of forensics practice. Following this introduction, the history of forensics in the twentieth century is presented. Chapter 2 traces the foundations of modern forensics in the public oratory era and its emergence as a powerful educational form. Chapter 3 examines the evolution of forensics after World War II into the technical era with particular focus on how the role of a national championship influenced forensics practice and how a divisive controversy about ethics, practices, and outcomes led to an increasingly fractured competitive landscape. Chapter 4 identifies the behavior of various forensics organizations and examines the challenges those organizations faced in bringing coherence to a very individualistic activity.

Part II unpacks the uneasy tensions that confronted forensics and the relationship of forensics activities to other constituencies. Chapter 5 traces the theoretical issues that created schisms in both the forensics community and communication disciplines almost immediately after the popularization of forensics at the turn of the twentieth century. Chapter 6 continues that analysis by describing the growing tension between forensics supporters and different groups within the communication discipline. Chapter 7 examines the complicated relationship between high school and college forensics.

Part III discusses the sociocultural dimensions contributing to the evolution of forensics and identifies their role in shaping practice. Chapter 8 considers the importance of the social dimensions of forensics competition, including the value of forensics as a form of play. Chapter 9 reveals the socioeconomic challenges of race, while chapter 10 exposes issues faced by women as they sought access to competitive forensics. Finally, chapter 11 unites the various themes, poses the question of whether a new, postmodern era has begun, and concludes with a rationale as to why forensics endures as a significant educational force.

REFERENCES

Allen, B. J. (2005). Social constructionism. In S. May and D. K. Mumby (Eds.), *Engaging organizational communication theory and research: Multiple perspectives* (pp. 35–53). Thousand Oaks, CA: Sage.

Auer, J. J. (1959). *An introduction to research in speech.* New York: Harper and Row.

Berger, P. L., and Luckmann, T. (1966). *The social construction of reality: A treatise in the sociology of knowledge.* New York: Doubleday.

Burke, K. (1961). *The rhetoric of religion: Studies in logology.* Berkeley: University of California Press.

Burnett, A. (1996). Good people speaking well: Delta Sigma Rho–Tau Kappa Alpha. *Argumentation and Advocacy, 33* (2), 87–88.

Burr, V. (1995). *An introduction to social constructionism.* London: Routledge.

Buzzanell, P. M. (1995). Reframing the glass ceiling as a socially constructed process: Implications for understanding and change. *Communication Monographs, 62,* 327–54.

Cerling, L. R. (1995). The fate of eloquence in American higher education, 1892–1925. Unpublished dissertation. Iowa City: University of Iowa.

Deetz, S. A. (1992). *Democracy in an age of corporate colonization.* Albany: State University of New York Press.

Dovre, P. J. (1965). Historical-critical research in debate. *Journal of the American Forensic Association, 2,* 72–79.

Fryar, L. (1984). A brief history of individual events nationals. *National Forensic Journal, 2,* 73–83.

Gergen, K. J. (1985). The social constructivist movement in modern psychology. *American Psychology, 40,* 266–75.

Hellman, H. E. (1942). The influence of the literary society in the making of American orators. *Quarterly Journal of Speech, 28* (1), 12–14.

Jacob, B. E. (1928). History of the National Forensic League, *Bulletin, 3* (2), n.p.

Klumpp, J. (2000). Organizing a community and responding to its needs: The first fifty years of the American Forensic Association. *Argumentation and Advocacy, 37* (1), 12.

Leeds-Hurwitz, W. E. (1995). *Social approaches to communication.* New York: Guilford.

Littlefield, R. S. (2006). Beyond education vs. competition: On viewing forensics as epistemic. *Forensic of Pi Kappa Delta, 91* (2), 3–16.

Mariner, S. D. (1969). A founder's recollections: The birth of Phi Rho Pi. *Persuader,* n.p.

Martin, G. (2012). History is bunk. Retrieved from http://www.phrases.org.uk/meanings/182100.html.

Nevins, A. (1962). *The gateway to history.* Garden City, NY: Anchor Books.

Nichols, E. R. (1936a). A historical sketch of intercollegiate debating: I. *Quarterly Journal of Speech, 22* (2), 213–20.

Nichols, E. R. (1936b). A historical sketch of intercollegiate debating: II. *Quarterly Journal of Speech, 22* (4), 591–602.

Nichols, E. R. (1937). A historical sketch of intercollegiate debating: III. *Quarterly Journal of Speech, 23* (2), 259–79.

Norton, L. (1987). *The history of Pi Kappa Delta, 1913–1987.* Peoria, IL: Bradley University.

Oliver, R. T. (1965). *History of public speaking in America.* Boston: Allyn and Bacon.

Perelman, C., and Olbrechts-Tyteca, L. (1969). *The new rhetoric: A treatise on argumentation.* John Wilkinson & Purcell Weaver, trans. Notre Dame, IN: University of Notre Dame Press.

Potter, D. (1944). *Debating in the colonial chartered colleges: An historical survey, 1642–1900.* New York: Bureau of Publications, Teachers College, Columbia University.

Review of Debating in the MSU. (1902, May 21). *M. S. U. Independent* [Columbia, MO], *9*, 8.

Santayana, G. (1905). *Life of reason: Reason in the common sense.* New York: Charles Scribner's Sons.

Sillars, M. O. (1949). History and evaluation of intercollegiate forensics at the University of Redlands. Unpublished thesis. Redlands, CA: University of Redlands.

Snyder, M., and Klein, O. (2005). Construing and constructing others: On the reality and the generality of the behavioral confirmation scenario. *Interaction Studies, 6,* 53–67.

Spiering, K. (2008). The impact of faculty perceptions on international students' adaptation to the United States. Unpublished dissertation. Fargo: North Dakota State University.

Stelzner, H. G. (1961). Tournament debate: Emasculated rhetoric. *Southern Speech Journal, 27* (1), 34–42.

Part I

THE HISTORICAL CONTEXT OF FORENSICS PRACTICE

The next two chapters provide a broad overview of forensics practice in the twentieth century by sketching the outline of the two dominant eras: the public oratory era, which began with the introduction of competition in the late nineteenth century and lasted until the end of World War II, and the technical era, which defined forensics after World War II. These chapters provide not a chronology of events but rather a comparison of the eras with regard to the development and maturity of the activity in the context of significant changes in educational institutions and social conditions during a very tumultuous century. Chapter 4 then reveals the influence of the honoraries in shaping the structures and practices of forensics.

2

The Public Oratory Era

In chapter 1, we described forensics as a life-changing educational activity whose development was strongly affected by its interrelationships with American culture and educational systems. This was shown through the following themes: (1) the eras of forensics history reflected assumptions about the purposes of the activity, (2) the relationship of forensics with higher education and the communication discipline was dynamic and uneasy, (3) the promise and intended and unintended consequences of forensics were variables in American education, (4) the relationship between collegiate and high school forensics was parallel but not necessarily symbiotic, and (5) the resilient and enduring educational form of forensics was characterized by fun, personal growth, and interpersonal interaction.

This chapter presents the foundations of contemporary forensics education. To lay the groundwork for the emergence of forensics as an American educational innovation, a brief overview of the social and historical forces at work during the late nineteenth and twentieth centuries is offered. In addition, the transformation of literary societies into competitive models is revealed, as is the parallel emergence of high school and college forensics. We begin by examining some of the dynamics influencing education and society during the first decades of the century.

FORENSICS IN THE PRECOMPETITIVE ERA

David Potter's (1944) landmark book *Debating in the Colonial Chartered Colleges* is the best source regarding the development of forensics from its introduction in colonial schools until the decline of the literary society movement in the mid-nineteenth century. The roots of public speaking and debate in Western society can be traced to the Greeks, the Romans, and later the Europeans. There is no doubt that debate training found a vital function in the communities of European immigrants to the New World. Nichols (1936a) observed, "Debate was a heritage. It belonged to us, then, as an English-speaking people. If it did not come to America in the Mayflower, it was not far behind. And came as the course of empire took its westward way over prairie, plain and mountain" (p. 214).

Nichols's implication that debate was a product of speaking English is indefensible, given its popularity in both Western and non-Western cultures. But his point about the popular embrace of argument skills illustrates the centrality of debate and discourse to the development of American democratic institutions.

Early Debating

Potter (1944) traced the role of debate in the colonial chartered colleges from their founding in the seventeenth century. These colleges, modeled after British universities, used debate training as an important pedagogical tool. The debate forms used in the colleges were obviously much different from those that emerged in the twentieth century. However, Potter described three distinct debate methods that evolved over the 150-year period of his study.

The original debate technique was the syllogistic disputation. Syllogistic disputations were debates, conducted in Latin, that followed very strict rules regarding the use of syllogisms in the construction of arguments. Borrowed from English university training, syllogistic disputations were designed to train future clergy (the primary vocational expectation of university students at the time) to effectively use Aristotelian methods to prove or disprove claims. A tutor would assign the student, the "respondent," a topic. The respondent would then affirm or deny the topic. The rest of the class would act as "opponents" and try to expose flaws in the respondent's reasoning (Potter, 1944, p. 5). The respondent would go about his task by writing a paper and then orally presenting his strongest arguments on the issue. Opponents would present their objections in syllogistic form (major premise, minor premise, and conclusion), and the respondent would counter by identifying a flaw in the opponents' use of reasoning. After each opponent had the opportunity to make an objection, the tutor would provide a critique of the exercise and additional teaching in the subject area.

A specific set of rules guided the disputations to ensure that the students were faithful to the process as a means of finding truth as opposed to discrediting the other debaters through triviality, sarcasm, or other means. An example of a frequently used subject for disputation was "Logic is the art of investigating and communicating truth" (Potter, 1944, p. 12). But colleges used a wide range of topics, not all of which were strictly tied to the study of truth and logic, at least insofar as the topic wording was concerned. For example, "Oratory should be free of homogenesis" and "Rhetoric is the art of speaking ornately" were two subjects illustrating a broader concern about the role of rhetoric, reflecting concerns raised by European scholars about the nature of rhetoric itself and whether the subject was worthy of study.

Potter (1944) observed that gradually the disputation subjects expanded beyond topics explicitly concerned with logic or rhetoric in the direction of topics with wider social and political significance. These broader topics reflected the growing conflict between Great Britain and the colonies and implicitly connected the use of debate as an important means of political discourse. In 1743, for example, Harvard student Samuel Adams affirmed the question "Is it lawful to resist the supreme magistrate, if the commonwealth cannot otherwise be preserved?" (Potter, 1944, p. 23).

By the middle of the eighteenth century, even prior to the Revolutionary War, syllogistic disputations fell out of favor. Potter suggested that students found the method restrictive and uninteresting and gravitated toward disputes and forms that could be conducted in less rule-bound ways and, equally importantly, in English rather than Latin. Fewer students attended the university to join the clergy, and changing social conditions, including the growing importance of civic engagement through town meetings and law courts, also contributed to the discontinuation of this debate form, which was replaced by the forensic disputation as the primary debate form.

The forensic disputation was introduced at Yale in 1747 and rapidly became popular and the major form of debate until the end of the eighteenth century (Potter, 1944, pp. 34–35). The forensic disputation in the colonial colleges was a much looser form and introduced many of the elements of contemporary debate. Both an emerging theory of British rhetoric (developed by Hugh Blair, Joseph Priestley, and Richard Whately, among others) and growing interest in legal reasoning and practice energized and informed this debate form.

Although there was not a consensus regarding alternating sides or direct refutation, both of those principles began to be commonly employed. The topics were broader than those used in the syllogistic disputations. In 1764, for example, Princeton debaters considered the topic "All dreams are not useless and insignificant," and, in 1768, "It is the interest of any nation, to have the trade of its new countries as free from embarrassment as possible" (Potter, 1944, p. 45). The successful revolution and formation of a new American government accelerated the interest in debating policy questions. The forensic disputation, like its predecessor, gradually lost popularity in the early years of the nineteenth century, although it remained part of some college curricula until 1900 or later. Potter (1944, pp. 61–63) suggested that an expanding curriculum, which made it less possible for students to devote sufficient time to both written and oral preparation, and the allure of the new literary societies as a means of finding both fellowship and the chance to argue about contemporary issues were factors contributing to the decline of the forensic disputation and its gradual removal from the college curriculum.

The Literary Society

The most immediate precursor to contemporary forensics was the literary society, which Potter identified as the third phase of debating in early colleges. The literary society was a critical element of public discourse in both colleges and communities for well over a century, and its faint traces can still be found in the twenty-first century. Literary societies were both a significant break from the restrictions of the preceding syllogistic and forensic disputations and the first sign of the significant changes that would come from the emergence of the residential college model of education after the Civil War.

The college literary society dates back to the early eighteenth century and was one of the few outlets for students in a highly regulated college environment (Potter, 1944, pp. 64–65). The literary societies were a combination of modern features: social fraternities, debating and speaking clubs, and private libraries. The early literary societies introduced forensic disputations that were later integrated into the formal curriculum. The literary societies utilized various forms of debate and a wide variety of topics in an environment free from the restrictive rules and close control of tutors and other college officials. Potter reported that the college literary societies were strongly encouraged by the colleges as an appropriate social and intellectual outlet for students, and the societies flourished until the end of the Civil War.

As informal gatherings, the debates used much less formalized rules and processes than the syllogistic and forensic disputations. A pattern eventually emerged. The meetings of the literary societies included formal sessions to conduct society business complete with parliamentary procedure, then declamations and other public speaking activities, followed by an actual debate using topics similar to those employed in the formal forensic disputations. As noted earlier, over time these debates adopted processes borrowed from English rhetoric and courtroom jurisprudence.

Colleges typically had two or more literary societies, identified by Greek names, that would compete vigorously (rhetorically, athletically, and prankishly) in much the same way that contemporary fraternities interact. The literary societies often created extensive library collections that included a much more liberal and extensive collection than would be found in the main college library. Their influence, particularly in training social and political leaders in the nineteenth century, cannot be underestimated. Hellman (1942) claimed that literary society training and experience was a vital cog in preparing a number of prominent leaders, a list of whose names would include Daniel Webster, Henry Clay, and Abraham Lincoln.

By the end of the Civil War, the era of the literary society was in decline, although societies continued to exist for many years. The reasons for the decline of the literary societies were complex: increased industrialization, the emergence of the residential colleges, the rise of newspapers, and the effects of war. The growing pressure toward industrialization and the emergence of the residential college structure at Cornell in 1869 began to change educational priorities. The residential college and the concomitant changes in secondary education initiated in the postwar era were inconsistent with the gentility of the literary society format. Residential colleges brought forth the fraternities as a new social system. Other observers point to the rise of newspapers as providing a consistent source of knowledge, replacing the need for students to discuss and debate to understand contemporary issues. Another reason might be the upheaval created by war, as a substantial number of young men were changed through their service and became less interested in discussion and more attracted to action.

A final factor may have been a decline in the quality of the societies themselves. Vigorous and well-prepared debates became less frequent, and more time was devoted to social interaction; parliamentary wrangling and the presentation of speeches and declamations failed to appeal to students (see Potter, 1944, pp. 91–93; "Missouri-Nebraska debate," p. 8). Regardless of the causes of their decline, the literary societies at the private colleges virtually disappeared in the latter half of the nineteenth century; ironically, they continued to flourish in rural communities and among particular groups in large cities, such as African Americans. The literary society never completely disappeared but was folded into new forensic societies in colleges and high schools and continued to serve as an intellectual and social stimulant elsewhere.

THE SOCIAL AND HISTORICAL FORCES SHAPING AMERICAN LIFE AND EDUCATION

The public oratory era of forensics lasted roughly sixty-five years, between about 1880 and the end of World War II. This was a time of significant change in American life and particularly in the structure and assumptions of American education. We first summarize the timeline of the public oratory era before discussing the social forces at work shaping the development and practice of forensics during that critical era.

A Brief Overview of the Public Oratory Era

After about 1870, forensics transitioned from the literary society format to the competitive version, which is the one we consider to be the foundation of modern forensics. There were two primary reasons: the interest in competition with other schools and a growing fascination with the debate format as a more formal style of speaking. We discuss the importance of competition later in the chapter, but the opportunity for students to represent their town or college blossomed with the rise of the residential college. Shortly after the introduction of the residential college model, the first speech competition—the Interstate Oratory Contest—began in Illinois in 1874; it continues to the present day.

Student members of the Adelphi Society at Knox College proposed a speaking contest originally conceived as including only students from local colleges (Schnoor, 1983). After discussion, an invitation was sent to several colleges in the Midwest inviting each institution to send an orator to Galesburg, Illinois, for the contest; the governor of each represented state would appoint a judge. Five colleges (Beloit, Grinnell, Iowa State, Chicago, and Monmouth) were represented. Fear of local favoritism led to the exclusion of Knox, the host, at the first contest. First prize was $100, and consistent with the tradition of the time, various social activities were connected with the contest. Charles Prather (1891), editor of the first compilation of the orations, described the event:

> The first contest in oratory took place in the evening of the 27th of February, 1874, in the City Opera House of Galesburg. The meeting was marked by the largest audience ever congregated in the city. The programme opened with an overture by the Grand Orchestra.
>
> F. I. Moulton, president of the Adelphi Society, then introduced Mr. H. C. Adams of Iowa College, Grinnell, Iowa. Subject: "The Student and the Mysterious," which the speaker rendered with true grace and eloquence. Mr. A. G. McCoy, of Monmouth College, Monmouth, Ill., followed Mr. Adams. His subject, "Conservatism," was of a political nature, and the speaker's style was energetic.
>
> Mrs. Chas. G. Hurd rendered the "Cavatina from Lucia di Lammermoor," an operatic solo that was highly appreciated, after which Mr. T. Edward Egbert, of Chicago University, Chicago, Ill., appeared. His theme, "The Heart, the Source of Power," won for him the first prize. Mr. Frank E. Brush, of Iowa State University, Iowa City, Iowa, next addressed the audience on the subject of "Ideas: Their Power and Permanence." It was an erudite production, and Mr. Brush a natural orator.
>
> The "Blue Danube Waltzes," by the Grand Orchestra was given next place on the programme, at the conclusion of which Mr. Geo. T. Foster, of Beloit College, Beloit, Wis., discussed the "British Rule in India," which was pronounced the second best oration. The last orator, Mr. W. W. Wharry, of the Illinois State Industrial University, Champaign, Ill., came forward with the subject of "Labor and Liberty; or the Mission of America," which he delivered in an easy manner, and retired amid applause.

While the judges, who had been appointed according to agreement by the Governors of the three states represented in the contest, withdrew for decision, Mrs. Hurd sang the favorite ballad, "Five O'clock in the Morning." The judges appointed were: Dr. A. Burns, president of Simpson Centenary College, Indianola, Iowa; Prof. A. Stetson of Normal University, Bloomington, Ill.; and Judge A. A. Smith of Galesburg, Ill. The prizes were awarded to Messrs. T. Edward Egbert and Geo. T. Foster. (pp. 9–10)

So popular and well received was the contest that the participating schools formed an organization, the Interstate Oratorical Association, that grew to more than sixty-three colleges by 1891. Eventually, the rules were standardized so that each state would have one representative in the national contest. The contest originally included both men and women, but later a separate contest was established for each sex. Included among the early participants of the contest were many who later became famous speakers: William Jennings Bryan, Robert LaFollette, Albert Beveridge, and Jane Addams.

In addition to enjoying the glory of competitive success, students began to demonstrate the desire to engage in more rigorous and formal debates. In literary societies, debates were secondary to the development of eloquence and oratory. In analyzing the beginning of competitive debate at the University of Missouri, an article in the *Independent* observed,

> The rise of debating in the University of Missouri is coincident with the rise and growth of the new University. Until recent years, oratory held undisputed sway, and the energy and enthusiasm of the older literary societies was directed chiefly toward the development of oratorical talent. The debate, it is true, was nominally a regular feature on the program of the literary societies, but it was always the "tail end" of the program and usually cut short because of the absence or lack of preparation on the part of the debaters. ("Missouri-Nebraska debate," p. 8)

In actuality, debates in literary society programs were more similar to group discussions and legislative debates than to the competitive debates that would replace them. But when was the first competitive debate held? The answer is elusive.

Thomas Trueblood claimed that debates between Harvard and Yale in 1892 were the first. Trueblood made the assertion possibly as a result of coverage of that encounter in the *New York Times* (Nichols, 1936a, p. 213). Other accounts identified earlier intercollegiate contests: records suggest that Knox College debated Rockford Female Seminary in 1883, and it is likely that debates were taking place in high schools even before they appeared in colleges. There is little doubt that wherever the first contest occurred, the competitive model spread rapidly throughout the United States, particularly in the East and Midwest, where many colleges, established before and during the transition to the residential model, were in close proximity and among which rivalries had begun to develop. Intercollegiate sports rivalries began during this period, and it was only natural for the competitive spirit that already existed between literary societies and other social groups on one campus to translate into competition with those of another nearby institution.

Competition provided students with an alternative to the restrictive classroom practices common in the nineteenth and well into the twentieth centuries. Because long lectures, memorization, and strict rules regarding campus life were the norm, outlets such as sports, music, theater arts, and debate began to emerge to flesh out what some considered a mundane educational experience. Debate was also a welcome alternative to the strictly structured oratory and declamation that dominated public speaking instruction at the time (Cerling, 1995, p. 190). The first modern theorist of what would become the study of argumentation, George Pierce Baker (1895), claimed that competitive debate was an intellectual sport and a worthy use of student time and energy. Baker wrote the first textbook devoted to this intellectual sport, and by that time competitive debate was in full swing at colleges and high schools across the nation.

Later in this chapter, we discuss the characteristics of debate competition during that time, but it is useful to note that early contests were unique experiences conducted without generally accepted rules and norms. All elements of the contest, including dates, format, topic, related festivities, and even housing and eating arrangements were negotiated between the parties. This process was time-consuming, particularly in the era before widespread availability of telephones, and there was almost immediate pressure to organize this wildly popular activity. Organizational structures to facilitate the competition emerged for both high school and college debate competitors between 1900 and 1920.

The date of the earliest high school debate contest is also unknown, but as suggested above, it may have predated college contests. Levin and Goodfriend (1914, p. 6) reported that high schools in the Boston area were participating in interscholastic contests as early as 1887. The activity quickly became popular, especially after the publicity given by the *New York Times* to the Harvard and Yale debates in 1892. Following the model of the Harvard and Yale debates, the Harvard-Yale-Princeton triangular debate contests in 1894, and the subsequent explosion of triangular and quadrangular collegiate debate leagues in the Midwest based on the relationship between Michigan and Wisconsin debate teams in 1893, high school debate societies formed and began holding interschool debates. High school debaters eagerly modeled many common practices associated with intercollegiate debate (e.g., use of a common question, identification of affirmative and negative issues, speaker order, forms of proof, and scheduling affirmative and negative teams from each school to meet each other). As a result, at the start of the twentieth century, high school debate flourished. Soon after, university administrators made the connection between developing programs to promote and coordinate high school debate activities and increasing their recruitment of high school debaters to their universities (Hayes, 1952). We discuss how universities developed their extension programs in chapter 7.

Two major social forces provided encouragement for the new competitive model of forensics: the impact of Progressivism on American society and the monumental shift in higher education to the residential college model.

The Progressive Era

The Progressive Era and the economic and political forces that focused attention on societal problems needing resolution strongly influenced the emergence of forensics in American educational institutions. After the Civil War and well into the early twentieth century, the United States underwent an extended period of population growth, industrialization, and political activism. The American frontier was irrevocably altered by the influx of immigrants, the introduction of the telegraph changed communication patterns, and the completion of the transcontinental railroad facilitated travel for an increasingly mobile society. This rapid transformation had a marked impact on American society, affecting the people in many ways (Broderick, 1989).

As farmers expanded their capacity to meet the growing needs of the population in urban areas and the world markets, they found themselves hostage to the railroad companies and grain elevators that controlled the distribution of their products to market. Family manufacturing shops found themselves displaced by legions of workers in the larger foundries, whose actual production capacity outpaced the ability of consumers to purchase and make use of their products. Women and children were regarded as cheap labor and given fewer rights and less regard than their male counterparts. Small business owners lost customers to larger corporations, just as banks in smaller venues lost out to larger banks, which became influential partners with the conglomerates amassing wealth and power through their economic empires, often at the expense of the American public. Lastly, consumers found themselves unable to pay high prices for what was commonly poor-quality merchandise. The people were victimized by economic forces over which they had little influence or control (Broderick, 1989, p. 2).

As members of the public came to fully realize their situation, they grew more and more discontented and impatient, seeking change from the status quo (O'Toole, 2005). However, rather than being viewed negatively for their attacks on the established power structure that was forming in industrialized America, these progressive individuals were described by Taylor (2004) as "the most creative, optimistic, and committed generation of democratic thinkers and activists in American history" (p. 2). They embraced issues of concern to Americans across the country, including greater popular rule, woman's suffrage, presidential primaries, popular election of senators, short ballots, campaign reform, referendum and recall, popular review of judicial decisions, minimal working conditions, social justice issues such as a living wage, increasing the value of the farmer and farm family, states' rights, protective tariffs, and the national regulation of the currency system (Broderick, 1989, p. 110). Specific policy issues were the focus of their attention because the merits or disadvantages of these policies had a direct bearing on the quality of life they and their families enjoyed. With few places to turn, they concentrated on the federal government, through its legitimate authority as vested in the Constitution, as they sought to "protest against, to curb, and to control" the "Big Interests" (Thayer, 1919, p. 348).

During this time, the federal government was not idle, despite being described by some as laissez-faire, or lacking in governmental regulation (Broderick, 1989). In the period known as the Progressive Era (1880–1914), voters sought to gain control of the forces confronting them by electing individuals who would represent their interests and empowering the federal government to act on their behalf. The central issue of Progressivism was "how should the United States 'work out a strategy for orderly social change' in the new order created by large-scale industrial and financial capitalism" (Broderick, 1989, p. 4). In response to this question, major legislation was passed during this era to shape the new order, including the so-called Granger Laws and the Interstate Commerce Act to regulate and supervise railroad practices, the Sherman Anti-Trust Act designed to prevent the monopolization of particular sectors of the economy, and the Pure Food and Drug and the Federal Meat Inspection acts regulating the quality of the food and medicine produced and made available to the public.

The people who initially led the charge of Progressivism were educated, middle-class people who recognized that something had to be done to control what was happening in America (Chandler, 1954, p. 1462). They believed that in order for democracy to survive, "only the character of the citizens" and "their willingness to bear the burden of democratic virtue" would be successful (Taylor, 2004, p. 9). This faith in the ability of the individual to rise up in the face of undemocratic forces was the basis for much Progressive Era activism. Those who accepted the mantel of Progressivism believed in their ability to "solve the problems raised by American society, by inventing institutions for the promotion of public health, by promoting the conservation of natural resources, by designing political institutions that would curb the corruption of political parties and promote a decent democratic politics. But the biggest project of all, the one that underlay all the others, was the project of promoting democratic citizenship" (Taylor, 2004, p. 23).

Those who subscribed to the Progressive philosophy found that it was not something that could be accepted halfheartedly. Rather, citizenship represented character and personal virtue in all aspects of life. In this manner the current of Progressivism found its way into the thinking and practices of students who not only used forensics as a means to consider pressing contemporary issues of economic, social, and political importance but also found the training in public speaking and argumentation skills to be the foundation for what they would need as they stepped off the campus and into the real-world democracy in which they lived.

Voluntary Associations for Civic Engagement

Literary societies, debate teams, and later forensics organizations benefited in part from their structural similarity to the voluntary associations that were an integral part of the American experience with democracy. Characterized by Schlesinger (1944) as a "nation of joiners," America provided an environment in which citizens came to believe early on that they were capable of thinking and acting in their own behalf to solve the problems that confronted them in their communities, regions, and nation.

From the Revolutionary era through the Civil War, Americans were drawn to civic and religious groups, as well as fraternal associations. Partially out of necessity and perhaps based on the individualistic orientation of Americans to be self-sufficient and independent, voluntary associations enabled individual citizens to be engaged and control decision-making processes at the local level. Americans were drawn to religious as well as political associations; the Great Awakening in the nineteenth century attracted thousands of Americans confronting the harsh environment of the American frontier with the promise of a new heaven on earth (consider Ann Lee and the Shaker movement). The fraternal associations were equally attractive, particularly as lodges became havens for young men who migrated to new regions of the country and established communities like those they left behind. The high level of involvement was so evident that during his tour of America in the 1830s, French aristocrat Alexis de Tocqueville found "a profusion of voluntary associations, vibrant religion, competitive elections, and decentralized government," making the United States "an unusually civic democracy" (Skocpol and Fiorina, 1999, p. 9).

As the nation expanded, people brought their voluntary associations with them to new locations, where they "flourished locally . . . in the absence of any strong national state" (Skocpol, 1999, p. 32). In addition to enriching their new communities, these transplanted associations provided the means for individuals to stay connected with others in their previous communities, as well as their regions and nation. These translocal connections were models for what would later become regional and national associations, enabling local citizens to affiliate with national leaders. In addition, Skocpol discovered a positive relationship in regions with more associations as having more effective governing arrangements. As local populations grew and greater demands were made on governments to provide stability and positive growth, in communities where citizens had more capacity in areas involving civic action, the local governments worked more effectively.

Following the Civil War, as a result of industrialization, larger associations took over the activities formerly managed by families and local groups. Some associations grew as a way for Americans and workers to unite against unfair or inhumane working conditions and low wages. As the middle class grew, so did its participation in the voluntary associations, from local community groups to national networks of individuals sharing a common purpose. Examples of these associations included "moral-reform movements, farmers' and workers' associations, veterans' groups, and many ethnic and African American associations" (Skocpol, 1999, p. 33). These associations were encouraged by the very nature of the American system of government that promoted citizenship and active participation in community affairs.

The structure of the United States government also served as an organizational model for the voluntary associations (Skocpol, 1999). For example, "The United States was put together as a federal republic, and both the nation and the states had written constitutions that spelled out rules for voting and representation; explicitly parceled out administrative, legislative, and judicial functions; and assigned levels of sovereignty to national, state, and local government" (Skocpol, 1999, p. 47). From this model, local units of an association were organized and connected with state or regional associations by the rules by which they operated. They also elected their officers and representatives to national bodies "just as U. S. senators were originally appointed by state governments" (Skocpol, 1999, p. 47).

Voluntary associations became an essential part of civic America partially because of this organizational relationship; they provided connections between the local community and the broader national landscape. Individuals often "were inspired to join endeavors to which they knew thousands of others across their state and nation were also committed" (Skocpol, 1999, p. 66). Communities rallied around the selection of delegates from a local club or unit to attend annual district, state, or national conventions. Publications were generated to publicize and report such events, and delegates were obligated to return and report to their fellow citizens what transpired at the "big meeting" and about "the sights in whatever city had hosted the meeting" (Skocpol, 1999, p. 66).

The nature of these associations is also relevant to the environment in which forensics emerged in that these groups provided opportunities for individuals to rise up through the ranks to become leaders. Previously, leadership positions had been reserved for those with financial resources, family pedigree, or educational training above that of the average citizen. With the rise of the middle class, voluntary associations became a place where the average citizen could move up the "mobility ladders" through the progression of leadership positions to the top of the association (Skocpol, 1999, p. 66). The democratization of the community through voluntary associations enabled individuals who were not traditionally considered to be among the elite to interact with those who formerly would have been inaccessible. In these leadership roles, members demonstrated public speaking skills, meeting-management skills, knowledge of parliamentary procedure, and general organizational skills.

The Role of Education in Citizenship Training

In pre-twentieth-century America, the facilitation of both training and practice opportunities for citizens to exercise their oratorical and performance skills was perceived as one of the civic purposes of colleges, high schools, and even local communities (Halloran, 1982). These educational institutions understood their role in teaching people to argue and effectively speak and perform in public and generated significant public good will through their encouragement of sound rhetorical training gained through participation in classroom speeches, literary societies, and informal debating clubs.

When colleges and universities first organized themselves in America, their purpose was "to produce a virtuous, decent person, capable of serving both in civic duties and in the professions (law and the ministry)" (Keith, 2007, p. 23). Those who populated these institutions were the children of elites or those with sufficient funds to support their educational endeavors. However, as the United States was flooded with immigrants during the late nineteenth and early twentieth centuries, politicians recognized the need to provide for the public education of all children, no matter what their socioeconomic status (Keith, 2007). In addition to providing public education for all minor children, the Morrill Act of 1862 established land-grant colleges to make postsecondary education available to a larger percentage of the population.

As student populations swelled, colleges and universities experimented with new models for creating a campus environment, including the residential college model. In 1869, Cornell University built the first such facility, named Sage Hall, "the most luxurious accommodations of any college dormitory in the United States" (O'Hara, 2009). Residents had access to a swimming pool, gymnasium, botanical conservatory, indoor plumbing, and "luscious" furnishings. Residential colleges differed from traditional colleges by having a dining hall, classrooms, a library, professional offices, and housing all within one building. Through the creation of this model, faculty led societies in each residential facility, providing the advantages of a small college within the environment of a larger university (O'Hara, 2009). This feature was particularly conducive to the expansion of

intraschool forensics activities in which different dormitories, or houses, competed against each other in debates, oratorical competitions, and declamation.

The public education of minor children, prior to their entry into college, was left
up to the local school boards to provide. In addition to the basic subjects, children
were taught platform skills: how to memorize great passages from literature, how
to stand in front of an audience with poise to speak or recite, and how to express
their thoughts about important issues of the day. The practice of engaging students
in speaking and performing activities stemmed from the belief that these skills
would prepare students to be more engaged as citizens. This was accomplished by
training children to present and defend positions on issues of importance to them
and by inspiring young people to become advocates for important issues.

THE INFLUENCE OF HIGHER EDUCATION
ON THE GROWTH OF FORENSICS

Herman Cohen (1994), in writing a history of higher education in the United
States, described the years from 1870 to 1944 as the "transformative" era of
American higher education. This was the period of the greatest innovation and
most substantial growth. The modern university was created, and that model remains the dominant structural paradigm to this day. Graduate education, general
university requirements, the residential college, and cocurricular education were
some of the innovations that spread across the country, reflecting a rapidly expanding industrial nation that needed educated and trained workers and citizens
to support swift growth and change.

Three distinct characteristics of the transformative era strongly influenced the
rapid expansion of forensics during the same time: the perceived importance of
cocurricular activities as means of training students for productive careers, the
intense competition between colleges and universities that nurtured the paradigm
of the competitive model of forensics to replace the earlier literary society, and
the emergence of speech as a distinct discipline coupled with the development of
graduate education necessary for training forensics educators.

Prior to 1870 cocurricular activities, including sports and forensics, were
virtually nonexistent because there was no perceived value for students or the
larger institution. At the same time, of course, there were virtually no spectator
opportunities beyond attending concerts, theater productions, or the occasional
political or other speech. There was little interaction between the college and
the surrounding community. College attendance was reserved for the wealthy or
determined upwardly mobile members of the middle class.

The new university model, introduced by Cornell and rapidly embraced and
expanded elsewhere, quickly changed the perception of the cocurriculum. Sports

teams (mostly for men) sprang up; fraternities, social clubs, and student newspapers were all created and justified as important for producing more holistically educated university graduates. Public speaking activities and debate fit this growing need perfectly, as they were essential elements of education long before the transformative period. Literary societies and other informal groups regularly debated social and political concerns, and the widely publicized and well-attended Lincoln-Douglas debates of 1858 sparked interest in the role of debate in public decision-making.

Colleges and universities, in the transformative era, were highly motivated by competition. Competition served several functions: forensics provided publicity for colleges and universities needing money and support to expand to meet the growing demand for education, and success in competition also equaled prestige. In an era of rapid growth, colleges needed to differentiate themselves, and competitive success, in whatever form, was perceived to be valuable.

The third factor influencing the rapid growth of forensics was the innovation of graduate education. Graduate education was crucial in encouraging higher standards of professional preparation and a much larger pool of faculty to teach in all levels of institutions. A side effect of graduate education was the narrowing of disciplinary focus. As more faculty members were awarded advanced degrees, specialization emerged. Formerly large omnibus departments began to specialize in smaller, more focused areas of study. One of those more focused disciplines was speech, which emerged formally after 1900, due in part to the great interest in competitive debate. Graduate programs in speech produced faculty interested in and trained to teach speech and debate; forensics as a subdiscipline, complete with scholarship and status, further nurtured the new competitive model. Successful debate coaches were prized and occasionally poached from one university by another.

THE CHARACTERISTICS OF THE PUBLIC ORATORY ERA OF FORENSICS

By the mid-nineteenth century, educational institutions afforded the greatest opportunity for American students to polish their speaking skills by marrying public oratory to competition in the form of debate and forensic speaking activities. This American innovation was actually a reinvention, as the task of training citizens in public oratory existed both formally and informally in colonial colleges, maintaining a long-standing British university practice, as detailed in chapter 1.

However, forensics spread quickly as an innovation because of its perceived characteristics (Rogers, 1995): (1) forensics provided comparative advantages over literary societies, (2) forensics was compatible with the value of civic involvement, (3) the complexity of forensics was not a deterrent to participation, (4) forensics could be tried before making a major commitment, and (5) forensics activities could be observed. Rogers (1995) argued that any of these characteristics might be enough to persuade someone to adopt an innovation. The fact that forensics subsumed all five of these characteristics demonstrated the compelling attraction of this academic innovation for students at a time when Progressivism, membership in voluntary associations, and the introduction of residential colleges converged during the late nineteenth and early twentieth centuries.

Students found forensics to be advantageous over the literary societies because of the added element of competition. Bruno Jacob, a debate manager at Ripon College and later the founder of the National Forensic League, said it best when he suggested that defeating the debaters from the next town was a great motivator for students. The deeply rooted belief that debate and public speaking prepared the student for citizenship in the American democracy was compatible with the expectations of the public that schools trained children to become engaged citizens. The format of debate was relatively simple and easy to master, following the syllogistic models used in the colonial colleges (Potter, 1944). The literary societies provided the venue for students to practice speaking, debating, and using parliamentary procedure. Being able to try the activity gave less experienced or confident students the chance to test their abilities at the local level before venturing out into intercollegiate competition. Finally, debate and forensic contests were public events that could be observed by trained and lay audiences alike. The focus of forensics was on the public, and keeping the activity externally driven helped to make forensics exceedingly popular prior to World War I.

Due to the attributes previously mentioned, from around 1880 to 1945, debate and speaking activities grew to be a staple of American high school and college education, as documented in school newspapers and yearbooks during this period. Characterization of this time as the public oratory era arose from the almost universal agreement, among participants, scholars, and the public, that forensics training was valuable exclusively as a means of preparing people for the duties of civic life, as advocates in their professions, and in the important tasks of public participation and governance. Forensics was, during this era, first and foremost a public good whose value did not stem from achieving competitive goals such as winning championships and bringing glory to a school, university, or community. While those were inevitably side benefits, there was never any publicly expressed belief that competition was justified for its own sake. Not until the onset of the Cold War did competition become an end in itself and not solely a means. During the public oratory era, other values, embodied in common practices and norms, were paramount, and those other values generated the rapid growth of participation, theoretical development, and public enthusiasm for competitive speech and debate.

Five characteristics of forensics during the public oratory era explain its popularity: the novel and largely unique role that students played as active agents in the growth of forensics; the popularity and prominence bestowed on participants of the era that often eclipsed the favor given to star athletes, musicians, and actors; the community embrace of forensics as a source of civic pride and responsibility; the audience-centered practices of forensics as a local, regional, and national activity; and the nurturing of significant experiential and practical innovations that adapted to student life during the era.

The Role of Students

The first unique characteristic of the public oratory era was the powerful role that students played in creating programs, organizing on-campus and off-campus events, and promoting the activity among various constituencies. Students were the organizers who formed debating societies, engaged in practical activities to stimulate their critical thinking and develop their speaking skills, prepared for and sponsored intersociety competitions, served as student managers, and actually coached themselves (Stone, 1893). Forensics was a bottom-up, student-initiated educational innovation. While faculty sponsors were sought out to provide legitimacy for forensics at their home institutions, the students actively worked to establish competitive programming and lobbied for academic credit for their efforts (Foster, 1904; Nichols, 1936a). Once faculty members were teaching argumentation and oratory for credit, students sought a change in the practical function of the faculty advisor. Team members realized that those students with faculty coaches tended to win more contests than those without faculty coaches (Cowperthwaite, 1946; Nichols, 1936a, 1936b; Sillars, 1949). Even with a faculty advisor, the practical operation of forensics programs typically was student run. A student manager scheduled competitions with other schools, negotiated the specifics of the competition (including the wording of the resolution, time limits, judges, and the location of the all-too-necessary banquet after the event), made the necessary travel arrangements, engaged in precontest coaching, and handled the public relations.

The Prominence Afforded by Forensics Participation

The public oratory era was also unique because debaters were afforded prominence and prestige within their schools and communities for their argumentation, oratorical, and competitive skills. Orators and debaters were very often popular figures and student leaders, causing the public to regard forensics as an elite activity and give it high status in schools and on college campuses. Anyone could join a literary or debating society. However, in the beginning, only the very best were chosen through local competitions to participate in intersociety or inter-school competitions (Levin and Goodfriend, 1914). The number of individuals actually traveling outside their state for forensic competition was even smaller (Nichols, 1936b, 1937).

Forensics and the Local Community

The third distinct characteristic of the public oratory era centered on the close association of forensics with the local community. While there were opportunities for interstate competition, forensics drew its initial strength from the actual demonstration of argumentation and oratorical skills in local schools and community halls in cities, towns, and villages. School campuses and surrounding communities served as the centers of activity and competition, and engaging in local contests and being selected to represent one's literary society or school against a neighboring school's best speakers served as its own reward, as Jacob (1928) described in his autobiographical sketch: "The sensation of defeating a neighboring city only half our size in a single debate was sufficient to make forensic interest the chief consideration in choosing my college and so I came to Ripon" (n.p.). Winning the top prize—a scholarship, gold watch, medallion, or cup—was an honor that made up for the fact there were usually few tangible rewards for competitive success (Stone, 1893).

Audience-Centered Focus

The public oratory era was distinct due to the audience-centered nature of the competition. The patrons of forensics (teachers, students, community supporters) required that substantial efforts be made to make forensics relevant to audiences. Forensics was considered an important entertainment outlet for communities starved for diversion. Initially, debaters and speakers were taught to use familiar historical and literary examples, in lieu of extensive reporting of facts or direct quotations, as those forms appealed more generally to local audiences. Speakers incorporated humor, sarcasm, and stylistic appeals as common strategies for creating audience interest (Foster, 1904).

As debaters sought to keep the interest and attention of their audiences, formal prepared speeches gave way to more extemporaneous and adaptive ones. Similarly, as audiences became less willing to attend debates lasting over two hours, the number of speakers on a team was reduced from three to two, and the speaking time for each speaker was shortened (Foster, 1904; *Harvard vs. Yale*, 1917). Since audiences often decided the winners of the early forensic contests, speakers adapted to what they believed audiences expected in order to gain their favor. Adaptation also was needed for community judges who were unfamiliar with conventions associated with particular forensics activities or contests (*Debating*, n.d.; Levin and Goodfriend, 1914).

The Emergence of Organizational Structures

The fifth characteristic of the public oratory era was the willingness of those involved to experiment with organizational structures and the ready adaptation of those structures to the vagaries of student academic and social life. Forensics was different from sports and other student activities. Taking place outside the confines of the regularly scheduled class, the activity necessarily adopted norms, practices, and structures consistent with the other elements of educational life.

The adaptation took numerous forms. The forensics season, for example, was clearly defined by the parameters of the traditional academic calendar—that is, prepare during the first semester, compete during the second (Nichols, 1936a; Stone, 1893). The preparation phase took considerable time due to the use of multiple debate topics of local or state interest, as well as the fact that the vast majority of students spent their summers working on farms or otherwise making money to subsidize their educations (Cowperthwaite, 1946). For the speech contests, orators selected their topics, wrote and memorized speeches, and practiced during the first semester. Some national groups sponsored annual competitions in response to significant world events or national movements (e.g., National Intercollegiate Peace Association, Interstate Oratorical Association), necessitating the adaptation of speeches to the particular rules set by the sponsoring group (Sillars, 1949).

During the second semester, competitions were scheduled on campuses, between neighboring schools, and in the form of debate and speaking tours. Student managers established reciprocal contracts with debate teams along a particular route or in a particular geographic area. For example, Ripon College debaters toured New England and debated Ivy League schools; the University of Redlands in California traveled to the Midwest and debated teams all along the way. The first transcontinental debate trip was made in 1916 when Columbia University traveled to Los Angeles, with a stop at William Jewell College in Liberty, Missouri (Nichols, 1937; Sillars, 1949). Typically, a school did not engage in more debates than football games, and there were fewer oratorical contests.

THE NATURE OF FORENSICS PRACTICE
IN THE PUBLIC ORATORY ERA

The public oratory era began when competition models supplanted the literary societies, when organizational structures emerged, and when argumentation and debate theories began to be developed. Later, competitive rules and norms were consolidated, and the broad framework of forensics competition and its uneasy relationship to the speech discipline became apparent.

The Emergence of Forensics Models

Four models of forensics emerged during the public oratory era: the intersquad tour, the tournament, the international, and the innovational. The intersquad tour was the original and dominant model of competitive forensics and the most popular throughout the era. As in athletic contests, a squad of debaters (an affirmative and/or a negative team) from one school traveled to another institution for a debate, or perhaps two, each taking one side of the agreed-upon resolution. The debates were public contests that often included other festivities, such as musical interludes, banquets, and speeches from notable local public figures (Littlefield, 1998).

Most squads had a student or staff manager whose responsibility it was to arrange the details of the debate(s). The manager would contact the other school and negotiate the time, place, and topic; the host school usually provided the judges. The judges were often prominent community members who took their responsibilities seriously, particularly with regard to being unbiased about either the participants or the merits of the resolution. The visiting squad traveled to the host institution and was greeted with some fanfare; the debate would then take place in front of an audience of students, faculty, and community members. It was not unusual for the host to hold a banquet honoring the debaters before or after the debate. The winning team would likely be given a trophy.

The costs and inconvenience of travel (mostly by train during this era) encouraged teams to conduct tours on which they debated various schools. The added complexity of scheduling tours encouraged the use of a single proposition so as to make it easier for the traveling team to prepare. For example, the 2008 movie *The Great Debaters* (Washington, 2007) embellished a true incident, a debate between a small historically black college/university (HBCU) and a large college, the University of Southern California (changed to Harvard in the movie version). The Wiley College squad (Marshall, Texas) participated in various debates on its way to Los Angeles in 1935. The local press reported the debates in El Paso and Albuquerque, and their coverage emphasized the uniqueness of African American versus Caucasian contests and the debating skills of the Wiley students.

Two important organizational structures emerged at the college level during this time: leagues and national fraternities. The league structure (e.g., triangular, quadrangular) was used throughout the country but most prominently in the Midwest as a means of facilitating regular debates with rival schools. This paralleled the growth of sports leagues. These leagues lent a sense of predictability and organization to the emerging contest format. Typically, the leagues sponsored home and away contests with an affirmative team from one school traveling to its opponent's site, while the opponent's negative team might make the reverse journey. There was not, however, a fixed organization for these events. The league contests did have some consistent characteristics.

First, they were public contests. The debates often occurred in front of large audiences attending an event with many different forms of entertainment (e.g., musical performances, speeches, and banquets). These combined to make the debates a lively evening of activity. The visiting team would sometimes be met at the train station by a large crowd and escorted to the event site. The debates were eagerly anticipated by a society steeped in the tradition of the Chautauqua and lacking the modern stimulation provided by the radio, television, or Internet.

Second, the rules and topics were negotiated beforehand, which helped ensure, but did not guarantee, a fair contest. The topics themselves were problematic. Lacking experience in topic construction, each team had an obvious incentive to suggest a topic favorable to its position or local views. League debates were occasionally cancelled due to strong disagreement about the topic or upon discovery that an opponent had prepared to debate on a topic different from that originally negotiated. The debate resolution appears to have been a more controversial issue than the judging. Generally the host school would provide the judges, who were civic, educational, or religious leaders. The judges appear to have taken their responsibilities seriously, but the lack of consistent judging standards made it likely that the judges sometimes evaluated the debate on the basis of their own opinions on the subject or the speaking skills of the debaters.

Third, the results of the league contests were often considered to be indications of institutional quality and educational preparation. Quality assessment in higher education was nonexistent during this time, at least in the sense of its role in the twenty-first-century educational world. Most colleges were fairly new and had no particular way to judge their own quality. Debate, as an intellectual sport, represented at least one comparative measure schools could use as a quality measure. So league results were carefully tracked and reported.

The other significant organizational innovation during this era was the creation of debate honor societies. Delta Sigma Rho was founded in 1906, Tau Kappa Alpha in 1908, Pi Kappa Delta and Zeta Kappa Xi in 1913, Delta Phi in 1915, and Phi Rho Pi in 1927. Delta Sigma Rho modeled itself on Phi Beta Kappa and emphasized establishing chapters in large and prestigious institutions. Tau Kappa Alpha was originally structured to include a single chapter in each state but eventually adopted the individual college chapter model. Zeta Kappa Xi and Delta Phi were established for women but disappeared when Delta Sigma Rho and Tau Kappa Alpha began admitting women (Nichols, 1936b, p. 599). Pi Kappa Delta and Phi Rho Pi were established to appeal to colleges ineligible for membership in the other honoraries. Pi Kappa Delta membership was centered on smaller and less prestigious institutions, and Phi Rho Pi was an honorary for junior colleges.

Each of the honoraries was organized around different principles. Delta Sigma Rho and later Tau Kappa Alpha emphasized academic achievement using the Phi Beta Kappa model. Pi Kappa Delta adopted the Masonic model of degrees and orders. Each of the organizations established publications to facilitate communication. They all initially faced severe financial constraints that took some years to resolve. With this timeline in place, it is important to discuss the significant social and intellectual trends that shaped how the newly discovered educational form would progress.

The Consolidation of Forensics Practices

After World War I, forensics norms and values became consolidated as new innovations began to replace the league and intersquad debate models. First, international debate became important. The grand tour of Europe or Asia by debaters was a characteristic of this era. The innovation of international debate is generally credited to A. Craig Baird and Bates College, which began debating British universities around 1905. Debates with Oxford and Cambridge held obvious appeal for universities seeking to enhance public perception of their quality, and many universities, particularly in the East and Midwest, sought either to host the British or to go themselves to Great Britain to debate and tour. The University of Oregon expanded on this model and achieved great notoriety by participating in an around-the-world tour in 1926.

The significance of international debating, which continued throughout the century, cannot be underestimated. During much of the century, both American and international students had limited opportunities to interact with or fully appreciate other cultures. Long before the creation of the United Nations and other contemporary forms of structured international interaction and negotiation, debaters from various nations were already modeling the values of debate both as a method for effectively managing disputes and as a means of breaking down the cultural barriers preventing meaningful understanding of diverse perspectives.

Forensics was the one activity that could easily translate between cultures, particularly in Europe, where there was an ancient history of debating as a form of student engagement. An additional benefit was that international debates were particularly popular in the African American colleges. LeMoyne College, for example, took a world tour and debated with white teams both in the United States and abroad, contributing to the pressure to fully integrate higher education and to recognize the intellectual equality of black and white students.

The second important innovation was event experimentation. As time passed, substantial experimentation and growth in the number and types of speaking and debating events occurred at both the high school and the college levels. E. R. Nichols's debate yearbooks described many instances. Radio debate, Lincoln-Douglas debate, cross-examination, storytelling, expository speaking, and a whole range of oral interpretation contests made their debut, and tournaments often competed to provide contestants with new outlets for their talents. When the public oratory era began, students competed primarily in team debate, oratory, and extemporaneous speaking. By the Roaring Twenties, the sky was the limit, fueled by the strong popularity of forensics on the college campus.

The third change was the introduction of the tournament. Travel and logistical challenges were the most likely factors in encouraging the growth of the tournament model, which had existed in rudimentary form, particularly at the high school level, for some years and gained popularity among colleges in the 1920s. There were two forms of the tournament model: the closed league system and the open system. The closed league system was the first tournament form and dates to at least the early 1900s. These leagues, which predated sports leagues, consisted often of three (triangular) or sometimes four (quadrangular) schools in regional proximity. These league debates were often hotly contested, as the competitive school spirit dictated either victory or failure. This led to not-infrequent squabbling over perceived rule violations or topic misunderstandings. As sports became more popular, the significance of the debate league model diminished, although it persists to this day.

Nichols (1936a) attributed the invention of the open tournament to Southwestern College in 1926. While there is not clear evidence to the contrary, it is probable that the model had been experimented with prior to that time, most certainly by high schools and Pi Kappa Delta, which had hosted a national convention with competition beginning in 1920. Wherever it began, the open tournament model rapidly gained adherence for a basic reason: it was highly cost-effective. The economic boom of the 1920s only trickled down to cocurricular activities. Colleges were much more intent on spending money on buildings, developing high-visibility curricular offerings, and a new interest in "financial aid" for students. Most forensics programs, as consistently cataloged by Nichols, who was the de facto commissioner of forensics, had few financial resources to cover travel and lodging costs. Being able to attend a tournament and participate in multiple rounds of competition was highly significant to the growth of the activity. The tournament model had several significant effects.

First, it expanded the number of students on a single squad who could participate in competitive forensics. In the earlier intersquad tour model, only a very select number of students could participate, and the competition for a spot on the traveling squad was often intense. The open tournament model allowed many more students to participate, which answered the high student demand for debate opportunities. Almost immediately after the tournament model became popular, tournaments began to divide their offerings by sex (men's and women's divisions) and skill (varsity and novice). Forensics transformed from an activity for the elite into one open to students of all skills and backgrounds. It became democratized in spirit, a change that went virtually unnoticed by the new speech discipline, many of whose leaders were already devaluing the activity because it insufficiently promoted civic engagement. We return to this issue in chapter 10.

Second, the tournament model expanded the need for professional coaching. Squads needed more coaching to prepare the greater number of participants for competition and had less need for a squad manager to negotiate arrangements with other squads. The forensics coach assumed the responsibilities of the squad manager and also organized practice debates and helped students gather evidence and create potential arguments.

Third, the tournament model significantly expanded professional dialogue, in journals and elsewhere, about rules, norms, and theories of competitive debate. Borrowing from a variety of different influences (e.g., rhetorical, legal, and parliamentary procedure), debate theory emerged to address competition-related issues. Some of this theory addressed ethical concerns, as we discuss later, and some scholarship simply expanded on existing concepts to fit theories (e.g., Whately's presumption) to the particular needs of competitive debate.

The unintended consequences resulting from the tournament model were far-reaching. The tournament model greatly aided the popularization of forensics but also necessitated standardization of formats and the use of a single topic so that attendees knew in advance what they would be debating. The tournament settled two persistent structural problems: whether students should debate both sides of the resolution and whether trained judges were to be allowed into the debating chamber. While single-side debating would last well into the technical era, it became more convenient and cost-effective to drive students to a tournament prepared to argue both sides. Also, the tournament model strengthened the growing belief that well-trained debaters needed professional coaches and that those coaches were a natural pool of judges when it became very evident that recruiting lay judges would make tournament hosting extremely difficult.

Fourth, the growing tension between the newly emerging communication discipline and forensics affected the evolution of the activity. The various published histories of the speech communication discipline generally devalue the impact of forensics students on actively lobbying colleges to offer speech courses and support debate programs, which assisted in the rapid expansion of the communication discipline after 1900. But while the popularity of forensics helped grow the number of college speech programs, the discipline, as it sought its own intellectual and academic footing, moved beyond forensics into both the humanistic study of rhetoric and the emerging social science–based research models. Almost immediately this created the fissures of disagreement between forensics and the communication discipline. This issue is considered in greater detail in a later chapter.

CONCLUSION

This chapter has revealed the foundations of contemporary forensics education through a discussion of forensics as an American educational innovation influenced by the social and historical forces at work during the late nineteenth and twentieth centuries. The transformation of literary societies into competitive models reflected the positive attributes of forensics during the public oratory era. The parallel development of high school and college forensics reflected the natural tendency of educational institutions to model similar programs with the capacity to benefit society during a time of civic engagement and progressive ideas. Finally, the emergence of the speech communication discipline in higher education signaled the desire of academics to resist the notion that speech education was all about elocution at the expense of content development.

Throughout this era of forensics history, the belief that forensics practice would prepare future citizens to be advocates for the changes needed to improve American democracy created an environment in which forensics thrived. Using the republican model of government as a framework, voluntary associations sprang up across the country in local communities, providing an opportunity for students trained in forensics to assume leadership positions, to use parliamentary procedure, to speak in public, and to engage in civic debate about the problems of the day and their potential solutions. Forensics was all about preparing people to engage in promoting the public interest, and the activity remained available to the public due to its external focus.

The next chapter identifies changes in the American educational system following World War II as having a dramatic effect on the nature of forensics activities. The influx of veterans into the collegiate environment, the growth of graduate education, and the focus of the federal government on creating educational policies are revealed in what we call the technical era of forensics. Chapter 3 delineates the rise of the competitive, extracurricular model of forensics and the use of trained critics as judges, as well as the advent of the American Forensic Association as an umbrella organization shaping what would be the evolution of forensics at the end of the century.

REFERENCES

Baker, G. P. (1895). *The principles of argumentation.* Boston: Ginn.

Broderick, F. L. (1989). *Progressivism at risk: Electing a president in 1912.* New York: Greenwood Press.

Cerling, L. R. (1995). The fate of eloquence in American higher education: 1892–1925. Unpublished dissertation. Iowa City: University of Iowa.

Chandler, A. J., Jr. (1954). The origins of Progressive leadership. In E. E. Morrison (Ed.). *The letters of Theodore Roosevelt* (pp. 1462–65). Cambridge, MA: Harvard University Press.

Cohen, H. (1994). *The history of speech communication: The emergence of a discipline, 1914–1945.* Annandale, VA: Speech Communication Association.

Cowperthwaite, L. L. (1946). History of intercollegiate forensics at the State University of Iowa. Unpublished thesis. Ames: Iowa State University.

Debating: History of the Harvard-Princeton-Yale Triangulars, 1909–1959. (n.d.). Available at Harvard University Archives: HUD 11320.959.

Foster, W. T. (1904). *Debating at Harvard University.* Cambridge, MA: Caustic-Claflin Company.

Gulley, H. F. (1954). Building audiences for debate. *Gavel of Delta Sigma Rho, 36* (4), 98–99.

Halloran, S. M. (1982). Rhetoric in the American college curriculum: The decline of public discourse. *Pre/Text 3* (3), n.p.

Harvard vs. Yale—Debate. (1917). Available at Harvard University Archives: HUD 11320 917.2.

Hayes, A. R. (1952). The influence and impact of Edwin Dubois Shurter on speech education in Texas. Unpublished dissertation. Austin: University of Texas.

Hellman, H. E. (1942). The influence of the literary society in the making of American orators. *Quarterly Journal of Speech, 28* (1), 12–14.

Jacob, B. E. (1928). History of the National Forensic League. *NFL Bulletin, 3* (2), n.p.

Keith, W. M. (2007). *Democracy as discussion: Civic education and the American Forum Movement.* Lanham, MD: Rowman & Littlefield.

Levin, A. N., and Goodfriend, H. B. (Eds.). (1914). *Harvard debating—1892–1913.* Cambridge, MA: Caustic-Claflin Company.

Littlefield, R. S. (1998). *Voices on the prairie: Bringing speech and theatre to North Dakota.* Fargo, ND: Institute for Regional Studies.

The Missouri-Nebraska debate. (1902, May 21). *M. S. U. Independent* [Columbia, MO], *9*, 8.

Nichols, E. R. (1936a). A historical sketch of intercollegiate debating: I. *Quarterly Journal of Speech, 22* (2), 213–20.

Nichols, E. R. (1936b). A historical sketch of intercollegiate debating: II. *Quarterly Journal of Speech, 22* (4), 591–603.

Nichols, E. R. (1937). A historical sketch of intercollegiate debating: III. *Quarterly Journal of Speech, 23* (2), 259–79.

O'Hara, R. J. (2009). The collegiate way: Residential colleges and renewal of campus life. Retrieved from http://collegiateway.org/news.

O'Toole, P. (2005). *When trumpets call: Theodore Roosevelt after the White House.* New York: Simon and Schuster.

Potter, D. (1944). *Debating in the colonial chartered colleges: An historical survey, 1642–1900.* New York: Bureau of Publications, Teachers College, Columbia University.

Prather, C. E. (1891). *Winning orations.* Topeka, KS: n.p.

Rogers, E. M. (1995). *Diffusion of innovations* (5th ed.). New York: Free Press.

Schlesinger, A. M. (1944). Biography of a nation of joiners. *American Historical Review, 50* (1), 1–25.

Schnoor, L. (1983). Historical summary of the Interstate Oratorical Association, 1873–1984. Paper presented to the Speech Communication Association, Chicago, Illinois.

Sillars, M. O., Jr. (1949). History and evaluation of intercollegiate forensics at the University of Redlands. Unpublished thesis. Redlands, CA: University of Redlands.

Skocpol, T. (1999). How Americans became civic. In T. Skocpol and M. P. Fiorina (Eds.). (1999). *Civic engagement in American democracy* (pp. 27–80). Washington, DC: Brookings Institution Press.

Skocpol, T., and Fiorina, M. P. (1999). Making sense of the civic engagement debate. In T. Skocpol and M. P. Fiorina (Eds.). (1999). *Civic engagement in American democracy* (pp. 1–23). Washington, DC: Brookings Institution Press.

Stone, A. P. (1914). Introduction (1893). Reprinted in A. N. Levin and H. B. Goodfriend (Eds.), *Harvard debating—1892–1913* (pp. 5–23). Cambridge, MA: Caustic-Claflin Company. Available at Harvard University Archives: HUD11320.914.

Taylor, B. P. (2004). *Citizenship and democratic doubt.* Lawrence: University Press of Kansas.

Thayer, W. R. (1919). *Theodore Roosevelt: An intimate biography.* Boston: Houghton Mifflin Company.

Washington, D. (Director). (2007). *The great debaters* [Film]. Beverly Hills, CA: Weinstein Company.

3

The Technical Era

World War II changed everything in higher education. The American educational system that began evolving at the end of the Civil War was transformed significantly with the return of thousands of soldiers, unprecedented government intervention into educational policy, and the opening of a Pandora's box of technology and science caused by the detonation of the atomic bombs. Enrollments in two-year and four-year institutions exploded as the GI Bill made it economically feasible for men and women who might otherwise have entered the blue-collar workforce to pursue the benefits of higher education, which had previously been limited to the middle and upper classes. The war finally ended the Great Depression, and in its aftermath there was a significant pent-up demand for consumer goods and other acquisitions, such as single-family homes in the suburbs, signifying progress toward the traditional dream of upward mobility.

Forensics changed as well. The activity entered a new technical era, comprised of the crossroads period, which would last twenty-five years and morph into the divergence period. Both of these periods involved a significant reconstruction of forensics practice from the public oratory era. Both periods would also see the apex of participation in forensics, measured by the number of programs, student participants, and activities; usher in the rise of national championships; and, ironically, see forensics transformed from a highly respected public good into a decidedly private activity devoid of audiences and consensus about the values and practices that students and forensics educators employed.

Forensics was not alone in its transformation during the Cold War and post–Cold War eras between 1945 and 1995. The entire nature of education would change in ways both good and bad. Science and technology would supplant (but not eliminate) the esoteric studies of the cloistered university. Racial and political unrest would dominate the beliefs and activities of generations of students. Organized athletics would become fiefdoms prized for their contribution to a university's public image and their ability to energize donors and alumni. Before considering the changes in forensics practice, we discuss two important social changes: the changes in the educational system after the war and the ongoing tension between practicality and intellectualism in American society generally and in higher education in particular.

THE CHANGING UNIVERSITY: SCIENCE, TECHNOLOGY AND GOVERNMENT INTERVENTION

Thelin (2004) provided a description of changes in higher education after World War II: "Following World War II, American higher education enjoyed a quarter-century of support marked by the 'three P's' of prosperity, prestige, and popularity. The unexpected good fortune was so heady that journalists and college administrators as well as historians have called this a 'golden age'" (p. 260). Thelin observed that this golden age was not without its financial, social, and intellectual challenges, but there is no doubt that the university and all its associated elements, including forensics, irrevocably changed in the immediate postwar era. Three significant factors influenced forensics directly and indirectly in this changing landscape: the substantially quantitative and qualitative change in the student body, the growth and change in graduate education and its resulting siloization of academic study, and government involvement in educational policy through encouragement of research universities and scientific study.

Changes in the Student Body Makeup

Prior to World War II the growth in the number of college students was gradual and reflected the change from an agrarian to an industrial economy. The end of the war saw an immediate and dramatic increase in the number of college students. Thelin (2004) noted, "By 1949–50, total student enrollments had ballooned to almost 2.7 million—an increase of about 80 percent in one decade. This was no aberration, for the figure increased to about 3.6 million in 1960 and then doubled again over the next decade" (p. 261). Many of these students took advantage of the unprecedented financial support provided by the GI Bill.

There were, however, other fundamental influences also at work. For example, an industrial economy began to transform toward a service economy, there was a significant increase in the number of white-collar government jobs, and the complexity of modern manufacturing created an immediate demand for college graduates with scientific and technical training. Public perception of education changed as well. A college degree came to be seen not as a luxury but as a necessity in the life trajectory of a successful person. Competing career paths fell away as the number of apprenticeships decreased, as there were fewer careers for which that method of preparation was appropriate. Pragmatically, universities and colleges relaxed entrance requirements to attract and meet the educational needs of returning soldiers and others seeking the opportunities associated with a college degree.

Initially, colleges anticipated that the new generation of students would be uninterested in traditional elements of college life. This did not turn out to be the case. While many students sought to complete their degrees quickly, many others were attracted to college life and actively sought out opportunities in cocurricular activities, including forensics. Cocurricular activities flourished and became wildly popular and important, particularly as the college curriculum evolved in the postwar era. Four key curricular changes accompanied the significant growth in student enrollment numbers: emphasis on the graduate curriculum, enhanced interest in science and quantitative study, greater differentiation of disciplinary distinctions, and greater urgency regarding accountability stemming from the burgeoning government dollars poured into educational systems.

Growth in Graduate Education

Emphasis on graduate education increased steadily in the twentieth century and became a major focus in the postwar environment. Graduate programs expanded quickly in all disciplines, and the number of graduate students grew steadily. A by-product of this growth became the expectation that college teachers would possess terminal degrees in a recognized and increasingly narrowly focused academic discipline. The reason graduate education expanded quickly was straightforward: higher education feared a shortage of qualified faculty to accommodate the anticipated growth in the student population, particularly as it became clear that a baby boom would guarantee a growing population of students for the long term. A rapidly expanding number of graduate students would also allow colleges to expand quickly with a ready-made teaching staff available to teach undergraduate students for a very modest cost as compared to the cost of paying regular faculty.

Gradually, research-intensive universities relied heavily on graduate students and turned over an increasingly substantial amount of their instruction to that group, leading to a new method of instructional delivery—that is, large lectures with smaller study groups—as well as impersonality in the educational system and a growing hunger for the kinds of close faculty-student interaction characterized by cocurricular activities such as forensics. The rapid expansion in graduate education began to peak sharply in the 1960s with a proliferation of programs in many disciplines, including communication.

One obvious side effect of the rapid increase in the production of graduates was the strengthening of disciplinary boundaries. The differentiation of disciplines did not start in the postwar era but became more prominent as more postgraduate degrees were awarded. As disciplines acquired more fixed boundaries, pursuits without fixed boundaries, such as forensics, began their gradual marginalization at the graduate level. While graduate students assisted with forensics coaching, much as they assisted with teaching other entry-level courses, coaching was increasingly judged to be a secondary activity, and graduate students were strongly encouraged to develop scholarly specializations in one of the more narrow disciplinary foci, particularly when pursing a terminal degree.

This pressure to specialize accompanied the well-documented phenomena of universities, particularly research institutions, placing substantially more emphasis on research than on teaching opportunities. While there were always research opportunities in forensics, those opportunities frequently were determined to be less valuable to the discipline as the activity was increasingly marginalized through characterization as an activity rather than as an outside-the-classroom learning environment.

Government Involvement in Educational Policy

The most profound change in education from 1945 to 1995 was federal involvement, which began even before World War II ended. The federal government asserted its influence on education in various ways: by promoting expansion of the student population through passage of the GI Bill; by expanding scientific and political bureaucracies, requiring technically trained college graduates; by creating large numbers of research grants to promote scientific research consistent with political needs generated by the Cold War; and by encouraging accountability in institutions of which there were only modest expectations prior to the war.

The GI Bill and related legislation, which expanded benefits to veterans and their families to provide financial support for military veterans who wished to attend college, constituted perhaps the farthest-reaching federal influence on higher education during the century. As noted earlier, the end of the war opened the floodgates of veterans taking advantage of the opportunity and quickly transitioning from soldiers to students. The legislation contained one important caveat. Benefits would only apply to students enrolled at accredited institutions, and accreditation took on added significance even as colleges rushed to provide physical, student-life, and academic opportunities. Millions of veterans used their benefits after the war, and this fueled rapid university expansion (U.S. Department of Veterans Affairs, 2012).

The second factor in the rapid growth of postsecondary education was the expansion in the size and complexity of all levels of government. An increasingly large number of jobs in public service emerged partially as a product of the war as well as New Deal programs. Entire support industries grew up as well to assist the government in managing its various activities. These industries needed well-trained employees, which they looked to colleges and universities to provide.

Government also began to invest public money to encourage research, particularly scientific research, to meet the perceived needs for technological and scientific supremacy during the Cold War. The global arms race, the development of civilian applications of nuclear power, and space exploration were only some of the urgent priorities for which a wide range of government agencies funded research activities. Government-funded research, virtually unknown prior to World War II, became a major source of support for universities and began a rapid expansion that continued virtually unabated through the rest of the century. By accepting research funding, universities had to build the required infrastructure, including labs and offices, as well as hire faculty, research associates, and other people to manage the paperwork.

This influx of research dollars also influenced national educational priorities. Schools at all levels were encouraged to emphasize mathematics and science education, and many disciplines, including communication, emphasized the use of empirically based research approaches. In the communication discipline, for example, communication theory grew rapidly and gradually replaced the more traditional rhetoric-based methodologies in significance.

While there were other times when the nature of higher education was transformed, they almost pale in significance to the postwar evolution of all areas of education. A significant influx of students seeking to find new jobs in an increasingly service-oriented and technology-driven economy was added to the new challenges posed by the Cold War and the demand for workers trained differently from those sought by factories during the prior industrial age. Universities grew rapidly, and the drive to expand graduate education began in earnest, peaking during the 1960s and 1970s.

As universities stressed disciplinary depth, the nature of campus life and undergraduate education evolved. These changing conditions affected all aspects of college life, and forensics was no exception. A second dynamic also led to a reshaping of education and forensics. This dynamic was a significant shift in one of the traditional fissure points of American political life, the balance between the public embrace and simultaneous distrust of intellectualism and practicality as forces in public life.

THE UNEASY RELATIONSHIP BETWEEN
PRACTICALITY AND INTELLECTUALISM

In the previous section we discussed the significant changes in education produced by a rapid expansion in enrollment and greater government influence on
educational structures. A second parallel change in education contributed to a
new, technical-oriented role for forensics in the postwar period. This change
was the consolidation of the trend, which began at the start of the century, of
evaluating educational structures in terms of their practical use while simultaneously distrusting the purely intellectual. Hofstadter (1962) addressed this
conflicting dynamic in his Pulitzer Prize–winning history *Anti-Intellectualism
in American Life*:

> During that decade the term "anti-intellectualism," only rarely heard before, became
> a familiar part of our national vocabulary of self-recrimination and intramural abuse.
> In the past, American intellectuals were often discouraged or embittered by the
> national disrespect for the mind, but it is hard to recall a time when large numbers
> of people outside the intellectual community shared their concern, or when self-crit-
> icism on this count took on the character of a nation-wide movement. . . . Primarily
> it was McCarthyism which aroused the fear that the critical mind was at a ruinous
> discount in this country. (p. 3)

Hofstadter (1962) identified some of the critical social forces associated with
what he detailed as an important conflict of the century surrounding the relationship between the influence of experts and elites and the demands and preferences
of "popular democracy" (pp. 197–229). The distrust of intellectuals is not new.
The conflict between modernity and tradition, science and religion, and popu-
lism and elitism has ancient roots and seems somewhat intractable. The relative
balance between these dichotomies ebbs and flows throughout history, and Hofstadter traced that ebb and flow regarding the relative value of intellectuals and
pure intellectual thought in American history. For a long time, the public enchant-
ment with the rugged individualist who conquered the frontier was ascendant.
Institutions of higher education, the greenhouses for unencumbered intellectualism, were considered the appropriate practical outlets for intellectual study and
reserved primarily for the children of the elite and for training students as pastors
and teachers. The excesses of the Gilded Age and growing public awareness of
the complexity of social problems late in the nineteenth century contributed to a
shift in perception of the importance of intellectuals and experts, which was one
of the foundations of Progressivism at the center of the storm of American political and social life through much of the century.

Progressivism, which we have already suggested was a significant influence
in inspiring and shaping the public oratory era of forensics, ushered in a new

emphasis on the role of government in making more use of people and mechanisms to balance the potential power of unfettered capitalism and the demands of
fairness. Hofstadter (1962) observed,

> To control and humanize and moralize the great powers that had accumulated in the
> hands of industrialists and political bosses [during the Gilded Age], it would be nec-
> essary to purify politics and build up the administrative state to the point at which it
> could subject the American economy to a measure of control. Of necessity, the func-
> tions of government would become more complex, and as they did, experts would
> be in great demand. In the interests of democracy itself, the old Jacksonian suspicion
> of experts must be abated. The tension between democracy and the educated man
> now seemed to be disappearing—because the type of man who had always valued
> expertise was now learning to value democracy and because democracy was learning
> to value experts. (pp. 197–98)

Debate training was particularly potent during the Progressive Era in contextu-
alizing public understanding of technical issues. As the significance of experts in
government and public policy expanded during the administrations of Theodore
Roosevelt, Woodrow Wilson, and Franklin Roosevelt, debate training was perceived as the path for preparing citizens to participate in an era of complex economic and political problems in which simple solutions rarely seemed feasible.
This was a central assumption of the public oratory era.

Hofstadter (1962) also traced the antecedents of modern education through
the long-standing argument as to whether the function of the university was to
be grounded in the pursuit of "pure knowledge" or "pragmatic problem solving"
(p. 204). During the time prior to the rise of the Progressives, the influence of
"academics" could easily be dismissed as irrelevant to the real demands of popular democracy. For a time, before the formal end of the New Deal with Franklin
Roosevelt's death in 1945, there was, with a brief interlude during the Republican
administrations in the 1920s, a rapprochement between experts, often college
professors and intellectuals, and public demand for effective problem solving.

The rapprochement did not last long. Growing unease about the perceived
power of intellectuals during the New Deal, coupled with frustration over the
slow economic recovery, upset the balance and ushered in a new period, after the
war, when the distrust of intellectuals dominated political thought to a significant degree. The 1950s represented a new divide between the intellectual (Adlai
Stevenson) and the pragmatic (Dwight Eisenhower), and the persistent whiffs of
Communist influence and Stalinist repression, which peaked with McCarthyism
and its claims of Communist infiltration of schools, universities, government
agencies, and the entertainment industry, contributed to persistent distrust of
anything without a clearly articulated practical application. This most certainly
affected forensics education.

As we shall see in a subsequent chapter, the wide gap between debate as an activity and the new interest in discussion as a method of civic engagement added to the dual pressures of changing assumptions about education and persistent distrust of intellectual elites. The divergent perspectives pulled the rug out from beneath the assumption that debate training was best understood as a public good and necessitated a subtle pedagogical shift, resulting in the dominant theme of the technical era: that forensics training was a private good and best understood as a tool to train problem solvers rather than citizens for participation in civic affairs.

FORENSICS PRACTICE IN THE TWO PERIODS OF THE TECHNICAL ERA

Forensics changed significantly during the two periods of the technical era. While an audience member attending a debate in 1920 would see some obvious similarities to a 1970 contest, that same observer would also have difficulty grasping the significant changes. The debaters would speak at a much faster, less comprehensible rate. Their arguments would be largely based on expert testimony gathered from books and articles rather than the philosophical and literary references common to debates in the public oratory era. The debate itself would occur in a classroom simultaneously with similar debates happening in other classrooms, each conducted in front of a judge likely trained in competitive norms who would judge many debates during a competitive season, which would encompass the entire academic year and culminate in a national championship tournament. The same observer, if watching individual speaking events, would see almost an explosion in the types of events and the numbers of students participating in them.

A new era began, which we label the technical era. The technical era, to a significant degree, resulted from forces that arose in the first half of the century and were accelerated by the changing social and educational dynamics present after the war. There was no conscious or intentional decision to reshape forensics practice; the changes illustrated Nevins's notion of the "consciousness of unity" in history. Nor were the changes accompanying the new technical era simply "aimless drifting"; rather, they were a fundamental reconfiguring of forensics practice necessitated by a world forever changed by war and the detonation of an atomic bomb.

The technical era had two distinct periods. The first, the crossroads period, lasted from 1945 to about 1970. During this period, forensics evolved significantly through the embrace of the competitive model, ending the long intradisciplinary dispute about whether competition could promote desired educational outcomes. During the crossroads period significant fissures emerged and rapidly expanded in the competition-inspired cauldron. Those people passionate about the value of forensics as public oratory training gave ground only grudgingly and focused on the devaluation of delivery as a perceived fatal flaw in technically grounded forensics.

These fissures and the inevitable pressures of the social upheaval of the 1960s led to a second distinct period, which we label the divergence period, encompassing the 1970s and 1980s and extending into the 1990s. This period witnessed a significant breakdown in the perceived shared values of forensics competition generally. There was extreme organizational devolution: the honoraries lost the ability to promote particular norms, the American Forensic Association (AFA) turned its attention to argumentation theory as a primary focus, and new organizations, created as reactions to competition-inspired excess, sprang up and tended, after a time, to revert to and reflect the alleged excesses they originally rejected.

Only in the mid-1990s did the pendulum begin to swing again, and only in terms of acceptance of the reality of a fractured organizational landscape and a growing fatigue with the effort required for opposition. The major competition-based organizations created a sense of détente and accommodation. A growing interest in nurturing new competitive venues, such as Urban Debate Leagues for high school students and new debate movements in Asia and Europe, created a postmodern era in which finding commonality was no longer a particular interest and was replaced by a sense of relativism through which competitive forms emerged, became popular for a short period, and then were again replaced by newer forms, increasingly separated from the communication discipline and the traditional rhetorical canons and pedagogies.

Trends during the Technical Era

Three significant trends in forensics emerged during the technical era, each of which reflected both the intentional choices of educators and the unintentional consequences of the significant changes in higher education occurring during this period. These trends began during the crossroads period and continued, often in subtly changed ways, during the divergence period.

Competition Emphasis Replaced the Educational Emphasis

The most profound change in the technical era of modern forensics was the supremacy of the competitive model as the major determinant of choices and practices in the activity for fifty years. Table 3.1 provides a description and the assumptions of the competitive model.

These are, to be sure, generalizations about the direction of practice. But the fact that there was an actual paradigm shift in the activity after World War II is inescapable. The forensics tournament became the central focus of teaching and

Table 3.1. Differences between the Public Oratory and Competitive Models

Public Oratory Model	Competitive Model
• Forensics was primarily a form of student training in oral public discourse. • Competition was an incentive for student participation.	• Forensics was a game. • Success was measured by winning competitions.
• Forensics was a cocurricular activity. • The purpose of forensics was to accentuate classroom learning in public speaking and reasoning.	• Forensics was an extracurricular activity. • Its purpose was extraneous to the classroom experience.
• The audience was universal. • The educated public intellectual was preferred.	• The audience was particular. • The highly trained forensics professional was preferred.
• Evaluative standards were grounded in classical principles of rhetoric. • Standards were absolute and generally accepted.	• Evaluative standards were grounded in game theory. • Standards were relative and accepted only in particular organizational, educational, and social contexts.

learning. Prior to World War II (and well into the 1950s), there was an intense scholarly debate about whether tournaments and competition should be the focus of forensics education. Many educators, such as Brooks Quimby of Bates, decried the tournament format as undermining the educational aims of forensics (Abernathy, 1942; Mills, 1960; Nobles and Cohen, 1959; Padrow, 1956; Walsh, 1957). Public oratory advocates focused on debate as citizenship training, a point made in the previous chapter. The growing movement to teach discussion grew in part out of the fissure created by widespread disagreement about the role of competition (Keith, 2007).

The decision by the United States Military Academy to host a "national championship" debate tournament in 1947 signaled the beginning of the end for serious questioning of the value of debate tournaments and began to align forensics with the emerging trends in higher education. Tournament success could easily be communicated to constituencies seeking empirical measures validating institutional quality. The tournament model was cost-efficient for institutions grappling with unexpected infrastructure costs caused by the flood of new GI Bill–financed college students. Efficiency was, as noted in the previous chapter, one of the most significant attractions of the model in the first place. Pi Kappa Delta (PKD) schools, generally less affluent than those schools that were members of Delta Sigma Rho (DSR) or Tau Kappa Alpha (TKA), invented tournaments as a cost-saving measure and not primarily because of their intrinsic preference for this format over the league or public debate models, which dominated the landscape.

By the beginning of the technical era, the relative balance of power between the three four-year college fraternities was shifting. Delta Sigma Rho, in particular, was suffering financial pains and declining membership. DSR leaders, such as Quimby, were the most vocal critics of the tournament format, and the organization did not host a national tournament to compete with the PKD national tournament that began in 1920. PKD came through World War II relatively unscathed and resumed its full range of activities soon after the war. PKD had always embraced the tournament format and used various means, such as publishing transcripts of debates and winning orations, to further acceptance of the tournament model.

The decision to host a national championship debate tournament was the result of a long deliberation between West Point and coaches throughout the country. Windes and Kruger (1961) suggested that "the tournament is a creation and an instrument of the entire forensics community" (p. iii). The tournament, from its inception, was always conceived as a de facto national independent debate championship, separate from the tournaments and conventions hosted by the various honoraries. The willingness of General Maxwell Taylor, the West Point superintendent, to provide financial and logistical support made the difference. The West Point Debate Society polled over one thousand colleges and universities to ascertain their support for a national championship. Given that only a fraction of that number of colleges supported an active debate program at that time (as it took many colleges some time to resume regular programming of forensics activities after the war), Windes and Kruger's (1961) claim of "overwhelming approval" of the idea must be put in some context.

Given the vitality of the existing PKD and Phi Rho Pi (PRP) national tournaments, the antipathy toward tournament debating among many DSR and TKA schools, and general financial weakness in many colleges recovering from the Great Depression and the war, it seems questionable that there was a true groundswell of support for the idea. But the tournament was unquestionably successful, achieving wide public recognition even in its first year and successfully branding itself as the national championship of debate for fifty years.

While only a limited number of schools with active debate programs regularly qualified for the tournament, which in 1967 moved from West Point because of financial constraints caused by the Vietnam War, the true significance of the tournament was that it focused attention on the competitive model as the primary delivery means of forensics education. The West Point tournament standardized norms for tournament pairing, inspired creation of a national circuit of competition, and finalized, after a few years, the general acceptance of a single national debate resolution.

The West Point tournament, as one of its innovations, divided the nation into nine geographic districts for the purpose of inviting teams. Each district received a number of teams that would be invited to West Point. Coaches from the districts selected those teams. While there was always some controversy about the appropriateness of the number of bids assigned to a district, the bid system further entrenched the tournament model. To demonstrate their qualification caliber, teams aspiring to attend the West Point tournament needed to be visible and successful at tournaments in their own region and, increasingly, in other districts.

The initial attraction of the West Point tournament was the opportunity to participate in a truly national tournament, and the tournament occasionally took pains to financially support teams from the West that found the expense difficult to justify. Often teams from the West would replicate a common practice from earlier years and "barnstorm" across the country, attending tournaments on their way to West Point. The West Point tournament also instituted the practice of bringing hired judges to the tournament to expand the judging pool and reinforce the idea that the tournament was the true national debate championship.

As the National Debate Tournament (NDT) began, conversations about the advisability of a national professional organization for debate coaches continued. There were various motivations behind the idea, with the basic one deriving from the influences of the rapidly changing educational environment. Higher education and, to an almost equal extent, secondary education found themselves responding to the demand for accountability and professionalism. It was obvious that in the postwar environment, educational institutions would support and reward faculty and activities demonstrating concern for professional growth and educational enhancement. It would no longer be enough simply to assert that a particular form of education was desirable; evidence would be required. While the sea change in exploding quality and quantity in graduate education was not yet visible everywhere, there was sufficient evidence to convince many debate coaches that they would need to upgrade their professional standards and demonstrate a more robust professionalism.

At the same time, the communication discipline was expanding rapidly, particularly regarding interest in the application of social science to communication phenomena. Where once the professional journals such as the *Quarterly Journal of Public Speaking* provided sufficient space and access for professional and scholarly discussions of debate-related issues, there was growing competition for limited pages in those publications. Much of the early scholarship in debate found its way into print in the privately funded and printed publications of Egbert Ray Nichols.

Nichols was easily the most prolific debate scholar of the twentieth century. From the time he began his professional career at Ripon College in 1913 until his retirement from Redlands University in 1953, Nichols wrote articles and books; published transcripts of debates and a debate magazine that was the de facto network for debate coaches to learn of trends as well as the comings and goings of their colleagues; edited the *Forensic of Pi Kappa Delta*; found time to successfully coach generations of debaters; and is credited with the innovation of direct refutation by the negative in a debate round, revolutionizing debate as a particular form. As he approached retirement age, Nichols had, for practical purposes, served as the commissioner of debate for his entire career. It could not have escaped his colleagues' notice that there would be a leadership void at whatever point Nichols left the scene.

Accreditation was another issue facing forensics during the technical era. Regional accrediting agencies filled a vital role in helping to assure the federal and state governments that educational institutions could establish and enforce standards without government regulation, which was common in Europe. The North Central Association of Schools and Colleges issued a report in 1949–1950 that included a recommendation that secondary schools stop participating in competitive speech activities. These recommendations energized the movement to establish a national organization of forensics coaches, and under the auspices of the Speech Association of America (SAA), a meeting was called in Chicago, and the American Forensic Association was founded.

The AFA filled the void and addressed various needs. The association established various publications aimed at providing cutting-edge knowledge and publication opportunities for debate coaches, began work on creating codes of ethics, and became the liaison with West Point regarding the NDT. The association assumed responsibility for promoting the selection of an annual debate topic in conjunction with the SAA and published a newsletter, the *Register*, providing members with the kind of information formerly provided by Nichols's *Debater's Magazine* (Blyton, 1970, pp. 13–16).

The AFA became an affiliate organization of the SAA. This formalized a relationship with the speech communication discipline that significantly formalized the association of forensics programs with communication departments despite the fact that many programs were unconnected with the communication curriculum. While there was always a connection between the communication discipline and forensics, the formal association of the new professional organization with the national communication organization entrenched forensics leadership by people associated with speech communication departments and influenced the direction of scholarship toward alignment with disciplinary trends and values. The impact was soon felt: the harshest critics of debate training during the technical era were communication scholars who argued that debate practice deviated from its ideal as was practiced in the public oratory era. We will return to this criticism shortly.

Forensics as a Private Good Replaced Forensics as a Public Good

When the tournament model became the dominant educational delivery means for debate and public speaking after the war, a significant transformation occurred in the forensics community's perceptions of the educational role of forensics competition. In the public oratory era, forensics training was believed to be a means of training for civic participation. Civic participation was a public good. Society required well-trained advocates to serve both public and private sectors. The competition element of debate and oratory was generally considered secondary to the public elements. Debaters would on occasion participate in tournaments or league competitions, but the main focus continued to be on public events. A healthy forensics program conducted a substantial number of debates and speeches in front of campus and community groups. Many schools had active intracampus activities, such as oratory contests.

This is not to say that schools did not take great pride in the competitive successes of their forensics programs. Winning tournaments and league events was cherished and widely publicized on campus and in the community. By the end of the public oratory era, forensics had slipped behind competitive athletics as a source of eager anticipation, but schools continued to perceive a successful debate program as one sign of a successful educational program. If athletics involved occasional excess from some weak student athletes recruited for their athletic rather than academic skills, overeager alumni, and a sense that sports were more important than academics, part of the antidote was the ability of the institution to point to the success of the debate team as evidence that there were smart and capable students on campus as well.

The relationship between competitive sports and competitive speech changed during the public oratory era from equality to competition. The relationship would further evolve in the technical era as forensics faded from public view. On the increasingly fewer occasions when the public took note of forensics, such notice emphasized intellectual competition and competitive success as understood from the perspective of competitive athletics.

As a result, forensics went underground and out of the public eye. Debate in particular evolved toward a much more private good. Programs embraced the competitive model, the number of tournaments expanded in the 1950s, and the tournament model increasingly crowded out the public service dimensions of programs. This switch was not immediate and not universal. Some programs maintained active campus and community service. But for many programs the community and service elements became secondary to competition. Service, for example, would be relegated to times after the season or would be the province of students who were not part of the traveling squad.

Debates themselves changed. As discussed in the next section, the classical canons of invention and style dominated debate practices in the periods of the technical era, and other canons (most notably delivery) were pushed to the side or ignored. This shift in emphasis was the product of changing needs in the educational system. Education was becoming more technically oriented; many institutions (and students, for that matter) saw career training as more important than general education. To echo Hofstadter, the practical was preferred to the purely intellectual. Furthermore, growing emphasis on assessment and scientific training attracted institutional and government support at the expense of other priorities. Competitive debate changed along with these other institutional and social practices.

The community understanding of forensics during the technical era focused on the private benefits to the student participant as opposed to the public benefits emphasized during the public oratory era. Argumentation textbooks for the first time began to justify debate training in terms of its benefits to the individual (McBath, 1963, pp. 11–12).

Table 3.2. Public versus Private Benefits of Forensics Training

Public Oratory Era	Technical Era
• Focus on community benefits: leadership training, public advocacy	• Focus on individual benefits: skill at research, argument invention, and "critical inquiry"
• Balance of emphasis on rhetorical canons	• Emphasis on invention; de-emphasis of other canons, especially delivery
• Success measured through positive audience response	• Success measured through repetition and tournament success

Invention and Style Dominated Competitive Forensics

The third change of the technical era was the gradual shift in teaching emphasis regarding the role of the classical rhetorical canons. The canons have served an important pedagogical function for centuries, as the method guiding creation of good rhetoric. That does not, of course, imply that there was always a balance in emphasis when teaching the canons. There was controversy in medieval times about whether the study of rhetoric was itself too broad and in need of division. Medieval universities came to separate the study of invention from the other canons, and that division persists in some forms to the present. Furthermore, the elocution movement in the nineteenth century, with its emphasis on preferred methods of delivery, caused a push-back from students desiring greater study of invention and alternate methods of style. This ultimately became one of the major reasons why competitive debate replaced oratory and the literary societies at the end of the nineteenth century. Students perceived oratory, declamation, and other elements of elocution as too stilted and confining, particularly as compared to the openness and challenge of debate at a time when society was open to challenges to traditional thought and inquiry, as exemplified by Progressivism.

Early debate training, as originally introduced by Baker (1895) and other early theorists, sought to reestablish a balance among the rhetorical canons and to teach argumentation and debate to students as a holistic skill set, the mastery of which would prepare the student for active civic engagement. Debate training during the public oratory era emphasized a strict adherence to balance. Students were instructed in well-known theories of formal reasoning and identification of fallacies. There was suspicion of an overreliance on argument by authority. The necessity of speaking to diverse audiences required practice in effective organization and delivery skills.

Forensics during the technical era gradually shifted away from the holistic practice toward a fractured worldview. This fracture initially came from a change in emphasis in competitive debate away from the balance between the rhetorical canons toward a preference for information-processing (invention) and spread debating (style) at the expense of delivery. The first fracture came in the form of splitting public speaking away from debate through a much more intentional emphasis on individual events competitions. While these initially celebrated the value of audience-centered style and delivery, ultimately the same competitive forces that influenced debate to move away from an audience-centered orientation also affected individual-events style as well.

Even within the debate community, further fracturing occurred, as there came to be a strong push-back against the perception that mainstream debate was over-emphasizing information processing and a preferred style grounded in rapid delivery. By the beginning of the 1990s, there was a wide diversity in debate forms and a lack of consensus about debate practice and values, which led to the end of the technical era and the beginning of the postmodern era, whose main focus has been on the diversity of practice itself, seeing value in having many forms of practice and rejecting the need for a single, preferred competitive form.

So how did the emphasis on information processing and rapid delivery style come to dominate debate practice? There are multiple factors at play. First, it was probably inevitable, given the shift in academic life we have discussed. As science and the investigation of science began to dominate education, empiricism as a paradigm became more prominent. Science education emphasized the scientific method, even if that method was not necessarily part of the curriculum. Evidence and proof took on a new meaning in a science-influenced culture. As the discipline of communication embraced the social sciences through analysis of communication theory, group dynamics, and empirical research methods, debate also embraced that direction.

Debaters began to spend a greater amount of time in the library availing themselves of the resources available in the newly minted information age. Debate arguments became more complex as debaters gathered more and more information and relied on authority-based claims rather than the broader types of claims preferred in earlier times. There was inevitable pressure on debaters to pack as much of their newfound evidence and analysis as possible into debate speeches. Thus was born the spread strategy, whereby the canon of delivery was sacrificed in support of the canons of invention and style.

Second, the growing emphasis on national competition led to the development of competitive norms. As the national debate circuit emerged, a gradual consensus developed regarding preferred practices, which included expectations regarding the presentation of substantial amounts of authority-based evidence and analysis in a debate speech and the strong preference for expert testimony and empirical evidence over the literary and historical references common in the public oratory era.

Third, a multitude of new debate theories were introduced by a generation of debate scholars and teachers who recognized the importance of theoretical advances in argumentation and debate practice not only to strengthen the activity but also to give academic debate legitimacy in the broader academic community. The growing norm in higher education was the expectation that faculty must publish or perish. This dictum applied equally to those debate educators occupying tenure-track positions. Chapter 5 goes into greater detail about the theoretical innovations introduced during the technical period. However, a short list would include the Toulmin model, debate paradigms, counterplans, and the comparative advantage case, among others.

Effects of the Shift to the Technical Era

Forensics, by the end of the technical divergence period, was in a much weaker state than at the end of World War II, even accounting for the challenges of reinvigorating the activity in the new postwar educational framework. After the war, colleges and universities faced many challenges, including hiring trained faculty to teach the waves of incoming students, managing deferred maintenance and debt reduction from the Great Depression, and adapting to the demands of accreditation and government accountability. Despite those challenges, forensics rebounded sharply and between 1945 and 1970 saw its high point as measured by both the number of programs and the number of students participating in a burgeoning number of forensics activities.

In the quarter century after 1970, during the divergence period, forensics experienced a small but general decline in overall participation and a substantial flattening of the landscape. Before 1970, most programs emphasized policy debate, and students participated in individual events activities as a complement to their debate participation. By the 1970s there was an explosion of interest in individual events as a national competition form, and the debate activity devolved into a number of smaller associations, each of which pursued a different philosophy of forensics practice.

The civil rights and antiwar movements did not seem to affect the number of students participating in forensics. However, the significant upheavals caused by the movements of the 1960s did contribute tangentially to changes in forensics through their effects on both society in general and student perceptions of the role of cocurricular education in particular. One effect of these changes was to challenge dominant hierarchies and norms. Assumptions previously taken for granted became fair game for criticism. This was certainly the case in forensics in the latter part of the divergence period of the technical era.

By 1970, the technical crossroads period gave way to the technical divergence period. While the nature of modern debate and public speaking practice was generally fixed by 1970, organizationally and philosophically the activity changed. Forensics, which began as a homogenous activity inspired by Progressivism and a desire to create good citizens, gave way to an extremely fractured activity defined more by dissent than assent about philosophy and practice. There were several key indicators of this shift toward divergence.

Fractionalization of Shared Norms and Values

The most significant effect of the technical era, particularly during the divergence period, and its surrounding social elements was the shattering of consensus about dominant norms and values. The lofty values articulated by organizational leaders as early as the 1920s, which formed the basis for promoting the tournament model and its apex, the West Point NDT, did not survive the turmoil of the changing postwar university, the growing emphasis on forensics as a technically based activity, and the social upheaval of the 1960s. The forensics activity broke into pieces.

Was ever there true consensus about norms and values in forensics? Affirmation would likely be an overclaim. There was an established distrust among the honoraries and fear that each organization was trying to poach schools from the others. But from the founding of the honoraries and the widespread expansion of forensics after World War I, there was a détente of sorts. The honoraries devised specific rules governing school transfers and explicit promises to avoid encouraging organizational switches. The various factions came together to select an annual debate resolution, even as some schools stubbornly opposed the tournament model. The threats and opportunities of the postwar period led the various factions to form the AFA, and after a long courtship, DSR and TKA merged to preserve their shared values and to deal with persistent membership and financial difficulties. This détente seemed to hold together until the 1960s.

The first shift in the landscape was the growing popularity of individual events in the 1960s. Speech competition was not, of course, new. The earliest speech tournament may have been the Interstate Oratory Contest (1874). PKD first sponsored oratory and extemporaneous speaking events as part of their national tournament in 1924. The organization published transcripts of winning speeches (*Winning Orations*) in 1926, and the national archives contain transcripts from several national conventions. Nichols's yearbooks printed transcripts, and peda-gogical assistance for coaching speaking events was common in the various com-munication and forensics magazines and journals. Many high school and college tournaments offered a wide range of individual events competitions beginning in the 1930s. One example was Linfield College, which hosted one of the earliest college tournaments in the West, regularly offering a wide range of speaking, oral interpretation, and theater events ("Presenting Linfield College," 1946). But until the 1960s individual events competition was considered secondary to debate.

Competition in public speaking and oral interpretation events grew steadily during the 1950s and 1960s, and eventually interest grew in offering a national championship tournament. Raymond Beaty of Ohio University and Jack Howe of California State University, Long Beach, floated the idea of a national in-dividual events tournament and were, according to Beaty, "met with laughter from the debate community" (Fryar, 1984). The consensus was that insufficient interest existed to justify such an event. The American Forensic Association was already dealing with West Point's decision in 1966 to withdraw as the host of the National Debate Tournament. This decision, caused by financial constraints imposed by the Vietnam War, initially seemed to catch the AFA off guard. While the AFA was working to resolve the hosting issue and create a permanent struc-ture for rotating the NDT, the organization did not actively explore the possibility of an individual events national championship.

It was left to Seth Hawkins of Southern Connecticut State College to "unilater-ally invent a national championship in individual events, declare it official by fiat, and send invitations" in 1971 (Fryar, 1984). Hawkins's national championship, held at Ohio Northern University, attracted twenty-three eastern and southern schools whose students competed in prose, poetry, extemporaneous speaking, oratory, and after-dinner speaking. Despite the success of the event, Hawkins resisted efforts to create an organizational structure, preferring to maintain per-sonal management of the event. Other forensics directors drafted a constitution over Hawkins's objections, and the National Forensic Association (NFA) was established in 1974.

The obvious success of the NFA tournament (more than one hundred schools attended the 1974 event) sparked interest among the AFA leaders, who quickly moved to establish the National Individual Events Tournament (NIET) in 1978. Both national championships expanded their event offerings and grew steadily in the 1980s, with a relatively small number of schools active and successful in both the NDT and NFA/NIET circuits. The era of specialization had begun.

A similar fracture appeared in the debate community. The most significant challenge came from Jack Howe's creation of the Southwest Cross-Examination Debate Association (SCEDA) in 1971. Howe claimed that he was inspired to create the organization while driving home from a tournament and bemoaning the state of debate as a high-speed recitation of evidence that was, in his view, inaccessible to many college students. Howe was hardly alone in his negativity about the state of debate at that time. There was considerable criticism of debate practice in the communication literature and elsewhere. SCEDA became the Cross-Examination Debate Association (CEDA), as a complement to policy debate rather than an alternative. Howe maintained for many years that while he personally did not support the existing practices in policy debate, he was not seeking to supplant it.

The original structure of SCEDA was modest. A handful of tournaments offered a division of this event. The SCEDA and later CEDA divisions were different from the existing policy divisions. They reintroduced cross-examination into the debates, typically used value resolutions rather than policy resolutions, and encouraged experimentation with format. SCEDA's goal was to provide a debate format appropriate for novice or occasional debaters who were unwilling or unable to engage in the specialization required for success on the policy debate circuit. SCEDA introduced a tournament sanctioning system and a yearly cumulative sweepstakes. Howe, in his role as executive secretary, distributed regular sweepstakes updates with tournament results.

The organization grew extremely rapidly and soon began siphoning programs, particularly in the West, away from the NDT circuit. Despite Howe's initial claim that the organization was not intended to compete with the NDT, it soon did. The sweepstakes system (awarding one point for each debate round victory) ensured that novice and junior division competitors could contribute to a squad's success. The regular turnover in topics, initially monthly and later biannually, changing at mid-year, provided opportunities for students with other interests to catch up and significantly lessened the massive research burden of NDT debaters, who began researching their topic as early as July and necessarily continued their research until the April conclusion of the season.

CEDA also exposed the resource disparity among forensics participants. CEDA attracted many schools with smaller budgets and fewer students. Schools with the more substantial budgets necessary to successfully compete nationally dominated the NDT. Obviously there were exceptions in both organizations. But the clear perception, particularly in the early years of CEDA, was that CEDA was primarily an organization for smaller programs unable to compete successfully with their larger counterparts. There was considerable organizational animosity in the years (1971–1990) when CEDA was rapidly expanding and the NDT was shrinking, as measured by numbers of programs and policy debate tournaments.

After many years of discussion, CEDA chose to offer its own national championship tournament in 1986. This tournament was an open event that contrasted sharply with the NDT's highly restrictive qualification system. The early CEDA national tournaments were very well attended, initially used random judging assignment systems, and were early adopters of computerized matching and recording technologies. CEDA became the largest debate organization, although by 2000 the organization had formed much closer connections with the NDT and, for all practical purposes, reunited the two organizations, although each continued to offer its own national tournament. By the turn of the twenty-first century, both CEDA and the NDT used the same yearlong national topic, and their memberships substantially overlapped.

Other debate organizations also formed and expanded during this period, particularly as the stylistic and philosophical distinctions between the NDT and CEDA communities blurred. The most important new direction was the renewed national interest in parliamentary debate. Parliamentary debate, modeled after the common style used in Great Britain, existed for many years primarily on the East Coast, usually as a less formal, student-run activity. The informal groups came together in 1981 as the American Parliamentary Debate Association (APDA), whose purpose was to encourage the practice of parliamentary debate similar to its practice in Canada, Europe, and eventually other parts of the world. Ten years later, a counterpart organization, the National Parliamentary Debate Association (NPDA), was created, initially consisting of schools in the Rocky Mountains and western United States. The organization was created as a direct reaction to the movement of CEDA back in the direction of the NDT, and the NPDA became popular in the West quickly and throughout the United States gradually.

The most significant effect of the technical era was the fractionalization of forensics into smaller and more philosophically discrete entities. By the end of the divergence period, there was no single voice for forensics within the academic community. Each of the various national organizations sponsored its own national tournament and developed its own competitive norms; many even wrote their own codes of ethics. While some programs tried to compete actively in multiple competitive forms, those programs were fewer and fewer each year. Programs tended to gravitate toward whichever competitive form provided them the greatest competitive success or kept them affiliated with other geographically close programs that were participating in their organization of choice. The AFA moved away from building consensus about shared norms and values toward simply being a clearinghouse for tournament schedules. This coincided with a growing interest of the AFA, especially through its journal, in an emphasis on argumentation theory rather than forensics practice.

Marginalization within the Academic Community and Communication Discipline

A second outcome of the technical era was the marginalization of forensics within the academic community, particularly the communication discipline. While we discuss this issue later, it is important to note here that the forensics activity was transformed during the technical era from a cocurricular to an extracurricular activity. Debate and public speaking were the centerpieces of the communication curriculum during the public oratory era, but by the end of the technical era, it was easily possible for a student to earn a communication degree without ever having any debate training or experience or more than rudimentary training in public speaking.

The communication discipline embraced the social scientific and empirical methodologies after World War II, reflecting the larger changes in higher education. The shift in communication was heavily toward theoretical and experimental research and away from a strong emphasis on citizenship training. The discipline de-emphasized the study of communication as a liberal art, moving toward an emphasis on career preparation and research. This shift pushed competitive forensics to the margins. Programs were increasingly perceived as extracurricular activities unconnected to the mainstream of communication study.

As debate became more specialized and technical, it became easier for universities to de-emphasize the activity or eliminate programs entirely. Many programs moved from being housed in a communication department to student affairs or club status. Fewer graduate students found support for forensics education training and, after a short time, moved out of forensics toward the greener pastures of communication research, which gained more financial and moral support from the university community. Almost ironically, forensics continued to enjoy strong public support, particularly at the high school level. Without really knowing what skills were being emphasized, the public continued to believe that forensics training was valuable.

CONCLUSION

The end of World War II created a significant shift in forensics as part of a vastly different conceptualization of higher education. The influx of many new students, the demand for training for technical and service jobs, and a move toward federal government funding for scientific disciplines, leading to an escalating demand for graduate training, played a role in substantially altering forensics. Debate moved from being primarily a public good to being a private good, a way of mastering research and information-processing skills necessary for success in a new economy. The growing influence of competition motivated a growing fractionalization of the forensics community, as significant differences emerged between practitioners embracing the new emphasis on invention and style and those seeking a different formula for learning and exhibiting the skills that debate and public speaking provided. By the end of the era, there were clusters of smaller groups and very little consensus about fundamental values and assumptions.

REFERENCES

Abernathy, E. (1942). The criticism against speech tournaments. *Quarterly Journal of Speech, 28*, 354–56.

Baker, G. P. (1895). *The principles of argumentation.* Boston: Ginn.

Blyton, G. (1970). The American Forensic Association: A history. *Journal of the American Forensic Association, 7* (1), 13–16.

Fryar, L. (1984). A brief history of individual events nationals. *National Forensic Journal, 2*, 73–84.

Hofstadter, R. M. (1962). *Anti-intellectualism in American life.* New York: Random House.

Keith, W. M. (2007). *Democracy as discussion: Civic education and the American Forum Movement.* Lanham, MD: Rowman & Littlefield.

McBath, J. H. (1963). *Argumentation and debate: Principles and practices* (rev. ed.). New York: Holt, Rinehart and Winston.

Mills, G. E. (1960). Audiences and tournaments: Two forms of over-emphasis. *Speech Teacher, 9*, 95–98.

Nobles, W. S., and Cohen, H. (1959). The disjunctive premise about forensics. *Speech Teacher, 8*, 316–20.

Padrow, B. (1956). Let's stop calling them educational. *Speech Teacher, 5*, 205–6.

Presenting Linfield College. (1946). *Debater's Magazine, 2* (4), 238–39, 261.

Thelin, J. R. (2004). *A history of American higher education.* Baltimore: Johns Hopkins University Press.

U.S. Department of Veterans Affairs. (2012). *The GI Bill's history.* Retrieved from http://www.gibill.va.gov/benefits/history_timeline/index.html.

Walsh, G. (1957). Tournaments: For better or worse? *Speech Teacher, 6*, 65–67.

Windes, R. R., and Kruger, A. N. (1961). *Championship debating: West Point National Debate Tournament, final round debates and critiques, 1949–60.* Portland, ME: Walch.

4

❖ ❖

Organizational Structures and Their Influence on Forensics Practice

Forensics is unique in that no single organization oversees its practice. Unlike athletics, forensics never implemented universal national guidelines governing rules, norms, or ethics. While no shortage of disputes arose about a wide range of ethical and practical concerns, the activity always lacked systemic mechanisms for settling those disputes or even providing a forum for their discussion. It is somewhat ironic that an activity based on teaching democratic values and rational problem solving itself did not institutionally model how that process should function. Instead, the history of forensics organizations reflects the practices and intersections of a wide range of groups whose decisions were typically reactive and short-term in nature, and the failure of any single organization to guide the forensics community in setting norms and settling disputes was the primary cause of the fractionalization experienced during the technical and postmodern eras.

This chapter traces the various forensics organizations and practices during the twentieth century. We conclude that this organizational history reflects Nevins's vision of both the intentional and the unintentional nature of history. Organizational evolution during this time reflected the significant changes occurring in education generally and the emergence of a new discipline, speech communication, whose history both paralleled and was intertwined with the growth of forensics as an educational form. We discuss this major theme in the second part of the book. An apparent uneasiness existed between forensics educators and participants and organizations attempting to guide forensics practices, between forensics organizations that often felt jealousy rather than the urge for cooperation, and between forensics as a subdiscipline and the emerging broader discipline of speech communication, which itself was frequently fractured.

The most important organizational forces in the public oratory era were the honoraries. Their influence waned during the technical era as a centralized organizational entity that became the American Forensic Association (AFA) emerged to create a national structure to deal, in part, with the violent forces fracturing forensics into special interest groups during the last quarter of the century. We begin with the crucial role the fraternities[1] played in organizing forensics.

THE ROLE OF HONORARIES IN ORGANIZING FORENSICS

The context from which honoraries emerged provides insight into their role in the organization of forensics activities. When forensics competition began, individual representatives from high schools and higher education provided the impetus for negotiating contests between educational institutions. The process was cumbersome. Prior to the widespread availability of the telephone, negotiation occurred mainly through face-to-face contact or by mail. This process worked adequately when a small number of contests constituted the competitive season and occurred between schools that were close geographically.

As groups of schools began interacting on a more regular basis, beginning in the 1890s leagues were organized, and the competitive process became more predictable (Nichols, 1936a; Potter, 1954, pp. 3–19). Squad managers established a network and negotiated the precise details of when the debate(s) or competitions would occur, their format, the topics to be debated or the nature of the speaking events, and who would determine the winner (Nichols, 1936a). The host school organized the judges and the social amenities. As these debates and competitions were staged for the public, events such as banquets and predebate musical interludes, as well as public relations activities, were very important (Nichols, 1936a). Typically, in the early league debates, one school commonly sent its negative team to the opponent's location and hosted the opposing school's team.

The negotiation of these details was sometimes complicated. One of the main sticking points was frequently the resolution. Despite some awareness of topic construction principles left over from the literary societies, the exact wording of the resolution was perceived as crucial. While school rivalries provoked frequent disagreements about one side or the other gaining an advantage based upon topic selection, or what Cowperthwaite and Baird (1954) described as "foul play" (p. 261), most schools followed a detailed process whereby the host team submitted a proposition and the opposing team had two weeks to select the side it wanted to take or submit a new proposition.

These early debates were much different from those of the technical and postmodern eras, when adaptation to the analysis of the resolution by each side was expected. During the early years of the public oratory era, speakers for each side would prepare their speeches in advance with only minimal reference to the opposition's points. Thus, having a shared interpretation of the debate resolution was critical. In instances when the negative team arrived for the debate only to discover either that it had prepared for a different topic or that the affirmative team had interpreted the language of the topic in a different way, debates were often cancelled, and future contests were jeopardized.

While President Theodore Roosevelt was instrumental in the creation of a national organization for the oversight of athletics in 1905 (i.e., National Collegiate Athletic Association) due to the violent and combative nature of football (*Roosevelt Rough Writer*, 1998), his opposition to some debate practices—particularly allowing students to debate both sides of a resolution—was insufficient to persuade the forensics community to establish such a national organization to oversee the growing forensics activity (Roosevelt, 1913, p. 28). Perhaps debating both sides of a resolution lacked the seriousness of injury and death on the football field, or limiting how students should think and speak was considered educationally unsound. Whatever the reason, despite how George Pierce Baker and other early theoreticians characterized competitive debate as an academic sport (Baker, 1901; Redfern, 1960), the twentieth-century emphasis on academic freedom, particularly in the classroom, worked against any thoughts of regulation. Furthermore, the absence of a true national championship in debate kept the stakes low.

High school forensics was organized more formally by the early years of the twentieth century (see Gulley and Seabury, 1954; Lambert, 1948; Littlefield, 2008; Shurter, 1915; State High School Leagues, 1932; Stone, 1914). Leagues were established in large cities like Boston and Chicago, and state extension offices at universities were encouraging high school activity in rural areas (as noted in chapter 2 and further explained in chapter 7). Absent an umbrella organizing body, however, matters such as resolutions and rules required the same intersquad negotiation as that affecting forensics activities at the college level.

The Importance of Social and Fraternal Organizations as an Organizing Model

It is not an accident that the initial organizing model for forensics was the fraternity or social club. Fraternities and social clubs were a vital element of social life, particularly after the Civil War (Cohen, 1998, pp. 68–69). In describing the rise of African American social clubs in Chicago, Poe (1944) reported in the *Chicago Tribune*, "The roots of black social clubs are traced to the black burial societies, such as the Elks, the Masons and the Knights of Pythias, that were established shortly after the Civil War. The societies helped families raise money for burial plots, but they soon became social as well" (n.p.). During their heyday in the second quarter of the twentieth century, club members said several hundred black social clubs flourished in Chicago. Many were groups of about thirty or forty people who became friends through their work, neighborhoods, or families. Except for a few groups for couples, all were segregated by sex (Poe, 1994).

The social club and fraternity model was well developed by the time of its use in organizing forensics. The Freemasons, likely the oldest of the social clubs, dating back at least to the seventeenth century, came to the new continent with European immigrants (Tabbert, 2005). The Benevolent and Protective Order of Elks was founded in 1868 (Detweiler, 1898). Lions Clubs International (2013) began at roughly the same time as the forensics fraternities, founded in 1917. It is clear that this movement (among both prominent groups like the Masons, Elks, and Lions and less prominent ones within ethnic and other communities in large cities) played a variety of important societal roles. These organizations had a sense of purpose, pursued activities designed to promote the general welfare—broadly defined—and provided a sense of belonging to their individual members. This had an obvious impact as groups of teachers, leaders, and citizens began corresponding with each other around the turn of the twentieth century and finding a common urge to organize competitive forensics activities to promote values in which they believed.

The founders of the forensics fraternities were likely themselves members of other social groups and could easily adapt processes, such as initiation rituals and membership degrees, for use in forensics fraternities. Also reinforcing public appreciation for forensics was the similarity of these social clubs to other segments of society. They were, as the cliché goes, as American as apple pie. The combination of public approval for social organizations added to the public appetite and appreciation for speech and debate as a natural combination. Buehler (1963) observed, "Our founders must also have been sensitive to the unique role of public speaking in public life. Most of them lived at a time when William Jennings Bryan, Senator Bob LaFollette, Robert Ingersoll, Billy Sunday, Teddy Roosevelt, Senator Albert Beveridge, Russell Conwell, and a host of platform figures in the Chautauqua, were in their prime" (p. 13).

Honor societies were also a significant aspect of college education, beginning with the founding of Phi Beta Kappa in 1776 (Nagel, 1963, p. 58). They gradually expanded in number, and while Phi Beta Kappa evolved into a strictly academic society, others combined both social and academic activities.

There was a rush to create debate fraternities and sororities between 1900 and 1930, with five national fraternities successfully emerging: Delta Sigma Rho (DSR) in 1906, Tau Kappa Alpha (TKA) in 1908, Pi Kappa Delta (PKD) in 1913, the National Forensic League (NFL) in 1924, and Phi Rho Pi (PRP) in 1928. The creation of specialty fraternities was not confined to forensics; similar organizations were created for music, theater, and other disciplines. Fraternities and sororities were widely accepted, particularly at colleges, despite concerns from their earliest days about their negative social behaviors (Turk, 2004).

For four-year colleges, DSR, TKA, and PKD were the most significant organizational influences and counted the majority of colleges and universities with active forensics programs among their memberships, with the notable exception of the growing number of black colleges. These historically black colleges/universities (HBCUs) were excluded from membership in the fraternities, although black students could have been members of integrated college chapters, as the highly publicized controversy over the membership denial of the accomplished Bates student Benjamin Mays demonstrated (Branham, 1996). The road to equality was difficult, and truly integrating the fraternities entailed a long process.

The three four-year college fraternities initially organized themselves loosely on Masonic principles. Their founders established the fraternity to promote high ethical standards of speech and debate, and their organizational structures and processes reflected the high idealism early teachers and scholars envisioned for the activity in creating active citizens and public servants. But the organizations also were inherently exclusive in their membership policies. The founders of DSR and TKA, in particular, wrote their constitutions as much to keep potential members out as to create standards encouraging excellence in those accepted into the fraternity (Ewbank, 1935; Rarig and Greaves, 1954; Constitution, 1920, 1922). The distinction is important. It suggests an organizational culture, certainly found in other aspects of collegiate life, based on status and privilege rather than merit. In the case of DSR and TKA, this culture did not last forever. The pressures created by the growing influence of the tournament model, as well as the relatively greater inclusiveness of PKD and PRP, eventually led to philosophical changes aligning what would become a combined DSR-TKA with a postwar academic environment in which exclusivity became less desirable than inclusiveness.

Delta Sigma Rho

DSR was originally conceived as a parallel organization to Phi Beta Kappa, the venerated academic fraternity. DSR sought to establish a single chapter in each state located at the most prestigious institution. The organization was specific about its intended audience, often ignoring or delaying applications from teachers' colleges and less prestigious institutions and favoring the Ivy League schools and major universities in each state ("History of Delta Sigma Rho," 1956). The DSR founders made no secret of their desire to emulate the exclusivity of Phi Beta Kappa. The organization established strict standards for membership, and its members primarily emphasized student academic achievement, with success in debate and public speaking being a lesser concern. DSR was the slowest of the honoraries to embrace the tournament format, eventually creating a student congress in 1939, partially to blunt the growing popularity of debate tournaments (Blyton, 1970; Buehler, 1963, p. 17; "The History of Delta Sigma Rho," 1956).

Tau Kappa Alpha

TKA was inspired by DSR. The original organizational meeting in 1908 was held in the lieutenant governor's office in Indianapolis, Indiana, and originally consisted of students and alumni from Butler, Wabash, DePauw, Notre Dame, and Earlham (Layton, 1963, p. 10). TKA was unique among the forensic honoraries based on the role that alumni played in the organization's operation in its early years (Layton, 1963, pp. 10–11). Hugh Miller, lieutenant governor of Indiana, was its president, followed by Indiana senator Albert Beveridge, University of Vermont president Guy Potter Benton, Governor Charles Brough of Arkansas, Professor John Quincy Adams of Louisiana State, and author Lowell Thomas (Layton, 1963, pp. 10–11). Elected officers who coached debate or were communication professors conducted the day-to-day work of the organization, as was the case with the other organizations.

TKA published the first journal devoted to speech and debate, the *Speaker*, in 1913. This journal merged with the similar publication of DSR, the *Gavel*, in 1963 and has appeared continuously since its inception. TKA's membership was larger and drawn from a slightly wider range of liberal arts colleges and state universities than DSR's. It began offering a national convention and tournament starting in 1939. The organization also began honoring a speaker of the year in 1949 (Rarig and Greaves, 1954).

Pi Kappa Delta

PKD, the third honorary for four-year institutions, was founded in 1913 by a group of debate coaches from the Midwest. The founders represented students at small colleges who would not be accepted for membership in either DSR or TKA, but for whom the perceived cachet of membership in a fraternity held strong attraction. PKD used the Masonic model of orders and degrees and created a logo closely resembling a Masonic pin. One of the founders of PKD, E. R. Nichols, who was the debate coach at Ripon College, soon moved to Redlands in Southern California, where he spent the remainder of his career as the leading national organizational voice for forensics and one of the early activities' most successful coaches. He served PKD in a wide range of offices, including president, vice president, and historian. He was active from 1913 until his retirement in the early 1950s (Nichols Jr., 1952).

PKD differed from DSR and TKA in its aim to build the size of its membership rather than reserving membership exclusively to a smaller number of colleges and universities. This was motivated, in part, by the nature of its members: smaller colleges with limited financial resources. Lacking the prestige of elitism embraced by the other two organizations, PKD pursued strategies to strengthen its chapters and to encourage more colleges to join (Nabors, 1956; Norton, 1957).

PKD sponsored the first national forensics convention and tournament in 1920, with one of its purposes being to strengthen and reenergize chapters after World War I. PKD introduced three other significant innovations in the 1920s that proved significant to the growth and development of the forensics activity: regional organizations under the national organizational umbrella, the tournament format, and a standard national debate resolution.

Development of regional units

Pi Kappa Delta created the province structure in 1920 and refined its practices during that decade (Norton, 1987, p. 95). A province was a regional grouping of PKD chapters formed to facilitate communication and interaction among chapters between national conventions and to promote forensics generally within the provincial geographical area. DSR and TKA were more centralized organizations, although each had a state organization built into its original constitution. PKD's provincial structures effectively flattened decision-making by allowing each region to adopt its own constitution and to hold regional conventions and tournaments in the years between national biennial gatherings. Another benefit of the provincial structure came in response to the financial and travel challenges faced during the public oratory era. One of the original assumptions of the fraternity—that each active chapter would routinely attend the biennial national convention—was untenable for smaller schools and programs, especially when the national event rotated to different regions of the country. The province structure was more accessible to smaller schools that wished to maintain their national affiliation but were unable to attend each biennial convention faithfully.

Introduction of the tournament format

At a province convention in Winfield, Kansas, in 1923, the second innovation, the tournament, was introduced (Nabors, 1956, p. 62). The Southwestern College tournament was likely the first college tournament, and fourteen PKD chapters attended and participated in a total of fourteen debates. The tournament model gradually became popular as it answered a basic problem facing forensics programs, especially in the West and Midwest, that lacked easy access to leagues and opponents (Nabors, 1956). The tournament, emerging simultaneously with expanded and improved roads and automobiles, allowed schools to stretch scarce travel dollars more efficiently and greatly expanded the opportunities for more students to participate in more debates and speech contests (Baker, 1931; Nabors, 1956). Arguably, the introduction of the tournament was the most significant of all the innovations in forensics during the public oratory era for two reasons: the tournament model significantly changed the ways that forensics functioned organizationally, and the enhanced competition stimulated through tournaments altered forensics values and norms.

A national resolution for debate

The third PKD innovation was the introduction of the national debate resolution. While the new tournament model made the use of a common resolution desirable, the movement toward a single resolution actually began in 1919 with preparations for the 1920 convention in Sioux City, Iowa (Rose, 1969). Because forensics teams traveling to the convention wanted to arrange exhibition debates for their debaters to use as practice opportunities along the way, they became aware that having a previously agreed-on resolution would aid in that process. Prior to 1920, as noted earlier, it was the usual practice for squads to negotiate the resolution as part of the arrangements. Each debate had a separate resolution, and there were no consistent standards for topic area or wording.

In response to this call for a common resolution, the 1922 PKD convention adopted a motion to allow chapters to collectively select a national topic each spring for the following academic year. The exact wording of the resolution was occasionally imprecise and altered to conform to resolutions used by other organizations, and in the early years a separate topic was selected for men and women. There was still a persistent myth that women argued differently from men, necessitating a different resolution in the interests of fairness. PKD offered separate resolutions for men and women until 1938 (Norton, 1987, p. 262). In 1927 the first controversy regarding the national topic flared, when the PKD chapters voted to debate a resolution about ending Prohibition (Rose, 1969): "Resolved: That the essential features of the McNary-Haugen Bill be enacted into law." Several chapters, likely reflecting institutional and community pressures, declined to debate that resolution (Rose, 1969). Controversy would again occur in 1954 when some schools, most notably the military academies, resisted debating a topic about extending diplomatic recognition to Communist China: "Resolved: That the United States should extend diplomatic recognition to the Communist government of China" (see Burns, 1954; English et al., 2007; Greene and Hicks, 2005).

The evolution of the topic-selection process illustrated the tensions and challenges of the interactions of the various forensics organizations during that era. F. H. Rose, a PKD national past president and first chair of the topic-selection committee, wrote that the Pi Kappa Delta topic became the de facto national debate resolution by the end of the 1920s. However, the selection process was cumbersome: each chapter submitted potential resolutions, a committee was formed to craft specific wordings, and the potential topics were submitted to a vote of the chapters, with the one receiving the highest number of votes becoming the topic for the following year. Using the PKD resolutions as a model made it likely that other collegiate teams, particularly PRP members, would attend PKD tournaments. The old process of debating a separate resolution in each debate began to fall by the wayside, particularly after PRP voted in 1931 to accept the PKD resolution as the official one to be debated by its members in competition (Rose, 1969).

As more squads began to attend tournaments in which schools from different fraternities were participating, a growing discord about the topic-selection process became evident. Rose (1969) noted that non-PKD schools resented having to debate a resolution they had no voice in selecting. Pi Kappa Delta's official position was that the PKD resolution was designed as an option for PKD members and tournaments and was not intended to influence other schools. But since PKD members sponsored the largest number of tournaments, and PKD officer Nichols published debates, briefs, and handbooks on the PKD annual topics, there was little doubt that the PKD topic was the de facto national resolution.

The first major attempt of the non-PKD schools to challenge PKD's established national topic-selection process came from the Mid-West Debate Coaches' Association, a group consisting largely of DSR and TKA members who published a report in 1937 urging the creation of a topic-selection committee, with representation from all forensics organizations, to be sponsored by the National Association of Teachers of Speech (NATS). The expressed purpose of this committee would be the selection of an annual topic with an approved interpretation for national use. The report also urged that the topic be released in the spring to allow for the creation of handbooks to assist in research and analysis. Such an approach would require the participation of Pi Kappa Delta since the organization had such wide impact on debate and hosted the greatest number of tournaments (Rose, 1969).

In response, the 1938 Pi Kappa Delta convention in Topeka, Kansas, considered the proposal and, after assembly debate, adopted a motion to continue the current process for selecting a PKD resolution for two years (until the next convention), referring the Mid-West Debate Coaches' Association's proposal to the national council for further study. Rose (1969) noted that while there was strong support for maintaining a PKD topic, some organizational leaders, such as E. R. Nichols, supported a more inclusive topic-selection process. A series of organizational maneuvers followed between PKD and its challengers for control of the process. The basis for this maneuvering was constitutional, as TKA and

DSR leaders were empowered by their constitutions to act unilaterally on such matters as topic selection, while PKD leaders felt a strong need to defer to the wishes of their members as expressed through explicit decision-making at their biennial conventions.

Despite the growing external pressure, the 1940 delegates to the PKD convention in Knoxville again reiterated commitment to their topic-selection process. In response, TKA national council member Charles Layton of Muskingum College successfully persuaded the NATS to adopt a resolution on January 2, 1941, to appoint a special committee, chaired by Layton, to select a national debate topic (Rose, 1969). The committee was to consist of six members, two each from DSR, TKA, and PKD (ignoring PRP altogether), with Layton giving TKA an extra member. The resolution also mandated that committee members be NATS members despite the fact that a significant number of forensics directors, particularly ones coaching PKD and PRP schools, were not speech communication professionals or members of that organization.

The approach was doomed from the beginning since the NATS had no particular ability to mandate that PKD adhere to the process, and PKD leaders continued to maintain that the organization's topic-selection process could only be changed by legislation approved at the biennial convention, which would not meet again until the spring of 1942 in Minneapolis (Rose, 1969). However, then PKD president W. V. O'Connell of East Central State College appointed two representatives to the NATS committee in order to maintain lines of communication with that group while simultaneously rejecting any thought that PKD would stop selecting its own topic. Thus, during the 1941–1942 academic year, there were two topics, one selected by the NATS-mandated committee (including representatives from PKD) and the topic selected by Pi Kappa Delta (Rose, 1969, p. 24). The NATS topic was as follows: "Resolved: That the federal government should regulate by law all labor unions in the United States, constitutionally conceded." The Pi Kappa Delta schools debated the following proposition: "Resolved: That the democracies should form a federation to establish and maintain the eight Churchill-Roosevelt principles" (Rose, 1969, p. 24).

At their 1942 convention, PKD members again considered whether to participate in a joint topic-selection process. By this time, the NATS had extended the existence of the topic-selection committee for another year and presented PKD with a specific plan for establishing a permanent topic-selection committee. The PKD convention approved this proposal with specific amendments: the first amendment changed the NATS proposal from having NATS appoint the chair to rotating that position among the various member organizations; the second amendment clarified that the committee would create one resolution rather than multiple resolutions, ensuring that there would be a single national topic; the third amendment specified that each participating organization would cover the expenses of its representatives at the selection meeting. The convention also passed a contingent motion approving the continuation of PKD's existing topic-selection process if the NATS and the other honoraries did not approve the amendments (Rose, 1969). Layton, still representing NATS and TKA, agreed to the amendments, and the new topic-selection process was established. This process, with some changes relating to committee size and the inclusion of the new American Forensic Association as one of the member organizations, continued until the de facto merger of the topic-selection process of the National Debate Tournament (NDT) and the Cross-Examination Debate Association (CEDA) in the 1990s.

The creation of the joint topic-selection committee did not end organizational tensions. After the creation of the AFA in 1949, that new organization floated a proposal to create a single national forensics office by subsuming the organizational processes of the honoraries. This proposal was strongly rebuffed, as was another AFA proposal to assume responsibility for selecting the national high school topic (Rose, 1969). However, this clearly began the transition in power, reflecting the new technical era in forensics history.

The adoption of a new process for topic selection effectively shut down the systemic influence of PKD in setting competitive norms for debate activities, and the emerging influence of the new AFA, dominated by TKA and DSR members, combined with the declining membership and financial health of DSR, resulted in all three fraternities turning their attention inward to their own organizational needs. This vacuum left the larger concerns of the broader forensics community to the AFA, at first a seemingly powerful and effective voice for articulating the interests of the forensics community. However, while willing to defer some of their authority to the AFA, members of the fraternities remained vigilant about retaining control of their policies and practices. This vigilance came to a head following the annual meeting of the AFA in December 1968.

At that meeting, the AFA passed a motion declaring the organization's intention to assume responsibility for selecting the national college resolution. AFA president Gifford Blyton of the University of Kentucky sent a letter to the three fraternities—DSR-TKA (these fraternities had merged), PKD, and PRP—and the Speech Association of America (formerly NATS), stating its case. The letter included a very controversial line of argument: "The American Forensic Association sponsors and administers the National Debate Tournament. This tournament in a real sense sets the pattern for intercollegiate debating in the United States" (Rose, 1969).

The AFA proposal was summarily and angrily rejected by all the parties, especially regarding the claim that the AFA was entitled to select the topic since it administered the NDT. Each of the honoraries reiterated its belief that the AFA proposal was an attempt to consolidate power over the direction of forensics and, as such, directly threatened the autonomy and well-being of the various organizations. Whatever moral authority the AFA previously possessed ended with that significant overreach, and the stampede toward a fracture of consensus, the principal characteristic of the technical era's divergence period, became more pronounced. Following this challenge, the AFA itself began a gradual reorientation toward emphasizing argumentation theory rather than forensics practice.

Summary

In summary, prior to World War II collegiate forensics was governed, for practical purposes, by the actions of the forensic honoraries that were most influential. After World War II forensics was increasingly governed by the various organizations sponsoring national championships. But in neither of these contexts was the governance of forensics anything like that exercised by the National Collegiate Athletic Association in athletics, especially after World War II. The predisposition of college forensics programs to affiliate easily between different forensics organizations, even in the public oratory era, seriously limited the ability of any particular group to enforce rules. Forensics organizations oriented themselves toward creating as small a set of rules as possible and relying on peer pressure and other forces, such as competition judging standards, to regulate behavior.

THE PUBLICATIONS AND SCHOLARLY ACTIVITY OF THE HONORARIES

The publication outlets for forensics scholarship came primarily through the honoraries that sponsored forensics activities. While not designed as forensics publications per se, the *Quarterly Journal of Public Speaking* (later the *Quarterly Journal of Speech*) and the *Quarterly Journal of Speech Education* were the early primary scholarly outlets for forensics educators, most of whom had an affiliation with a forensic honorary. These journals, sponsored by the young National Association of Academic Teachers of Public Speaking, published extensively about debate and speech practices and forensics topics of interest until after World War II, when speech expanded to include subfields of communication, increasing competition for publication space.

The forensic honoraries provided their own publication outlets, such as the *Speaker of Tau Kappa Alpha*, the *Gavel of Delta Sigma Rho*, the *Forensic of Pi Kappa Delta*, and the *Rostrum*, sponsored by the National Forensic League. An examination of the early volumes of these publications reveals specific organizational history, personal notes about members, features about member schools, news about trends occurring in different areas of the country, and the results of different contests and activities. If the forensics community faced particular issues, someone wrote an article addressing or explaining them. However, not until after World War II did these journals add space for more scholarly articles and reduce the intraorganizational information.

In addition to their individual publications, the honoraries participated in a collaborative publication organized and maintained by E. R. Nichols, who first introduced the *Debater's Magazine* as a way to connect the collegiate and high school forensics communities in order to revitalize forensics after World War II. The publication offered research-based articles, as well as general information about the state of forensics across the country. In an effort to appeal to a broad readership, reporters from each of the collegiate honoraries provided regular columns directed to their members. In addition, articles were written for the inexperienced coach or forensics student seeking insight into different events or forensics opportunities. Coaches in the NFL with collegiate affiliations also contributed to this publication, and many high schools took the magazine for its coverage of the high school topic and high school debate news (*AFA Register*, 1954). With the increased involvement of state high school activities associations in post–World War II forensics and out of a desire to widen its scope, Nichols changed the name of the publication to *Speech Activities*. Between 1944 and 1953, it changed from a mimeographed newsletter to a professionally printed magazine; it was the only forensics publication during the twentieth century that purposefully crossed all forensics organizations and participation levels from high school to college.

In 1948, Speech Association of America president James McBurney named E. R. Nichols to chair the committee to found a national forensics organization (the outcome was the AFA), specifically created to include high school and collegiate forensics educators (Blyton, 1970). Many of the early leaders in the AFA were members of DSR, and when Nichols, a proponent of PKD and the editor of *Speech Activities*, reached retirement age in 1953, his exit was marked by an offer to transfer his publication with a nationwide collegiate and high school circulation of four hundred subscribers to the AFA with no strings attached (*AFA Register*, 1954). The vacuum created by his retirement led to considerable disagreement between the introverted elements of the AFA leadership. To resolve the matter, a letter sent to all AFA officials to determine the course of action revealed "an even split on this issue with about half favoring adoption and the rest either doubtful or downright opposed. So there is no clear mandate one way or the other at this time. A poll of all members or action at our next meeting in Chicago seems to be the only way the issue can be resolved" (*AFA Register*, 1954).

The AFA officers eventually declined Nichols's offer and for a few years had no publication. In 1952, the *Register* was established as a mimeographed newsletter providing a forensic calendar, membership lists, special materials for high school teachers, and professional articles of general interest. The AFA president edited the *Register* until 1958, at which time John Rickey of Ohio State

University was appointed as editor, exclusively charged with this responsibility. From the beginning, this publication was conceived as "a house organ to report association business . . . but within a few years it began to also carry short articles about research projects or about such practical matters like judging debate" (Zarefsky and Sillars, n.d.).

Soon the leaders felt that if they published a journal, rather than a newsletter, the academic community would take the AFA more seriously. The pressures on forensics educators from their academic departments to produce scholarship eventually resulted in the 1964 decision by the AFA to publish its own journal, specifically focused on forensics and aptly called the *Journal of the American Forensic Association* (*JAFA*), renamed *Argumentation and Advocacy* (*A&A*) in 1988. As Blyton (1970) noted, "The growth and development of the Journal is one of the major publishing success stories in recent educational history" (p. 15).

Zarefsky and Sillars (n.d.) describe how *JAFA* changed during the latter part of the twentieth century. During its early years, about one-fifth of the journal was devoted to the business of the AFA. When the *AFA Newsletter* was created in 1978, the journal was freed of all matter dealing with the association, and more research articles were added. The original focus of the journal was competitive forensics activities, pedagogical issues, tournament practices, debate theory, and general argumentation theory. However, by volumes 28 and 29, no articles about competitive forensics were included, and by the end of the twentieth century, *A&A* largely focused on argumentation theory and theories critiquing the practice of argument in the public forum outside the contest setting.

In its place, specialized publications emerged that enabled those interested in competitive practices and forensics research to continue their scholarly pursuits. For example, the *CEDA Yearbook* provided articles about debate practices, and the *National Forensic Journal* enabled the emerging National Forensic Association to publish materials addressing competitive individual events and general topics of interest to forensics educators. By the end of the century, the four regional associations of the National Communication Association (NCA) were publishing journals, as were many of the state speech, theater, and communication associations. These were not dedicated to—nor did they exclude—manuscripts focused on forensics. However, as forensics experienced marginalization in the broader communication discipline, the focus of the mainstream communication journals included a broad range of topics, and forensics lost the prominence it enjoyed in the early years of the century.

An Overview of Scholarship about Forensics

Much scholarship has chronicled American forensics. Many articles, books, and academic disquisitions have detailed particular high school or collegiate forensics programs ("Fifty Years of Debating at Bates College," 1947; Harsh-barger, 1976; Johnston, 1917; Morrison, 1948; Potter, 1944; Roberts, 1978; Sillars, 1949) or provided histories about specific forensics activities, practices, and achievements (e.g., Baird, 1923; Busfield, 1959; Ewbank, 1935; Fernandez, 1959; Freeley, 1951; Jacob, 1931; Lambert, 1948). For the most part, accounts of forensics in particular states or regions of the country (e.g., Berry, 1928; Buehler, 1946; Diem, 1950; Littlefield, 1998; Montgomery, 1950; Moriarty, 1945; Schmidt, 1949; Wells, 1929) and ceremonial histories written at particu-lar milestones by representatives of national forensic honoraries (e.g., Blyton, 1970; Fest, 1956; Nichols, 1915, 1936a, 1936b, 1937, 1952; Norton, 1987; Trueblood, 1931) form the basis of what constitutes the historical record of forensics in American high schools, colleges, and universities. Unfortunately, many of these reference materials are not widely available, and most provide anecdotal information.

As we explored the publications about forensics, several general lines of re-search emerged, including the status and evolution of intercollegiate debate; the status and evolution of high school debate; the role and status of forensics in speech education, general education, and the communication curriculum; coach-ing and the management of forensics programs and finances; noncompetitive forensics; the personal value of forensics involvement; the role of minorities and women in forensics; student perceptions of forensics; the evolution of and changes in particular individual speaking events; the evolution of and changes in forensics organizations; the role of forensics in promoting civic engagement; tournament practices, awards, and judging; international forensics activity; and research in forensics. While not all of them were research-based, the publications identified the issues and struggles forensics educators faced as forensics evolved throughout the century.

From a methodological perspective, the nature of the scholarship ranged from anecdotal and descriptive to survey and experimental. Table 4.1 provides a general breakdown of methodologies used in forensics scholarship. Broadly, forensics scholars used four methodological approaches to reveal their research during the twentieth century: anecdotal, descriptive, survey, and experimental. The anecdotal scholarship provided individual assessments addressing personal or philosophical issues. Historical records and trends, as well as explanations of particular forensics practices, constituted much of the descriptive research. As forensics evolved, survey research methods recorded perceptions, trends, and practices in use across the country. Although not common, some quasi-experimental research was used to determine the effects of particular forensics practices. By and large, the earliest scholarship was anecdotal and descriptive as the leading figures in forensics education established the philosophical or practical foundations of the activity. As time passed, survey research enabled scholars to chronicle the impact of forensics. However, once forensics moved into the technical era, when academic departments preferred a more analytical and critical approach to scholarship, anecdotal and descriptive scholarship lost its value.

To provide a means to consider the themes, we used characteristics of the public oratory and technical eras as a framework. Table 4.2 provides the contrast in focus for themes reflected in forensics research.

Table 4.1. Methodologies Used in Forensics Scholarship

Type	Anecdotal		Descriptive		Survey	Quasi-experimental
Characteristic	Individual		Organizational	Practical	Patterns	Introduction of variables
Example(s)	Personal beliefs	Philosophical issues	Historical record	Particular forensics practices	Preferences, practices, and trends	Effects and tendencies

Table 4.2. Framework for Considering Influences on Forensics Research

Public Oratory Era	Technical Era
Education versus competition based	Competition based
Dominance of honoraries	Dominance of American Forensic Association
Philosophical	Practical, analytical, and critical
Centrality of forensics within speech departments	Marginalization of forensics within communication departments
Audience/public/community focus	Tournament/private/individual focus

Education versus Competition

The tension between education and competition framed the systemic evolution of theory in forensics. This tension was the dominant element that shaped the activity, as well as the scholarship, throughout most of the century. From the beginning, the skills gained through participation in forensics were viewed as foundational to the education of students. Thus, the early publications addressed pedagogy. However, as competition made forensics unique as an educational innovation, maintaining those elements that enhanced competition became a countervailing emphasis in the forensics and communication journals.

The Influence of Organizational Philosophies

Reflecting the dialectical tensions between education and competition, the teachers and scholars supporting the educational and competitive positions formed honoraries, and their scholarship and activities reflected their philosophical perspectives. Those who formed the organizations with more restrictive entry requirements (DSR, TKA) endorsed the educational or philosophical aspects of forensics, minimizing and often eschewing competition. The scholars in organizations with less restrictive entry requirements and a grassroots perspective (PKD, NFL) presented scholarship with a practical or more applied focus to promote and enhance the competitive side of forensics.

Later, the AFA aspired to be a national umbrella organization to unify the divergent forensic honoraries and provide legitimacy for forensics as a presence within the emerging communication discipline. The honoraries continued to function as entities within the AFA, and emergent scholars from the various organizations under the umbrella vied for the soul of the uniquely American innovation that was competitive forensics.

Philosophical versus Practical

The earliest forensics activities emerged from literary societies in which the best students from one group were identified to participate in debates and speaking contests with another. While competition was an inherent part of forensics in this early period, its elite nature kept the focus on the educational benefits of the activity. The noble purpose of preparing lawyers, ministers, and civic leaders was reflected in the writings and practices of early scholars. In fact, the creation of DSR and TKA as more introverted-reserved societies predisposed their spokespeople to promote the higher goal of education over the common practices of competition. Similarly, the elitist character, as reflected in which and how many students were actually able to engage in competitive forensics, enabled the activity to retain what these selective societies considered to be its early educational focus.

As forensics expanded and scholars and teachers sought avenues for participation, practical and applied scholarship resulted. The grassroots nature of these expanding forensics activities fit more closely with the introverted-expansive philosophy of PKD and NFL. The emergence of scholarship at both ends of this dialectic further separated and defined the evolution of forensics in the technical era. As the competition-based grassroots scholarship explored the how-to questions, the educational elites were advancing the why questions.

Centrality to the Discipline

The origins of forensic theory were pedagogical in that they focused on debate and argumentation as a way to learn the skills required of an active citizen in a democracy. Within this category, during the public oratory era, forensics was central to speech departments as the activity provided a way to teach effective communication within the public sphere. This emphasis was consistent with the educational theme. As forensics competition became more technical and the emphasis shifted from communal to individual benefits, actual forensics practices became antithetical to what communication departments viewed as effective speech practices. The marginalization of forensics pressured coaches and educators to shift their scholarship to produce research studies that legitimized the activity and/or placed the practices within educational paradigms that would keep forensics more closely associated with what academic departments viewed as their changing missions during the latter half of the century.

Shift from Communal to Individual

As previously described, the benefits of forensics during the public oratory era were community based—that is, the nature of the audience influenced forensics practices and reflected the partisan aspects of public debate and declamation. With the rise of the technical era, efficiency prevailed, and tournaments replaced public debates as the means by which debate and individual speaking events occurred. The shift between these periods was clearly evident in the scholarship pertaining to which forensics practices should prevail.

Implications of Forensics Scholarship

The characteristics of each era of forensics shaped the scholarship that resulted. Systemically, the tensions between education and competition remained throughout the twentieth century as forensics scholars attempted to promote and justify their philosophies. The philosophies of the national organizations shaped the scholarship of their proponents as the philosophical/practical and analytical/critical dimensions of forensics emerged. As the competitive practices of forensics changed for what some considered to be the detriment of the activity, the centrality of forensics to academic departments and the discipline prompted coaches and scholars to overcompensate with applications of theory to practice in an effort to keep from being marginalized further. Finally, as the focus of forensics shifted from the community to the individual, scholars used their writings to justify their orientations and preferences.

Publication outlets existed for forensics educators, despite their evolution in response to different contexts. Methodologically, forensics research utilized a broad range of approaches, including anecdotal, descriptive, survey, and quasi-experimental designs. The themes of the scholarship reflected frameworks that characterized oppositional viewpoints associated with the essential conflict between those favoring educational perspectives versus those seeking to enhance the competitive aspects of forensics. Most importantly, forensics scholarship of the twentieth century developed in response to the evolution of the activity as it presented itself. The following five implications merit consideration as overarching characteristics of forensics research during the century.

First, the experimental nature of forensics as an evolving innovation prompted a wide variety of practices that were explained through the scholarship of forensics educators. When schools in one part of the country used a particular system for scheduling competitions or when leagues adopted a new method or ballot for judging, forensics educators shared their adaptations with the forensics community through the journals. The rate at which practices were adopted across the country demonstrated the impact of the early scholars.

Second, scholars shaped the way forensics evolved by confronting the issues facing the activity directly through their research and writings. Those associated with the honoraries had strong philosophical positions about the core issues associated with the activity. The nature of the organizations made them more or less inclined to accept particular approaches or practices. Thus, forensics scholars were not reluctant to make arguments regarding what direction they thought forensics should take as it developed. In the absence of any uniform, national guidelines for how interscholastic and intercollegiate forensics should be conducted, the persuasiveness of the arguments raised by forensics scholars resulted in the adoption of particular practices by individual forensics programs.

Third, those contributing to forensics scholarship often used the formats they taught as means of expressing their arguments. For example, when forensics faced particular turning points in its development, scholars used the pro/con approach with a third-party judge to put the arguments on display for the forensics community to consider. Arguments about whether decisions should be rendered in debate, whether arguments should be judged by a lay person or expert critic, whether tournament debating should continue, and whether interscholastic forensic competition should be abolished were made using the pro/con format, followed by a decision rendered by a third party to indicate which side had provided the most compelling argument. The practice of modeling the activity they valued was a uniquely characteristic way that forensics educators presented their scholarship.

The evolution of the journals' characteristics revealed the changing context of the academic community during the twentieth century. From the beginning, every national forensics organization had a journal that was used to present internal communication to its members and occasionally to publish the scholarship of its members in the form of anecdotal information, descriptive essays, or reports of surveys about practices and the status of programs in the organization. In the case of the National Association of Academic Teachers of Public Speaking, when the *Quarterly Journal of Public Speaking* began, the majority of its content focused on the issues facing those involved with debate and forensics activities. This focus continued throughout much of the public oratory era due to the composition of its members. However, following World War II, as the communication discipline divided into areas of specialization ranging from rhetoric to mass media, forensics scholarship was marginalized as competing interests claimed a greater percentage of the journal's content. This served as a signal for the honoraries, and their journals responded by reducing the internal communication in the journals and increasing the available space for articles formerly included in journals not solely dedicated to forensics.

Finally, despite the considerable disagreement about which particular practice or approach to forensics should be followed, when threatened by external forces, supporters of forensics were able to unite the community through their scholarship. The ethics challenge from Theodore Roosevelt, the call for the prohibition of interscholastic competition by the North Central Association, and the decision to stop military cadets from debating a resolution that violated U.S. policy galvanized the forensics community, and in each case, forensics prevailed. This inherent unity is a remarkable characteristic of resiliency and dedication to the activity.

The prominence of the collegiate forensics community in shaping the evolution of forensics for both higher education and high schools stemmed from the publications—scholarly and otherwise—that impacted the agency of its participants. We now turn to an examination of the typology and behaviors of the forensic honoraries. The nature of these organizations attracted educators with particular perspectives about competition and education and affected their practices.

AN ANALYSIS OF FORENSICS ORGANIZATIONAL TYPOLOGY AND BEHAVIOR

An examination of the organizational history of forensics reveals four types of organizations determined by two dimensions: degree of introversion versus extroversion and level of expansion versus reservation. Introversion is the degree to which an organization is internally focused and expends its energy primarily in maintaining and refining internal processes (e.g., rituals, degrees of membership, and so forth). An extroverted organization's energy is spent managing external processes (e.g., competition and tournaments, service projects, lobbying for political change, and so forth). The second axis is expansion versus reservation. An expansive organization seeks to find new members to expand its reach.

A reserved organization seeks to maintain its existing reach or degree of influence. Using this framework, four general types of forensics organizations can be identified as depicted in table 4.3: introverted-reserved, introverted-expansive, extroverted-reserved, and extroverted-expansive.

Table 4.3. Organizational Types and Classification of Particular Forensics Organizations

Introverted-reserved	Extroverted-reserved
Delta Sigma Rho	American Forensics Association
Tau Kappa Alpha	National Debate Tournament
NEDA	National Individual Events Tournament
	NPTE
Introverted-expansive	**Extroverted-expansive**
Pi Kappa Delta	Cross-Examination Debate Association
Phi Rho Pi	National Forensic Association
	National Forensic League
	Urban Debate League
	National Parliamentary Debate Association

The introverted-reserved type is the founding descriptor of American forensic fraternities. This model was especially associated with DSR and TKA. These groups were founded on the principle that membership should be restricted to select schools and individuals, and their focus was introverted, centering on their internal rituals and activities. Ultimately, adhering to this model weakened these organizations in the 1950s as the number of schools meeting their criteria for membership and the competitive model (an extroverted process) diminished.

The introverted-expansive model was the original PKD model. While PKD initially sought the same cachet as the other elite fraternities, when the founding PKD schools were rebuffed by DSR and TKA because they lacked the requisite prestige (Phi Beta Kappa and/or research university status), PKD created an introverted-expansive philosophy to recruit any four-year schools to wanting to join, always keeping in mind that the point of joining was to enjoy the benefits of fraternity membership (introversion).

The extroverted-reserved and extroverted-expansive models were the dominant models of the technical era and emerged later in the century as a product of the rising popularity of competition following World War II. Forensics organizations, including the fraternities, fundamentally changed from being introverted to extroverted. Their focus moved from rituals and memberships to competition and tournaments. Influencing this process was the AFA, founded as an extroverted-expansive organization but quickly devolving into an extroverted-reserved one. While the original purpose of the AFA was to provide a professional organization

appealing to the widest range of educators, whether actively engaged in forensics or not, and to promote forensics in all its forms, this did not account for
AFA's decision to adopt the West Point Debate Tournament as the National
Debate Tournament and to conceive of that tournament as the de facto national
debate championship. This perspective necessarily directed the AFA, over time,
to become an organization focused on external elements (the national championships in debate and individual events), while maintaining an invisible yet impervious reservation status. Anyone could join the AFA, but aside from receiving
the journal, there was no particular benefit unless an individual or school participated in the AFA National Debate Tournament or the AFA National Individual
Events Tournament.

Transition from Introversion to Extroversion

The transition in emphasis from the introverted-reserved and introverted-expansive to the extroverted-reserved and extroverted-expansive models is one of the
significant differences between the public oratory and technical eras. Why did
this change occur? Why did the honoraries need to alter their organizational practices after World War II? Was the change significant? We suggest two factors
contributing to this change in emphasis.

Changes in Higher Education

First, higher education changed. As discussed previously, the entire nature of
higher education changed dramatically after the end of World War II. While
many of the changes would have inevitably occurred, the influx of substantial
numbers of new students, many of whom served in the war, accelerated educational changes. These new students came to college with different values and
different priorities. They were less interested in the ceremonial trappings of the
honoraries and more highly motivated by the competitive opportunities provided
by tournaments.

Colleges and universities themselves were changing, placing greater emphasis
on empirical measures of educational success. Having a local chapter of a national forensics fraternity became less valuable for a university, on its face, than
sponsoring a successful debate squad in tournament competition. In the years
after World War II, all of the honoraries saw shifts in their membership, with de-
clines, at least in the short term, in their numbers of active chapters (see Nabors,
1956, pp. 22–23). This decline was most notable for DSR, the most exclusive of
the fraternities. The slowest to embrace the tournament model, DSR faced significant decreases in membership and financial strains that accelerated interest in
a merger with TKA, the forensics fraternity that shared a similar organizational

philosophy (introverted-reserved) but that had already begun the transition toward extroverted-expansive. Tau Kappa Alpha hosted a national tournament and convention in 1939, became more active in soliciting new chapters, and increased its national visibility through the creation of a National Speaker of the Year award in 1949. In 1953, TKA (as PKD had done previously) increased its scholarly visibility and enjoyed huge success with the publication of a well-received argumentation textbook.

The merger between DSR and TKA took many years to complete, despite the apparent desire of both organizations to strengthen their organizational health. But even after the merger was finalized in 1963, the overall health of the new combined organization remained, as measured by active members and chapters, only modestly healthy, as the number of inactive chapters grew and balancing the budget remained a challenge, despite a healthy endowment brought by DSR to the merger. This situation mirrored the challenges faced by Pi Kappa Delta.

The Effects of Competition

A second reason for a shift from introverted to extroverted emphasis resulted from the inherently zero-sum nature of competition. The significance of the shift from an audience-centered to a competition-centered activity cannot be underestimated, particularly as this change affected how forensics activities were organized. During the public oratory era, the fraternities coexisted by carving out their own philosophical and geographical domains. DSR sought to be the forensics equivalent of Phi Beta Kappa, with a limited number of chapters located at the most prestigious universities. TKA sought to be like DSR but located in the next, slightly smaller tier of institutions. In addition, TKA sought national prominence through its leadership pool and innovations, such as the Speaker of the Year award. In contrast, PKD embraced the competition model and recruited chapters from colleges and universities generally unattractive to DSR or TKA. Finally, PRP membership was exclusively among the growing number of two-year colleges. While occasional tensions arose (e.g., determination of the national debate resolution), the organizations generally maintained distance and respect. There was a gentlemen's agreement not to poach each other's members, the organizations' presidents often gave brief congratulatory speeches at each other's conventions, members of all four fraternities were included as authors for articles published in E. R. Nichols's magazines and yearbooks, and gradually most all members joined the NATS.

The creation of the West Point Debate Tournament in 1947 was the turning point and the second sign that the technical era was replacing the public oratory era. From the creation of a single national debate resolution to the merger of DSR-TKA, the handwriting was on the wall that the DSR model, grounded in primarily promoting academic achievement and secondarily promoting forensics competition (particularly through the student congress), was losing ground in the wake of the forensics community's growing preference for extroverted models, particularly given the rapidly expanding postwar growth in higher education. Ironically, some DSR members were active leaders in promoting the idea of a national debate championship, and while some in the organization strongly resisted the competitive model, DSR leaders figured prominently in the NDT and the soon-after movement to create the American Forensic Association.

The creation of the AFA was a crucial piece of the puzzle in the evolution of forensics from the public oratory to the technical model. The AFA, almost from its inception, sought to establish a dominant leadership position in forensics, at both the high school and the college levels. The AFA aligned forensics with the national speech communication community, which accelerated the diminution of forensics as an interdisciplinary activity. Forensics became increasingly a cocurricular activity under the aegis of individual communication departments or, where those departments did not exist, an extracurricular activity housed with other clubs and activities. The shift in emphasis during the technical era from interdisciplinary to cocurricular and extracurricular firmly seated competition as the preeminent value.

Cocurricular and extracurricular activities, almost by definition, were believed to be outside the centrality of the curriculum. Communication, as a discipline, was experiencing significant growing pains as the drive to expand graduate study and research methods overlaid the tensions between empiricism and rhetorical studies that had existed even prior to World War II but had become a central battleground for hearts and minds in the communication field. Forensics was caught in the vortex of this zero-sum battle. The activity increasingly justified its existence through competitive measures rather than educational ones. The effects of the popularity of the NDT, its influence in establishing competition-based educational practices and norms, and the role that the AFA played in promoting a singular rather than pluralistic view of forensics would dominate the activity during the fifty years of the technical era.

As the competitive model prevailed, the influence of the honoraries declined but did not disappear. They all began to move (at least slightly) away from introversion as their journals and communications de-emphasized rituals, exclusivity, and other trappings of the introverted models that were prominent during their emergence and zenith in the public oratory era. They all sponsored their own versions of national championships, highlighted the accomplishments of their prominent alumni, and were active voices in the discussion of competition, values, and ethical issues pertaining to their activities and programs.

While some leaders of the forensics fraternities recognized the need to embrace a more competitive model, the role of forensics fraternities as the leaders of forensics activities diminished. The numbers of programs, teachers, and students who formerly looked first to the honoraries as their measure of success declined during the technical era. Their success in introducing innovations to forensics (e.g., the tournament, the national debate resolution, the national student congress, the Speaker of the Year award) was not repeated in the technical era. The organizations became reactive rather than spearheading change.

Organizational Turmoil during the Technical Era

The constructive and destructive aspects of competition organizationally dominated the technical era. If the public oratory era could be described as a stable period marked by occasional conflicts, organizational behavior in the technical period was marked by upheaval and discord. One source of contention was external as the AFA was created partially in response to turmoil inspired by the actions of an accrediting organization and its threat to competitive forensics at the high school level. Another source of turmoil experienced initially by higher education came in response to the demands of the new information age.

Selection of the Recognition of Communist China Debate Topic

The first significant instance of turmoil in the technical era was the brief but publicly intense controversy generated by the debate community's selection of the 1954–1955 debate topic: "Resolved: That the United States should extend diplomatic recognition to the Communist government of China." Although this was not the first public controversy caused by the choice of a debate topic, it was a curious community decision, given the political events of the time. In a nation still gripped by the Red Scare, it would have been difficult to imagine a topic choice that would inspire more public anger and concern and necessitate greater scrutiny of two of the fundamental assumptions of American academic debate: that the value of debating a single national topic was a core educational principle and that students should debate both sides of a resolution, even if debating one of the sides required a student to put aside strongly held personal beliefs (for a discussion of the benefits of debating controversial issues, see Baird, 1955).

The conflict over academic freedom and the recognition of multiple potential truths reflected Hofstadter's (1962) theorizing that the 1950s represented a resurgence of anti-intellectualism and a growing preference for the tyranny of the practical. The decision to debate a controversial resolution with no possible chance of enactment by the federal government signaled to many in the country that academic debate was more an elitist exercise than a method of exploring controversial issues in the context of creating good citizens. In one single decision, the public capital of forensics was squandered, and the process of marginalization began in earnest, not to be halted until the very end of the century with the growth in interest in promoting forensics internationally and among traditionally underserved populations, such as schoolchildren in the inner cities.

The public controversy began with the November 16, 1954, announcement by West Point and Annapolis that cadet and midshipmen debaters would not debate the national resolution, citing that the affirmative position would contradict U.S. foreign policy. The announcement briefly reignited the ongoing Cold War controversies, and many universities immediately feared federal government censorship, particularly given the prominence of the service academy debate programs. If those prestigious programs opted out of debating the national topic, the outcome would be either to force the selection of another topic or to completely undermine the joint topic-selection process.

Another threat came from the divide within the communication discipline itself regarding the relative benefits of debate and discussion as problem-solving methods. One significant element of the technical era was the severing of discussion from debate beginning in the late 1940s (see Buehler, 1963, p. 17; Keith, 2007). We analyze this severing process in chapter 6. However, in short, discussion theorists were carving out a distinct theoretical and pedagogical role for discussion as a preferred means of teaching democracy. If consensus about a single debate topic broke down, more educators might abandon debate in favor of discussion.

Such an outcome, while in retrospect perhaps difficult to envision (e.g., group discussion never developed as a credible alternative to debate), there was far less consensus about the norms and values of competitive debate in 1954. Pockets of programs across the country resisted the tournament model; programs were already precursors of the more common model of the 1970s in which competitors regularly competed in individual events as well as debate; and voices expressed dissatisfaction with the impact of the West Point tournament on competitive norms. It is conceivable that with a different outcome to the China topic controversy, a tipping point might have been reached that would have led to a far different role for academic debate as an accepted method of leadership and citizenship training.

As it turned out, the tipping point was not reached. Almost immediately, the academies' decision came under intense scrutiny. Individually and collectively, college presidents announced that their programs would debate the national topic. The U.S. secretaries of state and defense denied that they had pressured the academies to renounce the topic. President Dwight Eisenhower reaffirmed the rights of college students to debate controversial issues. The association between the college debate topic and the First Amendment was firmly established by icon Edward R. Murrow during an episode of *See It Now* that aired on November 24, 1954. Finally, the NATS reaffirmed the use of the China topic at its annual meeting in late December. The crisis was temporarily averted, but the damage was done. Public support for forensics would never again be as intense or widespread.

While the ramifications of the China topic issue were slower to emerge, another issue, the growth of interest in individual events and the desire for a national individual events championship, represented the first signs of the technical era's divergence period. We traced the chronology of this process in chapter 3, but the eventual emergence of two competing national individual events championships provides insight into organizational behavior during the technical era.

The Emergence of National Championships in Individual Speaking

Competitive public speaking contests predated competitive debate. The precursor to the Interstate Oratory Contest, which remains the oldest continuous forensics contest, began in 1874. Public speaking competitions were very popular both in high schools and on college campuses. High school speech contests began in the 1890s and possibly earlier (see Secord and Thomas, 1946). By the 1890s, many colleges were sponsoring annual contests open to the student body, and sometimes between fraternities and other groups, with the winner receiving a cash prize and a loving cup. While there would eventually be competition in many different speech formats, the first contests were in persuasion and occasionally declamation. Other speech types, including oral readings, were present and sometimes included as part of the early public debate competition programming.

The first PKD national convention and tournament included a persuasive speaking contest with divisions for men and women. Soon after, extemporaneous speaking also became popular, due in part to its perceived value to debaters. After 1930, competition in individual events expanded to individual tournaments at the high school level as a result of NFL expansion and state leagues promoted by university extension offices (Rarig and Greaves, 1954). Gradually, tournaments offering competition in persuasive and extemporaneous speaking included oral interpretation and other speaking events.

While debate was the dominant competitive event, eventually eclipsing efforts to popularize student congress and discussion as competitive forms, individual events competitions grew in popularity at PKD, TKA, PRP, and NFL national tournaments, at the very popular Interstate Oratory Contest, and elsewhere. The introduction of the NDT for debate, however, did not inspire similar interest at that time for a national championship in individual speaking, and no movement in that direction occurred until the late 1960s. The reasons for the delay are unclear but might include the following: the demand for speech and oral interpretation training and experience was met by high school and college courses; the excitement of competition found through debating dominated student time and interest, and speech events may have seemed secondary; or until the nature of competitive debate devalued delivery as a primary objective, debates themselves provided a training ground for improving public speaking.

Whatever the reason, the emergence of what would become the National Forensic Association (NFA) and that organization's creation of a national championship tournament in 1971 demonstrated clearly the direction taken by leaders of the American Forensic Association to be the result of an extroverted-reserved orientation. The AFA saw itself in the 1950s and 1960s not as a force to expand the boundaries of forensics but as an organization seeking to grow the number of schools and individuals within the framework of NDT-style debate and, increasingly in the 1960s, to promote the theoretical growth of argumentation theory as a subdiscipline. Fryar (1984) reported that Raymond Beaty (Ohio University) and Jack Howe (California State University, Long Beach) were derisively rebuffed when raising the idea of an individual events national championship within the AFA. Whether their idea was dismissed on philosophical grounds or because others believed that insufficient interest in and support for it existed, the unwillingness of the AFA and the debate community to consider a national public speaking championship began the most important organizational development during the technical period: fracture.

THE ZERO-SUM COMPETITIVE ENVIRONMENT

After 1970, any consensus about the values and direction of American forensics rapidly dissolved as the forensics community split into various segments attributed to the zero-sum competitive environment. The "unilateral invent[ion]" by Seth Hawkins of a public speaking national championship tournament (Fryar, 1984) and the creation by Jack Howe of an alternative debate format to the NDT, whose popularity exploded after its creation in 1971, are but two significant examples created to promote various competition-based outcomes. The closed-shop environment nurtured by the AFA was replaced by a wide range of extroverted-expansive forensics organizations whose influence would rival and sometimes surpass the AFA's role in promoting particular norms and competitive practices in the final thirty years of the century.

Significant Examples of Extroverted-Expansive Forensics Organizations

To fully gauge the nature of the fracture that occurred in the community as forensics experienced differences of opinion about what constituted meaningful forensics competition, two extroverted-expansive forensics organizations were identified as influential examples: the NFA and CEDA. They were, first and foremost, extroverted in nature. These organizations actively innovated in response to the changing interests of students and forensics programs. The NFA, whose first tournament included contests in six public speaking and oral interpretation events, quickly expanded its recognized events to include a very wide range of contests and demonstrated a clear interest in innovation.

CEDA adopted a parallel extroversion in debate, experimenting with different debate formats, most notably cross-examination (Oregon-style) debate, which had been largely dormant during the rise in influence of the NDT. CEDA also experimented with different debate formats and topics, often using value propositions that changed monthly (and later more often) that clearly contrasted CEDA with the policy debate practice of selecting a single policy proposition that was debated for the entire year.

When organizers conceived of the NFA and CEDA, they characterized these organizations as expansive in philosophy (Howe, n.d.). Both organizations created few barriers to participation and actively encouraged new schools to join and compete, in sharp contrast with the NDT's and AFA's answer to the success of the NFA tournament, the National Individual Events Tournament (NIET), created in 1978. Like the NDT, the NIET created a complex qualification system that limited participation in an attempt to promote the prestige of the championship, as evidenced by the considerably smaller number of participants who competed in comparison to the NFA tournament. Similarly, within a very short time, CEDA membership significantly outstripped the NDT's and, in some parts of the United States, particularly the Rocky Mountain and northwestern regions, contributed to the virtual disappearance of NDT debate within a decade.

CEDA's commitment to expansiveness was best captured by the periodic sweepstakes standings published by the organization. Sweepstakes points were published for schools irrespective of their membership status. The organization generated revenue by requiring that tournaments, to count for sweepstakes points, had to be CEDA members and have their event sanctioned.

Another result of the shift toward the extroverted-expansive model was the emergence of an uneasy duality between zero-sum and non-zero-sum elements of the competitive landscape. After 1971, forensics organization included both significant pressures toward homogeneity in competitive practices and simultaneous pressure toward heterogeneity and the creation of new forensics forms. The founding of the NFA and CEDA threw open the floodgates for new visions and practices: whatever consensus existed about the role of forensics in education was replaced by "letting one hundred flowers bloom." More organizations were created, often out of reaction to perceived competitive excesses or the belief that greater competitive advantage would be gained by joining a different organization. Debate programs finding it difficult to compete successfully in NDT debate, for example, quickly moved to CEDA and then to other outlets such as the National Parliamentary Debate Association (NPDA).

There was a time during this period when some programs at both the high school and the college levels practiced comprehensiveness and attempted to compete successfully in multiple venues. One variation of this comprehensive program model often used at the high school level in some states was to compete in debate and speaking events during different semesters (e.g., debate in the fall, speech in the spring) (Littlefield, 1998). At the collegiate level, many programs, particularly in the West, regularly competed in comprehensive tournaments, and students participated in both debate and speech competition. While this model persisted throughout the technical and postmodern eras, in practice, collegiate programs attempting to be competitive in both debate and speaking events at the national level were exceptions due to the emergence of increasingly specialized requirements.

The Rise of Specialization

One important characteristic of the dominance of competition was the promotion of a zero-sum environment. While first seen in debate competition after the introduction of the NDT, this phenomenon quickly jumped to competitive speaking events. Beginning first at the national championship level and gradually percolating down to the local level, individual events became more technical and formulary. Norms for variables such as quantity and quality of cited supporting materials, the preferred nature and use of visual aids, and even de facto dress codes for contestants pervaded individual events tournaments. Normative pressures influenced the evolution in competition, within events, and regarding the introduction of new competitive events.

The most substantial growth among types of events chosen for inclusion at national tournaments was in oral interpretation. During the public oratory era, when oral interpretation was offered, either all genres of literature were accepted within a single competitive event, enabling contestants to choose one genre of literature to be read based upon their personal preferences, or contestants were allowed to combine prose, poetry, and dramatic selections into one unified program to illustrate a particular theme. This latter model initially disappeared with the introduction of the NFA and NIET national championships, when these new national tournaments abandoned the single interpretation event and added genre-exclusive oral interpretation events, with each event having conventions that soon become expectations (e.g., focal points in dramatic interpretation). Later in the twentieth century, programmed oral interpretation reemerged as an event in which students sought alternative events to demonstrate their ability to perform effectively across several genres.

The most important dimension of this evolution was not the introduction of new events themselves. Even during the public oratory era, tournaments often experimented with various interpretation and public speaking events. Events such as declamation, children's literature, and storytelling were included at most tournaments. But after the creation of the national tournaments, there was considerably less innovation in competitive public speaking. If tournaments added events, they included the national events to assist competitors in qualifying for the national tournaments. The NIET, in particular, established a precise and rigid system for at-large qualification that effectively required local tournaments to offer a fixed set of events. There was little incentive for students or programs to support experimental or nontraditional events as such participation necessarily would divert time and effort away from national qualification.

There were obvious exceptions to this zero-sum environment. Some programs oriented themselves away from the NIET or NFA as their primary focus, choosing tournaments in which students could try new events, regardless of whether they counted for sweepstakes points. By contrast, PKD offered experimental events at its national tournament, and competitors could earn tournament sweepstakes points for participation. While there were some exceptions, in reality the introduction of new events was sporadic and localized.

The Emergence of New Debate Organizations

The duality of homogenous norms and heterogeneous organizational choices that characterized the American debate community after CEDA introduced an alternative format to NDT debate. The organizational trajectory of CEDA illustrated this duality. CEDA's founder, Jack Howe, publicly maintained that he started the organization not to supplant the NDT but rather as a means to promote debate training for students and programs who could not or would not adhere to the rigid norms necessary to compete successfully in the NDT system (Howe, n.d.). But almost from the beginning, CEDA attracted programs that viewed its format as a way to achieve the success that they were unable to realize in the NDT system.

Geography initially played an important role in helping programs find success. Founded in the West, CEDA initially attracted western forensics programs geographically and financially isolated from the NDT community, which flourished in other parts of the country where travel distances were shorter and costs were lower. It was simply easier to operate a successful NDT debate program in the Midwest and the East. There were more tournaments, and those tournaments were closer to each other and required less travel time and expense. There were, of course, highly successful NDT programs in the West, but even before the creation of CEDA, the number of regional programs had begun to decline, which made it more imperative for successful NDT programs to travel the national circuit.

Hosting CEDA divisions was immediately attractive. Students could successfully participate without having to fulfill the substantial research burdens characteristic of the zero-sum norms of NDT debate. The sweepstakes system provided a tangible reward system for smaller programs needing to justify their budgets and existences in an increasingly zero-sum university world. Some programs and forensics educators embraced the organizational philosophy of CEDA as an extroverted-expansive organization whose focus was less on promoting homogenous competitive norms and more on making debate as open to as many students as possible.

The rise of CEDA occurred at a time when NDT debate was becoming controversial within the communication discipline and the larger academic community due to its highly technical nature, its rapid and often incomprehensible delivery practices, and its strong emphasis on maintaining its introverted-reserved philosophies. The NDT initially reacted to the emergence and popularity of CEDA by shifting emphasis away from its initial extroverted-reserved model, which encouraged participation, and becoming a more introverted-reserved organization. While not doing so publicly, many NDT program leaders attacked CEDA as lacking the intellectual rigor of NDT debate, and the NDT and CEDA communities became adversarial and publicly critical of each other's practices and norms.

The heterogeneity in debate practice between the NDT and CEDA did not last. CEDA gradually dropped many of the experimental practices that originally distinguished it from NDT. Choosing to debate policy propositions and offering their own national championship tournaments were instrumental steps in beginning the process of rapprochement between CEDA and the NDT. By the late 1990s the two organizations had, for all practical purposes, merged when the NDT community eliminated its long-standing topic-selection process and began debating the same topic as CEDA. By that time CEDA no longer debated value propositions. Debate practice in CEDA changed as well. Organizational norms moved away from a preference for communication-grounded debate practices toward the introversion of the highly technical and theoretical argument and debate practices that had driven programs away from NDT toward CEDA in the first place. This led to the emergence of a new debate format: parliamentary-style debate.

As many programs had moved from NDT to CEDA a generation earlier, a similar migration occurred in the 1990s from CEDA to parliamentary debate. A new organization, the National Parliamentary Debate Association, quickly became a major influence in debate. Like CEDA, the NPDA began in the western and Rocky Mountain regions and promoted itself as an extroverted-expansive organization. NPDA characterized itself as an alternative debate form emphasizing good communication practices, as accessible to beginning students, and as allowing students to participate in both individual events and debate. The initial norms of using a new resolution for each debate round, using a wide range of resolutions, and encouraging innovative argumentative techniques led to the same rapid growth as that experienced by CEDA. Similarly, as the organization became larger and more national in influence, the same zero-sum pressures influenced practice; the NPDA began to resemble NDT debate, and some forensics programs again began to search for alternatives.

CONCLUSION

Forensics began the twentieth century as a totally unorganized and organic activity conducted by students reacting to the stultifying constraints of literary societies and seeking the intellectual and personal growth found in competition. Students from one college sought out their neighboring institutions and slowly negotiated the terms of engagement. There were no standards, few academic resources from which to draw, and no models to emulate, since other student activities such as athletics were similarly unorganized. There was also no academic discipline available to guide practice. Yet the activity quickly became wildly popular, and the inevitable demand for participation and the order-guiding principles of democratic societies motivated the earliest attempts to bring structures that participants knew were necessary to achieve their personal and competitive goals.

The fraternity model fit the bill. The important role that social fraternities played in American life generally in the nineteenth and twentieth centuries inspired the template for organization. It was not a random choice to emulate the principles of the Masonic Order and well-respected existing societies such as Phi Beta Kappa. Those were important guides for meeting three important needs: for principles under which to justify and guide the emerging competitive debate activity; for fairness and level competitive playing fields; and for clear boundaries of membership, through which social bonds could be formed.

This model worked incredibly well during the public oratory era. Innovation flourished. Competitive speech and debate found an alternative to the literary society in the life of the high school, college, and university. Forensics became intellectually and socially acceptable and extremely popular. But the inherent competition and strain between the fraternities planted the seeds of dissension, eventually undermining the détente between the fraternities regarding competition and recruitment of new schools and members. By World War II, the model was breaking down as the tournament model prevailed and the number of alternative methods of recognition for student achievement expanded. With a centralized topic-selection process and the emergence of a de facto national debate championship, the fraternities ceded the foreground to a new model.

The new model, the professional organization model, fit the needs of the postwar era. In contrast to the earlier fraternities, the AFA was created for professional educators, not students. Furthermore, the AFA was created as an expert and intellectual organization at the very time when the public was reacting strongly against intellectualism. Attempts to centralize and control forensics activities were greeted with skepticism by a public that had begun to discount the value of debate training as citizenship training, an emerging speech communication discipline whose search for academic respectability led it far away from appreciating the value of debate and speech training at its roots, and an increasingly fractured forensics community that shared fewer and fewer values and could not transcend the zero-sum game of competition.

REFERENCES

AFA Register. (1954). AFA Collection, University of Utah Archives, Accn. 418, Box 8, Fd. 1: *AFA Register*, 1954–1957.

Baird, A. C. (1923). Shall American universities adopt the British system of debating? *Quarterly Journal of Speech Education, 9* (3), 215–22 (AN9204201).

Baird, A. C. (1955). The college debater and the Red China issue. *Central States Speech Journal, 6* (2), 5–7.

Baker, G. P. (1901). Intercollegiate debating. *Educational Review, 21,* 244–57.

Baker, J. T. (1931). Planning and working in the debate tournament. *Forensic of Pi Kappa Delta, 27,* 149–54.

Berry, M. F. (1928). A survey of intercollegiate debate in the Midwest debate conference. *Quarterly Journal of Speech, 14* (1), 86–94.

Blyton, G. (1970). This American Forensic Association: A history. *Journal of the American Forensic Association, 7* (1), 13–18.

Branham, R. (1996). *Stanton's elm: An illustrated history of debating at Bates College.* Lewiston, ME: Bates College Press.

Buehler, E. C. (1946). The Missouri Valley Forensic League. *Gavel of Delta Sigma Rho, 28* (4), 57–58.

Buehler, E. C. (1963). History of Delta Sigma Rho. *Speaker and Gavel, 1* (1), 12–18.

Burns, J. M. (1954, December 5). Debate over collegiate debates. *New York Times Magazine,* 12.

Busfield, R. M., Jr. (1959). The speech contest and the individual event. *Speech Activities, 6* (3), 136–37.

Cohen, A. M. (1998). *The shaping of American higher education.* San Francisco: John Wiley.

Constitution of Pi Kappa Delta. (1920). *Forensic of Pi Kappa Delta, 6* (1), 27–36.

Constitution of Pi Kappa Delta. (1922). *Forensic of Pi Kappa Delta, 8* (1), 16–25.

Cowperthwaite, L. L., and Baird, A. C. (1954). Intercollegiate debating. In K. R. Wallace (Ed.), *History of speech education in America: Background studies* (pp. 259–76). New York: Appleton-Century-Crofts.

Detweiler, M. D. (1898). *An account of the origin and early history of the benevolent and protective order of the Elks of the USA.* Harrison, PA: Harrisburg Publishing Company.

Diem, W. R. (1950). History of intercollegiate debating in Ohio. *Speech Activities, 6* (1), 5–8. Reprinted from *Central States Speech Journal*, November 1949.

English, E., Llano, S., Mitchell, G. R., Morrison, C. E., Rief, J., and Woods, C. (2007). Debate as a weapon of mass destruction. *Communication and Critical/Cultural Studies, 4* (2), 221–25.

Ewbank, H. L. (1935). Three hundred and eight Delta Sigma Rho alumni in Who's Who. *Gavel of Delta Sigma Rho, 16* (3), 52.

Fernandez, T. L. (1959). 108 years of oratory. *Gavel of Delta Sigma Rho, 41* (4), 51.

Fest, T. B. (1956). Golden jubilee citations. *Gavel of Delta Sigma Rho, 38* (4), 99–105.

Fifty years of debating at Bates College. (1947). *Gavel of Delta Sigma Rho, 30* (1), 9.

Freeley, J. A. (1951). A survey of college forensics. *Gavel of Delta Sigma Rho, 33* (3), 50–52.

Fryar, L. (1984). A brief history of individual events nationals. *National Forensic Journal, 2*, 73–83.

Greene, R. W., and Hicks, D. (2005). Lost convictions: Debating both sides and the ethical self-fashioning of liberal citizens. *Cultural Studies, 19*, 103.

Gulley, H. E., and Seabury, H. F. (1954). Speech education in twentieth-century public schools. In K. E. Wallace (Ed.), *History of speech education in America: Background studies* (pp. 471–89). New York: Appleton-Century-Crofts.

Harshbarger, H. C. (1976). *Some highlights of the Department of Speech and Dramatic Art.* Iowa City: University of Iowa.

The history of Delta Sigma Rho. (1956). *Gavel of Delta Sigma Rho, 38* (3), 70–78.

Hofstadter, R. M. (1962). *Anti-intellectualism in American life.* New York: Random House.

Howe, J. H. (n.d.). It's time for open season on squirrels. Retrieved from www.cedadebate.org/cad/index.php/CAD/article/download/76/64.

Jacob, B. E. (1931). First national high school tournament. *Gavel of Delta Sigma Rho, 14* (1), 15.

Johnston, V. D. (1917). Debating and athletics in colored colleges. *Crisis, 14*, 129–30.

Keith, W. M. (2007). *Democracy as discussion: Civic education and the American Forum Movement.* Lanham, MD: Rowman & Littlefield.

Lambert, A. E. (1948). Survey of state high school leagues. *Debater's Magazine, 4* (4), 195.

Layton, C. R. (1963). Fifty years of Tau Kappa Alpha. *Speaker and Gavel, 1* (1), 10–11.

Lions Clubs International. (2013). Our history. Retrieved from http://www.lions clubs.org/EN/about-lions/mission-and-history/our-history/index.php.

Littlefield, R. S. (1998). *Voices on the prairie: Bringing speech and theatre to North Dakota.* Fargo, ND: Institute for Regional Studies.

Littlefield, R. S. (2008). From state association to national association: The emergence and evolution of high school debate during the early twentieth century. Paper presented to the National Communication Association Convention, San Diego, California.

Montgomery, K. (1950). High school debating in the West. *Speech Activities, 6* (1), 8–11.

Moriarty, V. (1945). Speech activities in the Rocky Mountain area. *Debater's Magazine, 1* (3), 117–18.

Morrison, R. (1948). History of debate in American colleges [North Carolina]. *Debater's Magazine, 4* (3), 150–52.

Nabors. D. J. (1956). The historical development of intercollegiate forensic activities: 1915–1956. Unpublished dissertation. Norman: University of Oklahoma.

Nagel, R. H. (1963). Honor societies—past, present, and future. *Speaker and Gavel, 45* (4), 57–58.

Nichols, E. R. (1915). Pi Kappa Delta, a historical sketch. *Forensic of Pi Kappa Delta, 1* (1), 3–5.

Nichols, E. R. (1936a). A historical sketch of intercollegiate debating: I. *Quarterly Journal of Speech, 22* (2), 213–20.

Nichols, E. R. (1936b). A historical sketch of intercollegiate debating: II. *Quarterly Journal of Speech, 22* (4), 591–603.

Nichols, E. R. (1937). A historical sketch of intercollegiate debating: III. *Quarterly Journal of Speech, 23* (2), 259–79.

Nichols, E. R. (1952). American debating: Beginning a codification of its rules and customs. *Speech Activities, 8* (3), 47–51.

Nichols, E. R., Jr. (1952). Mr. Forensic. *Speech Activities, 8* (4), 101–4.

Norton, L. E. (1957). The present status of intercollegiate discussion. *Gavel of Delta Sigma Rho, 39* (3), 63–64, 80.

Norton, L. (1987). *The history of Pi Kappa Delta, 1913–1987.* Peoria, IL: Bradley University.

Poe, J. (1994, February 9). Role of social clubs changes with times. *Chicago Tribune*. Retrieved from http://articles.chicagotribune.com/1994-02-09/features/9402090159_1_social-clubs-clubmembers-societies.

Potter, D. (1944). *Debating in the colonial chartered colleges: An historical survey, 1642–1900*. New York: Bureau of Publications, Teachers College, Columbia University.

Potter, D. (Ed.). (1954). *Argumentation and debate: Principles and practices*. New York: Dryden Press.

Rarig, F. M., and Greaves, H. S. (1954). National speech organizations and speech education. In K. R. Wallace (Ed.), *History of speech education in America: Background studies* (pp. 490–517). New York: Appleton-Century-Crofts.

Redfern, D. D. (1960). George Pierce Baker's theory of argumentation. Unpublished thesis. Eugene: University of Oregon.

Roberts, D. D. (1978). *From the beginning: The tradition of Watertown public speaking activities*. Watertown, SD: Watertown Public Opinion.

Roosevelt, T. (1913). *Theodore Roosevelt: An autobiography*. New York: Macmillan.

Roosevelt Rough Writer. (1998, January 17). The newsletter for volunteers in park at Sagamore Hill, *1* (4). Retrieved from http://www.ncaa.org/about/history.html.

Rose, F. H. (1969). A historical review of debate resolution selection. *Forensic of Pi Kappa Delta*, *55* (1), 3–7, 24–31.

Schmidt, R. N. (1949). High school debating in the East. *Speech Activities*, *5* (1), 14–17.

Secord, A. E., and Thomas, R. H. (1946). Speech in the extracurricular program. *Debater's Magazine*, *2* (1), 5–9.

Shurter, E. D. (1915, April–October). State organization for contests in public speaking. *Quarterly Journal of Public Speaking*, *1*, 59–64.

Sillars, M. O. (1949). History and evaluation of intercollegiate forensics at the University of Redlands. Unpublished thesis. Redlands, CA: University of Redlands.

State high school leagues. (1932). *Gavel of Delta Sigma Rho*, *14* (4), 8–9.

Stone, A. P. (1914). Introduction (1893). Reprinted in A. N. Levin and H. B. Goodfriend (Eds.), *Harvard debating—1892–1913* (pp. 5–23). Cambridge, MA: Caustic-Claflin Company. Available at Harvard University Archives: HUD11320.914.

Tabbert, M. A. (2005). *American Freemasons: Three centuries of building communities*. New York: New York University Press.

Trueblood, T. C. (1931). The founding of Delta Sigma Rho. *Gavel of Delta Sigma Rho*, *13* (3), 5–6.

Turk, D. B. (2004). *Bound by a mighty vow: Sisterhood and women's fraternities, 1870–1920.* New York: New York University Press.

Wells, E. W. (1929). The Pacific Forensic League. *Gavel of Delta Sigma Rho, 11* (2), 7–10.

Zarefsky, D., and Sillars, M. O., Jr. (n.d.). A. F. A. support for research: Journals and conferences. Malcolm O. Sillars Collection, University of Utah Archives, Accn. 1997 Box 1, Fd. 2: American Forensic Association Publications.

NOTE

1. We use the terms "fraternity" and "honorary" somewhat interchangeably. As we note, these organizations began using the fraternal structure similar to that of social and residential fraternities and sororities, which were familiar at the time to the founders of the forensics organizations. Over time, concerns about gender equity and the sometimes poor reputation of social fraternities led the organizations to refer to themselves more commonly as honoraries.

Part II

TENSIONS SHAPING THE
EVOLUTION OF FORENSICS

The next three chapters delve into the tensions that shaped the forensics community during the twentieth century: the tensions within the community about whether competitive elements or educational benefits should dominate forensics activities; within the speech discipline about the nature and place of forensics in the curriculum and in academic departments; and among the collegiate and the high school forensics communities as they interacted throughout the century. These chapters rely on the scholarship of twentieth-century forensics leaders who were not unwilling to share their opinions and arguments supporting their positions. Ultimately, these tensions led to the fractionalization of the forensics community during the technical era.

5

Tensions That Shaped
the Evolution of Forensics

The history chronicling the evolution of forensics activities reveals that the status of those activities and the individuals who engaged in them as participants, coaches, and educators changed throughout the twentieth century. The shift in status occurred on many levels: participant, activity, department, scholarship, and discipline. On each level, the status of forensics was challenged and moved from a position of prominence to one of marginalization. Why did this happen?

Participants who had once been better known and more popular than athletes on their campuses or in their schools—due to the public nature of the activity, which was both entertaining and intellectually stimulating—became invisible and sometimes negatively stereotyped as the tournament format, more technical judging criteria, and more complicated arguments removed the audience and transformed the focus of the activity from a public to a private perspective. The activity that began with an emphasis on oratory and elocution, featuring the Aristotelian canon of style, shifted to one in which the analytical and technical aspects of the activity prevailed, prioritizing the canon of invention.

The status of forensics shifted from being central to the rationale justifying the creation of departments of speech and the addition of faculty lines to being marginalized as an extracurricular activity often housed outside academic communication departments. The academic responsibilities for those serving as forensics educators and coaches at research institutions shifted from directing debate and forensics teams and teaching courses related to those activities to taking on additional research responsibilities in order to publish and demonstrate their value and legitimacy in departments and academic programs.

Similarly, the scholarship of the emerging professional association of teachers of public speaking began to change soon after the discipline broke away from English. The original focus on forensics pedagogy filling its flagship journal, the *Quarterly Journal of Public Speaking* (later the *QJS*), shifted to research in the social, psychological, and cultural aspects of what were becoming the core areas of interpersonal, organizational, and media-related communication. The publication of forensics-related research in the major journals of the discipline became the exception, influencing the honoraries to change the focus of their publications from personal and anecdotal stories to include the forensics research being published by faculty fighting for tenure, promotion, and legitimacy in their academic departments.

Finally, the very rationale for forensics as citizenship training was challenged, and forensics lost much of the goodwill it enjoyed at the start of the twentieth century. Seismic social and political changes caused by depression and war led to the rise of a powerful intellectual movement that questioned whether engaged citizenship was better served by discussion—communication in a noncompetitive setting to reach the best solution to a problem—than by a competitive activity like debate, which ignored the right solution in favor of deciding who did the better job of debating. The forensics community misunderstood the underlying claim of the advocates of discussion and focused on discussion as merely another potentially competitive form rather than as an alternative problem-solving philosophy. As the communication discipline was evolving toward a greater focus on empiricism and social science perspectives, discussion and the study of group communication supplanted the study of argumentation and debate, which remained firmly rooted in the rhetorical tradition of the discipline. Departments further marginalized debate and forensics by removing them from the curriculum and assigning them status as extracurricular programs.

As forensics activities evolved throughout the public oratory and technical eras, forensics and nonforensics scholarship reflected that evolution and mirrored the tensions resulting from changes in higher education and the communication discipline. We introduced the focus of forensics scholarship during the century in chapter 4. Our focus in this chapter and in chapter 6 is on why these shifts occurred. We suggest that three major tensions influenced how forensics educators and participants shaped American forensics in the twentieth century: the tension within the forensics community about the impact of competition in influencing forensics practices, the tension within academic departments about how forensics fit into the emerging areas of specialization found within their curricular structures, and the tension within the communication discipline about whether discussion or debate was the more appropriate way to teach students the skills needed to function as engaged, articulate citizens in the American democracy. Each of these tensions was reflected through the scholarship of forensics educators and those outside the forensics community. We focus on the first of these tensions in this chapter, leaving the two macro-level tensions for chapter 6.

THE POPULATION OF THE FORENSICS COMMUNITY

The forensics community always included a very diverse population of students, faculty, and private individuals and/or groups who initiated, supported, or engaged in competitive debate and declamation activities. There was never unanimity about any philosophical or theoretical point of view. One of the earliest and most significant tensions dividing the community was very differing opinions regarding competition as a point of emphasis in forensics activities. Students were the first to populate forensics and have always been the central focus of forensics activities because of their role as participants. When students reached out to faculty members to chaperone, give advice, or coach, the forensics community expanded. As student demand grew for more debate and forensics activities, campuses responded by adding faculty and courses that gave students training and credit for their debate and practical, public speaking training. A result of this expansion of forensics from a student-driven activity to one involving faculty was the emergence of tension among the faculty over how much competition should be emphasized. The vast majority of students wanted competition, but the faculty members were divided: those actively involved in coaching the student activities supported competition as the primary focus of forensics, whereas others, who were often former forensics coaches or participants, opposed competitive formats and practices as noneducational and devaluing of forensics activities.

In this chapter, we chronicle the scholarship of the forensics community, focusing on the tension between education and competition as forensics evolved during the twentieth century and identifying reoccurring philosophical and practical disputes that framed forensics practices. This chapter is not meant to be an exhaustive discussion of all forensics scholarship during the twentieth century. However, our analysis is drawn from a broad review of the *Gavel of Delta Sigma Rho*, the *Forensic of Pi Kappa Delta*, the *Debater's Magazine*, *Speech Activities* (published independently by E. R. Nichols of the University of Redlands in California), the *Bulletin* and the *Rostrum* (published by the National Forensic League), and the *Register* and the *Journal of the American Forensic Association/ Argumentation and Advocacy* (published by the American Forensic Association).

THE INHERENCY OF COMPETITION IN FORENSICS

The unique innovation of forensics was the introduction of competition between different schools and institutions. Thus, the inherency of competition as the dominant theme of much of the scholarship throughout the century is not surprising. When Davis (1916) characterized competitive debate either as "a game" or as training for "the wise disposition of important matters in a democratic society" (p. 171), the activity was already twenty-five years old. The defense of these potentially conflicting perspectives became the focus of forensics scholarship during this early period of experimentation (Nichols, 1936). This dichotomy between competition and education manifested itself throughout the public oratory, technical, and postmodern eras of forensics, as coaches and teachers struggled to reconcile its competitive and educational aspects.

When debate and forensics spread across the country, some scholars viewed the perspective of debate as a game as an advantage due to the motivational impact of competition on both participants and audiences. For example, Professors Lardner and Sarett of Northwestern University acknowledged that their debaters "wanted to win" ("Forum," 1921, p. 280). Professor Merry of the University of Iowa added, "The pleasure [to defeat a neighboring institution whose athletic team had defeated his or her school] became all the more intense" ("Forum," 1921, p. 282). Baird (1923) defended the evolution of competitive debate, suggesting that the prospect of winning attracted participants and audiences to the activity. Additionally, he cited the "highest recognition of the sport" given by politicians, educators, and justices, suggesting that "the debate contest, rightly or wrongly, has been regarded as a gage [*sic*] of the intellectual efficiency of the college" (p. 219).

While acknowledging the role of competition, other scholars suggested that some debate practices diminished the real value of debate as a meaningful educational opportunity for participants to inform the public and to train debaters in collecting and effectively expressing arguments. Schrier (1929) identified some of these detrimental debate practices as the introduction of coaching, unfair debate practices (e.g., waiting to present an argument in a debate until it is too late for the opponent to effectively refute it), the creation of ill will among schools, the lowering of professional standards, the promotion of a star system of competition in which only the best students could participate, and the tendency to inflate a debater's sense of self. From these conflicting perspectives emerged a number of major issues that shaped how forensics evolved throughout the century, including debating both sides of the resolution, decision versus no-decision debating, audience/lay judging versus expert critic judging, tournament competition, and conflicting pedagogical justifications for alternative forensics practices affecting the competitive aspects of the activity.

Debating Both Sides of the Resolution

One of the first issues emerging in early forensics scholarship questioned the educational value of preparing teams to debate both sides of the resolution. When competitive debate began, pairs of schools competed with each other, determining the resolution to be debated and negotiating which side of the question each school would defend. The resolutions differed for each debate competition, and the participating schools prepared only one side of the question. As groups of schools formed debate leagues, the need to facilitate the competitive structure of the leagues required that member teams debate a common resolution in different locations. The adoption of common resolutions meant more teams from each school could debate simultaneously. Thus, debaters would need to be prepared to debate either side of the question.

The practice of preparing teams to debate both sides became controversial when what promoters of the practice described as "the educational value of doing more research and learning more" (Keith, 2007, p. 66) contrasted with what some in the public arena perceived to be a sophistic practice. In this instance, the values of enhanced competition and education united to justify the practice of preparing teams to debate both sides of the question, while the opposition came from the public at large.

Public figures—namely, Theodore Roosevelt and William Jennings Bryan—criticized the practice of preparing teams to debate both sides of a resolution as a product of a "flawed democracy" (Keith, 2007, p. 69). An article in the *New Republic* reporting Yale's simultaneous victories against Princeton on the negative and Harvard on the affirmative prompted critics of the practice to suggest that training students to support both sides of an issue would lead to increased levels of partisanship in the political arena. Among Roosevelt's (1913) criticisms was the belief that advocating both sides of a resolution reduced a debater's level of "sincerity and intensity of conviction," and he was "exceedingly glad that [he] did not take part in the type of debate [in college] in which stress is laid, not upon getting the speaker to think rightly, but on getting him to talk glibly on the side to which he is assigned" (p. 406).

The issue found its way to the *Quarterly Journal of Public Speaking* as its first editor, James M. O'Neill (1916), and other supporters of the practice argued that preparing to debate both sides was a technical requirement of debate and did not mean that debaters were without conviction (Musgrave, 1946). They cited the artificiality of the debate contest as similar to sports and games and contended that debates were judged on the basis of who did the better debating, not on the question being debated or the side to which a debater was assigned. O'Neill also suggested that most debate squads assigned different partners to represent the affirmative and negative positions, reducing the potential for debaters being compelled to argue against their convictions.

Baird (1923) asserted that America's unique practical and legal national experience shaped the competitive nature of debate: "Our collegiate style, in as far as it is original and virile, is the expression of our particular political and educational inheritance. Our faith in a rigid constitution, our exaltation of the Supreme Court, explain sufficiently the character and popularity of our judicial style of debate" (p. 221). His position reflected the claims that debate can be ethical; that students are able to argue the side of the issue they think is right; that most undergraduates do not have settled convictions anyway, so investigating both sides of a question is valuable; that debaters accumulate and weigh evidence in the same way a scientist investigates the tentativeness of truth; and that social discussion through presentation and decision is an appropriate educational outcome. Finally, Baird (1923) defended competition: "The debating game properly played should not necessarily produce Sophists, archaic militants, or unscientific investigators" (pp. 220–21).

The challenge from the public arena fueling the controversy about preparing students to debate both sides of the resolution was brief and united the emerging forensics community. The resulting scholarship from supporters of the practice rationalized that not only was researching and understanding conflicting positions educational but the practice also expanded opportunities for more students to get involved in competitive debate. However, the appearance of this unity was short-lived, as the manner in which the preparation to debate both sides manifested itself in other debate practices that divided the debate community. In particular, controversy arose about the educational value of having as the basis for judgment in a round of competition the quality of the actual debating between opposing teams versus arrival at the best argument or decision for the solution of a societal problem.

Decision versus No-Decision Debating

While the first debates were no-decision contests, decision debates naturally followed as participants and audiences demanded to know which team had won. The arguments justifying decision and no-decision forms of debate reflected the similar philosophical positions of those who advocated debate as a game versus those who viewed it as a training activity for civic engagement. This controversy dominated forensics scholarship during the first quarter of the twentieth century (Miler, 1930), fueled by the significantly conflicting beliefs held in the competitive and educational camps.

As intercollegiate debate spread across the country, its proponents endorsed the competitive format reflecting the debate-as-a-sport paradigm. As in all sports, winners and losers are determined by either qualitative or quantitative means. Baird (1923) justified decision debates, arguing that they (1) "raised the standards of forensics set by the older college literary societies"; (2) attracted audiences "at least as large as those of 15 or 20 years ago"; (3) appealed to "large numbers of representative university men" who wanted to know if they had won the debate;

(4) spawned "hundreds of intercollegiate contests"; (5) contributed to the growth of forensic debating fraternities, "demonstrating their vitality"; (6) had the support of successful individuals in a variety of professions, "giving highest recognition of the sport"; (7) served as a barometer of academic success and "intellectual efficiency"; and (8) promoted "educational discipline and mental activity" at the highest levels of critical thinking (p. 219). Most proponents of decision debates agreed that no-decision debates had more real-world application because they focused on arriving at the best solution rather than on which team demonstrated better debating skills. However, as Sarett concluded, "The debaters want a decision" ("Forum," 1921, p. 280). In an emerging discipline the student voice drowned out competing viewpoints, and there was obvious student attraction to the excitement of formal competition measured by wins and losses. High schools and colleges could use competitive success as a reflection of their institutional quality and engender community pride, resulting in stronger financial and tangible public support.

The reintroduction of no-decision debates in 1914–1915 by six Midwestern Big Ten universities seeking to redirect the focus of debate away from its competitive roots was an effort to eliminate competition and reflect debate's educational objectives. Those opposed to decision debates raised several arguments through their scholarship in an attempt to persuade the forensics community to abandon the competitive paradigm. These arguments included saving money, eliminating coaching, and focusing on real-world practices.

Opponents, such as Professor Merry from the University of Iowa and Professors Trueblood, Hollister, and Immel from the University of Michigan, claimed no-decision debates would save money for school programs ("Forum," 1921), as the growth of debate and the potential for schools to field multiple teams increased travel budgets. With no-decision debates, the funds used to pay for judges could be diverted to defray other team expenses. Opponents of decision debates viewed coaching as a negative consequence, as the losing debate teams sought the advice of faculty and more experienced, successful debaters about strategies that would help them to win future debates. The departments of speech also used coaching as justification for their existence, putting pressure on coaches to create successful teams to prove their value as faculty members. Not only did the need for a decision divert the educational value gained when debate was "largely an outgrowth of the students' own development, ability, and interest" ("Forum," 1921, p. 281), but, as Professor Woolbert from the University of Illinois put it, decision debates also resulted in the "contest slavery that curses so many teachers of speech" ("Forum," 1921, p. 288). As teams from different schools met in competition, they used their win-loss records to justify receiving additional funds from their school administrations to increase the size and quality of their programs. Woolbert viewed this trend negatively because faculty members were diverted from "scholarship and academic dignity" ("Forum," 1921, p. 288).

The recurrent argument raised by opponents of decision debates stressed the importance of eliminating competition from the activity and viewing debate as a way to inform the public about issues of the day and a means to train debaters in collecting and expressing arguments. Davis (1916) stressed the need to keep debate focused on making a real difference in the world because providing training for the debaters to engage in the civic context after graduation should be the reason for engaging in debates. Thus, he argued that the debate activity should exist to enable students to acquire the skills necessary "for the wise disposition of important matters in legislatures, public gatherings, club and society meetings—wherever men [*sic*] collect, as they must be constantly doing, at least in a democracy, for counsel and effective action" (p. 173). Davis extended his position, suggesting that if the game metaphor is taken too far, questionable tactics—"devices, strategy, speciousness"—result, placing "a premium upon mere cleverness, upon *argument ad homines* [*sic*]; upon the ability, when occasion serves, to make the worse appear the better"; instead, he believed, debate should be conceived of as "an artificial but a genuine means of arriving at the just determination of important matters [placing] a premium upon genuineness, integrity, and sincerity" (1916, p. 178).

While the experiment with no-decision debates was short-lived, the motivation for opposing the competitive paradigm stemmed from the belief that as the debate activity expanded across the country, the potential for the spread of questionable tactics related to winning a judge's decision would further contaminate the pursuit of educational values associated with "preparing citizens to participate in the work of living and governing, of deciding intelligently and confidently the serious questions which from time to time arise" (Davis, 1916, p. 179). In retrospect, the intentions of those seeking to strengthen the educational values associated with debate were sincere. However, their approach may have been part of the reason why decision debate continued to dominate the forensics activity. Nichols (1936) provided an explanation:

> All would have been well had not the advocates of the new idea felt that abuse of the old way was essential to the progress of their plan. Abuse of the old system angered those who still adhered to it and were satisfied because they had made good records under it. A schism arose which divided the debate world into hostile camps—the decision and the non-decision cohorts. The more the reformers criticized and invented new forms, the more the devotees of the old plan clung to their time honored methods and ideas. (p. 269)

The divide between those supporting and opposing decision debates was not reconciled, as the uniquely American innovation retained its competitive characteristic of awarding the decision to the team doing the better job of debating. Without the support to change the direction of the debate-as-game paradigm, those favoring the strengthening of the educational value of debate next turned their attention to the quality of the decisions being rendered. This prompted scholarship examining the educational value associated with the person or persons who awarded the decision: an audience, lay judge, or expert critic.

Audience and Lay Judges versus Expert Critic Judging

Despite the considerable efforts exerted by individuals supporting the introverted-reserved orientation to reduce the emphasis on competition and eliminate decision debates as noneducational, the evolution of debate, and later forensics, during the twentieth century demonstrated the underlying popularity derived from the competitive elements of the activities. As Berry (1928) noted, student interest waned whenever competition was de-emphasized. Clearly, competition was the one characteristic of forensics that served to perpetuate the activity and shape its focus.

The preference among participants and audiences for decision debates established the need for judges to determine the winners. Thus, forensics scholarship focused on who should judge and the basis upon which decision(s) should be made. McCroskey (n.d.) identified fifty significant articles drawn from twelve publications (excluding the *Speaker* and the *Forensic*) suggesting the high level of scholarly concern regarding this issue essential to the competitive nature of forensics. Generally, the theme of the early scholarship centered on identifying the best method for judging and improving the quality of the judge's decision.

Before we present more specific information about these two issues, an observation is in order. From all accounts, no universally accepted judge-selection process emerged during the public oratory era. Because experimentation characterized this period, the level of competitiveness desired by school officials hosting the actual debate or forensic competition determined the judge-selection process (Berry, 1928). Gilman (1928) described the breadth of judging models available to early debaters: "We have tested the audience vote both on skill in debating and on the merits of the question, the shift-of-opinion ballot, four judges, three judges, the paid critic-judge, and the no-decision debate, in our search for a system that will give satisfaction" (p. 556). Bauer (1955) clarified what he perceived to be the real issue: "the problem of finding competent judges" (p. 40).

Those who advocated audience judging believed that debaters should speak to the observers using arguments that appealed to the general public. Audience-centered presentation skills and arguments that resonated with the general public were the hallmarks of this approach to judging. The actual practice of audience judging varied, with audience members sometimes asked to vote at the end of the debate for the side they believed had won or to provide the debaters with feedback about where they succeeded and failed in persuading the audience. Some competitions used what was referred to as the "shift-of-opinion" ballot or format (Woodward, 1915; Utterback, n.d., pp. 315–16). Those using this method took a poll before the debate began to determine where audience opinion stood on the question. Then, after the debate concluded, a similar poll was taken. Using a mathematical calculation, the side with the greatest shift of opinion was declared the winner. A disadvantage of the audience decision system was the perception among debaters and coaches that poor-quality decisions were often made. For example, the team making the best case might not win because the skills of the opponents were such that the latter persuaded the audience members to believe their weaker argument was superior.

During this time, panels of lay judges adjudicated most of the public debates. The term "lay," in the judging context, operationally referred to individuals drawn from the general public who were educated and capable of rendering a decision. In the early years, when schools engaged in dual or triangular debates, the local hosts arranged the judges. These debates occurred only once or twice a year and were highly anticipated. Hence, civic and religious leaders were approached and willingly served as distinguished judges from the community. Typically, a panel of three or four judges was selected, entered the auditorium where the debate took place, listened to the debaters present their constructive and rebuttal speeches, left the room to confer with each other, and returned to announce and present the award to the winning team. This system had its benefits for the activity, as superintendents, school board members, and other influential members of the community were often called upon to judge, and they could—at first hand—observe the benefits of debate for the participants and observers (Bauer, 1955). These individuals were often the ones who later supported forensics programs when additional resources were needed to provide for travel and other tournament-related expenses.

However, the lay judge approach was not without its critics, mostly after the fact, when the losing team and its coach rejected the partisan decision as due to home advantage or as groundless. This criticism caused forensics scholars to question whether lay judges provided an advantage over trained educators as judges of debate and forensics. Additionally, as the popularity of debate increased and the number of debaters needing to be judged grew, securing judges became more difficult, as civic leaders were less willing to volunteer on a regular basis.

In 1917–1918, a series of articles in the *Quarterly Journal of Public Speaking* presented the controversy regarding who should judge debates. Hollister (1917) advanced the position that to remain interested in forensics, students needed to have faith in the judging of the contests. He argued that trained educators should be used because they would ensure that the best practices associated with each event were rewarded: "A trained judge is regarded in all walks of life as better than an untrained one. A trained judge is apt to recognize and weigh carefully a larger number of factors than an untrained one" (Hollister, 1917, p. 238). O'Neill, the first president of the National Association of Academic Teachers of Public Speaking (NAATPS), supported this position, believing that without "the professionalization of the speech profession" (Keith, 2007, p. 71), anyone could judge a debate. This opening of judging to untrained observers would weaken the primary justification for the creation of departments of public speaking to teach the specific skills that debaters and speakers should use to engage in the forensic arts and ultimately to become active citizens of the democracy.

This position became the spark that ignited the most sustained debate about who should judge debates: the juryman or the expert critic. To understand what ultimately prevailed in the controversy, the second issue that shaped forensics scholarship about judging—the proper basis for the decision rendered by the judge—must be considered. Once that was established, the "Who should judge?" question would become clear. Table 5.1 provides the contrasting perspectives of those supporting the juryman and the expert critic.

The position advanced by Wells and others supporting the juryman perspective argued that the question being debated should be the basis for deciding who won. Because debate should mirror democratic institutions, citizens should advocate for what is best for the general public. Any citizen or juryman should be able to

Table 5.1. Contrasting Perspectives of Juryman versus Expert Critic

Juryman	Expert Critic
Debate should mirror democratic institutions.	Debate is a classroom experience.
Debate is central to civic life, in which the responsible citizen advocates for what is best.	Debate is a game in which participants engage in the art of debating.
The question should be the basis of the decision.	The practice of debating should be the basis of the decision.
The debate should be directed to the public decision of the audience.	The debate should be directed to the private decision of the judge.
Anyone should be able to judge a debate.	An individual with professional training and expertise in argumentation and debate should be the judge.

understand the issues underlying the question and make a decision. Those who endorsed using the juryman—operationally understood to be a member of the general public capable of deciding the strongest argument—as judge thought that the debate winner should be determined solely based on the quality and rightness of the argument, not on technical prowess, which may demonstrate debate skill but not an understanding of the question being debated. Wells (1918) advanced the analogy that the quality of a painting is judged by the finished product, not based on how the artist painted it. Similarly, a debate should be judged by the quality of the final argument, not by how the debaters engaged in the practice of getting to it. Using the example of the Lincoln-Douglas debates, he suggested that Stephen Douglas won the debate but Abraham Lincoln won the argument about slavery.

Advocates for the expert critic based their arguments on the premise that debate was an extension of the classroom experience and that the art of debating should be the basis for deciding who won or lost. Because debaters demonstrated particular skills, one of which was the ability to present a case capable of withstanding the attacks of opponents, expert critics trained in argumentation and debate should be the judges. As such, the opinion of the judge about which debaters prevailed superseded the public opinion about what position on the question was right or wrong.

O'Neill's (1918) position that the expert critic was the preferred judge for debates inherently developed through his promotion of the NAATPS and his argument that the practice of debate, not the question being debated, should be the basis for the decision. He argued that using the quality of the argument as the determinant factor would unjustifiably give the decision to debaters who may have been given a case or an argument by their coach or who may have "stumbled upon a strong or sound argument" without having to think on their feet, demonstrate critical thinking skills, refute the arguments of their opponents, or function effectively within the timed context of a debate round. O'Neill argued (1918) that the best debaters should prevail because they were able to demonstrate stronger preparation and attention to the multiple variables that could influence the decision in a round of debate. Thus, the need for the expert critic-judge resulted because the range of elements affecting a debate decision would be better understood and applied by someone trained in determining which team did the better job of debating. O'Neill's analogy used a musical performance as its basis. When deciding which soloist performed a musical selection more effectively, the critic would consider the many aspects pertaining to how the solos were performed, which would include choice of selection but not rely exclusively on that one aspect as a basis for decision. Extending this analogy to forensics, debaters or speakers should be judged by how they conveyed their material, not by their choice of material as the sole basis for the decision.

While the debate between these two sides continued, proponents of the critic-judge position ultimately prevailed because they effectively argued that the critic-judge could subsume the juryman while the juryman could not subsume the critic-judge. The juryman stressed that the strong argument should win the debate. The critic stressed that the best debaters would develop the strongest argument within the context of the debate, while also demonstrating a range of other skills that conveyed their debating prowess. Only the critic-judge could effectively evaluate those other skill sets.

The proponents of this view reminded their readers that all criteria are potentially significant and can be used as a basis for debate decisions. However, because these varied and often conflicting criteria will be differently interpreted within the context of each debate, the individual judge should determine their respective merit. Johnson (1935) provided a simplified version: "[Voice and delivery, arguments and subject matter, and effectiveness and power as a speaker] as generally used are of equal merit, each considered one-third. However, each judge may give greater weight to one or more, but should never give more than 50% to any one of the three" (p. 398).

After Wells and O'Neill, others weighed in on the subject of who should judge. Seeley (1930) rendered a judge's perspective, favoring expert, trained judges, comparing them to athletic officials who knew the rules and were paid to make sure they were followed: "An individual who has made a study of debating should be a more competent reviewer of opposing abilities than three individuals who have not made such preparation" (p. 20). Just as in medicine, law, engineering, religion, education, music, and even technical skills such as plumbing, "a demand for qualified opinions even at the expenditure of a fraction of the amount drafted for athletics, will result in strengthening forensics" (Seeley, 1930, p. 20).

As competition for the trained judges' decisions became more refined, debaters discovered the need to adapt to a range of judging tastes, which would be a characteristic of the activity even when judging standards became more homogenized in the technical period and the relationship between judge and competitor flipped from the competitors exclusively adapting to the judge to the judge also being expected to adapt to the community norms emerging from the establishment of national championship tournaments. Westfall (1933) alluded to the presence of different judging paradigms when he wrote, "It is unfair to the debaters for a judge to hold them rigidly to his own criteria. The next judge may have a different set" (p. 6).

Not until later in the century would the full array of judge paradigms emerge in forensics scholarship. However, even in the early debates about the basis for a decision, three judging paradigms were identified: (1) punish the debaters if they did not perform the skills correctly or follow the rules of debate, (2) assess the arguments of the debaters to determine which position was right, or (3) critique the debaters to provide feedback on how they functioned in the debate. The skills paradigm came to describe those judges who punished; the stock issues and narrative paradigms reflected the juryman's approach to the establishment of the strongest argument; and the critic became the policymaker, hypothesis tester, or games player judge, considering multiple perspectives as he or she made a decision about who won the debate.

While the situation remained that a debate decision could always be questioned and there was little agreement about which particular element(s) of debate should weigh more heavily in a judge's decision, support grew for expert critics in order to provide a more technical and analytical approach to judging debate. By the 1930s, the critic-judge system was the predominant system of judging in forensics, with the heaviest use in the Midwest and some use in the far West, occasional use in the South, and rare use in the East (Holcolm, 1933, pp. 37–38).

The Introduction of the Tournament

As noted in chapter 2, the introduction of the tournament to competitive forensics was prompted by economic and social factors that challenged the traditional means by which debates and speaking contests occurred. Miller (1958) claimed, "The only important change in intercollegiate debate has been the addition of the debate tournament . . . born of the depression, as a method of providing many debates at little cost . . . kept alive during the war when travel restrictions made it easier to attend a tournament than to travel to several institutions for debates; . . . and perpetuated by the extreme conservatism of debate coaches, who apparently feel that change must not invade debate" (p. 7).

When intercollegiate competition commenced, debates were singular events. That is, schools contracted with each other to engage in dual meets (Keith, 2007). Once arrangements were made, students and their chaperones from one school traveled to the host school to debate. The host was responsible for all arrangements, including the selection of the judges. Judson (1938) explained, "Dual meets were popular because they fostered good will, inter-campus friendship, as well as [provided] for the exchange of intellectual currency" (p. 35). With an increase in the number of schools with debate teams came the introduction of round-robins (in which a group of three to five schools met and debated the teams of each of the other schools) and debating leagues (Hansen, 1949).

Further expansion of debate activities necessitated the introduction of a different means by which students engaged in forensics activities. The tournament format was introduced in 1923 at Southwestern College in Winfield, Kansas, as a way to facilitate increased participation. Judson (1938) suggested that in the beginning, when tournaments were small, they provided benefits for participating schools. Because a central location could be identified and multiple schools with coaches could attend, a system of tournament scheduling developed, whereby two school teams could debate and be judged by a coach from a different school. This third-party judging arrangement helped to minimize the problem of finding enough expert judges with knowledge of the topic.

At the 1924 convention, Pi Kappa Delta (PKD) adopted the plan for a national debate tournament to be held at the 1926 convention scheduled for Estes Park, Colorado (Hansen, 1949). Those who favored the tournament format justified the practice in their scholarship, describing the format and management practices to familiarize those who had not yet participated in a tournament, as well as offering testimony about the advantages associated with this format. The popularity of tournament debating was widespread; for example, by 1937, 185 teams from fifty-seven colleges in ten states debated in a double-elimination format at the Southwestern College tournament. With over fifty teams and more than five hundred people coming to the little town of Winfield, the tournament organizers rightly described Southwestern College as the "debate capital of the United States" (Hansen, 1949, p. 154).

Newman (1955) refuted the arguments raised against tournament debating, stating that (1) tournaments offered debate training to more students than did audience debates, (2) promoting competition was an inappropriate reason to discontinue debate, as the value of competition already had prevailed in the forensics community, and (3) the abuses being cited as occurring at tournaments were not unique and could be found in any system of competition. He further suggested that the value of learning the techniques of research, gaining knowledge of contemporary problems, learning to evaluate evidence critically, building argumentation skills, developing broadmindedness, and acquiring public speaking expertise were all benefits of preparing to engage in tournament debate.

Those opposed to the tournament format cited numerous faults, including the elimination of the public element from the debate activity by "burying debating in the back-halls and cubby holes of our campuses" (Lull, 1948, p. 109) and the marginalization of the forensics community even further from those in mainstream communication departments. Lull (1948) concluded, "No wonder there is no faculty or student support of debating in many schools. They never hear a debate" (p. 109). Judson (1938) argued that, on a large scale, tournaments were regimented and too intense, and they dehumanized the conduct of the debaters. Barnard (1937) cited the lack of time to assimilate ideas from round to round, indiscriminate pairings, switching sides, and the absence of an audience as other major defects. Constans (1949) offered additional criticisms, attacking the practice of limiting entries at tournaments to one or two teams per school and suggesting that tournaments produced boredom for judges, who had to hear the same issues round after round, and debaters, who experienced "the law of diminishing returns" in the absence of new arguments (p. 153).

Another source of tension was the nature of the tournament. Initially, local and regional tournaments were sufficient to bring together teams from schools in a particular geographic area. As schools repeatedly met the same opposing teams at local and regional tournaments, the desire to experience competition in other areas of the country grew. Those programs with the financial resources and desire to travel outside their localities or regions were exposed to different teams, new arguments, and new practices. When they returned to their local and regional tournaments, these teams integrated their newfound knowledge to win their debates.

Some forensics coaches embraced the new arguments and competitive practices; others rejected them as unfamiliar and ineffective. The division of provincial versus national circuit programs had a definite impact on forensics during the last quarter of the century. Due to the higher costs associated with traveling around the country to national circuit tournaments, high school programs either cut down their squads to smaller traveling teams or divided their large squads into teams comprising the more competitive and accomplished students (who traveled) and the less competitive students (who competed locally and/or on a limited basis).

Much of the controversy over national circuit debating was played out through related scholarship about the value of summer debate camps geared toward national circuit debating, the explosion of prepared materials in the form of handbooks and supplemental materials developed for high schools by colleges hosting summer debate camps, and the relationship between high school and collegiate forensics programs and the use of college students as high school coaches and judges. Because high schools needed judges, who were often collegiate debaters, and colleges needed high schools to keep producing debaters for their programs, the tensions between provincial and national circuit elements of the debate community festered beneath the surface.

Collegiate programs faced a slightly different dilemma with regard to tournaments. As financial resources at campuses diminished, programmatic decisions were made to increase success, and specialization occurred. For example, in Pi Kappa Delta programs, schools typically offered comprehensive forensic opportunities in both competitive speech and debate. During the latter half of the twentieth century, as specialization occurred, forensics programs began to make choices in order to increase their potential for success. For example, debate teams that previously had been successful on local or regional levels found that they were unable to win against teams with more resources and national exposure. The result was an inability to qualify for the highly competitive National Debate Tournament (NDT). While some schools continued to participate using the NDT format, over time, schools began to discontinue their debate programs, and without sufficient teams to run a division, local tournaments stopped offering debate. This shift contributed to the further division of schools as long-standing debate programs expanded their travel to attend the tournaments in which debate was offered and reduced the size of their travel teams to manage the economic issues facing them on their home campuses.

By World War II, the dual-triangular-quadrangular formats were reserved for exhibition purposes, and the tournament format of forensics was firmly entrenched. The eventual outcome of the tournament format was the establishment of national tournaments. Pi Kappa Delta, Phi Rho Pi, and the National Forensic League (NFL) were leaders in creating national tournaments. As previously noted, as the technical era progressed, the American Forensic Association and other individuals and entities established national tournaments to increase the prominence of their organizations.

The North Central Association Threat

Once the majority of the forensics community endorsed competition as the central element of forensics activities, the tension within the community focused primarily on balancing competition with educational benefits to avoid the excesses of overly competitive practices. However, in 1950, when a report by the North Central Association favoring the abolition of extracurricular speech activities at the high school level opposed competitive forensics, the forensics community spoke with one voice to confront what it perceived as an external threat to its existence. There is some disagreement about whether this was an attack on forensics from outside forces (e.g., administrators and professional educators) or, as Mills (1950a) inferred, the opponents were using many of the same arguments that reformers within the forensics community had used twenty years earlier.

Just as the comments from Roosevelt and Bryan united the debate community in justifying the educational benefits of debating both sides of the topic, the North Central report galvanized the competitive forensics community in support of the educational value of forensics. Some forensics scholars chose to write rebuttals to the report, while others acknowledged the opportunity the report provided for those involved with forensics activity to review their practices. Lull (1950) made the point, obvious to many in the community, that there was some truth to the report in that one can always find abuses and problems to address.

Whatever the motivation, voices from the forensics community produced a massive response, and the report's recommendations were not adopted. The collegiate organizations rallied, and the NFL used the *Rostrum* to persuade its chapter sponsors and district organizations to get involved in presenting information about the value of forensics competition in a democratic society (see "Inside Story," 1950; Mills, 1950b; "On the North Central Front," 1951; "Resolution

Approved," 1951; Secord, 1951; Tucker, 1950). This theme resonated in articles found in all of the forensics journals, and forensics educators used these materials as the state associations and entities reconstituted their activities during the post–World War II years. This was the last systemic challenge to competitive forensics in the twentieth century, in part due to the steady work of the NFL to build awareness and support among the superintendents and principals of their member schools and in getting the endorsement of the National Association of Secondary Administrators for competitive forensics.

Summary

The power of student interest in competitive forensics activities provided impetus for those advocating the role of competition in debate and public speaking contests. Arguments were advanced about how preparing to debate both sides of the resolution provided more opportunities for competition while enhancing the educational benefits of having a more complete understanding of the topic. Making the decision about who won or lost a key focus of the debate not only motivated participants to win but also encouraged them to expand their educational knowledge by researching and preparing arguments that would appeal to judges. Accordingly, when they lost debates, competitors wanted to know the reason for the decision in order to make corrections before the next round of competition. As debate practices and arguments improved and the tournament format became a standard for competition, the need prevailed for better-trained and informed judges to function within the system. Eventually, when threatened by the North Central Association with the elimination of competitive forensics, the community stood in support of competition as an educational activity for student participants.

IMPACTS AND IMPLICATIONS OF COMPETITION

The conflicts that surfaced within the forensics community about how much competition should influence forensics activities reflected the disagreements of strong-minded and strong-willed individuals who wanted the activities to reflect their perspectives. As these individuals came together and formed national forensics organizations, those who joined with them accepted their perspectives and contributed to the furtherance of their beliefs and established practices. The impacts of these competitive practices were significant in terms of how they affected student interest, the unity of the forensics community, the scholarship produced by faculty involved with forensics, and the specialization that occurred.

Student Interest

Students created the forensics model and competition kept them interested and involved in the activity. The students who engaged in debates and speaking competitions enjoyed the intellectual competition and the thrill of victory, and the students who populated the early audiences enjoyed the competition for entertainment purposes and as a show of school spirit. While students almost universally acknowledged the positive impact of forensics experiences on their lives, from the faculty perspective, finding a balance that allowed for students to enjoy the thrill of competition without sacrificing educational quality was critical.

Competition was embedded in forensics, and no matter how educational reformers tried to make the activities, as long as students could compete, they continued their participation. The following points illustrate the preference of students for competition: they enjoyed preparing both sides of the resolution because doing so was challenging, fun, and demonstrated their expertise; they wanted decision debating in order to know who won; they preferred more specific criteria for judging to improve the quality and consistency of the decisions provided by the judges; they appreciated knowledgeable and expert judges who understood norms and accepted practices; and they enjoyed tournaments because they reduced costs and enabled holding more debates at a single location.

In short, each well-intentioned effort to increase the educational benefits of debate at the expense of competition resulted in a decline in student interest and participation. When competition was made a central feature of forensics, students were drawn to the activity. This construction of forensics as a student-based activity, enhancing the education of those who participated, kept it associated with high schools and colleges and universities.

A Split in the Ranks

The tension between competition and education created the initial split in the forensics community between those valuing each perspective. The issue came down to a focus on how forensics activities were to be made available to larger numbers of participants. When debates and speaking contests were scheduled between rival schools and limited to the few exceptional student speakers who were in training for professions requiring higher levels of thought and expression, the educational aspects of forensics provided justification for participation, and the competitive elements were secondary. In contrast, as greater numbers of schools engaging in forensics activities sought ways to increase the opportunities for their students to participate, competitive practices and structures—such as preparing to debate both sides of the topic, securing a judge's decision, and engaging in tournaments—were necessary to accommodate student demand. The formation of forensic honoraries reflected these differing perspectives, and the construction of their activities demonstrated how they viewed their commitment to their student members.

Those involved in forensics continued the process of self-examination about their competitive practices and ways of recognizing students and coaches, resulting in the introduction of alternative forms of forensics activities thought to provide more educational benefits. Struggling somewhat with growing tensions, the forensic honoraries attempted to keep unity in their ranks by negotiating with each other to maintain common structures and practices. The formation of the American Forensic Association was another effort to coordinate all forensics activities through one organization. However, despite their best efforts, as the technical era of forensics progressed, those who disagreed with particular competitive practices broke away and formed their own organizations and offered events reflecting their particular flavor of educational forensics within a competitive context.

Forensics Scholarship

When the forensics community was constructing its structures and practices, attention focused on coaching and teaching students. Conducting and publishing forensics research was not an expectation. However, as forensic honoraries formed and began publishing journals and other publications, and the national organization for public speaking teachers established itself as an independent entity within the academic community, faculty took advantage of the need and opportunity to share their knowledge and practices in whatever publications were available.

As this chapter has demonstrated, despite considerable tension expressed over the educational benefits and competitive practices of forensics, one effect of this tension was the prevalence of forensics scholarship with a practical focus. Sharing practices to help participants, coaches, programs, and forensic groups compete more successfully was common. In addition, the emergence of national speech and forensics organizations produced the need for publications that their members could use to communicate with each other about educational values, norms, and competitive practices. While the early forensics journals focused on organizational history, business, contest results, and team news, the *Quarterly Journal of Public Speaking* (*QJPS*) was the main outlet for teachers of public speaking, debate, and argumentation to share their views about what was happening in forensics at the state, regional, and national levels. Forensics-related articles were common in the *QJPS* in the early years of its existence. However, once the focus came to rest on competition as an inherent dimension of forensics, fewer articles found their way into the main journals of the emerging academic discipline of speech communication.

Competition Led to Specialization

As forensics became more competitive, debate became more specialized and technical. Teams became more sophisticated in their argumentation and strategies, necessitating more qualified judges and more sophisticated criteria for deciding winners. The educational value of preparing arguments for the lay judge was superseded by the competitive value of having an expert who knew the rules and topic making the final decision. As the two camps became more entrenched, the composition of the forensics community shifted. Those valuing lay judges saw the overemphasis on competition as reducing the educational value of the activity; those valuing experts saw the educational value of the activity lessening if judging decisions were made by untrained and uninformed critics.

There were many consequences of this split, but one that particularly influenced how forensics evolved in debate was the construction of the national circuit on both the college and the high school levels. Those schools with more resources sought competitive outlets through which they could debate similarly resource-rich schools. As these schools traveled across the country to tournaments and became more familiar with each other, they established common practices that were accepted by the trained critics whom they used as judges. Ultimately, the national circuit culture conflicted with that of the more parochial teams when the two groups interacted. Depending on the judge assigned to the debate, teams had to adapt in order to be successful. The judges who frequented the national circuit expected a particular level of competitiveness; similarly, the judges who were not part of the national circuit and unfamiliar with accepted practices were unwilling to accept particular lines of argument that might otherwise have prevailed. Thus, when the teams and judges from the national circuit mixed with parochial teams and judges, the tension among the two groups exacerbated the conflict between those seeking a more educational framework for debate and those comfortable with competition-based practices.

CONCLUSION

This chapter has focused on what we consider a fundamental tension shaping how forensics evolved in the twentieth century. The challenges associated with finding a balance between competition and education kept forensics educators striving to construct a model that would unify the forensics community and maintain the activity's popularity and prominence among participants and observers. We conclude here with the position that competition was the originating element that captivated student interest in the activity. Thus, it was not surprising that those wanting to engage and involve students in forensics activities would support structures and practices catering to that interest. However, in the process of seeking to improve the quality of the competitive experience, leaders within the forensics community sought to influence how that competition should be structured. This process led to more advanced and sophisticated levels of competition that were challenged by external forces but ultimately endorsed by the forensics community. In the next chapter, we move on to explore the macro tensions that forensics faced as the activity jockeyed for position with newly emerging academic departments and that forced an abdication of one of its principal values associated with training individuals for engaged citizenship in the American democracy.

REFERENCES

Baird, A. C. (1923). Shall American universities adopt the British system of debating? *Quarterly Journal of Speech Education, 9* (3), 215–22 (AN9204201).

Barnard, R. H. (1937, May). A deserter pleads his own defense. *Gavel of Delta Sigma Rho, 19* (4), 59–60, 63.

Bauer, O. F. (1955). A century of debating at Northwestern University: 1855–1955. Unpublished thesis. Evanston, IL: Northwestern University.

Berry, M. F. (1928). A survey of intercollegiate debate in the Midwest debate conference. *Quarterly Journal of Speech, 14* (1), 86–94.

Constans, H. P. (1949). The role of intercollegiate debate tournaments in the post war period. *Speech Activities, 5* (4), 151–54.

Davis, W. H. (1916). Is debating primarily a game? *Quarterly Journal of Public Speaking, 2* (2), 171–79 (AN9223589).

The Forum: The decision-less debate. (1921). *Quarterly Journal of Speech Education, 7* (3), 276–91.

Gilman, W. E. (1928). Can we revive public interest in intercollegiate debates? *Quarterly Journal of Speech, 14* (4), 553–63 (AN9249083).

Hansen, J. D. (1949). Origin of debate tournament. *Speech Activities, 5* (4), 154–55. Reprinted from *Forensic*, October 1949.

Holcolm, M. J. (1933). The critic-judge system. *Quarterly Journal of Speech, 19* (1), 28–38.

Hollister, R. O. T. (1917). Faculty judging. *Quarterly Journal of Public Speaking, 3* (3), 235–41.

Inside story of NCA resolution. (1950). *Rostrum, 25* (3), 3.

Johnson, T. E. (1935, June). How should debates be judged? *Quarterly Journal of Speech, 21* (3), 396–99.

Judson, L. S. (1938). Editorial: An indictment of large-scale tournaments. *Gavel of Delta Sigma Rho, 20* (2), 35.

Keith, W. M. (2007). *Democracy as discussion: Civic education and the American Forum Movement.* Lanham, MD: Rowman & Littlefield.

Lull, P. E. (1948). Enemies of academic debating. *Debater's Magazine, 4* (3), 109–10.

Lull, P. E. (1950). I speak for the NCA Contest Committee. *Speech Activities, 7* (1), 10–11.

McCroskey, J. C. (n.d.). Fifty articles in fifty years: A selected annotated bibliography on debate judging, 1915–1964. Retrieved from www.jamescmccroskey.com/publications/10.htm.

Miler, E. (1930). I believe in decisions. *Rostrum, 5* (3), n.p. Reprinted from *Gavel of Delta Sigma Rho*.

Miller, N. E. (1958). The status of debating. *AFA Register, 7* (2). AFA Archives, University of Utah, Accn. 418 Box 8, Fd. 2: *AFA Register*, 1958, 1959.

Mills, G. E. (1950a). Reply to North Central Committee. *Speech Activities, 6* (4), 147–48.

Mills, G. E. (1950b). Abolish high school speech contests? *Rostrum, 25* (2), 4–6.

Musgrave, G. M. (1946). The Wells-O'Neill controversy. *Debater's Magazine, 2* (4), 218–20.

Newman, R. P. (1955). Tournament debating should not be abolished. *Gavel of Delta Sigma Rho, 37* (3), 56–60, 68.

Nichols, E. R. (1936). A historical sketch of intercollegiate debating: I. *Quarterly Journal of Speech, 22* (2), 213–20.

On the North Central front. (1951). *Rostrum, 25* (7), 4–5.

O'Neill, J. M. (1916). Game or counterfeit presentation? *Quarterly Journal of Public Speaking, 2* (2), 193–97.

O'Neill, J. M. (1918). Comment on judge Wells' last ms. *Quarterly Journal of Speech Education, 4* (4), 410–21.

Resolution approved by the Illinois Speech Association. (1951). *Rostrum, 25* (5), 11.

Roosevelt, T. (1913). *Chapters of a possible autobiography*. New York: Outlook.

Schrier, W. (1929). Shifting the emphasis: An argument for no-decision debating. *Quarterly Journal of Speech, 15* (3), 365–75.

Secord, A. E. (1951). Speech in the extra-curricular program. *Rostrum, 25* (5), 10.

Seeley, K. B. (1930). Who is best qualified to judge debates? *Gavel of Delta Sigma Rho, 12* (2), 20.

Tucker, L. M. (1950). Committee blasts contests. *Rostrum, 25* (2), 2–3.

Utterback, W. E. (n.d.). News and notes: News of the departments. *Quarterly Journal of Speech Education*, 315–16.

Wells, H. N. (1918). Juryman or critic: A final reply. *Quarterly Journal of Speech Education, 4* (4), 398–409.

Westfall, A. (1933). The critic judge arrives at his decision. *Gavel of Delta Sigma Rho, 15* (3), 5–7.

Woodward, H. W. (1915). Debating without judges. *Quarterly Journal of Public Speaking, 1* (3), 229–33 (AN9221034).

6

Departmental and Disciplinary
Tensions Shaping Forensics

During the twentieth century, the relationship between forensics and the academy was uncertain, strained, and highly contentious. The fault lines were many and complicated. Was forensics a curricular, cocurricular, or extracurricular activity? Where was the appropriate disciplinary home for forensics? Was competition an appropriate educational tool? In many ways, these controversies reflected the long-standing insecurity of the communication discipline since its emergence from English departments in the early twentieth century.

As the field of communication (the very term itself being relatively new as a disciplinary descriptor) evolved during the century, the twists and turns of the changing field manifested themselves in an evolving relationship with competitive speech and debate. The connection with the larger discipline of speech, speech communication, communication, rhetoric, or however else the study was labeled, started out strong and interconnected, but over the years the connection became frayed. A new discipline in the early twentieth century that would have believed it inconceivable not to provide students the opportunity for speech and debate training through competition found itself at the end of the century marginalizing forensics.

In the previous chapter, we suggested that challenges from within and outside the competitive forensics community contributed to its decline in prominence. The tension resulting from dissent among the faculty about how much competition should be part of forensics led to continual changes to improve the quality of debate. The tensions resulting from departmental and disciplinary differences of opinion were largely responsible for the marginalization of forensics activities and those who engaged in them.

The composition of the forensics community had something to do with how the tensions were revealed. The interaction of students, faculty, honoraries, and those without organizational affiliation influenced the way the forensics community structured and aligned itself as it dealt with difficult issues throughout the twentieth century. In the beginning, the competitors were the community, with acceptance of the initial rules and practices of the first debaters becoming the qualification for membership in the ranks. Those later joining forensics as intercollegiate debaters adopted those rules and practices eagerly. However, as the forensics community grew and faculty became involved, disagreements among an increasing number of voices about the educational value of particular competitive practices became heated and caused substantial internal realignment in the forensics world. These issues drew the attention of the entire speech discipline as debate played a significant role in its separation from English.

As noted in the previous chapter, there were two different camps when it came to evaluating the role of competition. Those who accepted competition as a necessary part of forensics sought to remedy problems as they manifested themselves. That camp stressed the experimental nature of the events and, in typical American fashion, willingly changed questionable rules and practices to immediately elevate the perceived quality and educational value (i.e., by adding extemporaneous style for constructive speeches, clearer guidelines for judging, and the use of trained critic-judges) (Cowperthwaite and Baird, 1954). For those persistent critics of competition—such as Overstreet, Mangum, and Shaw—who found particular competitive practices lacking in educational value and therefore, by extension, considered all forms of competition antithetical to education (Baird, 1955), their philosophical and practical separation from the competitive ranks of the forensics community within the emerging speech discipline enabled these critics to devalue debate and either remove it from speech departments entirely or develop from a distance noncompetitive alternatives to replace it. Adding to the tension within the forensics community were the distinct philosophical positions held by the forensic honoraries.

The honoraries—Delta Sigma Rho (DSR), Tau Kappa Alpha (TKA), Pi Kappa Delta (PKD), and Phi Rho Pi (PRP)—were expanding their memberships, setting their rules and processes, determining their relationships with each other on such matters as which school should be accepted into which organization, and generally beginning the process of identifying standards of teaching and scholarship. Each of the organizations began publishing a journal at about the time that the *Quarterly Journal of Public Speaking* was first published. The journals served various purposes. Foremost, they represented a communication tool at a time when there was not a viable broadcast alternative for simultaneously communicating with a wide number of people. So the journals reported financial information, membership names and numbers, minutes of meetings, and results. The journals also included pedagogical articles that were vital in the early days of competition to initiate conversations about what would become argumentation and debate theory, as distinct from classical theories of rhetoric. These early articles were not peer-reviewed in the modern sense. They were opinion pieces written by teachers and students before the modern standards of scholarship emerged and reflected varied anecdotal perspectives authoritatively, often without the benefit of research data or substantiation. That DSR and TKA philosophically came down on the side of discussion, favoring education over competition, whereas PKD promoted debate, originating the tournament format and selecting the national debate topic each year, should not go unremarked. Whatever their affiliation, feelings ran deep among the coaches and faculty, and organizational affiliation likely had everything to do with which side of the discussion-debate issue a forensics program aligned itself.

Because the faculty were just feeling their way along as the honoraries formed and established themselves within the context of the emerging speech discipline, the difficulties of communication and the press of daily life made it less likely that college or university teachers could devote the time and energy to both the new discipline and their interest in competitive debate. Furthermore, from the very beginning, debate was extremely popular in smaller colleges and universities, whose members were less attracted to participation in the new organizations. For many of these teachers, their institutions did not value scholarly research to the same degree that the larger ones did. Their bread and butter was teaching, and their colleges encouraged debate training in response to student demand for those courses and cocurricular experiences before there was a clear sense of what a formal discipline of speech would encourage and require in a curriculum. Thus, the diverse composition of the forensics community contributed to the tensions that would arise as the new speech discipline defined what would and would not be included within the scope of its teaching and research activities.

In this chapter, we focus on the macro tensions facing forensics on the departmental and disciplinary levels. First, we examine the tension within departments about what place forensics should hold in the emerging communication field. Then we move on to explore the discussion movement within the discipline and its effect on the status of debate as the principal way to promote engaged citizenship in the American democracy. We argue that the result of these tensions was twofold: forensics activities were marginalized within academic departments and the speech discipline, and the forensics community accepted its lesser status in these domains.

ACADEMIC DEBATE AND THE EMERGENCE OF SPEECH AS A DISCIPLINE

To understand the tensions that resulted when academic departments navigated the unchartered waters of identifying their curricula and establishing themselves within the academy, we first look to the relationship between academic debate and the emergence of speech as a discipline. Rarig and Greaves (1954), Cohen (1994), and Keith (2007) discussed the various influences and events leading to the creation of the early national professional organizations in speech after the turn of the twentieth century. However, their accounts were inconsistent. Rarig and Greaves (1954) almost took for granted the relationship between the emergence of academic debate as a popular and influential educational tool and increased interest in creating a distinct national organization in speech. Cohen (1994), on the other hand, virtually ignored the relationship and argued that the need for research in speech—as distinct from the English discipline—motivated the drive for a separate national organization. Keith (2007) took the middle ground, paying homage to the significance of the emerging forensics movement but suggesting that debate, as a form of civic training, was ultimately unsatisfactory in meeting the need to train the greater population and gave way to training in discussion. Keith's thesis is consistent with ours, revealing the flaws in an emerging speech communication discipline that sacrificed pedagogy in debate and public speaking in favor of theoretical research aimed at establishing the unique significance of communication as an academic discipline. However, we extend Keith's analysis, suggesting that while interest in forensics may have served to influence the formation of a new speech discipline, the forensics community itself failed to capitalize on this opportunity because of its inability to come together and collectively agree on the value of its pedagogy.

We begin our explanation of the tensions dividing departments regarding the presence of forensics activities with three instructional perspectives that provided the foundation for the emerging speech discipline in higher education. Then we focus on how student interest in forensics supported the addition of more courses and reasons supporting the creation of separate speech departments to manage those courses. In addition to student interest and faculty support, we describe the construction of the National Association of Academic Teachers of Public Speaking (NAATPS) and conclude this section with a discussion of factors that ultimately caused the marginalization of forensics activities within speech departments.

The Foundations of the Speech Discipline

While the study of rhetoric dates back to antiquity in both Western and non-Western societies, the study of the characteristics of oral speech probably began in Great Britain during the eighteenth and nineteenth centuries and did not become a distinct area of study in the United States prior to the emergence of three branches of public speaking: homiletics, elocution, and the Delsarte tradition. Homiletics, or the application of rhetoric to preaching, was a very old and significant area of study in European universities and monasteries that became a central subject in colonial schools and colleges. Pastoral training was a major focus of colonial colleges, and students learned and regularly practiced homiletic skills that included rudimentary instruction in public speaking (Dargan, 1922). As noted earlier, the strictly regulated academic instruction led students to seek out opportunities for more lively engagement, which they found through membership in literary societies.

Another source of speech training emerged during the eighteenth century in the form of elocution. One of the most important elocutionists, Thomas Sheridan, published a series of lectures on elocution in 1762 and oral reading in 1775, which speakers used to mark and prepare literature for public presentation. Another elocutionist, John Walker, published *Elements of Elocution* in 1781, providing instruction on voice control, gestures, pronunciation, and vocal emphasis. With the publication of these works, elocution gained support as a viable means for preparing entertainment for the masses.

As the middle class in Western countries demanded more access to public education, elocution became a staple of the school curriculum. Collections of literary selections were published together in the form of anthologies, commonly known as "speakers," to provide material students could use to improve their elocutionary skills. By the end of the nineteenth century, public school students in the United States had several options, including *McGuffey's New Eclectic Speaker* (McGuffey, 1858), *A Manual of Elocution and Reading: Embracing the Principles and Practices of Elocution* (Brooks, 1882), and *The Delsarte Speaker, or Modern Elocution Designed Especially for Young Folks and Amateurs* (Northrop, 1895). In addition to the literary materials included in each speaker, the pictorial depictions of body movements and gestures added additional training insight.

A third aspect of speech training in nineteenth-century America built upon the entertainment aspects associated with elocution. François Delsarte (1811–1871), a French voice and speech coach with vocal training from the famed Paris Conservatory, formulated a method of acting that connected the inner emotions of an actor with specific gestures and movements (Delaumosne, 1893). His method of acting gained prominence due to its association with the elocutionary movement (Kirby, 1972). In 1839, he opened his first course, and many artists enrolled, including Steele MacKaye. MacKaye, Delsarte's only American student, introduced the Delsarte system to students in the United States as part of his system of "applied aesthetics." By the end of the century, the Delsarte system of oratory "was the most popular single method for speech training in the United States" (Kirby, 1972, p. 55).

Both elocution and aspects of the Delsarte method were influential in the emergence of speech training in late-nineteenth-century America. Speech schools and classes were introduced, and itinerant teachers regularly offered instruction

in public speaking presentations. Those literary societies that were still functioning embraced these elocutionist ideas and moved their emphasis toward public
speaking events, contests, and theatrical performances. The emphasis of speech
training on the Aristotelian canon of delivery at the expense of the other canons,
particularly invention, was pronounced.

Colleges and universities that began introducing speech training did so by offering courses very heavily grounded in elocution. For example, Bauer (1955)
reported that the founder of the School of Speech at Northwestern University,
Robert Cumnock, "was not interested in how to construct a speech. His main interest was in teaching how to deliver a speech" (p. 50). Cumnock typified the roots of
an emerging discipline, as coaching students to deliver a message with emotional
undertones became the basis for instruction. Cumnock was extremely active in
elocution education and a frequent participant in Chautauqua programs. While he
eventually founded what became the School of Speech, he never taught courses
beyond the study of elocution and retired prior to the formal emergence of the
speech discipline. In short, the interest in homiletics, elocution, and the Delsarte
tradition shaped the initial speech offerings available to students in the classroom.

The Influence of Student Interest

As previously suggested, the literary societies within schools and colleges provided the outlet for students to practice their oral performance skills outside the
classroom. However, the decline of literary societies at the end of the nineteenth
century and the preoccupation of new speech departments with elocution at the
expense of formal training in other areas contributed to a sudden interest in competitive debate among the student population. Both factors were crucial in defining the early relationship between forensics and the new discipline.

Debate training began outside the formal structure of the academy. Students, as
noted in an earlier chapter, initiated debate competition and pursued that interest
without input from the faculty (Cowperthwaite and Baird, 1954). The universities
did not distinguish between the old literary societies that traditionally operated
outside the curriculum and the new debate clubs that were rushing quickly to fill
a gap the students saw between the sophistry of informal speaking competitions
sponsored by the literary societies and the rigidity of the elocution-based curriculum emerging in the new departments of rhetoric and oratory in various colleges. The intersection of the new interest in competitive debate and the chafing
of faculty interested in speech, as distinct from the existing English department
curricula, seemed almost coincidental, despite what appeared retrospectively to
have been a vital unspoken synergy.

Information revealing the nature of that synergistic relationship between
the founding of the speech communication discipline and the simultaneous

blossoming of competitive debate is limited. In his essay, Smith (1954) drew on primary and secondary sources to trace the emergence of college speech departments, suggesting that the modern idea of an academic department could be traced to 1890. The academic department was a natural outgrowth of the growing specialization of colleges that began with the Morrill Act of 1862 and the introduction by Cornell University of the residential college model in 1869.

The emergence of the departmental model was critical in promoting curricular specialization and the laying of disciplinary boundaries. This foretold the emerging conflict within the English discipline between written and oral rhetoric. What was the role of public speaking in an English department? The answer is revealed by an examination of how public speaking was characterized. By 1890 and progressing quickly in the following years, there was growing dissatisfaction with elocution as the organizing principle behind training in oral communication and an emerging belief that practical "speech" deserved its own area of specialization. The quotation marks around "speech" are deliberate. An early challenge facing this new discipline—one that never disappeared—was determining the name for this area of study. Among the choices were rhetoric, speech, public speaking, elocution, oratory, expression, rhetoric and speech, English and speech, and dramatic arts (Smith, 1954, p. 462).

However the discipline was named, Smith (1954) documented the growing popularity of discrete offerings in a wide range of speech courses after 1900 and their continuing, steady growth through the years immediately following World War II. The distribution of courses changed over time; courses in argumentation, parliamentary law, speech correction, radio, and the speech sciences that were nonexistent in 1900 became widely available by 1930. This reflected the growing pains of a new discipline seeking its place in the academy, as Cohen showed in his discussion of the historical roots of the discipline. Whereas Cohen (1994) ascribed the changing curriculum to reasoned disputations among scholars, Smith identified another force that was equally helpful in explaining the direction of the new speech discipline: student demand. In a long passage, Smith (1954) drew the relationship between student demand and curricular change:

> The opportunity [for study in speech-related courses] was to be reestablished both by the development of coursework in speech, and the development of new forms of extracurricular speaking activity. The coursework was often directly related to the activity. Intercollegiate debating, which developed generally after 1894, marked one new line of activity and by 1910–1920 coursework in debate had become the most popular speech offering. Intercollegiate oratory was another activity to develop and the appearance of the college theatre in the twentieth century claimed the interest of many students. Courses in theatre, after a few beginnings in the decade 1910–1920, developed spectacularly after 1920. These student activities, with their demonstrated appeal to student interest, were to form the basis, first, for the development of

coursework designed to give academic recognition to the educational significance of the activity, and second, for the formation of speech departments to direct both the activities and courses associated with them. (pp. 458–59)

Smith traced examples from various colleges and universities (e.g., Michigan, Mississippi, Wabash, and Minnesota) that responded to student demand by creating speech departments.

The creation of speech departments also reflected the relationship between the discipline and the wider societal forces at work in higher education:

The modern department of speech was a reflection of the forces that were shaping American higher education in the 19th and 20th centuries. But not until the 20th century did the impact of science and utilitarianism, of student interest and curricular specialization, begin to be fully realized in the curricular area of the languages and literature. Speech departments, accordingly, came into being as an expression of the great forces that were changing the American educational scene, as those forces converged with the interest and energies of men [*sic*] who made the teaching of speech their profession. (Smith, 1954, p. 459)

Clearly, student interest in practical speech training was influential in the formation of the speech discipline. While Smith (1954) cautioned against overclaiming that student interest was the primary reason for the creation of departments of speech, the addition of courses in argumentation, debate, and public speaking stemmed from student interest and activity, and those who directed, coached, or taught those courses were the faculty who sought academic status and administrative autonomy for speech.

Motivation for the Separation of Speech from English

The forensics community and the speech discipline were always interrelated, and when needs intersected, they worked together. When tensions were identified, they often stemmed from the dual roles performed by the faculty, who served as debate coaches in the forensics community and speech professionals within the national speech organization. Despite the potential for coordination and cooperation, there was never a time when those in competitive debate and the speech discipline acted in complete harmony.

As noted earlier, at the turn of the twentieth century, academic departments were a relatively new phenomenon resulting from changes in higher education. While a number of factors contributed to their emergence, the drive to create distinct academic departments stemmed, to a significant extent, from student demand for professional training in debate (Smith, 1954). But the forces that caused colleges, particularly the smaller ones, to create stand-alone speech departments did not best explain the nationalization of the speech discipline that emerged after 1914. While initially embracing competitive debate, the national movement began to distance itself from the activity almost immediately, and while it never threw debate overboard, the discipline was moving in distinctly different directions by the start of World War II.

Three forces pushed speech teachers to organize nationally and to advocate for a distinct discipline: perceived inferiority within the English discipline, public demand for training in discourse, and fear of disciplinary marginalization through perception that speech was a practical art rather than an intellectual pursuit.

Perceived Inferiority

When the push to create distinct academic departments within colleges and universities began in the last quarter of the nineteenth century, speech was most generally grouped with English due to their shared rhetorical roots. The study of rhetoric had flourished since colonial times and was an influential and popular area in many colleges throughout the nineteenth century. However, during the nineteenth century, it became identified with literature and literary criticism, using the work of Hugh Blair and focusing on the reading of old speeches (Smith, 1954).

In addition, the study of rhetoric did not, at that time, significantly distinguish between oral and written elements, although the classical canon of delivery was emphasized less than the other four, due in part to its prominence within the elocutionary movement and probably to cherry picking in the sense of only teaching certain rhetorical principles or tracts and ignoring those in which delivery, in particular, was emphasized (Smith, 1954). Gray (1954) summarized the state of teaching speech prior to 1890: "The field of speech up to 1890 had been for the most part disorganized, and in the hands of the professional elocutionists who apparently had no concept of the educational values in the subject. Rhetoric was essentially concerned with writing; and other aspects of speech were either neglected or unknown entirely" (p. 424).

As a new discipline, English was trying to navigate between pressures to be a truly scholarly discipline with distinct research methods and lines and to prepare students to be successful workers by teaching them writing style and grammar. (The term "English" itself is a convention, as would be the case in "speech." The term "English" was an inclusive one, covering literature, grammar, writing, and speaking.) Adding to this need, the continuous influx of immigrants to the United States necessitated instruction in English to improve oral and written literacy (Littlefield, 1998). The dispute within English departments was contentious and doubtless created a sense of frustration among all members of an extremely eclectic discipline.

One aspect of departmentalization was the greater prominence of rewards systems within universities. Promotion, pay, and perks were then, as now, important inducements in academic life. Even within the highly contentious atmosphere of English departments, the oral English/public speaking faculty found themselves largely shut out of the reward system and at significantly higher risk in terms of benefits and security than their counterparts teaching literature or writing. Winans opined, "Many heads of English departments will refuse to promote teachers of public speaking" (Rarig and Greaves, 1954, p. 498). Public speaking faculty were lowest in prestige and thought by their English department colleagues to be teaching in an area lacking intellectual body and content (see Kitzhaber, 1990, p. 42; Gray, 1954). To faculty outside speech, public speaking was simply a technical skill with no justification for serious academic preparation. There were no post-baccalaureate programs in speech, and the success of itinerant public speaking teachers, as well as elocutionists, suggested that speech was unworthy to be considered part of the emerging concept of the liberal arts as taught in colleges and universities.

Public Demand

A second factor was the intense public appetite for training in public speaking as part of students' preparation for civic engagement. As the nineteenth century closed and a new century began, many people believed that oral communication was fundamentally much more important than the written form. The Chautauqua movement was at its peak and provided nourishment for the public soul in ways that books or newspapers did not. Citizens listened to their leaders speak rather than reading about their activities. The journalism of 1900 was considerably different from that at the end of the twentieth century. While there was always an appetite for great works of literature, in a growing industrial society that still had a huge agricultural employment base, the number of people who were actually engaged in regular reading was small and probably very select. One of the basic premises of the residential college movement was to address the need to create citizens capable of active civic participation, and while college faculty and leaders early on began to conceive of the university as a place for introspection and research, that was not the vision of a citizenry that saw a college education as preparation for great things. Doing great things required skill in public speaking, and demand thus chased supply not only within the college cloisters but also in trade schools and other places where a public teaching speaker could be enticed to set up shop.

Colleges certainly were not immune to market pressures. They hired more faculty members to teach public speaking and debate but faced the reality that, lacking the matrix of graduate education, it would be a challenge to hire qualified faculty while simultaneously reinforcing the perception that the role of a university was to encourage research and reflection. So colleges tended to hire faculty without significant academic credentials with the expectation that those faculty would teach for a short while and then move on, to be replaced by a fresh wave of young faculty. This model worked well in some ways, especially for debate coaching. The earliest coaches were often alumni who returned to their alma maters briefly to help coach the team before pursuing their life's work in law, business, or education. Even before the modern notion of the teaching assistant emerged, a similar model was in use for teaching public speaking and debate at the college level.

Disciplinary Marginalization

The third force pushing speech faculty toward carving out their discipline was the fear of intellectual marginalization. Despite its popularity in some circles, according to Rarig and Greaves (1954), the move of elocutionists toward academic respectability with the creation in 1892 of a national professional organization—the National Association of Elocutionists (later changed to the National Speech Arts Association in 1906)—was perceived as a threat by teachers of practical speech or public speaking, and the entire elocution movement was considered as being intellectually shallow and meaningless. While they did not come out and criticize elocution per se, the lack of participation by many speech teachers, particularly at the more established institutions, in the activities of the National Speech Arts Association was telling.

Further, even at institutions where elocution teaching was well established, such as Northwestern and the University of Michigan, activities such as competitive debate were organized independently. No other speech-related activity was as antithetical to the work of the elocutionists as competitive debate. The roots of the latter activity sprang from student dissatisfaction with literary society practices that were reflective of elocutionism. The emphasis, even in early debate training and the works of early scholars, such as George Pierce Baker at Harvard, on the other rhetorical canons of invention and organization intellectually overshadowed elocutionism and presaged the quick disappearance of that intellectual tradition by the end of World War I.

But in the first two decades of the twentieth century, the preference for a more robust rhetorical and scholarly based speech study was hardly a given. The elocutionists, led by Trueblood at Michigan and Cumnock at Northwestern, were well-respected academic leaders. The general public familiarity with elocution and the popularity of theater, which often reflected the Delsarte influence, contributed to a sense that speech study was somehow at the margins of intellectual life at the very same time that its popularity as a pedagogy was unassailable.

The Formation of the National Association of Academic Teachers of Public Speaking

Despite the significance of these forces, the actual decision by a small group of speech faculty to create a national organization was very similar to that of the debate coaches to form their honoraries. In each case, a small number of visionaries implemented their choices without any real expectation of success. For the speech professionals, there was still considerable fractionalization between those wanting to maintain their positions within English, those who adhered to the elocutionist perspective, and those for whom any change would cause distress and uncertainty.

The new association formed in 1914 was anything but a national or inclusive one. While its membership rules were drafted to be open, it was clear that elocutionists or teachers of public speaking not associated with a high school, college, or university were unwelcome—or at the very least subject to greater scrutiny by the membership committee. As Rarig and Greaves (1954) noted, "The word *Academic* in the Association's name pointedly indicated [that nonacademics were not welcome]" (p. 499; italics in the original).

Additionally, the highest objective of the association was to promote research and disciplinary independence created by published scholarship or through publication of a scholarly journal. The new association was very clear in its emphasis on being research based and scholarship oriented, as Rarig and Greaves (1954) revealed: "The Association promptly set up a Committee on Research to encourage the study of public speaking as a 'scholarly subject with a body of verified knowledge and a professional tradition and ethics'" (p. 506). The first editor of the *Quarterly Journal of Public Speaking* actually gave priority to all scholarship coming through this committee. This research emphasis reflected the schism in the English discipline at the time over the appropriateness of "the German Ph.D. ideal" for public speaking (Rarig and Greaves, 1954, p. 498), as well as the growing interest of those who saw the primary role of the university, particularly the larger land-grant public universities, as increasing primary knowledge rather than teaching students about that knowledge.

The competitive debate movement was well represented in the initial days of the new association, although it is less apparent whether it perceived its interest in the association as coming from or in spite of its members' role as debate coaches. At its inaugural meeting, the first president, James O'Neill, provided four aims to be included as focus areas for the new association: the correction of speech defects, debating, declamation and reading, and oratory or original speeches (Gray, 1954, p. 423). Thus, when independent departments of speech formed, they initially took on these areas—particularly debate, declamation and reading (later oral interpretation), and practical speech writing—as essential to their forensics activities for students.

While one hundred years later one might envision a group of wise men (there were no women among them) sitting around a table and creating the association, these founders were more likely relatively young and inexperienced people who, although doubtless intelligent and passionate, came from a wide range of backgrounds, had very different ideas about speech and education, and taught a wide range of courses at a wide range of institutions at a time when there was very little consensus about the nature and purposes of higher education. They likely did not know each other particularly well personally, as they would only regularly communicate by mail and see each other at occasional professional conferences. They were feeling their way along, and so it is entirely possible that they created the National Association of Academic Teachers of Public Speaking without the intellectual and moral certainty that Cohen (1994), in his description of the time, seemed to imply.

This intellectual uncertainty was reflected in the early publications in the *Quarterly Journal of Public Speaking*. Cohen (1994) effectively documented how the journal became the place where difficult analytical problems were aired, and the fundamental assumptions about what speech would become emerged from the cauldron of discussion. Controversies such as the role of science and empiricism in speech research versus the long rhetorical tradition, whether sociology and other social sciences should be the model for speech education, and appropriate pedagogical practices for debate training all appeared and certainly occupied the attention of the nascent discipline. To borrow a metaphor, it was the Wild West, where the rules were not yet firmly fixed and a wide range of ideas was being tossed into the mix.

While debate and practical speech training may have been part of the initial impetus for the creation of departments of speech, other related areas of study within the discipline soon emerged. Baird (1937) described the complex interests coming together in the early speech departments. Some faculty believed that rhetoric and the classics should form the basis for the curriculum. Another group promoted the practical skills needed to reason and function in society. Those interested in the speech act itself and ways of correction wanted to include other physical and physiological dimensions of speech in the curriculum. Some advocated speech as a way to promote democracy and civic engagement, and almost from the start, some faculty turned their attention to behaviorism and psychology as natural extensions of communication. Finally, the progressive educators in the group advocated social experimentation in order to prepare students for life. Within this collection of interests, debate and forensics did not neatly fit. As Baird (1937) noted in his speech presented to members of the National Association of Teachers of Speech, referring to the scholarship from 1917 to 1937, "The problem, then, is this: into what one of these seven or eight schools of thinking will our speech activities and our curriculum best fit?" (p. 2).

The Marginalization of Forensics

As speech departments formed and the conflicting perspectives vied for dominance, two factors contributed to the gradual divergence of forensics from the
mainstream: (1) the movement of the speech discipline to reward the use of new
research methods in areas unrelated to forensics over research associated with
teaching and coaching forensics, and (2) the continued association of forensics
activities with elocution and the privileging of delivery or style over the other
traditional canons. However, it is important to be precise about the nature of the
divergence before listing its causes.

Debate was an important component of the growing interest in speech training
after 1890. Courses in debate were among the first speech-related ones added to
college curricula across the country. Almost every early taxonomy of speech as
a discipline included debate, and that relationship was central to the early years
of the national association and the creation of college departments of speech.
While competitive debate as a form of communication would (and still does)
remain a part of the speech discipline, after 1920 and in accelerated fashion after
World War II, forensics was increasingly marginalized within the discipline and
ultimately pushed to the side as either an extracurricular or a cocurricular activity
led by a non-tenure-track instructor.

With the need to establish themselves within the academic community, departments of speech began rewarding research over teaching. The new speech
discipline wanted to be serious and to be taken seriously. This preference for research was meant not to devalue the activities of dedicated and actively engaged
scholars but to reinforce the high degree of uncertainty as to what precisely the
speech discipline should encompass. Woolbert (1923) explained the problem:

> A university most deserves that name when it carries on research and publishes its
> findings. What have the university graduate schools done for the broad subject of
> speech? About as little as for any discipline in the whole curricula. Most university
> graduate school leaders are still skeptical of the notion that speech is worthy of seri-
> ous consideration as graduate study; it was not taught when and where they took their
> doctoral degrees, therefore it must be of doubtful value at best. Worse than this, as an
> undergraduate discipline in the university of liberal arts, it has been often turned over
> to the English department where scholarship is frankly and specifically possible only
> as the study of philology, except where in recent years degrees have been allowed for
> literary criticism and the history of some man or period. (p. 12)

The challenge was the derivative nature of communication. The discipline has always been more a quilt than seamless whole cloth. The artifacts and tools employed
by communication scholars were shared elsewhere. Leaving the English department
for the speech department, before there were any graduate programs in the field,

made it important for the new scholars to demonstrate a commitment to research methods and products that distinguished speech from English or the social sciences.

This created an immediate paradox for those scholars interested in competitive debate and what would come to be recognized as argumentation. Competitive debate, with its long-held commitment to practices grounded in the law (e.g., presumption and burden of proof) and its subject matter necessarily drawn from current political and social issues rather than the philosophical and esoteric subjects argued in colonial classrooms or literary society salons, seemed to position debate squarely on the firing line between the rhetorical tradition at the heart of the history of speech and the new interest in social science. The activity did not fit neatly in either place, making it particularly difficult to carve out a clear research direction independent of the pedagogy of teaching argument and debate, which was outside the direction in which the new *Quarterly Journal of Public Speaking* and the leaders of the new discipline wished to head.

The second factor behind the tensions in academic departments about the placement of forensics within the curriculum was the remnants of the elocution movement that were still in full view. The reaction against the movement, primarily from those interested in the psychology of speech making, further separated debate from the speech discipline. In discussing the development of speech as a discipline in 1923, Woolbert stated the case against elocution in providing part of the rationale for a science-based study of speech:

> Contributing to this preoccupation with German standards was the suicidal extravagance of the old-line elocutionists, assuming to have a scientific basis for their doctrines, but not willing to pay the price for scholastic thoroughness; giving themselves vastly more to art than to science, and at a very time when art was on the defensive and science arrogant and all but despotic. Instead of seeking out laboratories for their science, each old master—an artist fundamentally—thundered out his pet hobbies and called them eternal principles, leading all his followers, often in evangelical or crusading mood, to proclaim him the greatest original and all others base imitators or even mountebanks—a charge not always actionable for slander. Instead of presenting the solid front that scientific investigation inevitably produces, the elocutionists and expressionists fought each other to disruption, or else found common meeting ground only in speech art, never in speech science. (pp. 9–10)

As noted earlier, several of the most prominent figures in speech education were elocutionists, and while the popularity and influence of the movement was in decline by World War I, there was still a significant following for that approach. Almost from the beginning of the publication of the *Quarterly Journal of Public Speaking*, scholars began to seriously advocate for investigation of the psychological dimensions of speech, leading to the vigorous and multidimensional study of persuasion, which became one of the signature research lines in the field.

Despite the antithesis of debate and elocution, the violent opposition to elocution also influenced the relationship between the speech discipline and debate. The discipline, while trying to establish its academic credibility, frequently argued that the lack of formal training for the debate coaches (many of whom were alumni) was similar to the self-training of many of the elocutionists, as well as the substantial number of informal "store front" speech schools prevalent at the time. That anyone under any guise could claim to be a speech teacher was one of the most difficult problems the speech discipline wanted to address. It was, of course, only modestly successful in that regard, as the history of speech training flourished despite the efforts to discredit those teachers for lacking the proper scientific foundation for their work.

Typical of those nonscientific practitioners was Dale Carnegie, whose work remains well known today. Carnegie apparently participated in debate while an undergraduate at the state teachers college in Warrensburg, Missouri. After graduation and a successful sales career, Carnegie gradually moved full-time into the speech-training industry and published his most famous work, *How to Win Friends and Influence People*, in 1936. Carnegie's huge popularity reflected everything the new discipline opposed, as the Carnegie approach did not make any particular effort to integrate the research findings being regularly incorporated into the discipline and published in scholarly journals and books.

Equally troubling was likely the disinterest of the forensic honoraries in discussing training standards for debate coaches. None of the publications of the honoraries addressed this issue, and while possessing a graduate degree gradually became more common, the notion of creating a professional certificate or standard for forensics coaching never was seriously considered. Thus, at the heart of the matter, even when forensics was with the speech discipline, it was not of the discipline. The interdisciplinary character of debate especially contributed to the inherent separation from the discipline that was never overcome. The speech discipline, obsessed with achieving academic and intellectual standing in higher education, always faced forensics activities that were wildly popular among students, relatively impervious to the demand for standards for teaching practitioners, and able to exist and prosper outside the speech department.

Eventually, departments made structural changes within their curricula, resource allocations, and programs in order to marginalize forensics activities. This marginalization process was gradual, more characteristic in larger universities, and sometimes related to the particular person responsible for the program. It was always the case that individual forensics directors played a significant role in maintaining their programs over time. Their eventual retirement presented the opportunity to divert the faculty position in another direction or replace the tenure-line director with an instructor or teaching assistant. Table 6.1 illustrates the nature of this marginalization.

Table 6.1. Structural Marginalization of Forensics within Speech Departments

Structural Category	Central to Department	Marginal to Department
Curriculum and instruction	1. Program directed by tenure-track faculty. 2. Activity considered a part of the ongoing curricular offerings of the school and department. 3. Academic credit given for participation in forensics activities.	1. Program directed by non-tenure-track instructor or graduate teaching assistant. 2. Activity considered extracurricular and might be located outside a department in student affairs or as a club. 3. No academic credit given for participation.
Resources	1. Travel budget allocated from academic budget and stably provided. 2. Scholarship or financial aid provided regularly for participation. 3. Students not expected to significantly subsidize their own participation.	1. Travel budget allocated outside regular academic budget and subject to variance. 2. No scholarship or financial aid provided to participants in forensics. 3. Students expected to do outside fund-raising or to subsidize their own participation.
Program status	1. Department and institution regularly report on program success and participation to various constituencies. 2. Department and institution use program as indicator of quality and prestige.	1. Activities of program are unreported by department and institution. 2. Program is not referenced as an indication of quality or prestige.

Summary

The tension within the emerging speech discipline about its place within the academic community affected the status of forensics activities within the academic departments in which they were housed. As departments struggled with what the content of the discipline should include, the pressures to create graduate programs and publish research advancing the field generated tensions among the faculty, many of whom had been drawn to speech through the vehicle of debate, either as participants or as coaches. Because competitive forensics fell between art and science, faculty who sought legitimacy within their departments either began fashioning research agendas encompassing forensics and argumentation or accepted the relegation of forensics to a marginalized place within their department's programs.

While the forensics community coped with departmental tensions associated with establishing legitimacy within their academic units, additional tensions emerged as the debate community was assailed by those who challenged the legitimacy of debate as the basis for citizenship training. In the next section, we reveal the emergence of the discussion movement and the various ways the forensics community responded.

THE DISCUSSION MOVEMENT'S IMPACT ON DEBATE

At the heart of the tensions between the forensics community and the larger speech discipline was the issue of control over the curriculum and the associated activities. Forensics activities, particularly debate, had demonstrated the potential to attract students, and faculty seeking to create a discipline distinct from English and legitimate within the academic community took advantage of that student interest as they broke away in 1914 and started their own national association. However, once in place, as debate and forensics became more important in the collegiate environment, critics began to challenge forensics as the foundation on which the new discipline should be based.

At first, because forensics did not fit into the new areas of study emerging in the field, critics were able to marginalize the activities through means previously discussed. In addition, since forensics relied on some of the rhetorical theories and practices associated with former English departments from which the new speech departments were anxious to distance themselves, scholars minimized forensics as tangential and extracurricular. Despite this relegation, interest in competitive forensics persisted as coaches self-policed the activity, corrected bad practices, and constructed new ways to deliver the fun and challenging activity to receptive participants.

In addition to self-correction, the forensics community also used a number of arguments to defend itself, one of which was the position justifying forensics as a means by which students were prepared for active citizenship in the American democracy. This justification became the next target for those scholars seeking to eliminate debate or replace it with an alternative format. Establishing the supremacy of discussion over debate became the focus of the discussion movement that emerged during the second half of the public oratory era and extended into the first decades of the technical era.

In this section, we first provide some background on the basis for the discussion movement. Next, we introduce the Trojan horse of citizenship training that drew the forensics community into an unnecessary and damaging philosophical conflict and critique the claims used by pro-debate and pro-discussion advocates in their arguments justifying their activity as the best means to prepare citizens for civic engagement in the American democracy. We conclude by providing our understanding of the effects of this tension on the forensics community, which ultimately became further marginalized within the discipline.

Background on the Discussion Movement

The discussion movement had its origins in the 1910s, even though Ehninger (1949) placed the start of the movement around 1935. While discussion events did not appear regularly until the mid-1930s, Nichols (1945) suggested that the impetus for this movement came when coaches "who were not too successful in achieving [winning decisions]" identified questionable practices occurring in debates as the cause for their dissatisfaction and broke ranks (p. 104). These individuals focused their energies on criticizing debate as lacking educational merit and proposed a series of alternatives (e.g., no-decision debates, symposiums, group discussions, open forums) as a way to improve the activity. While Nichols (1945) characterized the established debate community as willing to improve its practices and to extend the olive branch to discussion advocates, he wrote that the other side "largely scorned" these actions: "The answer to this generosity of spirit on the part of many of the former non-decision crowd, many of whom are now discussionists, is to attack tournaments. It has been quite the style in some quarters to revile them, sneer at them, make fun of them, or speak all manner of evil about them" (p. 105).

By this time, Nichols had established himself as a something of a commissioner of debate, having founded a national forensic honorary, served in several executive forensics offices, coached debate, and published forensics history, news, and competitive practices for nearly forty years. From his vantage point, Nichols (1945) described the schism caused by this controversy over discussion versus debate as a family squabble: "No one admires a family that is continually running to the neighbors with charges and counter-charges against other members of the family. The total effect is loss of respect in the neighborhood—and some speech teachers are wondering why speech does not have a higher standing in administrative circles. Well maybe someone is waiting for us to make up our minds what we stand for—maybe we might gain by getting together on our story" (p. 106).

Because the forensics community was so divided on the debate-discussion issue—McBurney (1948) actually described the differences as "the cleavage"

(p. 59)—when coaches or teachers changed at a school or college, the institution's perspective toward forensics often correspondingly changed. This constant changing of forensics program emphasis, based on the philosophical perspective of the coach, had adverse effects on departmental and collegiate administrative support for forensics programs as decision-makers asked, "Which perspective is right?"

The disagreements among members of the forensics community were not lighthearted or easily dismissed. Ehninger (1949) described the disagreements between pro-debate and pro-discussion advocates as a "knock 'em down and drag 'em out fight" in which combatants often "spoke without sufficient knowledge of the methodologies they were attacking and defending" (p. 54). Many in debate saw no value at all in discussion, and discussion advocates ignored the value of debate as a tool of social decision. The extreme positions polarized the forensics community and threatened the future of competitive forensics.

When World War II broke out and resources were diverted to the war effort, many schools and colleges saw their forensics programs severely curtailed. Fewer students populated the debate squads, and travel budgets shrank. The forensics community dealt with the same constraints experienced by the greater American society at the time, and some wondered if the activity would ever enjoy the same level of popularity and support as during its earlier decades of growth and development. In this context, the question of discussion replacing debate became less important than the issue of whether forensics would survive. The tone of the arguments between pro-discussion and pro-debate advocates became less strident, and rather than forcing a choice of one or the other, some suggested the value of both. From the tone of the articles and speeches delivered during and after the war, the vitriolic debate over the issue changed to a practical discussion of the problem.

When the war ended and the forensics community was regrouping, Nichols began publishing the *Debater's Magazine* (later changed to *Speech Activities* to be more inclusive of all forms of forensics activities). In the first year, he commissioned a number of articles addressing the general state of forensics, particularly focusing on the discussion-debate controversy. Baird, characterized as the godfather of forensics (Hellman, 1945), and others saw value in both discussion and debate, advocating the integration of both into the curriculum (see Jacob, 1951; Lahman, 1947; Lull, 1948; Quimby, 1953). What soon followed was a proposal to create a national association for high school and college coaches involved in all forensics activities.

With the formation of the American Forensic Association (AFA), and as the forensics community entered the decade of the 1950s, unofficial interest groups developed within the forensics community. As a matter of practice, coaches aligned themselves with the groups that best represented their interests and perspectives. For example, debate coaches supported the creation of the National Debate Tournament at West Point, and coaches favoring discussion supported the first national contest in public discussion (Thompson, 1952). Later, with the expansion of individual events tournaments, coaches selected tournaments reflecting their preferences for events and types of debate. The result was the start of fractionalization affecting individuals who made up the larger forensics community: instead of being a whole, the forensics community became the sum of its parts. In the next section, we provide an explanation for why this split between debate and discussion originated.

The Trojan Horse of Citizenship Training

Making the tension more complicated regarding whether discussion should have supremacy over debate was the fallacy that revealed how the forensics community bought into its logic. From the beginning, debate was king of forensics. Although contests in speaking predated the first intercollegiate debates, once competitive debate emerged as an activity, those who debated were the most highly regarded of the forensics participants. Debate flourished, and those aspiring to a career that involved the welfare of the public were expected to have debated at some point in their academic careers. As an example, throughout the twentieth century, politicians used their debate training as a credential for being able to successfully articulate an argument, advocate a position, and persuade others.

From this position of power, debate was identified as the principal way to prepare students for active engagement as citizens in the American democracy. Thus, as departments separated themselves from forensics as a central focus for their curricular offerings, speech faculty increasingly came to perceive that competitive debate was failing in its duty to train students for civic engagement. Keith (2007) argued that debates about debate were important to the new discipline in trying to identify the inherent center of speech education: Is it training, or is it a liberal art? Such a dispute did, of course, harken back to Plato and Aristotle and has always been an issue whose resolution was elusive. The attacks on debate practice were rooted in the assumption that the primary purpose of debate was civic training and that the failure of the activity to achieve a narrowly defined set of standards rendered it unjustifiable and thus unworthy of support. We examine each part of this syllogism individually.

The first premise suggests that civic training was the primary purpose of debate. Acceptance of this idea was a *post facto* justification for the popularity of the activity and the perception that simply having fun and learning argument skills was, on its face, insufficient justification for debate. Life prior to World War I was a serious matter, in the sense that Progressivism created a sharpened awareness of societal ills and the strong belief that the role of government was to address those ills. This elevated civic engagement to a higher position than it previously held. Prior to the advent of the Progressives, for example, there was far less attention paid to the role of the individual citizen in the voting booth. The great city machines (e.g., Tammany Hall) supplied a dependable number of voters who pulled the lever for whomever the machine demanded. U.S. senators were chosen not by popular vote but by state legislatures, whose own seats were likely gerrymandered to ensure that a proper balance between competing political parties was maintained. That there was a reformist's zeal in the air was undeniable; Progressivism was growing, and due to a popular Progressive, Theodore Roosevelt, some headway was made against the financial trusts and monopolies. But the claim that suddenly a new educational form that lacked a long history, a set pedagogy, or even trained instructors should be measured against its ability to train properly prepared citizens created an unassailable bar against which to succeed.

The problem, of course, was that the new debate community, particularly the honoraries, bought into this attractive but ultimately deadly trap. Universities with newly minted debate programs could enhance their own credibility by pointing to the virtues of having a debate team. Debate as an abstraction held great sway. The Lincoln-Douglas debates had taken place only two generations earlier, and textbooks romanticized debates, such as that between Daniel Webster and Robert Hayne leading up to the Civil War. That these encounters and others like them could be judged as failing to live up to an artificially set standard was irrelevant. Once the notion became fixed in the public mind that competitive debate was to be judged valuable insofar as it prepared students for civic life, other, more nuanced standards were not considered.

The second premise was that debate, as practiced, failed to meet the civic preparation standard. The failure was determined by three of the most important controversies played out primarily in the 1920s: that debate as a form of competition was unworthy, that debating both sides of a resolution was unethical, and that using untrained judges was uneducational. The first issue, that competitive debate was unworthy, stemmed from the comparison of debate competition to athletics, especially football, whose rise in campus popularity paralleled debate and competed with it for the attention of students and audiences. Football was very controversial in its early years due to the sheer violence of a game played with few rules and only rudimentary equipment. Calls to ban football included one by President Theodore Roosevelt, who was no stranger to the rough-and-tumble. Football and sports were never weighed down by the need to justify their existence through fulfillment of a particular academic need. They existed to entertain and to provide valuable public exposure for colleges and universities. The connection between athletic success and alumni and friend donations was made quickly, and most colleges introduced a wide range of athletic programs.

George Pierce Baker (1896), the first to characterize debate as an "academic sport," was undoubtedly trying to provide audiences unfamiliar with the new activity a point of reference. Unfortunately, the relationship stuck. Public debates were very popular in the public oratory era, and colleges and universities used competitive successes to enhance their reputations and fund-raising prospects. But this interconnection came at a cost of creating dissonance between the civic-minded Progressives, who were the intellectual and academic leaders in the new speech discipline, and their perception that sports competition, including debate, was inappropriate training for a new generation of civic leaders. While competitive athletics would later attempt to remedy the notion that it did not train civic leaders (particularly as West Point football stars rose through the military ranks and, like Dwight Eisenhower, became political leaders as well), during the 1920s there was little attempt to change that perception. This created a view that debate competition was a waste of time for individuals truly committed to self-improvement, and the defects of its practices, such as switch-sides competition and professional judging, further devalued its importance.

The second problem cited with debate as civic preparation was the belief that asking students to debate both sides of a resolution violated ethical principles since, presumably, students would be forced to argue a position contrary to their beliefs. The utter fallacy of this position seems obvious. At no point in academic debate history were sides in a debate selected by the ethically based choices of the students, and even during the disputations practiced in colonial colleges, researching both sides of any idea was considered an intellectually sound and morally neutral practice. But the contention, again fueled by Theodore Roosevelt, that debating both sides was flawed continued to generate controversy in intellectual discourse about debate practices. Roosevelt (1913) wrote,

> What we need is to turn out of our colleges young men with ardent convictions on the side of the right; not young men who can make a good argument for either right or wrong as their interest bids them. Our present method of carrying out debates . . . encourages precisely the wrong attitude among those who take part in them. There is no effort to instill sincerity and intensity of conviction. On the contrary, the net result is to make the contestants feel that their convictions have nothing to do with their arguments. (p. 406)

The response from the debate community did not expose Roosevelt's fallacious reasoning or note that he provided no evidence for his sweeping indictment. Instead, O'Neill suggested that debate was merely a training method: "It probably very rarely happens that a student who has ardent convictions talks against them in an intercollegiate contest. But it would not undermine his moral character if he had. 'So is it artificial?' Yes, certainly—in the same way that other games, sports, modes of training and practice exercise are artificial; just as similar contests between chess teams, glee clubs, track teams and football elevens are artificial. But it is no indictment of debating" (O'Neill, 1916, p. 79).

Unfortunately, O'Neill's response was not a defense. Rather than developing a more nuanced understanding of the role of debate in civic life, O'Neill and others after him simply relegated it to practical training, which made it considerably easier to discard or devalue when other forms of training, such as discussion, were introduced into the curriculum.

The third and final problem was the issue of professional judging. This controversy was probably the most significant issue that competitive forensics faced and continued to be a source of wide controversy throughout the century. What was the role of the judge? This was a complicated issue prior to the emergence of the tournament format in the late 1920s. The judging problem was closely related to the wider issues of whether there should be win-loss decisions in debate rounds and the proper role of the coach. There was a strong point of view that no-decision debating was intellectually preferable and could avoid the moral weaknesses of competition in training citizens. Keith (2007) argued that this controversy was at the heart of the concern of the new association as to whether speech was truly a professional discipline. If lay audiences could appropriately judge debates, it was believed, then there was no point in establishing scientifically based professional standards. On the other hand, civic training required students to learn the ability to appeal to untrained audiences—a position that supported Keith's ultimate claim that the movement toward discussion would ultimately be the discipline's answer to the perceived deficiencies in debate training.

The problems of no-decision debates and the role of coaching were persistent issues throughout the century. The possibility of the misuse of competition always dominated discussions about forensics. As discussed earlier, the fracturing of debate and individual speaking into various organizations and styles in the 1960s was a direct product of the belief that the prevailing competitive styles overemphasized competition. One theme of the technical era was the ethically based concern that an activity justified by its personal benefits to students rather than its role in promoting citizenship training devalued debate training and made it more a game than a simulation. Stelzner famously labeled debate "emasculated rhetoric" in 1961, a view consistent with that of critics who persisted in their claims that the only role of debate was to train citizens using a very narrow definition of what that training entailed. Starting with the founding of the Cross-Examination Debate Association and the National Forensic Association, forensics reform took on alternative styles and formats to the mainstream in the hope of using style and format to remedy the perceived ethical weaknesses, such as the failure of debaters to adapt to the audiences. Ultimately, each of the reforms reverted back to the one it replaced, complete with the accompanying weaknesses, which in turn inspired a new reform effort in an unending cycle.

There also has been persistent concern about the role of coaching. This was a particularly acute problem at the beginning of the century with the formation of the new speech discipline. As earlier observed, one of the first problems the speech association faced was how to interact with casually trained practitioners, such as the alumni debate coaches who were largely self-taught and the itinerant speech teachers whose training was often based on elocution and Delsarte methods. The results of this coaching were often stereotypical and artificial speakers lacking authenticity or believability. Even as standards for teaching speech and debate emerged in the 1920s, there was no shortage of scholarly dispute about the role of the coach in helping students prepare for debates and speaking competitions. Partially, that concern was a reflection of a wider societal concern about ghostwriting of speeches, which was still perceived to be inappropriate, if not unethical. In later years, there would be disputes about whether it was appropriate for coaches to assist with research or construction of debate materials, such as briefs and theoretical arguments. The specific dispute as to judging standards retreated from being a central concern as the tournament format took hold and made it necessary for a trained pool of judges to be available for effective tournament management. But the issue never disappeared, and the concern for diversity in judging standards continued to be a forensics community discussion item throughout the century.

The conclusion of the syllogism was clear: if debate has failed to prepare students for civic engagement, it must be replaced with a better alternative. The debate over which method best trained students for democracy consumed the forensics community. In the following section, we discuss the comparisons made by pro-discussion and pro-debate advocates about the value of their activities.

Debate versus Discussion as Preparation for Civic Engagement

The advocates for discussion built their arguments on the assumption that competitive debate was not an educationally sound or effective way to provide students with the skills they needed to become actively engaged in civic life after they graduated. Their criticisms of debate were not new. In fact, as Rickey (1956) suggested, they were the same as those used in 1915–1916:

> 1) The judge and his decisions are weaknesses in debating. 2) Should debate be considered a "sport" or a "counterfeit" of a real situation? 3) Debate should be a search after truth instead of an attempt to win a point. 4) The style of debate should be changed. 5) Debate discourages holding first hand convictions. 6) Debate encourages undesirable speaking processes. 7) Certain actions of debate coaches are undesirable. 8) There is a class of criticism which has no real foundation. (p. 38)

After reviewing each of the criticisms, Rickey (1956) concluded, "There is really nothing new in the censuring of debate" (p. 38). Even as debate was preparing to enter its sixth decade of existence, critics described it as too "technically complex and highly competitive," too focused on "standardized tournament training," too attentive to "judge approval . . . rather than clarity and soundness of argument and effectiveness of rebuttal," and no longer relevant, as evidenced by the "dwindling audience before which the potential debater might speak" (Fest and Schindler, 1957, p. 29).

In addition to portraying debate negatively, "the more rabid discussionists made wild claims for the supremacy of their method as a tool for lubricating the machinery of all human relationships. Discussion was the magic key" (Ehninger, 1949, p. 54). Nichols (1945) described the situation as follows: "Discussion was all good and debate was all bad, or vice versa, depending on which team you lined up with" (p. 54).

Since proponents of debate and discussion defended their activities' educational benefits for those who participated, the academic community sought some reference or criteria by which the activities could be evaluated to determine which should be emphasized within the curriculum and extracurricular activities. The question of which format was best able to promote democracy became that point of reference. Baird (1945) identified five educational needs that were widely associated with the promotion of skills needed by students to function effectively in the American democracy: (1) "widespread education on current problems," (2) "techniques adequate for the analysis and solution" of problems, (3) strengthening of "the processes of straight thinking," (4) understanding of the American social structure and "methods of cooperative thinking and action," and (5) "improvement in oral and written communication" (pp. 1–2). Baird (1945) and Sattler (1945) used these needs as a framework to justify the supremacy of discussion over debate in the promotion of democracy, as depicted in table 6.2.

Instead of focusing on one fixed resolution in depth, discussion enabled students to have a broader exposure to a wider range of current social problems facing the American society. Dewey's reflective thinking process, focusing on relevant issues using pertinent evidence, provided a framework for analyzing and solving problems. The capacity for immediate, short, and direct interaction between participants to clarify arguments and correct ambiguity and misdirected emphasis promoted straight thinking, whereas the fixed speeches of debate allowed confusion to remain unresolved. In a democracy citizens must understand the social structures in which they function and work together to solve problems, making the process of a meeting of the minds through discussion a more desirable outcome than identifying someone or some team as the winner or loser of a debate.

Furthering this need to function within social structures, discussion was promoted as more democratic since a larger number of people could join in

Table 6.2. Characteristics Used as a Basis for Advocating Supremacy of Discussion over Debate for the Promotion of Democracy

Discussion	Debate
Open-ended question allows participants to take different positions seeking the best solution to a current societal problem.	Fixed resolution commits participants to specific positions testing the wisdom of a certain solution.
Reflective thinking process serves as organizing framework for investigation of relevant issues, pertinent evidence, and analysis (multidirectional).	Affirmative and negative speeches serve as organizing framework for presentation of stock issues, evidence, and analysis (bidirectional).
Shorter speeches allow for interaction without time limitations.	Longer speeches focus on presentation of positions within strict time limitations.
Outcome is characterized as a "meeting of the minds."	Outcome is the identification of a "winner" of the debate.
A variable number of participants interact depending on context.	A fixed number of participants interact depending on format.
Cooperation is used to describe process.	Competition is used to describe process.
Willingness to yield a position is possible.	Willingness to yield a position is impossible.

the process, whereas debate was elitist in that a limited, fixed number of participants were involved in the interaction. Similarly, in a democracy, citizens needed to be able to yield to the perspectives of others in order to solve problems. Discussion allowed for such compromise, while compromise in a debate setting meant defeat. Finally, democracy was characterized as depending on articulate citizens who could speak and write effectively. Both discussion and debate had the potential to provide participants with the opportunity to refine their communication skills. However, the ongoing criticism of debate that coaches prepared the briefs and materials used by their students suggested that the other characteristics associated with the reflective thinking process and more interactive nature of discussion would reveal the actual speaking and preparation skills of the participants.

In keeping with this line of reasoning, Thompson (1945) suggested that discussion was group action to find the best solution, while debate tested the wisdom of a certain solution. In essence, "debaters should be considered as co-workers and not as antagonists" in "the process of subjecting a proposition to a rigorous test" (Thompson, 1945, p. 9). The resulting truth to be found through this process of investigation would be the reward and establish the value of debate in a de-mocracy. Not everyone agreed with this position, as Hellman (1945) articulated: debate should not "bow respectfully and retire to a seat in the back row or bow out entirely. . . . Debating is debating and is not 'a fourth type of discussion' . . . that can be employed only after a great deal of preliminary discussion has taken place" (p. 14).

In countering the position that discussion was a more accurate reflection of how democracy functioned, Hellman (1945) argued that debate offered a more realistic way to teach the essence of democracy: "Are we not called upon to function ten times as 'decision makers' to once as 'solution finders'?" (p. 17). That debate was more essential to decision-making for citizens than discussion justified his position:

> In their theorizing about discussion, its proponents also theorized about democracy, and so wandered from reality concerning both. They lost sight of the fact that we the people do not "rule" in this republic, but rather only decide between alternative courses of action—or more accurately (and even more simply) we decide to accept a proposed course of action or reject it and do nothing (i.e., stand by the status quo). In this there is very little of the "problem, hypothesis, deduction," etc. and "the essential phases of the scientific method of John Dewey" with which the discussion theorists would have us and our students preoccupied. But there is in it everything of the debate process, the "old fashioned" debating process, including antagonists, persuaders, a good stiff contest, and usually good wholesome hunks of sophistry on both sides! Such is democracy as it is. (Hellman, 1945, p. 18)

Others shared Hellman's belief that debate was best suited to the real democracy that citizens experienced in America (see Aarnes, 1946; Crocker, 1946; Eistenstadt, 1951; McBurney, 1948).

Clearly, from an observer's standpoint, the parties involved could not resolve the tension within the forensics community brought on by this controversy. The battle raged, and not until both sides acknowledged that forensics was big enough for both groups to have their own preferences and identities did the rhetoric become less hostile. Unfortunately, as Nichols predicted, those speech faculty and administrators observing this thirty-plus-year war of words from outside the forensics community were perplexed and frustrated by the disputes and the strong philosophical positions that often caused forensics programs to change their educational focus and professional affiliations based on who was coaching the team. The result of this controversy was an administrative detachment from the needs and problems faced by forensics programs. While administrators considered forensics activities valuable—many of them were alumni of forensics teams—their attention was better spent elsewhere until the forensics community got its act together. The ramifications of this detachment haunted forensics directors throughout the remainder of the twentieth century, as the majority of the forensics community often felt at the mercy of the more vocal members of the discipline representing opposing philosophical perspectives about what forensics should be and how activities should be offered.

Supremacy versus Coexistence

By 1940, some of the respected leaders in the forensics community who wanted to maintain the viability of competitive activities within the speech discipline took a more moderate position and shifted from an either-debate-or-discussion perspective to a debate-and-discussion point of view. Members of the community began speaking out against the extreme positions pro-debate and pro-discussion advocates were taking. Thompson (1945) argued that the critics should know what they are talking about regarding discussion and debate, warning that "loose thinking and loose talking about the objectives of discussion and debate endanger both the value and prestige of courses offered in these techniques" (p. 1). He went on to provide an explanation of what discussion was and was not, as well as what did and did not constitute debate. While not everyone agreed with Thompson's interpretation of these practices (see Hellman, 1945), the call for a more informed dialogue about the values associated with debate and discussion demonstrated the efforts of some forensic leaders to come together to resolve, at least partially, the dispute between the warring factions.

Lahman (1947) furthered the position that fairness was needed when comparing debate and discussion: "Neither is easy. Both require careful preparation of content and training in method. Both may be poorly done. Consequently, it is unfair to compare a good specimen of one with a poor specimen of the other" (p. 4). Attempting to resolve the controversy, Nichols (1945) suggested that both activities be valued for their contribution to the education of forensics participants: "Why not face the truth honestly—which probably is that both are on the whole good activities, but in no real sense whatever satisfactory substitutes one for the other" (p. 104).

In further support of the claim that both debate and discussion were valuable activities, Lahman (1947) cited the relationship between the United States and Russia to make his point:

Are Russia and the United States rivals or allies? Would you agree that they can be either, depending on the wisdom shown by the leaders of both nations? The same is true, in my judgment, of debate and discussion. In the hands of nationalistic teachers and directors they can be bitter rivals, with atomic arguments and counter-arguments creating widespread discord. In the hands of internationally minded directors they can each make their own contribution, supplementing and complementing each other in a strengthened, vital forensics family of nations. (p. 5)

J. H. McBurney (1948), dean of the School of Speech at Northwestern University, summarized the position of many seeking a more moderate position on the debate-discussion question: "Discussion and debate are different but complementary methods, both useful in the schools, and both of great social importance" (p. 59). Perhaps it was the persistence of these techniques that led to a realization that they served a demonstrated purpose and could coexist.

Impact on Forensics

The impact of the decades of conflict over discussion versus debate reflected an entropic unwillingness to promote a common set of beliefs and values associated with forensics. This was manifest in various ways. Argumentation textbooks repeated commonplaces about the value of debate training without providing support as to the uniqueness of that preparation. What defenses were provided did not differentiate between debate and other forms of speech training, such as discussion and group process. While the onset of World War II provided a golden opportunity to explain the role of debate as citizenship training, the need for schools to eliminate debate competition for the duration of the war due to the war's impact on resources reinforced the growing belief that the activity was peripheral. Further, during the public oratory era (1920–1940), the disagreements among the honoraries overwhelmed any efforts to provide a united front in promoting common values. As noted in chapter 3, the squabbling over who should manage the topic-selection process divided the honoraries, and much of their interaction, while ostensibly collegial, still focused on charges of membership poaching and unsupported claims of academic or competitive superiority of one honorary over another.

Would a united front have slowed or reversed the divergence? There is no way to tell. Competitive forensics remained popular and even grew in size as the fractures within the speech discipline became more obvious. With a growing activity that emerged from World War II larger in size, with a drive to create national championships and a rapidly expanding base of high schools in organizations such as the National Forensic League, there was little perceived need to confront such issues. Even as large universities moved forensics to the periphery, particularly by assigning coaching responsibilities to instructors and teaching assistants, the healthy financial state of the university system, coupled with the strong public perception of the value of forensics, despite the rapidly changing practices of the technical era, contributed to the belief that the activity was strong and would, as it always had, continue to prosper even as it uneasily coexisted with a rapidly changing speech discipline.

After World War II, as the technical era of forensics began, a shift in the speech discipline placed greater emphasis on the social science dimensions of the field. More scholars began describing their discipline as communication rather than speech. Media studies took a more prominent place in public perception of the field, particularly with the instantaneous popularity of television. The various journals continued the trend of featuring experimental research in persuasion, group process, and interpersonal communication.

After 1950, there was, as previously discussed, a rapid growth in graduate programs in speech and communication. Even in the subdiscipline of rhetorical studies, Aristotelian criticism was rapidly replaced with a much wider range of critical rhetorical models. The field was growing and changing, and as part of that evolution, the long-standing trend toward separation with competitive forensics continued. Particularly in the larger universities, forensics was increasingly marginalized and disappeared from view in some of the traditionally strong programs, especially those that had rewarded graduate study in argumentation and forensics. Forensics was further isolated by the significant change toward greater interest in argumentation as a social process in contexts such as political communication and the studies of reasoning processes at the expense of interest in the pedagogy of forensics.

Summary

The discussion movement was a major development in the history of forensics caused by the dissatisfaction of members of the forensics community with the supremacy of debate and its associated practices. Fueled by "an overstating of the legitimate case for each" (Ehninger, 1949, p. 54), the controversy grew in scope and intensity for over thirty years as the forensics community divided itself into pro-discussion and pro-debate forces that seemed unwilling to compromise. Eventually, when World War II became a game changer, forcing the forensics community to consider how it could remain a viable part of the education of students, moderate voices prevailed, suggesting that forensics was big enough for both groups to coexist. The birth of the AFA created an umbrella organization under which all honoraries and interest groups could affiliate. From outside the forensics community, using Nichols's metaphor, observers had watched a family squabble and attack itself for more than thirty years over an issue that ultimately ended in a draw. The resulting apathy toward the forensics community and its characterization as always being in turmoil over issues related to competition, placement within the curriculum, and legitimacy within the discipline resulted in a loss of prestige for the forensics community.

CONCLUSION

This chapter focused on the macro tensions that influenced how forensics evolved. We began by exploring what place forensics should have within academic departments through a look at the relationship between debate and the emergence of the speech discipline. While the impetus for the National Association of Teachers of Speech may have been based partially on tensions felt by speech teachers within English departments, the impact of student demand for courses in speech based upon a growing interest in intercollegiate debate is undeniable. As the new field of speech established its content and research traditions, a variety of approaches found their way to the departmental table, and because forensics did not neatly fit into any one of the approaches, other than some of the rhetorical traditions and methods associated with the English departments from which speech faculty were distancing themselves, the marginalization of forensics activities began and intensified as coaches retired and departments had the opportunity to redirect resources.

We then moved to the conflict between discussion and debate to consider how this controversy affected forensics. The conflict started when debate exploded across the country and some of the practices associated with competition resulted in uneducational and unsatisfying outcomes for some of the participants. For those who found these outcomes intolerable, opposition to debate became their channel for change. Those who ultimately became pro-discussion advocates criticized debate, often relying on past transgressions to fuel their current arguments against the activity. Both sides had extremists who saw no good in the other's activity. As the conflict escalated, the use of citizenship training became the criteria by which the two activities were evaluated.

The debate community accepted this *post facto* criterion, which proved to be its Trojan horse. Ultimately, both activities were recognized as forms of argumentation requiring research and presentation. The difference was that debate resulted in a decision (product of a decision) reached by an external critic-judge, while discussion resulted in a common agreement about how to solve a problem (process of reflective thinking to a solution). While debate may have been king, discussion was certainly a baron seeking more territory and power within the kingdom. Moderate heads prevailed, due to the need to preserve forensics as a part of the students' academic experience. The standoff between these groups resulted in the start of a fractionalization of the forensics community that was enabled by the creation of the AFA. As special interest groups formed, those who populated these groups accepted their placement as part of the whole, further marginalizing themselves within the forensics community. This attitudinal acceptance shaped the way future forensics leaders viewed themselves and their roles within the greater forensics community.

In the next chapter, we explore tensions of a different kind. While the collegiate forensics community dealt with departmental and disciplinary tensions affecting its ability to function, the high school community was establishing its own framework for competition. The parallel development of the collegiate and high school communities produced a number of tensions that influenced and were influenced by their similar but different constituencies and practices. We intend to show that the presence of the collegiate and high school forensics communities may be part of the reason why forensics activities survived during the twentieth century and continue today.

REFERENCES

Aarnes, H. (1946). Debating from Aristotle to atoms. *Debater's Magazine, 2* (4), 215–18.

Baird, A. C. (1937). The educational philosophy of the teacher of speech. Speech delivered at the National Association of Teachers of Speech, New York City. A. Craig Baird Collection, Box 2, Problems in Public Speaking, Special Collections Department, University of Iowa Libraries, Iowa City, Iowa.

Baird, A. C. (1945). Debate and discussion in post-war service to democracy. *Debater's Magazine, 1* (3), 1–5.

Baird, A. C. (1955). The college debater and the Red China issue. *Central States Speech Journal, 6* (2), 5–7.

Baker, G. P. (1896). *The principles of argumentation.* Boston: Ginn.

Bauer, O. F. (1955). A century of debating at Northwestern University: 1855–1955. Unpublished thesis. Evanston, IL: Northwestern University.

Brooks, E. (1882). *A manual of elocution and reading: Embracing the principles and practices of elocution.* Philadelphia, PA: Eldredge and Brother.

Cohen, H. (1994). *The history of speech communication: The emergence of a discipline, 1914–1945.* Annandale, VA: Speech Communication Association.

Cowperthwaite, L. L., and Baird, A. C. (1954). Intercollegiate debating. In K. R. Wallace (Ed.), *History of speech education in America: Background studies* (pp. 259–76). New York: Appleton-Century-Crofts.

Crocker, L. (1946). Democracy thrives on debate. *Debater's Magazine, 2* (2), 83–84, 110.

Dargan, E. C. (1922). *The art of preaching in light of its history: The Holland lectures.* New York: George H. Doran Company.

Delaumosne, M. L. (1893). *Delsarte system of oratory* (4th ed.). New York: Edgar S. Werner. Retrieved from http://www.gutenberg.org/files/12200/12200-h/12200-h.htm@p4-08.

Ehninger, D. (1949). What has discussion taught us about debate? *Speech Activities, 5* (2), 54–55.

Eistenstadt, A. (1951). Education and debate. *Rostrum, 25* (7), 8–9.

Fest, T. B, and Schindler, B. (1957). Can forensics survive the educational revolution? *Gavel of Delta Sigma Rho, 39,* 27–30.

Gray, G. W. (1954). Some teachers and the transition to twentieth century speech education. In K. R. Wallace (Ed.), *History of speech education in America: Background studies* (pp. 422–46). New York: Appleton-Century-Crofts.

Hellman, H. B. (1945). Debating is debating—and should be. *Debater's Magazine, 1* (4), 14–19.

Jacob, B. E. (1951). New plan for high school debate. *Speech Activities, 7* (1), 3–5.

Keith, W. M. (2007). *Democracy as discussion: Civic education and the American Forum Movement.* Lanham, MD: Rowman & Littlefield.

Kirby, E. T. (1972, March). The Delsarte method: 3 frontiers of acting training. *Drama Review, 16* (1), 55–69. Retrieved from http://www.jstor.org/stable/1144731.

Kitzhaber, A. R. (1990). *Rhetoric in American colleges, 1850–1900.* Dallas, TX: Southern Methodist University Press.

Lahman, C. D. (1947). Debate and discussion—rivals or allies? *Debater's Magazine, 3* (1), 3–5, 27.

Littlefield, R. S. (1998). *Voices on the prairie: Bringing speech and theatre to North Dakota.* Fargo, ND: Institute for Regional Studies.

Lull, P. E. (1948). Enemies of academic debating. *Debater's Magazine, 4* (3), 109–10.

McBurney, J. H. (1948). The role of discussion and debate. *Debater's Magazine, 4* (2), 59–60, 70–71.

McGuffey, W. H. (1858). *New eclectic speaker.* Cincinnati, OH: Wilson, Hinkle and Company.

Nichols, E. R. (1945). Editorially speaking. *Debater's Magazine, 1* (4), 104–6.

Northrop, H. D. (1895). *The Delsarte speaker, or modern elocution designed especially for young folks and amateurs.* Cincinnati, OH: W. H. Ferguson Company.

O'Neill, J. M. (1916). Game or counterfeit presentation? *Quarterly Journal of Public Speaking, 2* (2), 193–97.

Quimby, B. (1953). But is it educational? *Speech Activities, 9* (2), 30–31.

Rarig, F. M., and Greaves, H. S. (1954). National speech organizations and speech education. In K. R. Wallace (Ed.), *History of speech education in America: Background studies* (pp. 490–517). New York: Appleton-Century-Crofts.

Rickey, J. T. (1956). Persistent criticisms of debate. *Gavel of Delta Sigma Rho, 38* (2), 37–41.

Roosevelt, T. (1913). *Chapters of a possible autobiography.* New York: Outlook.

Sattler, W. M. (1945). Discussion as preparation for debate. *Debater's Magazine, 1* (2), 14–17.

Sheridan, T. A. (1762). *A course of lectures on elocution: Together with two dissertations on language; and some tracts relative to those subjects.* Lon-

don: W. Straham. Retrieved from http://books.google.com/books?id=X81Zd
TkY2I4C&dq=A+course+of+lectures+on+elocution+together+with+two+dis
sertations+on+language&hl=en&sa=X&ei=OpcRUtCAF6X12QX5jYGIAQ&
ved=0CC8Q6AEwAA.

Sheridan, T. A. (1775). *Lectures on the art of reading; second part: Containing
the art of reading verse.* London: J. Didsley, Pall-Mall; J. Wilke, St. Paul's
Church-yard; E. and C. Dilly, in the Poultry; and T. Davies, Ruffel-Street,
Covent-Garden. Retrieved from http://www.abebooks.co.uk/Lectures-Art-
Reading-Second-Part.

Smith, D. K. (1954). Origin and development of departments of speech. In K. R.
Wallace (Ed.), *History of speech education in America: Background studies*
(pp. 447–70). New York: Appleton-Century-Crofts.

Thompson, W. N. (1945). Discussion and debate: A re-examination. *Debater's
Magazine, 1* (4), 1–12.

Thompson, W. N. (1952). National contest in public discussion. *Speech Activities, 8* (2), 41–42.

Walker, J. (1810). *Elements of elocution.* Boston: D. Mallory and Company.
Retrieved from www.books.google.com.

Woolbert, C. R. (1923, June). The coach versus the professor. *Quarterly Journal
of Public Speaking, 9*, 234–35.

7

❖ ❖

High School Forensics

The Growth and Development of Competitive Forensics

In earlier chapters, we discussed the interrelationship of forensics with social and cultural forces that swept across America in the late nineteenth and early twentieth centuries. With the rise of the middle class following the industrialization of America after the Civil War and the increased need for engaged citizens to be able to articulate their concerns and evaluate the proposed solutions advanced by leaders at all levels of government, competitive forensics became one way for young people to develop the cognitive and behavioral skills necessary for active participation in the American democratic experiment. Forensics provided the tools considered by many to be essential for democracy, emphasized free speech and active citizenship, trained leaders, improved the speech of the general public, and evoked values supporting progress. These characteristics formed the fabric of the public oratory era and continued into the technical era of forensics as the United States found itself in ideological conflict with the Soviet Union and other adversaries.

This chapter focuses on the forces and tensions contributing to the growth and development of forensics at the high school level. Specifically, it presents (1) the influence of adult education movements in response to the demands of the public for more information about the world around them, prompting the introduction of forensics activities in high schools; (2) the emergence of statewide competitive forensics activities resulting from demands for more coordination among participating schools; (3) the influence and impact of the National Forensic League (NFL) and the tensions within the high school community as interstate competition and national tournaments became a year-end goal for many programs; (4) the relationship and tensions resulting from the influence of collegiate forensics on high school programs; and (5) the related quasi-competitive forensic opportunities made available by civic groups and voluntary associations seeking to engage young people in contests designed to promote citizenship and democracy. Each of these areas affected how high school forensics evolved and thrived in the twentieth century.

THE INFLUENCE OF ADULT EDUCATION
MOVEMENTS ON FORENSICS

The Progressive Era galvanized the American public because it came in response to needs expressed by citizens wanting to confront and control the social, political, and economic forces that negatively impacted their lives (Woytanowitz, 1974). Citizens rose up and proposed innovative and perhaps revolutionary solutions, using the voting booth as a way to elect officials who would respond to their demands for change. The elites and those in positions of power recognized this growing activism and determined that in order for the uneducated masses to make informed choices, additional educational opportunities must be made available (Borchers and Wagner, 1954; Woytanowitz, 1974).

Prior to this time, the public received education through a limited number of institutions. The elementary, or "common," school existed to teach young children in every community. In this setting, children learned the basic skills of reading, writing, spelling, and arithmetic (Borchers and Wagner, 1954). At the other end of the educational process, the private colleges focused on the liberal arts and specialized professions (medicine, law, religion, education), and later the public universities addressed the agricultural, technical, scientific, and practical arts society required. Between the common school and higher education, some private secondary or preparatory high schools existed to provide more advanced training for those children with the ability or resources to pursue higher education. However, high school was not compulsory, and depending on the circumstances, most children stopped their formal education after learning the basic skills needed to read, write, and count.

As the population increased and families moved into less-populated regions of the country, thousands of one-room schoolhouses were built. However, older children and adults had very few educational opportunities or connections with what was happening in other parts of the country. In this context, civic and university leaders sought and developed ways to provide greater educational opportunities. These innovations in adult education and extension work took the form of the lyceums, Chautauquas, the university extension movement, and the Cooperative Extension Service (CES). All of these efforts addressed the perceived need to increase the educational capacity of the general public and stemmed from a combination of efforts by voluntary associations and university personnel. The impact of their efforts was the creation of an environment in which communities took considerable pains to create opportunities for their children to learn, audiences appreciated the public display of critical thinking and speaking skills, and individual students learned the necessary skills to become engaged members of their communities.

Lyceums

One of the earliest extension efforts to reach the American public was the lyceum movement, led by Josiah Holbrook. In 1826, Holbrook contended that lyceums would provide practical information to the public, improve social morality, educate the growing number of citizens becoming engaged in political activity, and improve the common schools (Bode, 1956). As news of this innovation spread, local communities started lyceum series, bringing in speakers who provided educational and entertaining programs to citizens.

As originally constituted, lyceums were voluntary, education-based associations and extremely popular because "no tax funds were required and no one who did not attend had to pay" (Woytanowitz, 1974, p. 18). However, by the end of the Civil War, the nature of the lyceums had changed, and entertainment replaced education as the understood purpose. An indirect consequence of the lyceum movement, with it focus on education and purpose of bringing some of the best minds of the day as speakers for the general public, was greater community support for local schools and the public libraries (Bode, 1956).

Chautauqua Programming

The Chautauqua movement contributed to the next phase of American community adult education, influencing the future of forensics in high schools. With its roots in the Methodist Church, the first Summer School and Sunday School Institute drew its name from its geographic location, meeting at Lake Chautauqua in 1873. Led by Bishop John H. Vincent (1886), the original Chautauqua was based on the belief that "it was almost sinful not to continue one's education throughout life." As such, the "obligation to learn" became "sacred" and "a part of the Protestant ethic" (Woytanowitz, 1974, p. 19).

The format of the first Chautauqua was similar to what is now known as a summer school, with resident, qualified faculty. The program of events included classes on different topics of interest, sacred literature, public lectures, concerts, and other forms of entertainment. The influence of religion was evident in some of the rituals and practices (e.g., hymn singing). However, Chautauqua was a school and not a church, so secular university professors seeking summer employment did not hesitate to accept the opportunity to participate (Woytanowitz, 1974).

Although locally managed, the organization of the Chautauqua programs provided college and university educators with the ability to exert some institutional
influence on the attending publics. The Chautauqua movement and its format,
bringing together university professors and the people in structured learning
communities, continued into the twentieth century as a way for local leaders to
enhance the knowledge levels of their adult populations about the world around
them. In addition, some colleges and universities adopted the Chautauqua summer school model and "began to print bulletins, establish reading courses, and
hold short courses" for adults interested in continuing their formal education
(Sanders, 1966, p. 17).

The Extension Movement

As a natural outgrowth of the lyceum and Chautauqua movements, extension
programs emerged as an organized way to bring courses and structured programs
to the public. Some independent community groups acting through their local
libraries developed extension programs. Other programs came from university
departments or government entities seeking to improve the lives of individuals
struggling to cope with the changes brought about by industrialization. Whatever
the means for delivering these programs, the American extension movement offered the public advanced knowledge with the potential to improve the quality
of their lives.

Early American variations of extension programming followed the British
model of university professors offering a series of off-campus lectures, readings,
written assignments, discussion, and testing (Kelly, 1962). James Stuart from
Cambridge University delivered the first such extension series in 1867 (Woytanowitz, 1974). It was so successful that university administrators gave Stuart
permission to offer additional courses of study off campus, officially adopting
the system of extension education in 1873 (van den Ban and Hawkins, 1996).
As American educators learned more about the extension movement in England,
they found the practice of taking the university to the general public consistent
with American efforts to provide adult education to the growing middle class
and to promote enhanced levels of civic engagement in the democratic process
(Chapin, 1894). They proposed that extension efforts should be "a blend of university scholarship and popular adult education" (Woytanowitz, 1974, p. 8).

Efforts to Serve Rural America

In contrast to the rise of independent associations promoting adult education,
congressional passage of the Morrill Act of 1862 and the second Morrill Act
of 1890 had a profound effect on increasing educational opportunities for the

"industrial classes in the several pursuits and professions of life" (Kelsey and Hearne, 1949, p. 27). Through the passage of these acts, public land was dedicated in each state for at least one college to be built, and "federal funds were to 'be applied only to instruction in agriculture, the mechanic arts, the English language—with *special reference* to their applications in the industries of life'" (Kelsey and Hearne, 1949, p. 28; italics in the original).

The purpose of the land-grant institutions was to increase the opportunity for the children of the working public to secure a higher education. Thus, the idea to provide practical instruction for those not physically attending universities naturally followed. The CES emerged as an innovative way for land-grant institutions to bring their universities to the public and fulfill their mission (Rasmussen, 1989).

In 1914, the passage of the Smith-Lever Act established the structural and financial foundation upon which the entire system of cooperative extension work was built. While the general concept of extension drawn from the British model reflected the focus of the university to bring the campus to the general public, the practical development of extension programs in America took a different path. The CES was developed as a system of county, state, and federal units united through the U.S. Department of Agriculture (USDA) to enhance the education of farmers and ranchers about improved agricultural production methods and the practical arts. The CES approach differed from that of university extension efforts to be discussed later in this chapter.

The CES, headquartered at land-grant institutions, provided training and development programs for adults and children at the county level. Brunner and Yang (1949) explained the impact of CES on the rural family: "better homes and better farms with which to feed, clothe, and strengthen the nation, and better organized and functioning communities" (p. 1). Agents of the university resided in the counties they served, establishing strong ties between the institution and the local population.

As agents worked with the rural populations, they often found the adults somewhat resistant to some of the new ideas being developed at the universities. However, the agents found the younger people more inclined to experiment with new ideas and techniques and later share what they learned with their older family members. The 4-H Club for boys and girls emerged as a major focus of the CES to diffuse research about new farming and production methods ("4-H Story," 2009). The attention to youth outside the school setting reinforced the development of civic responsibility and engagement that was characteristic of the Progressive Era. The 4-H Pledge reflected this focus on citizenship development: "I pledge my head to clearer thinking; my heart to greater loyalty; my hands to larger service; and my health to better living, for my club, my community, my country, and my world" ("4-H Story," 2009). The focus on training young people for civic engagement was clearly evident in the CES.

University Extension Efforts

While the passage of the Smith-Lever Act centralized and formalized cooperative extension under the auspices of the land-grant institutions and the USDA, the university extension movement did not have a national mandate to standardize the delivery of extension programs. Each institution and association seemed to have its own vision about what should be done to bring the university to the people. Early efforts in the 1890s by the American Society for the Extension of University Teaching to promote a uniform method of delivering extension programs were unsuccessful (Rasmussen, 1989). Communities and universities appeared to have their own unique approaches to extension and accomplishing the objective of educating the public.

In 1891, the American Society called a national conference on university extension attended by college presidents, faculty, and representatives from twenty states (Woytanowitz, 1974). The purpose of the conference was to establish the American Society as the center of extension efforts in the United States and to hear reports from extension advocates from around the country about best practices in delivering extension programming. The reports from the different entities were extremely diverse, and there was no agreement on what extension was or consensus about a particular method of organization.

Woytanowitz (1974) explained the different approaches to extension: "At Brown, Rutgers, and California, extension was an organic part of the university a year before Harper's University of Chicago adopted that system. At Michigan, the faculty proclaimed their readiness to teach courses, while in Indiana, Minnesota, and Ohio, the public had seized the initiative. There were city societies in Detroit, Toledo, Cleveland, and elsewhere, state societies in Connecticut, Ohio, and Wyoming, and even a national society in Philadelphia" (p. 53). This diversity meant that American extension efforts would be locally determined and under the leadership of individuals with their own visions for what was and was not effective programming. William T. Harris, the U.S. commissioner of education, called on extension groups to focus on secondary education, which he described as "the weakest rung of the educational ladder" (Woytanowitz, 1974, p. 45). However, while some institutions created programs and networked with high schools in their regions, others believed that extension programs should be solely for the adult population.

The university extension movement proved instrumental in the promotion of competitive high school forensics. The tensions resulting from the public seeking more information and educational opportunities about the world around them resulted in university faculty extending their involvement off campus and into communities. As the next section discusses, universities organized and promoted competitive opportunities for high school students. The resources provided by the extension divisions to high school teachers and coaches proved instrumental in

democratizing competition. In all, because university extension division administrators met periodically and developed publications and materials for distribution,
the state debate and oratorical leagues that developed through university extension efforts were strikingly similar.

THE EMERGENCE OF STATEWIDE
COMPETITIVE FORENSICS ACTIVITIES

Prior to 1900, the extension efforts developed through universities and private
groups were modeled after the British system of extension—that is, they took the
university class or practice to the public. Three of the most influential extension
programs developed at three universities: Wisconsin, Chicago, and Kansas. Their
approaches varied, but each contributed to the framework that would later emerge
as a means by which forensics activities were promoted at the high school level.

Woytanowitz (1974) provided a detailed accounting of the organization, programs, and motivations of these three university extension programs. Table 7.1
provides the unique characteristics of each. As the table demonstrates, university
extension programs established different patterns of organization, ranging from
no central office to fully integrated programming to the creation of an independent School of University Extension. Some programs offered lecture series and

Table 7.1. Comparison of Characteristics of Early State Extension Programs

	Wisconsin (1885)	Chicago (1891)	Kansas (1891)
Organization	No central office	Organic to institution	Separate School of University Extension
Programs	Farmers' institutes Lectures	Lecture study Class work Correspondence Examinations Library and publications	Courses for credit
Motivation	Mitigate citizen demands for an agricultural college in the state Progressivism	University not complete without extension	Keep up with schools in the east Recruitment Compete with University of Missouri

institutes pertaining to a specific topic, while others created courses that could be taken for credit away from the university setting. While all extension efforts were viewed as central to the Progressive agenda of creating a more informed and engaged society, extension programs served the pragmatic needs of institutions to present themselves favorably as compared with other universities.

Despite their best intentions, the extension programs at Wisconsin, Chicago, and Kansas as originally constituted were unsuccessful. However, as the Progressive Era continued into the twentieth century, University of Wisconsin administrators made a concerted effort to reform their extension program. A separate Department of Extension was formed and took as its focus a commitment to agriculture and service-oriented higher education. The effect was dramatic: "Between 1900 and 1915, 22 institutions established or made over extension departments on the Wisconsin model; 17 of these were state universities" (Woytanowitz, 1974, p. 151). One result of the growth of university extension programs following the Wisconsin plan was the creation in 1915 of the National University Extension Association (NUEA). Extension units became service departments for their universities, and their directors focused attention on how to reach out to the public, particularly to the high schools from which potential students might be forthcoming.

In his thesis for a master of arts degree at the University of Wisconsin, Highsaw (1916) provided a thorough history of the extension efforts in states following the Wisconsin plan. He suggested that three types of state organizations promoted competitive forensics: "First, those states having leagues under the auspices of their state universities and managed through some agency of the university, either the literary and debating societies . . . or the department of extension. . . . Second, those states having leagues under the auspices of some private college . . . and third, those states having leagues not under the direction of any educational institution" (pp. 376–77).

The one state Highsaw (1916) identified as leading "all the states of the Union" was Texas, due to the organizational efforts formally begun in 1910 by Dr. E. D. Shurter (p. 367). Other states Highsaw identified as having well-developed debate and forensics activities for high school students were North Dakota (1910), Oklahoma (1913), Kansas (1910), North Carolina (1912), Oregon (1907), and South Dakota (1915). Because the ways in which these university extension departments developed and promoted high school debate and forensics are remarkably similar, we have chosen to focus the following discussion on how Texas established its statewide forensics activity program.

Texas—a Representative Example

From the beginning, competitive forensics for secondary students was considered an important tool in preparing young people for the responsibility of engaged citizenship. Community leaders and educators believed that in a democracy, citizens needed to be trained to argue their positions in a responsible and dignified manner, regardless of whether they received a college education. As Shurter (1915) wrote, "The purpose . . . is to foster in the schools of Texas the study and practice of public speaking and debating as an aid in the preparation of citizenship" (p. 60). The public schools were viewed as places where all students could be given the opportunity to develop their speaking skills. Thus, opportunities within the schools for students to practice debate, public speaking, parliamentary procedure, and declamation were cultivated.

As university faculty and officials observed the content of high school curricula, they soon exerted their influence. Because the curricula in public schools in the early twentieth century did not include training in oral reading or public speaking, university professors with debate and oratorical expertise sought a means of affording students such experiences. In Texas, the Department of Extension provided a means to organize schools to provide training in debate and public speaking (Shurter, 1915).

Additionally, faculty also realized the potential that educated, well-spoken students held for the institution as future students. The recruitment of these trained students was reason enough to be interested in promoting forensics. As Hayes (1952) described, "Competition among these institutions for larger enrollments and for spheres of influence forced them to seek new methods of attracting high school graduates, and new avenues for expressing their usefulness as institutions to the public. It was then that the idea of interscholastic contests emerged as an instrument in the hands of the progressive institutions of higher learning" (p. 182). In addition to recruiting of students, the University of Texas promoted debate at the high school level to serve as a feeder system for university debate teams (Hayes, 1952, p. 186).

As a way to organize and coordinate these efforts, the Department of Extension was charged with publicizing the university and promoting the debate and forensic contests and programs. Following his death, Mrs. E. D. Shurter wrote about her husband's perspective on the use of contests to promote forensics activities: "He knew the value of contests. He ever had in mind the children of the far districts. A contest would be an incentive and an opportunity for these students—pupils—to meet the pupils of other schools. It would be good for the teachers. The winners of the contests would come to the University for the finals. . . . In short, the League would help boost enrollment at the University of Texas" (A. B. Shurter, 1950). The operations of the Department of Extension were comprehensive, involving recruitment of schools to participate in the programs, publicity about all aspects of the programs, preparation and dissemination of materials that could be used by students in the debate and speech contests, introduction of correspondence courses for teachers to improve their ability to teach debate and public speaking, organization of statewide competitions, and the recording and dissemination of results after the contests (Annual Faculty Report, 1900–1901, p. 54).

The rapid, uniform growth of high school debate in Texas was due to the infrastructure established by the Department of Extension to promote the competitions. County-level involvement of school and community leaders ensured that the contests were available to every student who wanted to participate. In Texas, Shurter (1915) reported, county forensics organizations to oversee the various contests had been established in 126 of the 256 counties in the state. The county organizations had officers (often teachers), who were appointed by the university.

County boards were expected to meet regularly, promote the contests within their counties, and oversee the contests. Shurter (1915) believed that the county organization of schools "had a marked influence in promoting school and community spirit" (p. 60). The directors of extension were well known among the county leaders and helped to promote the value of all schools participating. When the district contests began, Shurter knew each of the contest directors personally. Hayes (1952) explained, "He selected them because of their interest in the promotion of public speaking and because they were well known in their respective communities. Practically all of these early district directors were either graduates or ex-students of The University of Texas" (p. 205). Shurter believed this also performed a service for the university in that it established an excellent means of keeping alumni "interested in their alma mater and of affording them a state-wide network of practical functioning in her behalf" (Hayes, 1952, p. 206).

Once in place, the format for debate and public speaking contests was institutionalized, partially because those in charge remained in their positions for extended periods. For example, historical records suggest that after the departure of Shurter in 1922, Roy Bedichek directed the forensic contests until he retired in 1959 (a span of more than three decades). With leadership firmly established within the Department of Extension, the contests retained a consistent format.

The contests were timed to occur during the spring of the school year. Following the school and county contests, the state of Texas was divided into sixteen districts. A central town or city in each district was used as the contest site, and an executive committee appointed by the Department of Extension was established to oversee the competition. The district winners advanced to the university on "the first Friday and Saturday in May of each year for the final state contests" (Shurter, 1915, p. 61).

Thus, once the formula for statewide contests was shown to work, it was followed routinely every year. Because there were few changes in the rules and formats for the contests, teachers and public school administrators became familiar with the programs and knew what to expect. The annual routine made it easier for teachers to learn how to coach their students and for administrators to understand all aspects of the forensic contests. This familiarity was later cited as one of the reasons why public school administrators resisted some of the changes introduced by school coaches affiliated with the NFL. As Capel et al. (1975) contended,

> Historically, changes in the [Texas] League structure, procedures, and events have been accomplished through a statewide vote of high school principals. Since most schools had no specified speech or debate or drama teacher, the principals had no one to ask about the advisability of change. Most remembered happy days when declamation winners came from their own schools. They did not know of changes that were developing over the nation. So they would vote down proposals to eliminate declamation. (p. 26)

Another factor influencing the nature of high school debate in Texas was the development of the University Intercollegiate League (UIL). The Texas High School Debating League and subsequently the UIL developed in a manner similar to how leagues in other states in the Midwest were forming based on the University of Wisconsin model. In 1895, the Wisconsin State High School Lyceum Association encouraged the growth of triangular debating leagues among its member schools (Bedichek, 1927, p. 72). The university's extension department was instrumental in publicizing and providing "bulletins of information on public questions and hundreds of package libraries which are widely used" (Highsaw, 1916, p. 365).

Neighboring states adapted Wisconsin's model, including Minnesota. The University of Minnesota Extension Department was the first to develop debate contests on a statewide basis in 1902 (Hayes, 1952, p. 183). Other Midwestern universities patterned their contests after these two models: "The Midwestern universities, seeing the opportunity of bringing the high schools of their states into closer touch with them, seized upon the interscholastic meet with state-wide contests in debating, declamation, and athletics as the best means of assuming effective leadership" (Highsaw, 1916, p. 365).

By the time Shurter formed the Texas High School Debating League in 1910, there were fifteen state examples and precedents (Hayes, 1952, p. 184). As soon as the University of Texas president recognized that the debate league "would attract students to the University," "afford the University ever-increasing contacts through the high schools of Texas," "help to popularize general education as well as speech education throughout the state," and "be an excellent means of expanding and [advertising] the work of the Department of Extension," he pushed the proposal through the Texas Board of Regents (Hayes, 1952, p. 198).

With the debating league in place, Shurter began promoting the UIL. He produced a constitution in the form of a bulletin published by the Department of Extension and sent it out to all Texas high schools. There was such a positive response that rules immediately were instituted so that the debate competition could be held within the year. In addition, high schools were invited to attend a meeting of the Teacher's Association in Abilene, Texas, to discuss the league rules (*Texan*, 1910, cited in Hayes, 1952).

When the Department of Extension began organizing statewide activities, schools gravitated to the UIL. According to Capel et al. (1975), the number of schools grew dramatically from 1910, when 28 schools participated (primarily in debate), to 1912 with 248 schools, 1917 with 2,268 schools, and 1922 with 3,637 schools (360 of which participated in forensic contests leading to the state competition).

School administrators were encouraged to join the UIL and to participate, according to its rules and guidelines. As was often the case, the first high school debate coaches were often the school superintendents or principals. The importance these administrators placed on engaging in activities associated with the universities in their states may have been part of the reason for their commitment, reinforcing the earlier attention given to building alumni relations. In addition, school administrators often compared the successes of their students. Having the top debate or public speaking students at one's school often provided bragging rights to the superintendent or principal who was also the coach.

Emerging from these characteristics is an understanding of the importance the early promoters of debate and forensic contests attributed to their role in maintaining this opportunity for high school students to compete. As such, their establishment of competitive systems and contest rules was very systematic, evolving into a routine practice that had the grassroots support of high school administrators and coaches. As these coaches increased their own competencies, their interest in organizing state associations and leagues to support their efforts grew.

The relatively uniform and rapid growth of interscholastic debate and public speaking contests in Texas suggests that justifying the activity was essential. The promotion of democracy and citizenship gave high school debate a legitimate purpose beyond pure competition. The intervention of university faculty and administrators in the high schools through departments of extension offered a legitimate role for higher education in the formation and promotion of high school competitions. College professors, with their status conferred through their academic leadership skills and the credibility generally assigned to those with knowledge of debate and public speaking skills, afforded these individuals the ability to promote their visions and philosophies with the willing participants in the high school community. In addition, the range of services provided by the university was a significant resource that high schools could draw on through their involvement in forensics. By including alumni and county and district educators in the program, a network of committed individuals developed. The loyalty to the university reinforced commitment to offer debate and forensic contests for students. Throughout these early years, stability in the rules and procedures created an advantage for forensics because the familiarity with the format encouraged teachers and administrators to become and stay involved. Over time, their competency as coaches and teachers of debate and forensics increased. Finally, to enable the school coaches and administrators to become more engaged in the organization of the contests, the formation of a state league (or, in the case of Texas, the UIL) contributed to state unity and ultimately afforded opportunities for professional association on the national level (e.g., NFL).

Emergence of Forensics in Other States

The case study of Texas is not unique. For example, almost simultaneously, North Dakota developed in a strikingly similar manner (Littlefield, 1998). With the altruistic purpose of providing a way to promote citizenship among its newly arrived immigrant population, in 1910 the University of North Dakota, through its extension department, created a statewide system of contests for debate. Local officials were involved as a network of competitions were scheduled, culminating in a state competition on the university campus during the first weekend in May each year. The organization of the contests remained relatively constant until after World War II, as only two individuals directed the competitions for most of that period. Over the years, hundreds of debaters were brought to the university, and many of them returned as undergraduate students.

Similarly, the Kansas High School Debating League organized in 1910, and the extension division provided a substantial amount of service. Once formed, the extension division began bringing various groups to the campus: engineers, business people, health officers and physicians, attorneys, teachers, superintendents, and principals. The *University Kansan* of March 21, 1911, revealed the motive for hosting events for superintendents and principals: "It was frankly stated by its organizers that its object was 'to increase the interest of the high schools in the University'" (Stockton, 1956, p. 11).

One of the original departments of the University of Kansas Extension Division was Debating and Public Discussion. The department assisted adult societies and clubs that were interested in debating, the director of the division was instrumental in forming the Kansas High School Debating League in 1910, and the league's constitution and bylaws created a connection between the league and the extension by making the director of extension the secretary-treasurer of the league.

While Texas, North Dakota, and Kansas created their state contests in 1910 in somewhat different ways, their programs represented a pattern of development. In an earlier work, we suggested that the network of coaches and students at the collegiate level created an infrastructure that promoted the expansion of collegiate speech and debate activities across the country within a relatively short time frame. As university educators began to understand the impact that becoming involved in the promotion of forensics contests could have on their own forensics programs, as well as university enrollment, the infrastructure may well have served as a conduit for the movement into high schools and the further expansion of high school forensics.

As the century progressed, following World War II, the scope of the university extension departments changed. While one function of the extension departments may have been to stage forensic contests as a way to recruit high school students to attend the university, when the war ended, thousands of soldiers returned, and the need to spend time, money, and energy on recruitment dissipated. University extension departments shifted their focus back to one of their original areas: providing access to instruction for those not able to be on campus. Distance education and special courses replaced forensics contests. When this happened, many states leagues found themselves without individuals with tournament management experience.

National Federation of State High School Athletic Associations

To fill the void left by the abandonment of forensics by university extension offices, teachers and coaches turned to another entity with roots at the high school level since the early 1920s: the National Federation of State High School Athletic Associations (NFSHSAA). Officially founded by representatives of state high school athletic associations from Illinois, Iowa, Michigan, and Wisconsin and named in 1922, the association provided national consistency in the supervision and oversight of high school athletic team eligibility rules and school group regulations. Because every state with an activities or athletic association governing its athletic events was a member of the national federation, and because these associations promoted and ran education-based interscholastic sports, when the vacuum in forensics tournament management left by university extension presented itself, the NFSHSAA expanded its oversight to include other activities, relieving the governing tensions, particularly for the fine arts and forensics.

The national federation began publishing rules and providing support for state associations that sponsored forensics coaching clinics and administering statewide competitions. In states where public and private schools were affiliated with the high school athletic associations (HSAAs), all were included in NFSHSAA activities. Where the extracurricular activities of public and private/parochial schools were separated (e.g., Texas, where the UIL and the Association of Private and Parochial Schools were in place), the public entity (UIL) was recognized by the national federation, while the private entity (Association of Private and Parochial Schools) was not. Because all high schools with athletic teams and activities became associated with the national federation, forensics was included as an extracurricular option for students within their individual states. However, modeling their collegiate counterparts, many high school coaches felt the tensions associated with finding ways for their students to compete in interstate and national competitions. The National Forensic League emerged as a vehicle to provide national recognition and competition for high school students seeking to go beyond their local and state contests.

NATIONAL FORENSIC LEAGUE

The Progressive Era had ended by the time the National Forensic League (NFL) was founded in 1925. However, the same power of individual and collective action that defined Progressivism provided the impetus for the creation of the most influential high school forensics organization in America. This section includes a brief history of the NFL, as well as a description of its aims, the features of the league contributing to its popularity, and the impact of the organization on high school forensics.

Brief Early History

Through a series of letters and other correspondence written primarily by Bruno E. Jacob (the founder of the NFL), Ray Cecil Carter (an English teacher at Albany High School in New York State), and other interested high school and collegiate supporters, the idea of creating a national forensics organization for high school students evolved. Jacob (1928) described this process: "In September the organization was undreamed; in June it numbered twenty-four chapters from coast to coast, well named, well ordered under a strong constitution, well officered, and well symbolized in a splendidly designed emblem of sterling silver" (p. 5). By all accounts, the establishment of the foundation for the NFL was carefully planned and executed under Jacob's leadership.

The NFL produced its own account of its early history in the *Bulletin* (later the *Rostrum*). However, several aspects merit inclusion here. First, the impetus for the creation of the NFL came from a high school teacher who was familiar with Pi Kappa Delta (PKD), Tau Kappa Alpha, and Delta Sigma Rho. Ray Cecil Carter's question—"Do you know of any association of debaters membership in which high school students are welcome to?"—prompted Jacob to respond, "If we felt that there was a real and sufficient interest among high school students and coaches we would, I am sure, be willing to go to considerable effort to sponsor such an enterprise" (Jacob, 1928, p. 1). Jacob was a member of the Wisconsin Alpha Chapter of Pi Kappa Delta at Ripon College, and his creative and organizational abilities as a student leader and team manager/coach were well established.

In addition, his friendship with the founders of Pi Kappa Delta, as well as his familiarity with the honorary's constitution and organizational structure, gave Jacob the confidence and ability to move forward in founding the first national high school forensic league.

Second, Jacob moved methodically but with surprising swiftness, continuing his correspondence with interested parties throughout the process. He secured verbal and monetary support from school administrators for Ripon College to serve as the sponsor for such a national organization. He resurrected his earlier plan to create a Wisconsin state league, with a system of credit points and four degrees of membership, as the basis for a new proposed constitution for the national organization. Essentially, students earned a set number of points for every round of competition or public presentation that accumulated throughout their high school careers. Coaches received a percentage of the points earned by their students. These points contributed to chapter school strength in decision-making within the NFL organization. Students and coaches enjoyed watching these point totals grow. As a distinct emblem separating the high school organization from the collegiate honoraries, Jacob proposed a silver key. In the process of finding an acceptable name for the organization, he communicated with the state superintendents of schools in the forty-eight states to discover that "while thirty-four states had no statutory prohibition against non-secret Greek-letter societies in high schools, several states did have such laws and in a number of the rest regulations of school boards in practice were just as prohibitory" (Jacob, 1928, p. 2).

Third, Jacob identified and built grassroots interest among those who shared his vision for a national high school forensic association. With the basic elements in place, Jacob identified high school teachers in every state with strong debate programs, sent a letter introducing the new national high school forensic league, and invited them to participate in the formation of the organization. There were fifty-five positive responses. From that point, Jacob coordinated the final drafting of the constitution by mail. Preliminary drafts were circulated, and responses were gathered. When particular issues were solidified, Jacob converted them into propositions that were voted on by interested participants from throughout the country. The process of voting followed a preferential balloting system (ranking options 1, 2, 3, and so forth) that is still used by the NFL. The anglicized name National Forensic League was chosen over the National Debaters' Society, National Forensic Society, National Forensic Honor League, and American Forensic Union (Jacob, 1928).

When all issues were resolved, the constitution was printed, and on March 28, copies were submitted to the schools for ratification. Twenty schools were needed to put the NFL constitution into effect. By June 1925, twenty-four schools had ratified the constitution. Within a year, another 125 chapters were added.

Aims of the NFL

While the NFL was instrumental in expanding the opportunities for high school students to engage in competitive debate and forensics activities at the district and national levels, the tensions associated with this competitive feature of the organization were viewed by its founders as less important than the higher objectives of "furthering interest in the various forms of public speaking and in developing a better and more universal speech training in America" (Mundt, 1935, p. 2). In an essay written on the tenth anniversary of the NFL's founding, Karl Mundt (1935) articulated a higher goal for the organization in actively working to promote improved speech training for all high school students "so that the general level of American speech can be raised to more effective and more accurate standards" (p. 2).

Mundt (1935) suggested three specific aims of the NFL beyond providing opportunities for high school forensic competition: the creation of a required speech course taught in every high school by teachers with specific speech training as part of their academic preparation; the elevation of speech and debate coaches to the level of athletic coaches in terms of monetary compensation, release time, and preferential treatment from school administrators; and recognition that teacher training in speech and the creation of departments of speech in high schools and colleges should be placed on an equal level with the "older and more established" departments of English, history, and mathematics. Mundt stressed that the NFL, during its first decade, had been committed to these aims and considered "speech training in America" to be "one of the most vital services offered by the progressive and up-to-date High School[s] and College[s]." Ultimately, the NFL viewed its role as helping America "become a nation of better speakers and more influential and competent citizens" (Mundt, 1935, p. 3).

Features of the NFL

The popularity of the National Forensic League throughout the twentieth century was not fleeting. Several organizational values contributed to the success of the NFL in promoting its mission and recruiting new schools and members. Two important features were commitment to democratic participation and maintenance of a public focus.

Democratic Participation

From its creation, the NFL has emphasized democratic principles. As earlier described, the constitution and the early organizational efforts were constructed through the interaction of people from across the country. Those who crafted the constitution did so collectively. The organization of the NFL used a local-district-national model with high schools forming teams, schools competing in districts, and district winners advancing to national competition. The local coach, the district committee comprised of coaches elected by their district peers, and the national tournament run by an executive board of coaches elected by the local coaches reflect the American democratic governance model. The organization has remained attractive by giving school members an active voice in decision-making.

In addition to this structure, the NFL rules have promoted open participation in sponsored tournaments and events. The league has been coeducational since its founding, unlike some of the college organizations. Even the decision to allow students in the top two-thirds of their class to become members was a conscious decision to expand the opportunity to participate beyond the academically gifted or elites of the school.

Focus on the Public

The main characteristic of the public oratory era was the emphasis on forensics as a public good. This principle influenced the organization's philosophy as the successor to the state extension offices' view of the values of forensics. Both its size as a national organization and its grassroots governance systems insulated the NFL from being overtaken quickly by national circuit competitive norms, which were prevalent at the college level after the establishment of the National Debate Tournament in 1947. The organization maintained competitive rules such as multiple-judge elimination-round panels and the inclusion of lay judges (jurymen) to try to promote the value of forensics as a public good. The large size and open nature of the annual NFL championship tournament assisted in maintaining the commitment to promoting openness, even as high school forensics was subject to the same competitive demands and homogenization of practice found at the college level and disseminated to the high school level by college competitors serving as coaches and summer institutes training high school competitors in strategies and philosophies commonly found in college events.

But beyond the competition, to maintain the support of school administrators and sponsors, the NFL increased its visibility through the creation of resources available to member schools or schools seeking membership in the league. NFL membership was open to all high schools, and once a member, a school immediately participated in local and district events.

NFL's Impact on High School Forensics

The National Forensic League impacted high school forensics in two major ways: by encouraging participation through student recognition and through the creation of a national league of high schools. Each of these impacts reflect a focus on increasing visibility with the public and expanding opportunities for students and coaches to develop their communication skills. These attributes helped to sustain the NFL as it moved through different phases of its history.

First and foremost, the NFL's impact on high school forensics was an opportunity for high school teachers and coaches to provide recognition for their students competing in forensics activities. From the initial inquiry of a high school English teacher who wanted to provide national recognition for his students, the underlying motivation behind the expansion of the NFL has been to bring honor to those students who participate. The point system was chosen as a way for students to monitor their progress. The more students participated and the better their skills became, the more points they earned. As they earned points, they rose through several degree categories (e.g., merit, honor, proficiency, distinction, highest distinction) and received a certificate and seals marking each level of achievement. Additional rewards came to the coach, with a percentage of the students' points converted into coaching points that resulted in recognition (e.g., diamond levels based on fifteen hundred, three thousand, and six thousand points) based on years of coaching and point totals. Recognition for achievement was earned at the local level, making participation the means to success. No other high school forensics organization established a similar structure, capacity, or commitment for sustained recognition.

A second impact came from the creation of a national league. As previously discussed, the creation of state leagues occurred as part of the expanded university extension efforts of the early twentieth century. As state leagues formed, an explosion of high school debate and forensics programs followed (Highsaw, 1916). As high school programs grew, the number of teachers and coaches who got involved in forensics increased. However, these were intrastate networks of high schools with no way to connect with other state leagues. With the creation of the NFL, high school coaches and programs interested in competing at an interstate level found a way to do so. The formation of a national league enabled the local school to retain its autonomy regarding the forensics activities it would support. However, the school's affiliation with the NFL enabled its students to participate in district and national tournaments. Local control with national opportunities was a particularly attractive feature of the NFL, making its impact on high school forensics significant.

While the NFL increased the opportunities for high school students to engage in national competition, it must be recognized that tensions emerged between public schools and private religious schools, particularly in the eastern United States. Issues pertaining to which schools would control the management of the district tournament, which schools would have the necessary strength to elect coaches from their schools to serve on the district committee, and which students would have the opportunity to compete at the National Debate Tournament resulted in the formation of a second national high school forensics organization, originally founded as the Eastern Catholic Forensic League and later named the National Catholic Forensic League (NCFL).

The Impetus for the National Catholic Forensic League

While little is documented, a major figure in high school forensics who was an active coach in both the NFL and the NCFL indicated that NFL executive secretary Bruno Jacob and NFL president Senator Karl Mundt were public school advocates personally affiliated with many conservative senators from the Midwest who were uncomfortable with Catholic education in the United States. Anti-Catholicism was still prevalent, even though most visible discrimination against Catholics had disappeared by the end of the 1950s (Byrne, 2000). As late as 1949, a bestseller titled *American Freedom and Catholic Power* by Paul Blanshard argued that the "Catholic religion undermined the basic tenets of American Society" (Byrne, 2000).

Despite his personal views regarding Catholicism, Jacob was interested in building the NFL, particularly on the East Coast, where there were many more schools. While there were fewer Catholic schools in comparison to public schools in the Midwest (e.g., in Wisconsin there were fewer than ten Catholic schools in the three largest cities, compared with fifty to sixty public schools), on the East Coast and in larger metropolitan areas, Catholic schools were more prevalent. Eventually, in northern and southern New Jersey, New York, and Massachusetts, Catholic schools were granted charters in the NFL. Once chartered, the private Catholic schools actively participated in forensics tournaments.

One unique feature of participating on a forensics team at a private Catholic school was the ability to engage in more rounds of competition than students from public schools. For instance, in the late 1940s and early 1950s, Catholic school students were attending and competing at regular forensics tournaments sponsored by public schools on Saturdays; then, through Catholic youth organizations, these same students were entered in speech and debate tournaments on Sundays after mass. This particular circumstance gave students from Catholic schools two days' worth of NFL competition points each weekend, compared with only one day of points possible for public school students. As a result, Catholic school students were able to quickly amass points and degrees, a key criterion used to justify the granting of charters to new schools. As more charters were granted to Catholic schools, they quickly became a majority of NFL chapters in a number of districts on the East Coast. While some public school coaches expressed concern about the growing number of private Catholic schools chartered in their districts, tensions did not escalate until the Catholic schools began electing individuals from their schools to the district committees and as district chairs, for these individuals managed the district tournaments, secured individuals for the judge pool, and had access to information from other NFL district and national leaders.

As the Catholic schools gained power, it was the New Jersey public school coaches who first complained to the NFL board. During the 1950s, the Executive Council had been aware of this growing concern among the public school members of the NFL and had debated this issue in an attempt to determine the organization's response. The national board's deliberations eventually resulted in a January 9, 1965, decision "to refer charter applications from Catholic schools to the National Catholic Forensic League until such time as the number of Catholic schools holding NFL charters equals the percentage of Catholic schools among the secondary schools in the country" ("Executive Council actions," 1965, p. 9). While there were a few exceptions in the context of the original motion, the decision to refer applications resulted in some push-back from Catholic school coaches wishing to seek membership in the NFL, so a committee of the NFL council met with the officers of the National Catholic Forensic League and reached an agreement. The action was subsequently ratified by the Executive Council voting by mail to allow for Catholic schools to enter the NFL according to the following formula: "District committees be authorized to grant one charter a year to a private school if 20% or less of the charters in that district are held by private schools; one charter to a private school every second year (1966, 1968, etc.) if more than 20% of the charters are held by private schools; one charter every third year (1966, 1969, etc.) if more than 50% of the charters in that district are held by private schools" (Jacob, 1965, n.p.). In addition to this formula, Regulation No. 23—which described how students could earn NFL points—was amended "to provide that no point be recorded for debates or contests held on a Sunday" (Jacob, 1965, n.p.). This effectively stopped the use of Sunday tournaments as sources of NFL points for the private, Catholic school students.

While some may have considered this formula to be discriminatory, the NFL leaders argued that this policy was not so much an anti-Catholic attack as a response to the public schools in the districts that considered themselves at a disadvantage because they couldn't compete on two days each weekend and therefore were losing influence in district decision-making. The Executive Council defended its position that the formula and rule change were not an attack against their Catholic colleagues, stating, "Over 200 Catholic schools now hold NFL charters. Some have been with us for thirty years. Their membership record is as good as that of the public schools. They are respected and valued members. Their charters are in no wise [sic] affected by this directive. They may hold them as long as they meet the requirements for renewal" ("Executive Council actions," 1965, p. 9). Throughout the controversy, the NFL leaders stressed that the issue was making sure parity existed between public and Catholic schools.

Many Catholic educators perceived discrimination in this policy, since their numbers were effectively limited simply because public schools did not want, or were not ready, to join the NFL. Fueled by their frustration with the NFL's policy, a group of coaches founded the Eastern Catholic Forensic League (ECFL). The ECFL started as an opportunity for Catholic schools to organize themselves into diocesan leagues from which they could compete with other Catholic school teams. The new organization originated on the heavily Catholic East Coast. The ECFL was conceived as a purely Catholic league, but soon a bitter debate ensued about accepting public schools. The ECFL resisted for a time, but later, as the organization moved westward (although still east of the Mississippi), public schools were invited to participate in the league's activities to increase numbers and to sustain the Grand National Tournament held each spring. The name later changed to the National Catholic Forensic League to reflect the broader membership base.

The NCFL model provided that each Catholic diocese should have a league of schools that would host several tournaments during the year. Member schools attended these diocese tournaments but were also allowed to attend other public school– or university-sponsored tournaments. At the end of each season, there would be a final diocesan tournament, with student qualifiers advancing to the Grand National Tournament. The appeal of the NCFL resonated with many of the Catholic school coaches because in some cities there were more private Catholic schools than public schools, and these coaches felt that if charters were being denied to some schools, there would be high-quality students who could not qualify for the NFL National Tournament due to chartering constraints on parochial school members.

Because membership was open to all public and private secondary schools in the United States and Canada, the NCFL was extroverted-expansive. The NCFL was not national in scope. Rather, local leagues were organized geographically along the diocesan lines of the Catholic Church. Even at the end of the twentieth century, only thirty-five states and the District of Columbia had NCFL diocesan leagues in place, totaling about sixty-five active local leagues. As the NCFL was largely a confederation of schools rather than a federation (e.g., NFL), the major benefit of participation was the ability to attend a national tournament at the end of the school year.

Since most of the early NCFL leaders were also NFL coaches, the purposes of this group mirrored those of the NFL and included encouraging and assisting in the development of articulate leaders; promoting curricular and cocurricular speech and debate activities in Catholic, private, and public secondary schools; establishing, maintaining, and coordinating a system of diocesan leagues to administer schedules of interscholastic speech and debate activities; assisting individual schools in which no diocesan league existed; and sponsoring and administering the annual Grand National Tournament of the league.

The NCFL (2013) described itself as "an all-volunteer organization, run for coaches, by coaches. We offer a low-cost alternative to larger organizations that have paid staff and offices." There is an obvious allusion comparing the NCFL and the NFL, as the latter had an office and paid staff to run the organization. Other differences included the point system used by the NFL to reward individual achievement and participation versus the school-based focus of the NCFL, whereby, based on the number of schools in the diocesan league, allocations for the Grand National Tournament were made. Despite the differences, the NCFL and the NFL coexisted primarily because so many high school coaches in the metropolitan areas were involved in both organizations.

Diocesan leagues were obligated to have a person to serve on the tournament staff, participating schools were obligated to supply judges, and teams were obligated to stay in the tournament hotel blocks. Failure to comply resulted in significant fines that, if not paid, would lead to the exclusion of the league from subsequent Grand National Tournaments.

Generally, NCFL leaders came from cities with large Catholic populations and multiple high schools. Similarly, the early Grand National Tournaments were held in larger cities, including Brooklyn, Pittsburgh, Cleveland, Philadelphia, Chicago, New York City, Baltimore, and Washington, DC.

The Impact of the National High School Leagues

Coaches who wanted to provide a national competitive experience for their students founded the NFL and NCFL. These leagues modeled the collegiate practice of holding national tournaments, and ultimately a national circuit of high school tournaments developed to provide practice opportunities for these teams. Not all coaches chose to join these national leagues, relying on their state high school activities associations to provide the rules and supervision for their competitive experiences. While the National Federation, NFL, and NCFL coexisted throughout the latter half of the twentieth century, there were tensions at the state level when conflicts between HSAA and league rules occurred. In most cases, the HSAA policies prevailed because of the ramifications for school athletic teams if a forensics coach chose to ignore the ruling of the HSAA in favor of NFL rules regarding a forensics matter. Of course, the modeling of collegiate forensics by NFL and NCFL schools was another source of tension associated with national competition, as the following section discusses.

THE IMPACT OF COLLEGIATE FORENSICS

As described in chapter 1, high school and collegiate forensics experienced a parallel but not necessarily symbiotic relationship during the twentieth century. For example, the NFL was modeled after PKD and initially led by former members of that honorary, but at the end of the twentieth century it was playing a leadership role in the initiation of a partnership with PKD to promote collegiate forensics among the ranks of the NFL. The interplay of factors, in which the high schools provided potential recruits for summer debate and speech institutes or collegiate forensics teams, and in which college programs provided student competitors as hired judges and assistant coaches, as well as college faculty as judges and coaches at high school competitions, demonstrates the continued relationship between the two groups.

Historically, at the collegiate level, while perhaps not the first intercollegiate debate, certainly the first notorious one occurred in 1892, when debaters from Harvard University met Yale at Cambridge (Cowperthwaite and Baird, 1954, p. 259). However, Stone (1914) suggested that the participants in the early intercollegiate debates actually got their start at the secondary level: "As early as 1887 joint debates were held among the schools in and around Boston, the Boston Latin School, Cambridge Latin School, Roxbury Latin School, Newton High School, and Dorchester High School being among the schools participating. It is undoubtedly true that the men who took part in these interscholastic debates were the men who afterwards started the intercollegiate debates" (p. 6).

Despite the controversy, the pattern of intercollegiate debates set by Harvard and Yale beginning in 1892 and by Harvard, Yale, and Princeton in 1894 (*Debating*, n.d.) served as a model for Michigan and Wisconsin, as well as other Big Ten institutions, to begin intercollegiate debating using the triangular format. Hayes (1952) suggested that as word spread among the collegiate ranks, the triangular and quadrangular became standard formats for organized debates. Using this model, after 1895, debate contests were soon adapted for use in secondary education (Hayes, 1952, p. 181).

The relationship between collegiate and high school debate is intertwined and complex. While debate and declamation may have been simultaneously available to students at both levels, the role of universities in the promotion of forensics in high schools is clear. In the beginning of this relationship, both groups partnered to provide students with the opportunity to become better citizens and public speakers. Later, as university promoters of forensics began to exert pressure on high school teachers and coaches to adopt new practices and perspectives as part of a more competitive model, the relationship deteriorated.

One specific example of this pressure that compromised the relationship between high school and collegiate forensics involved the increased demonstration and acceptance of high delivery speeds in debate. During the public oratory era, debates were largely oratorical, with persuasion and audience adaptation forming core components of the activity. After World War II, as debate became more technical and the quantity of information and arguments advanced by a team became the basis for the decision, the debater best able to speed-read was praised over the debater who presented her arguments effectively but too slowly to cover all the attacks.

The practice of accelerating the speed of delivery originated at the collegiate level, and as college debaters migrated to the high school coaching ranks as assistants and head coaches, they encouraged their debaters to adopt this delivery style and rewarded those who excelled at this strategy with wins over those who did not. The encouragement of this practice among high school debaters angered the older, traditional coaches, who tended to stop listening or following if debaters spoke too rapidly. From the collegiate perspective, the judges who punished with losses those debaters who spoke too rapidly were out of touch with contemporary debate practices. From the high school perspective, collegiate debaters and national circuit coaches and judges were polluting the pure practices of high school debate with poor and ineffective communication practices.

The tensions between the high school and college forensics communities may have been due to their vantage points. The high school forensics community accepted and justified forensics as extracurricular competition, whereas the collegiate forensics community struggled with where to place forensics within the curriculum and the justification for that placement. The resulting scholarship from the collegiate level pertaining to this struggle may have seemed superfluous to the high school community, for which that ship had already sailed. The tensions about this and other issues between high school and collegiate forensics educators continued into the twenty-first century (Littlefield and Venette, 2004) and resulted in the creation of a new form of public forum debate designed to reward effective communication for a lay audience. Public forum debate's survival into the twenty-first century will be determined by the ability of the high school community to maintain its focus on audience-centered debate.

ADDITIONAL QUASI-COMPETITIVE OPPORTUNITIES

Other competitive opportunities were extended to high school students complementing, and occasionally competing with, state or NFL activities. These quasi-competitive opportunities took the form of national contests promoted by organizations such as the American Legion and Veterans of Foreign Wars (VFW). These competitions were used by the organizations to involve young people in national causes and to promote citizenship. At a time when democracy was being challenged at home and abroad, national organizations like these sought ways to involve high school students in what they perceived to be a fight for the American way of life.

Developing a deeper knowledge and appreciation for the U.S. Constitution was the focus of the American Legion Oratorical Contest, started in 1927, at which students spoke on one of the articles or amendments, presented an original oration, and responded to questions from judges. Students won scholarships as they proceeded from local competitions to state and ultimately national finals. The purpose of the contest was to promote leadership qualities in students, to generate awareness of the U.S. Constitution, and to develop the ability to think and speak clearly, as well as understand the duties, responsibilities, rights, and privileges of American citizenship.

The Veterans of Foreign Wars created the Voice of Democracy audio-essay competition after World War II in 1947 to foster patriotism among America's youth. Local VFW post winners were chosen from their districts and advanced through state levels to a national competition. The prizes for winning included scholarships and, for the state winners, an all-expense-paid trip to Washington, DC.

Throughout the twentieth century, speech-related competitions were sponsored by fraternal and social organizations, including the Benevolent and Protective Order of Elks, Optimists International, the Independent Order of Odd Fellows and Rebekahs, Lions Clubs International, and Rotary International. These competitions used the promotion of good citizenship and the development of effective public speaking skills as key reasons for their existence. However, it should be noted that the judges for these contests were often members of their organizations with little or no training in speech construction or delivery.

CONCLUSION

This chapter focused on the tensions and forces that contributed to the growth and development of forensics at the high school level. We cannot understand how high school forensics developed without understanding the influence of adult education movements on local communities. When community leaders expanded the educational opportunities for their citizens through lyceums and Chautauqua programs, they did so through public programs and speakers. The introduction of the university extension efforts to organize and offer programs for communities resulted in more support for local schools and libraries. The format for all of these efforts represented a public focus and fostered the cultivation of the platform skills needed by citizens who would debate issues of importance to their communities, states, and nation.

As university extension departments refocused their efforts toward serving their institutions and state audiences, they appealed to the interests of high school students. Competitive debate and forensics activities in every high school were encouraged through the development of state leagues. As the university extension programs transformed after World War II into units promoting distance learning and special educational programming, high school activities associations in many states assumed responsibility for statewide forensic contests.

As the high school programs grew in number and scope, the attention of the teachers and coaches was drawn to an innovative organization designed to recognize and support forensic participation at the local and national levels. Modeled and inspired by the collegiate honoraries, the NFL and NCFL provided the means by which such recognition in forensics could be achieved at the high school level. This relationship between collegiate forensics and high school programs is intertwined and complicated. However, their symbiotic bond provided mutual support as the social, political, economic, and cultural events of the twentieth century shaped the world. In the third section of this book, we move to a discussion of how competitive forensics survived the tensions that shaped its evolution throughout the century, exploring the fun inherent in the activity and why forensics appealed to those who engaged in it, as well as how African American students and women found their place in the competitive forensics environment.

REFERENCES

The 4-H story. (2009). Retrieved from http://4-h.org/4history.html.

Annual faculty report of the University of Texas. (1900–1901). Austin: Center for American History, University of Texas.

Bedichek, R. (1927). Interscholastic non-athletic contests. Unpublished thesis. Austin: University of Texas.

Blanshard, P. (1949). *American freedom and Catholic power*. Boston: Beacon Press.

Bode, C. (1956). *The American lyceum: Town meeting of the mind.* New York: Oxford University Press.

Borchers, G. L., and Wagner, L. R. (1954). Speech education in nineteenth-century schools. In K. R. Wallace (Ed.), *History of speech education in America: Background studies* (pp. 277–300). New York: Appleton-Century-Crofts.

Brunner, E. D., and Yang, E. H. P. (1949). *Rural America and the extension service: A history and critique of the cooperative agricultural and home economics extension service.* New York: Bureau of Publications, Columbia University.

Byrne, J. (2000). Roman Catholics and the American mainstream in the twentieth century. Retrieved from http://nationalhumanitiescenter.org/tserve/twenty/tkeyinfo/tmainstr.htm.

Capel, R., Emery, E., Larson, P. M., Tolliver, C., Streeter, D., Abernathy, E., et al. (1975). *A history of the Texas Speech Communication Association, 1923–1975.* Corpus Christi: Texas Speech Communication Association.

Chapin, A. J. (1894). University extension. In M. K. Oldham (Ed.), *Eagle: The Congress of Women: Held in the Woman's Building, World's Columbian Exposition, Chicago, U.S.A., 1893* (pp. 393–97). Chicago: Monarch Book Company. Retrieved from http://digital.library.upenn.edu/women/_generate/authors-C.html.

Cowperthwaite, L. L., and Baird, A. C. (1954). Intercollegiate debating. In K. R. Wallace (Ed.), *History of speech education in America: Background studies* (pp. 259–76). New York: Appleton-Century-Crofts.

Debating: History of the Harvard-Princeton-Yale Triangulars, 1909–1959. (n.d.). Available at Harvard University Archives: HUD 11320.959.

Executive Council actions. (1965, January). *Rostrum, 39* (5), 8–10.

Hayes, A. R. (1952). The influence and impact of Edwin Dubois Shurter on speech education in Texas. Unpublished dissertation. Austin: University of Texas.

Highsaw, J. L. (1916). Interscholastic debates in relation to political opinion. *Quarterly Journal of Public Speaking, 2* (4), 365–83.

Jacob, B. E. (1928, October). History of the National Forensic League. *Rostrum, 3* (2), 1–5.

Jacob, B. (1965, March 13). Unpublished minutes of the meeting between a committee of the NFL council and officers of the National Catholic Forensic League. Original copies held at the NFL Office, Ripon, WI.

Kelly, T. (1962). *A history of adult education in Great Britain.* Liverpool, UK: University of Liverpool Press.

Kelsey, L. D., and Hearne, C. C. (1949). *Cooperative extension work.* Ithaca, NY: Comstock Publishing Associates.

Littlefield, R. S. (1998). *Voices on the prairie: Bringing speech and theatre to North Dakota.* Fargo, ND: Institute for Regional Studies.

Littlefield, R. S., and Venette, S. J. (2004). Perceptions of high school opinion leaders about the role of college debaters in the high school debate community. *Argumentation and Advocacy, 4* (4), 259–66.

Mundt, K. E. (1935). Objectives of NFL. *Rostrum, 9* (6), 2–3.

National Catholic Forensic League. (2013). How to join. Retrieved from www.ncfl.org/join.

Rasmussen, W. D. (1989). *Taking the university to the people.* Ames: Iowa State University Press.

Sanders, H. C. (Ed.). (1966). *The cooperative extension service.* Englewood Cliffs, NJ: Prentice Hall.

Shurter, A. B. (1950, March 17). Letter to Arthur R. Hayes. Correspondence. Personal Files, Arthur R. Hayes, Center for American History, University of Texas, Austin.

Shurter, E. D. (1915, April–October). State organization for contests in public speaking. *Quarterly Journal of Public Speaking, 1*, 59–64.

Stockton, F. T. (1956). *The pioneer years of university extension at the University of Kansas.* Lawrence: University of Kansas Press.

Stone, A. P. (1914). Introduction (1893). Reprinted in A. N. Levin and H. B. Goodfriend (Eds.), *Harvard debating—1892–1913* (pp. 5–23). Cambridge, MA: Caustic-Claflin Company. Available at Harvard University Archives: HUD11320.914.

Van den Ban, A. W., and Hawkins, H. S. (1996). *Agricultural extension* (2nd ed.). Oxford: Blackwell Science.

Vincent, J. H. (1886). *The Chautauqua movement.* Boston: Chautauqua Press.

Woytanowitz, G. W. (1974). *University extension: The early years in the United States, 1885–1915.* Iowa City, IA: National University Extension Association and the American College Testing Program.

Part III

THE SOCIOCULTURAL DIMENSIONS CONTRIBUTING TO THE EVOLUTION OF FORENSICS

In this section, we identify dimensions of forensics that have received less attention from scholars due to the nature of their content. First, in chapter 8, we examine the social side of forensics as it drew participants into its ranks and provided the enjoyment that enabled competitive activities to survive the tensions previously discussed in part II. Next, in chapters 9 and 10, the clouded side of forensics is revealed through an examination of the experiences of African Americans and women as they confronted legal and structural barriers to participation. The "absent history" that never made it into the books is an essential part of the evolution of forensics during the twentieth century in America and provides a context for challenges that will continue to face forensics in the future.

8

The Social Dimensions of Forensics

Up to this point, much of our focus on forensics has considered the activities associated with it solely in intellectual terms, as training in argument or preparation for career or citizenship. That perspective misses what we consider to be the more profound significance of forensics. Put simply, students benefited from and participated in forensics because the activity was enjoyable as well as educational. This inherently epistemological dimension of forensics activity provides an explanation for why forensics is perceived as fun by those who participate as competitors, judges, coaches, teachers, and audiences: "Play is simultaneously a source of relaxation and stimulation for the brain and body. A sure (and fun) way to develop your imagination, creativity, problem-solving abilities, and mental health is to play with your romantic partner, officemates, children, grandchildren, and friends" (Kemp et al., 2012).

The relationship between play and social and intellectual development is well known. We play "to learn," "to create," "to feel challenged," "to pass time," "to calm and focus ourselves," "to win," "for the fun of it," and "for the joy of it" (Kemp et al., 2012). There is a strong positive correlation between enjoyment and the acquisition of new skills and knowledge.

The National Institute for Play (2010) described various types of play, each of which serves a particular role in human development. One of those types, transformative-integrative and creative play, characterizes the relationship between forensics, as a playful activity, and its role in helping stimulate creativity and thought. Some have suggested that Albert Einstein engaged in transformative play he imagined himself riding on a sunbeam at the speed of light while theorizing quantum physics. Similarly, forensics, as a form of transformative-integrative play, has long emphasized the importance of the activity in strengthening intellectual, personal, and moral development. Our argument is that there has been a fundamental overemphasis on justifying forensics primarily in intellectual terms and a failure to appreciate the activity's value as a critical tool in the interpersonal and social growth of students. In this chapter, we (1) develop the way educators overlooked the fun of forensics as they attempted to justify their own emphasis on its intellectual benefits for students; (2) highlight the three dimensions of forensics as play—simulation, socialization, and conversation and community—whereby students practiced skills in an artificial setting, interacted with other participants, and built social capital to strengthen the forensics community and impact higher education; and (3) analyze how the nature of fun changed as forensics evolved into a more technical activity.

The Justificatory Overemphasis on Intellectual Benefits of Forensics Training

Even before the end of the public oratory era, defenders of forensics emphasized the intellectual and societal benefits of forensics as training in argument and logic and preparation for citizenship. During this era, forensics was considered a public good because participation yielded concrete benefits. As the public oratory era ended and the periods of the technical era began, scholars turned their attention to justifying forensics as a means of improving skills such as policy analysis, critical thinking, and research (Allen, 1963; Beckman, 1956; Brembeck, 1947; Gruner, Huseman, and Luck, 1971; Huseman, Ware, and Gruner, 1972; Jackson, 1961). Studies purporting to document those values were published in academic journals and reified in many argumentation and communication textbooks (Freeley and Steinberg, 2009).

Unfortunately, the evidence of purely intellectual benefit from forensics competition was sometimes contradictory, often anecdotal, and muddled in the sense that it has never been particularly clear which elements of the forensics experience contributed to a particular outcome. This is not, of course, unique to forensics. Virtually every level and type of educational experience shares the same difficulty in defending its presumed benefits and outcomes. How does one determine what subjects a fifth grader should learn and how she should learn them? Is a college education valuable? How should we assess the qualities of a good teacher? These questions are simultaneously ancient and modern.

The problem for forensics always has been its inferiority complex about being a cocurricular as opposed to a strictly curricular activity. As previously noted, the earliest antecedents of argumentation training were rigidly undertaken in the classroom in colonial schools and colleges. The literary society arose as a reaction to rigidity and truly was the earliest form of cocurricular education (Potter, 1944). The modern movement toward competitive speech and debate was a reaction to the excesses of the literary society. In the early years of the twentieth century, students clamoring for systematic training lobbied schools and colleges to add formal instruction in debate and public speaking as an integral part of the emerging discipline of speech communication (Smith, 1954).

As previously argued, the schism between forensics and the communication discipline began almost immediately after the founding of the various professional organizations in communication as communication departments, intellectually and financially, had to allocate scarce resources (Cohen, 1994). World War II became an important turning point, as the pressures on universities to meet highly specialized technical training demands and the similar pressures on high schools to properly prepare students for college created a maelstrom of contradiction. High student demand for speech and debate training and competition faced a system that provided less and less reward for teachers and college instructors to deliver that training and an increasingly technical set of competitive rules and norms that required increasing specialization by both teachers and students.

Forensics was pushed, especially at the college level, to the margins and became, in many institutions, a cocurricular activity rather than an integral curricular need. The overriding influence of tournaments interjected play into the equation and accelerated the drift of forensics from the curricular to the cocurricular and extracurricular classification. Competitive play generally was not considered an appropriate curricular strategy, and competitive forensics lost the tether to the curriculum and was increasingly perceived as fungible, along with sports, activities, and clubs, primarily valued as a diversion for students rather than as an essential educational element.

Forensics educators constantly pushed back against that perception, but their efforts met with limited success. When the North Central Association report recommended discontinuing speech and debate in high schools, the forensics community successfully brought pressure to bear to withstand implementation of the recommendation by stressing the educational benefits over forensics' popularity or the enjoyment it provided (Blyton, 1970). The new American Forensic Association and its members actively published scholarly books and articles justifying the educational benefits of forensics. As empirical data explaining the unique benefits of forensics training remained elusive, scholars relied on anecdotal evidence and self-reported data to argue, essentially, that we can't explain why forensics is beneficial or which particular elements are most beneficial, but since students self-report its significance in their later lives, it must be good. The consistent element absent in the argument was the activity's most obvious value of being a fun and playful way of learning, for there was a persistent fear that playfulness was an insufficient and almost unseemly way of explaining the success or importance of an activity increasingly isolated from the regular university and secondary school curriculum.

Forensics as Play

What is the value of playfulness, and how does this idea help explain the significance and value of forensics? Psychologist Peter Gray (2008) summarized the literature to identify the characteristics of play: "(1) Play is self-chosen and self-directed; (2) play is activity in which means are more valued than ends; (3) play has structure, or rules, which are not dictated by physical necessity but emanate from the minds of the players; (4) play is imaginative, non-literal, mentally removed in some way from 'real' or 'serious' life; and (5) play involves an active, alert, but non-stressed frame of mind." Gray noted that the essence of play lies in the perception of the player and that all of these characteristics might not be present for playing to occur.

Does forensics meet Gray's definition, and if so, what are the specific implications of this classification? A cursory examination confirms, at least at the definitional level, that competitive forensics constituted play for those who engaged in its activities.

Play Is Self-Chosen and Self-Directed

Students have always chosen to participate in forensics activities rather than having their participation required. While an occasional college department or school may have required students to experience competitive forensics, the vast majority of participants were self-enrolled. Justifications for the activity emphasized the role of personal motivation and self-direction in influencing competitive success.

Play Is Activity In Which Means Are More Valued than Ends

Forensics participants consistently were instructed that the process of debating and speaking outweighed the end product: competitive success. While participants frequently may have confused ends and means at particular points, overemphasis on competition generally was treated as outside the acceptable norms.

Play Has Rules Not Dictated by Necessity But Emanating from the Participants

The rules governing competitive forensics were arbitrary and developed over time. Rules about speaking times for individual speeches, speaking order, and appropriate speaking behaviors were never necessary but merely convenient and subject to constant evolution and change. The participants generated rules in order to facilitate the advancement of the play based on experiences and preferences associated with particular ways of engaging in the competitive fun.

Play Is Imaginative, Nonliteral, and Mentally Removed from "Real" Life

The first National Developmental Conference on Forensics, in its report, described forensics as a laboratory for argumentation and communication (McBath, 1975). The nature of forensics as a simulation has been well understood, even from the inception of competitive forensics prior to 1900. The clear dividing line between real argument and debate, such as political debates or campaign speeches, and the simulated context of college and high school forensics was always part of the rationale for why forensics could exist in the ways that it did.

Play Involves an Active, Alert, But Nonstressed Frame of Mind

While some would argue that participants, judges, and coaches must be active and alert in order to effectively engage in the play of forensics, some observers would likely take issue with this fifth element in the context of forensics as it relates to the second part of this element: the nonstressed frame of mind. Gray (2008) described this dimension:

> This final characteristic of play follows naturally from the other four. Because play involves conscious control of one's own behavior, with attention to process and rules, it requires an active, alert mind. Players do not just passively absorb information from the environment, or reflexively respond to stimuli, or behave automatically in accordance with habit. Moreover, because play is not a response to external demands or immediate strong biological needs, the person at play is relatively free from the strong drives and emotions that are experienced as pressure or stress. And because the player's attention is focused on process more than outcome, the player's mind is not distracted by fear of failure. So, the mind at play is active and alert, but not stressed. The mental state of play is what some researchers call "flow." Attention is attuned to the activity itself, and there is reduced consciousness of self and time. The mind is wrapped up in the ideas, rules, and actions of the game. This point about the mental state of play is very important for understanding play's value as a mode of learning and creative production. Play encourages conditions conducive to encouraging creativity and skill acquisition.

This is the most problematic issue in describing forensics as play. As forensics embraced competition during the technical era, a tension between outcome and process emerged. For some, the stress of having to speak quickly, take notes, find evidence, construct arguments, and answer questions in a technical environment took some of the enjoyment out of the forensics experience. However, for others, these technical demands and high-stress situations were exhilarating and part of the fun of competition. The difficulty for the forensics community became finding a middle ground in which both kinds of participants could have fun. This proved problematic for a number of reasons. We will return to this point after outlining the three dimensions of forensics that characterize the activity as play.

THREE DIMENSIONS OF FORENSICS AS PLAY

Why do students continue to participate in forensics when there are many other play forms vying for their time and attention? This may be one of the most persistent and fundamental questions underlying the history of forensics. Students have found forensics competition difficult and demanding of thoughtful and time-consuming preparation. Yet even as the dominant competitive forms and accompanying norms have changed (public debate to policy debate to individual events and multiple debate models), the popularity of the forensics activity has remained strong. A simple explanation might be the participants' recognition of the educational value of forensics as play. However, that explanation does not seem to be complete, as people do not always make rational choices even when they have adequate information. A more complete explanation must include three play-related elements of the activity: simulation, socialization, and community and conversation.

Simulation

Forensics is, first and foremost, a simulation. Most forms of forensics competition were grounded in the opportunity for students to practice or simulate skills necessary for active civic participation. Simulation is, of course, an example of active learning. The benefits of simulation and active learning are not new. Confucius identified their importance: "I hear and I forget. I see and I remember. I do and I understand" (Thum, 2012). Despite simulation's obvious benefits, education traditionally underutilized both it and play as teaching tools. Traditional models in both high school and college settings depended on lecture and memorization. Active learning was rarely used. This was one of the major reasons for the decline of the literary society movement in the late nineteenth century (Potter, 1954). Students began to rebel against the stifling environment caused by the narrow parameters of elocution, a point developed in chapter 2.

The emergence of competitive debate, as a fresh and new alternative to elocution and declamation prized by the remaining literary societies, grabbed the interest and attention of students and revealed the promise of active learning as a critical dimension of post-nineteenth-century education (Nichols, 1936a). Students could merge the stimulation of play with the simulation of civic preparation. Rather than simply reading about the law or politics, students could practice the necessary skills.

The significance of this transformation cannot be underestimated. The nineteenth-century college classroom often was boring. The literary society had emerged in colonial times because the sixteenth-century classroom was even more boring due to the rote manner of learning being practiced. Employing simulation, through competitive debate, was a welcome, fun antidote to the passive lecture and laboratory experiences common to high schools and colleges.

The rules of forensics contests evolved to support the simulation properties of the activities. Basic debate rules, such as turn taking, speaking time limits, and process rules like disallowing new arguments in rebuttals, closely paralleled the rules of courts and legislative debates. The rationale for these rules was found in the belief that simulation was the most important form of preparation for real-life experiences, not unlike a practice game in a sporting event.

Socialization

The second element of forensics as play came from the facilitation of socialization. Students traditionally participated in forensics as much for the relationship experience as for the learning. This is not, of course, unique to the forensics activity. Socialization is an important dimension of all team contexts. Players learn to cooperate for the success of the team. The opportunity to bond and socialize with like-minded people is a crucial human motivator. The socializing effects of forensics were evident in group settings (e.g., social organizations and competitive school teams), as well as on an individual level (e.g., intrapersonal and interpersonal contexts). In all, participants had considerable flexibility in self-selecting the aspect of forensics they found most enjoyable in order to retain their interest in the activity.

From its earliest precursor, the literary society, competitive speech and debate emphasized socialization. In the earliest literary societies, students would gather outside the classroom and combine social interaction with public speaking and debate. There would be banter, alcohol consumption, singing, and friendship. The participants had fun. They interacted with people who shared their interests and passions and made lasting friendships, the very heart of the socialization process.

When the competitive model emerged, the relative importance of socialization effects became even more pronounced. Debate teams were formed and became part of squads whose members spent considerable time together preparing and, after the tournament model became popular, traveling to tournaments. For many students, the travel opportunity was very attractive. The chance to see what they perceived to be exotic places, to wear formal clothes, to share a hotel room, to eat at a restaurant, and to meet people from different high schools or colleges who might have very different beliefs and values was a virtual cauldron of socialization (Engleberg, 1993; Friedley, 1992; Paine and Stanley, 2003).

The nature of competition invariably created interpersonal conflict. The zero-sum nature of tournament competition left one person or team, at least in the short run, unhappy. Losing became, to cite a cliché, a teachable moment. Gracefully accepting defeat, accepting personal responsibility rather than placing blame, and supporting the shortcomings of others could be learned and improved upon on a regular basis, as certainly would be true of any competitive endeavor such as sports. The difference between forensics and sports was the frequency with which defeat was encountered. Every single competitor would lose a debate or be outshown in a speech round. The reasons for a loss would not always be evident to the loser. The nature of judging forensics competition was inherently imprecise and impressionistic. The opportunity for any single competitor to infer unfairness was always there, and such inferences were common. However, the fact that competitors returned again and again to competitive settings demonstrated that there was something enjoyable in simply engaging in the activity, despite the outcome.

Involvement in forensics affected the personality development of its participants and built self-confidence. Mayer (1948) cited examples drawn from his experience of several ways forensics enhanced personality development, including the development of self-control, sportsmanship, improved judgment, deference to cooperation, enhanced initiative, greater courage, improved tact, honesty, and demonstrated leadership. While forensics could enhance these characteristics, Beaird (1937) aptly described how forensics empowered participants through competition: "The feeling of inferiority is eliminated through participation in the contests, and we often find students who have learned faith in themselves through facing and dealing with the difficult situations often afforded by the competitive contest" (p. 4).

Forensics not only affected the individual participants but also promoted community within a campus or school team, created a social fabric of participants from different schools, and established a professional social structure that spanned the country. Participation in forensics promoted the development of loyalty and social cohesiveness for teams, often providing first experiences for the participants, as Ewbank (1951) noted: "my first meal on a diner, my first night in a Pullman" (p. 3). Many students held among their fondest memories the social relationships developed while on the school team. One participant reminisced, "I'd love to gather up the old gang of 1942–44 and go on another debate trip to Denver or the Missouri Valley Tournament. Gee, we had a good time" (Olson, 1948, p. 67). One reason for the development of strong team loyalty and affiliation was the amount of time spent by the team while engaged in forensics. Buehler (1963) explained, "I saw much of the U.S.A. with my debaters. We traveled far and wide by train, bus, plane, and automobile. . . . More important are the scores of deep and abiding friendships . . . which grew out of squad meetings and the many forensic experiences" (p. 60).

The loyalty of students to their coaches and teammates surfaced regularly as particular milestones were reached. For example, when Alan Nichols of Southern California celebrated his twenty-fifth year of service in debate, more than two hundred gathered to pay tribute, because "in retrospect the victories are not nearly so important as the fellowship that developed between men twenty years apart who could feel close together because of the single common experience of having worked with [Dr. Nichols]" ("USC Testimonial Dinner," 1947, p. 61).

In addition to building team unity, forensics also created a social fabric of participants who shared the common experience of competition. The socialization that occurred was purposeful. At tournaments, students and coaches were more than adversaries; they were friends. As such, social opportunities in the form of banquets and dances were built into the competition schedule ("Special Feature," 1945).

As friendships formed, a network of forensics information was established through the numerous forensics publications that developed. College newspapers and literary magazines generated by debaters who were often journalists became the source of ideas and knowledge about people, programs, records, and activities across the country (Nichols, 1936b). The national network of forensics programs expanded as publications, such as the *Debater's Magazine* and *Speech Activities*, offered special features about a college or high school program making some distinct contribution to forensics activities or gaining a reputation for excellence. Often schools reflecting very different institutional sizes and missions were showcased, including Bates College (Maine), Ottawa University (Kansas), Boston University (Massachusetts), Bradley University (Illinois), Linfield College (Oregon), Manchester College (New Hampshire), Montana State University, Rutgers University (New Jersey), the University of Florida, the University of Michigan, the University of Redlands (California), Southwestern Louisiana Institute, and Southwestern College (Kansas).

Also promoting the social network of forensics teachers, coaches, and participants were regular columns titled "News, Notes and Personals," published in the *Debater's Magazine* and *Speech Activities*. This personalized publicity about individual and team successes in Delta Sigma Rho, Tau Kappa Alpha, Pi Kappa Delta, Phi Rho Pi, and the National Forensic League (NFL) came from correspondents whose job it was to report about individuals, their activities, and their organizations. The personal news (e.g., birth announcements, obituaries, promotions, new positions, alumni achievements) kept forensics colleagues and participants informed and connected. The inclusion of information about all of the honoraries in each of these early publications provided for a more interconnected community than existed during the latter part of the twentieth century, when the various forensics national groups became more self-focused in their publications.

Forensics provided opportunities for students of like mind and interest to associate with others on the road to leadership in their schools, communities, and nation. The historical records from every state and region of the country are replete with the names of individuals who became statesmen, teachers, educational leaders, textbook authors, forensic directors, journalists and broadcasters, lawyers and justices, doctors, preachers, businesspeople, homemakers, and leading citizens, to name a few (Ewbank, 1951; Fernandez, 1959; Fest, 1956; "Fifty Famous Alumni of Pi Kappa Delta," 1963; Quimby, 1952). Often their forensics experiences transcended several levels of education—from high school to college to graduate school—and provided for ongoing leadership opportunities. In a survey of 255 Nebraska alumni who participated in forensics from 1895 to 1945, "over 78 percent of the [163] people who returned the questionnaires thought that debate enabled them to take a greater position of leadership on the campus and in civic life" (Olson, 1948, p. 66).

The uniqueness of this competitive experience was also characterized by Constans (1949): "There is a certain value in actual inter-collegiate participation that comes to the individual, a stimulus . . . that he [sic] seldom, if ever, gets from practice debating in the classroom. Intercollegiate competition . . . provides the real test of his ability" (p. 153). Another aspect of community building involved the way forensics educators helped to facilitate competition and created structures for governance. Initially, as forensics activities sprang up around the country, universities functioned as facilitators for competition (Highsaw, 1916). For example, the University of Texas organized and coordinated the University Intercollegiate League forensic contests for Texas high schools (Hayes, 1952). Similarly, other universities (e.g., North Dakota) formed high school declamation leagues and debating unions. At the collegiate level, triangular, quadrangular, and pentagonal leagues were common as coaches sought venues for student competition (Perrill, 1935). Forensics teams regularly scheduled debating tours, as Jacob (1928) described: "Desiring a little travel farther than our customary debates into Illinois and Iowa and especially anxious to witness a presidential inauguration, I persuaded our department to let me schedule a debating tour into New England. Those jaunts are now common among colleges and not unheard of at all among high schools, but in the day it was about the first venture of the kind" (n.p.).

As the interest in forensics activities grew and the Great Depression and limited funds restricted schools' ability to travel great distances, the tournament format emerged, in which, at a designated site, hundreds of students from dozens of schools could participate in public speaking, debate, and the performing arts (Hanks, 1948).

Researchers have only modestly examined the socialization effects of forensics (Friedley, 1992; Paine and Stanley, 2003). This is due in part to the justificatory preoccupation with defending the activity on its intellectual values and the imprecision with which socialization effects are understood and measured. There is no shortage, however, of anecdotal evidence on the question. Participants have always fondly reminisced about friendships, travel anecdotes, "war stories" from particular tournaments, debates, and speeches.

Community and Conversation

The third play element of forensics centers on how play encourages a sense of community and conversation. A recurring theme in the history of forensics is the presence and importance of the community and how various communities have encouraged forensics conversation and interaction. Sociologists have typically defined a community as a group of people interacting in a common location who share, to some degree, common beliefs and values. The power and value of communities is evident. Communities create a shared sense of belonging and commonality with others that is essential to good health and well-being.

Portes (1998) described social capital functionally, quoting Coleman's definition: "a variety of entities with two elements in common: they all consist of some aspect of social structure, and they facilitate certain actions of actors . . . within the structure" (p. 5). From this perspective, social capital could take any form in order to facilitate interaction between individuals, groups, organizations, or cultures. Portes concluded that social capital was neutral, but positive or negative results could occur depending upon how individuals chose to use it. Putnam (2000) was more directional in his focus, suggesting that social capital had value and played a key role in the preservation of democracy, which he suggested was declining in the United States as evidenced by a lower public trust in government and lower levels of civic engagement. He also suggested that social capital could be measured by the amount of trust and "reciprocity" in a community or between individuals.

One of the qualities of forensics as play was its role in creating social capital through the shared experiences and interactions of its participants. Even the title of Putnam's (2000) acclaimed book, *Bowling Alone: The Collapse and Revival of American Community*, established this point. Putnam noted the loss of bowling leagues in society as evidence that people were less engaged with each other. Putnam's point was not simply the absence of the leagues themselves but also the opportunities for engaging with other people and finding and reinforcing community values. Much as Putnam claims that the value of bowling leagues goes beyond the sheer interactivity occurring, forensics has always been much more than simply a competitive outlet for talented participants. Forensics in each historical era has led to the building of social capital, albeit in different ways.

Creation of Social Capital during the Public Oratory Era

During the public oratory era, the connection between forensics and play and the creation of social capital was straightforward. The explicit rationale for forensics was grounded in creating connections between people. This was a lingering by-product of the literary societies. Those societies were among the critical interpersonal connections of the evolving university environment (Potter, 1954). The societies were created in large part to provide the opportunity for students to interact outside the stilted classroom environment. Debating public issues, even when shrouded in larger philosophical questions, not only developed the arguing and decision-making skills of participants but also helped them forge relationships with other potential leaders and create connections. The connections could be either enduring political or social partnerships or shared bonds of trust among adversaries. The bond of trust was the expectation that even in disagreement over policies, an underlying respect and personal relationship would keep the disagreement from either becoming violent or threatening the destruction of the relationship. A fundamental aspect of much of American political history was the idea of "disagreeing without being disagreeable," which came into being, in part, through the literary society debating process and the social capital created through debate as a form of play. This fundamental contribution of the literary society to democracy cannot be underestimated.

When the literary societies declined in popularity, due in part to moving away from the sharpness of intellectual dispute through debate toward more formalized contests in elocution, competitive debate and public speaking emerged and included practices that contributed to the creation of social capital. Early debate contests were highly social occasions. There was considerable pomp and circumstance surrounding the actual debate, creating interest and excitement. In rural areas, communities were very interested in public forensic events. A professor at the University of North Dakota explained,

> North Dakota is a state of small towns and when a debate concerning grain elevators, parcel post, working men's compensation, is held by two rival schools, the citizens are really interested. . . . Last winter, in a certain town, the train bringing the opposing team was six hours late. It was a bitter cold night, but the audience waited until 12:30 p.m. [*sic*] We then began the debate—nobody left—and followed it with a banquet. It was 5 a.m. when the last toast was finished. (Highsaw, 1916, pp. 374–75)

High school debaters joined college teams in providing their communities with exposure to forensics through public debates. Highsaw (1916) reported that between 1902 and 1912, "It is safe to say that if we consider the entire 48 states and the various local interscholastic debating leagues, it is probable that 5,000,000 people have listened to these [high school] debates in the last decade, or 5% of the entire population" (p. 381). In the early years of the century, communities responded enthusiastically when local high school students were successful or needed support. In one instance, when a student won a national championship at the NFL National Tournament, "the school was so appreciative of [her] national victory that they declared a holiday, the chamber of commerce honored her at a special program, and the town had a parade" ("National Forensic League Contests," 1946, p. 164). The ability of forensics to stimulate intense feelings of partisanship and promote new experiences for students and communities remains a significant cause of its popularity during this era.

Social capital is grounded in the premise that people appreciate a larger world than their own. It is easy to see how forensics, particularly during the public oratory era, aided in building that appreciation. Students involved in forensics activities were exposed to topics in a wide range of disciplines beyond just the social science frameworks of policy disputes. Students studied the humanities, as well as significant social, political, economic, and international issues of the day. For example, in participating in public speaking and oral interpretation events, students needed to find and select appropriate material from literature or explore philosophical perspectives useful in unprepared events, as well as learning from the work of famous orators.

Jones (1954) shared the influence of the humanities on his education: "My teachers always stressed the need for good material, and we were encouraged to read widely in both classical and modern literature. The study we made of some of the world's great orations was especially stimulating" (p. 17). Participants also confronted significant issues of the day and used forensics as a way to express their thoughts and emotions. Secord and Thomas (1946) explained, "When a farm boy writes an oration about some phase of the Federal farm program which is within his grasp; when a negro [*sic*] student writes an oration entitled, 'On Being Black'; when any thoughtful high-school student writes an oration concerning juvenile delinquency; those are orations. They come from the heart and emotions are involved" (p. 7).

The role of students

Several characteristics of forensics significantly contributed to the creation of social capital. The first characteristic was the powerful role that students played in creating programs, organizing on-campus and off-campus events, and promoting the activity to various constituencies. Students were the organizers and enjoyed forming debating societies, engaging in practical activities to stimulate their critical thinking and develop their speaking skills, preparing for and sponsoring intersociety competitions, serving as student managers, and actually coaching themselves (Stone, 1914). Competitive forensics was a bottom-up, student-initiated educational innovation. While faculty sponsors were sought out to provide legitimacy for forensics at their home institutions, the students actively worked to establish competitive programming and lobbied for academic credit for their efforts (Foster, 1904; Nichols, 1936a; Smith, 1954). Once faculty members were teaching argumentation and oratory for credit, students sought a change in the practical function of the faculty advisor. Team members realized that those students with faculty coaches tended to win more contests than those without faculty coaches (Cowperthwaite, 1946; Nichols, 1936a, 1936b; Sillars, 1949). Even with a faculty advisor, the practical operation of forensics programs was typically run by students. A student manager scheduled competitions with other schools, negotiated the specifics of the competition (including the wording of the resolution, time limits, judges, and the location of the all-too-necessary banquet after the event), made the necessary travel arrangements, engaged in precontest coaching, and handled the public relations.

A position of celebrity

During the public oratory era, debaters were treated as celebrities, not unlike the admiration given to contemporary athletes in schools and colleges today. Orators and debaters enjoyed the fun of often being popular figures and student leaders, causing the public to regard forensics as an elite activity and uplifting its status in schools and on college campuses. Anyone could join a literary or debating society; however, in the beginning, only the very best were chosen through local competitions to participate in intersociety or interschool competitions (Levin and Goodfriend, 1914). The number of individuals actually traveling outside their state for forensic competition was even smaller (Nichols, 1936b, 1937).

An emphasis on local prominence

During the public oratory era, forensics was closely associated with the local community. While there were opportunities for interstate competition, forensics drew its initial strength from the actual demonstration of argumentation and oratorical skills in local schools and community halls in cities, towns, and villages. The school campuses and surrounding communities served as the centers of activity and competition, and engaging in local contests and being selected to represent one's literary society or school against a neighboring school's best speakers served as its own reward, as Jacob (1928) described in his autobiographical sketch: "The sensation of defeating a neighboring city only half our size in a single debate was sufficient to make forensic interest the chief consideration in choosing my college and so I came to Ripon" (n.p.). Winning the top prize—a scholarship, gold watch, medallion, or cup—was an honor that made up for the fact there were usually few tangible rewards for competitive success (Stone, 1914).

In addition, debaters and speakers ventured out into local communities to speak and perform at the meetings of various civic groups (e.g., Knights of Columbus, the YWCA, Lions Clubs, and the Sons of Norway) (Schrier, 1930). The value of these extension efforts was noted: "The college debater can do more than any one group to establish their [the community's] public understanding of the college and its work, and it is upon such understanding that favorable public opinion depends" (Cortright, 1933, p. 9). High school students also extended themselves into the surrounding communities through speaker's bureaus. During World War II, many high schools "furnished high school students as speakers for civilian defense programs, bond sales drives, salvage drives, and other emergency efforts" (Secord and Thomas, 1946, p. 8).

A focus on the audience

The audience-centered nature of forensics during the public oratory era made a crucial contribution to creating social capital. The diverse views of patrons of forensics (teachers, judges, students, community supporters) required that participants make substantial efforts to adapt their arguments and speeches to audiences. Forensics was considered an important entertainment outlet for communities starved for diversion. Initially, debaters and speakers were taught to use familiar historical and literary examples, in lieu of extensive reporting of facts or direct quotations, as those forms appealed more generally to local audiences. The feature film *The Great Debaters* (Washington, 2007) provided clear examples of this process. Speakers incorporated humor, sarcasm, and stylistic appeals as common strategies for creating audience interest (Foster, 1904).

As debaters sought to keep the interest and attention of their audiences, formal prepared speeches gave way to more extemporaneous and adaptive ones. Similarly, as audiences became less willing to attend debates lasting over two hours in length, the number of speakers on a team was reduced from three to two, and the speaking time for each speaker was shortened (Foster, 1904; *Harvard vs. Yale*, 1917). Since audiences often decided the winners of the early forensics contests, speakers adapted to what they believed the audience expected in order to gain their favor. Adaptation also was needed for community judges unfamiliar with conventions associated with particular forensics activities or contests (*Debating*, n.d.; Levin and Goodfriend, 1914). While the relationship—both individually and collectively—between social capital and forensics was very clear in the public oratory era, this close connection was less clear during the technical era, although it did not altogether disappear.

Creation of Social Capital during the Technical Era

The technical era roughly corresponded to Putnam's (2000) timing of when the breakdown of social capital creation became evident. This was not a coincidence,

as forensics became focused less on the very social capital elements that characterized the public oratory era in favor of an emphasis on the individualistic and
personal benefits of forensics. Scholars shifted their emphasis toward attempting
to validate the personal benefits of forensics competition and virtually ignored
examining the social value of forensics. As noted earlier, as the activity evolved,
so did the students who participated in its various events. What had been enjoyable in the public oratory era gave way to a new kind of enjoyment as participants
found personal advancement and individual achievement appealing.

The significant numbers of research reports in the public oratory era that emphasized the public benefits of forensics participation on preparation for public
service were replaced by research activities designed to demonstrate the value
of forensics training in enhancing critical thinking skills and other personal
benefits. The growing trend in communication research toward a preference
for empiricism fueled this tendency. Communication theory, perceived in some
quarters as a fuzzy or imprecise field, felt compelled to justify its existence
through increasingly narrow and specific research emphases. The subdiscipline
of rhetoric, with a heavy emphasis in the public oratory era on public address
studies, evolved into the highly technical study of various critical methods
prized for their ability to deconstruct the meanings of messages rather than appreciate the aesthetic and social values of public discourse. A key change in the
technical era was the fading of the traditional relationship between forensics
and social capital toward a new model emphasizing the personal benefits of
forensics. In the public oratory era, forensics was justified because the activity
created a social or public good. In the technical era, forensics became a vehicle
for private or personal good.

As discussed in the previous section, in minimizing some aspects associated
with forensics that might have been fun for participants, educators justified the
activity as an important means of training for students to become active citizens
and societal participants. In this model, dominant terms included "audiences,"
"persuasion," and "holistic preparation." In the private-personal model of the
technical era, forensics was justified as an individualistic training that helped
students become better thinkers and critics. The dominant terms included "critical thinking," "research," and "strategy." This is not to suggest that the role of
building social capital was nonexistent in the technical era, only to be revived in a
post-technical era, but merely that its importance was sublimated to the perceived
demands of a scientific and technical world in the fifty years after the conclusion
of World War II.

Debate topics gradually became more specific and technical in nature during
this time, and an emerging argumentation and debate theory emphasized students
learning and appreciating arcane debate theories, such as judging paradigms,
counterplans, and counterwarrants, as means of winning debates without much

regard to the value of such theories in promoting debate training as a means of generating social capital. Competition in public speaking and oral interpretation events, while still an enjoyable aspect of forensics for the participants, similarly devolved toward a preference for form over content, and students adapted.

An important intellectual influence helps explain this significant change in emphasis: the emergence of critical thinking as an emphasis in higher education and, more specifically in forensics, the introduction of the Toulmin model (Brockriede and Ehninger, 1960; Toulmin, 1958).

The fun of critical thinking

Glaser (1941) first introduced the concept of critical thinking as a human construct and educational goal. In describing critical thinking, he suggested,

> Critical thinking calls for a persistent effort to examine any belief or supposed form of knowledge in the light of the evidence that supports it and the further conclusions to which it tends. It also generally requires ability to recognize problems, to find workable means for meeting those problems, to gather and marshal pertinent (relevant) information, to recognize unstated assumptions and values, to comprehend and use language with accuracy, clarity, and discrimination, to interpret data, to appraise evidence and evaluate arguments, to recognize the existence (or nonexistence) of logical relationships between propositions, to draw warranted conclusions and generalizations, to put to the test the conclusions and generalizations at which one arrives, to reconstruct one's patterns of beliefs on the basis of wider experience, and to render accurate judgments about specific things and qualities in everyday life. (p. 6)

In essence, critical thinking enabled forensics participants to engage in complex thinking that challenged them and provided great joy when used effectively to win. Glaser's work influenced other scholars and fit nicely with the drive to promote science and empiricism in 1950s America.

The relationship of critical thinking to education was not new. Dewey (1916) advocated that approach at the beginning of the century. The belief that debate training could enhance critical thinking was quickly adopted by debate scholars and just as quickly became the new rationale for the activity. If critical thinking were the key skill necessary for living in a technologically sophisticated world, and if debate training could improve critical thinking, that would make debate training an important educational tool. Whether the premises and conclusion of that syllogism are correct is beyond the scope of the current discussion, but the linking of the critical thinking movement to forensics changed the fundamental assumptions of the activity and pushed the earlier beliefs in the power of debate training as crucial to generating social capital out of the spotlight.

Toulmin's model

Toulmin's contribution to intellectual thought in various fields is well documented, but his work was particularly salient in argumentation theory when his ideas were introduced to American audiences by scholars, including Robert Newman, Wayne Brockriede, and Douglas Ehninger. Toulmin's early writings focused on the flaws of absolutism in traditions of formal logic. Toulmin (1958) reinforced the importance of relative rather than universal truths because universal ones could not be upheld because they had no practical value.

While always controversial in philosophy and other disciplines, the communication discipline almost immediately adopted Toulmin's work. Traditional rhetoric and formal logic, the foundations of argumentation theory in the public oratory era, were, in a relatively short time, replaced by an emphasis on arguments influenced by the nature of appropriate data, warrants, and claims. This approach fit perfectly with educational systems seeking to teach critical thinking and research skills. The particular audience replaced the universal audience, and it became necessary to increasingly focus forensics training on an increasingly narrowly conceived set of variables.

This sea change was not unique to debate and certainly not universally accepted. Critical thinking also was, in a more general sense, part of the rationale for the emergence of empiricism and the new influences in communication theory that supplanted the traditional humanistic approaches of rhetoric in the communication discipline after World War II. A few debate scholars and critics began a critique of the changing nature of debate in the 1950s and strongly urged a return to the more traditional practices of the public oratory era. Perhaps the most vehement of critics was Stelzner (1961), one of whose criticism titles in 1961 reflects this view: "Tournament Debate: Emasculated Rhetoric." Stelzner's views typified an increasingly isolated group of debate scholars whose views would disappear for some years only to gradually reappear when the schisms in the debate community emerged after 1970.

THE CHANGING NATURE OF FORENSICS AS FUN

While not as heavily emphasized, social capital processes were present in the technical era. These processes were the source of fun for early participants in forensics, and the various processes of the public oratory era helping to generate social capital did not completely disappear during the technical era, even as they were supplanted by the emphasis on critical thinking and personal growth. There are several examples of important social capital building processes.

First was the attempt to adapt debate to television. Even before the Kennedy-Nixon presidential debates of 1960, there was interest in televising college debates, due in part to the fact that debates had been broadcast over the radio for decades, dating back to the 1930s. As a mass medium, television was still relatively new and exciting. Critics, such as Newton Minow, characterized the medium as a "vast wasteland" (McBath, 1964). However, the attraction of audiences to the Kennedy-Nixon debates accelerated interest in televised debates, resulting in a sixteen-week series, *Championship Debate*, in 1962. The series was telecast as a daytime educational program and pitted college debate teams and three judges in a half-hour format with a new topic each telecast. The program was well regarded but did not draw a particularly large viewing audience (McBath, 1964). Two important groups viewing the debates included college and high school classes, raising the profile of debate as an educational tool, which doubtless contributed to the role of debate training as a means of creating social capital.

Second was the emergence of regional, national, and activity-particular (e.g., debate leagues) competition circuits. One important change in the technical era was the emergence of various competitive circuits of tournaments. These circuits, based on the earlier idea of triangular and quadrangular leagues, were created primarily for competitive reasons but also became an important opportunity for competitor and educator interactions. The circuits likewise gave rise to the emergence of competitive norms, which were a significant defining characteristic of the technical era. The emergence of competitive norms created a clear tension in the social dynamics of forensics between adaptation to local norms and the need to conform to broader, more national competitive norms. This tension was an important issue during the technical era.

The competitive circuits, in which forensics programs tended to concentrate their activities, emerged in the 1930s with the popularization of tournaments, but they did not reach their full significance until after forensics reemerged from World War II. The obvious initial cause of these emerging circuits was logistical. It simply was easier and less costly to attend nearby tournaments. The concept of circuits was institutionalized by West Point in the structuring of the National Debate Tournament (NDT). West Point allocated invitations using a regional system to ensure that the tournament was truly national in character. Selected forensics directors from the eight regions were invited to nominate teams for the West Point tournament. This system, in various permutations, became the basis for national tournament participation and was very similar to the system already in place for high schools through the NFL.

The circuit system and the competitive-season-defining West Point national tournament, in addition to the coalescence of the various honoraries around a single national topic chosen in a highly organized and predictable manner, shaped the competitive landscape. Forensics programs could begin to budget in a predictable way, as it became easier to predict costs and plan for competition. Tournaments expanded the use of experience-based divisions when tournament size warranted. The early Pi Kappa Delta practice of separating men's and women's divisions continued until the 1970s, although it became increasingly more common for women to participate in the men's division, and the practice generally disappeared by the 1960s.

The forensics tournament itself was an opportunity for building social capital, initially through judge adaptation. As the technical era progressed, the role of the contest judge changed. In the public oratory era, the emphasis in judging was on providing a wide range of judges for competitive rounds, including lay judges untrained beyond familiarization with contest rules, whose focus was primarily on delivery and style with less emphasis on the technical qualities of the arguments except in their broadest rhetorical sense. Debate ballots often consisted merely of a place to indicate the winner of the contest. That individual judges would apply often wildly different standards was a given, despite the objections of scholars early on that judging ought to be more standardized and predictable, so as to enhance the educational experience.

One by-product of the competitive circuit was the opportunity for competitors to familiarize themselves with the vagaries of judges, whom they might encounter at other tournaments during a season or at the same tournament in the following season. Debaters became more conscious of the need to adapt their arguments and strategies to the judges' proclivities. At the same time, participating in circuit tournaments meant that they might debate another team multiple times in front of different judges. This contributed to the fun and popularity of tournaments. The intellectual and strategic opportunities multiplied exponentially. Determining why you lost a particular debate to a particular team in front of a particular judge became the basis for preparing for the next tournament. The particular audience and situation replaced the universal audience and situation.

A preoccupation with the particular audience rather than the universal one was not, of course, confined to debate and speech competition. Advertising, audience analysis, public relations, and opinion polling were also gathering steam during this time. Advertisers were creating more focused and nuanced messages, and politicians were learning to measure and adapt to the preferences of voters. In this context, the idea of judge adaptation was a useful training tool preparing students for social participation. Unfortunately, in the context of competitive debate and speaking during the technical era, the adaptation to the particular audience led to another unanticipated outcome: the preferred audience.

The preferred audience standard describes a phenomenon that grew rapidly during the technical era, when competitors were increasingly compelled to conform to an idealized competitive standard that reflected competitive preferences at the margin rather than the center of the educational objectives of the activity. Judging evolved toward finding homogeneity in preference, reflecting practices at the national circuit level rather than the local. The three most prominent elements of this preferred audience standard were the shift toward norms of rapid delivery in debate, preference for expert testimony as the strongest form of evidence in reasoning, and highly standardized practices in competitive public speaking and oral interpretation events.

Doubtless the most controversial aspect of debate in the technical era concerned delivery, a point discussed earlier in chapter 7. Rapid delivery, commonly referred to as the "spread" style of debate, in which the debater attempted to present as much content as possible in the hopes of overwhelming the opponent, was not a theoretical change that happened after considerable scholarly discussion, in the way that other innovations, such as the Toulmin model or the comparative advantages case, emerged at roughly the same time. The spread style of debate became popular over time, particularly on the national circuit level; as more debaters adopted it and more judges accepted it, this style became the norm, which percolated down through the local college level and, inevitably, to the high school level. Rapid delivery became the preferred norm, even as the larger academic community pilloried it (Christopherson, 1960; Friedman, 1957; McBath and Cripe, 1965; Stelzner, 1961; Swinney, 1968).

Controversy over the spread style was a major factor in causing the schisms of the technical era, when there were major defections from policy debate toward more substantial emphasis on public speaking and oral interpretation and, later, nonpolicy debate. Eventually, as the technical era gave ground to the postmodern era, emphasis on the spread style began to wane, although it had not disappeared by any means by the end of the century.

The preferred audience standard was the defining characteristic of the national circuit beginning to emerge in the 1950s and which was very influential for the rest of the technical era. The antecedents of the national circuit can be traced back to the earliest days of the public oratory era. During that time, from roughly 1900 to 1930, there were three competitive forms: the single-occasion dual debate between schools, the triangular or quadrangular leagues, and the debate tour. During a debate tour, a squad would travel long distances, usually by train, and debate various other squads along the way. The debate tour was popularized during the period when the honoraries began to host national conventions, and the tour gave squads the chance to meet and debate other schools while presumably mitigating their travel costs by being supplied a place to stay and an occasional banquet meal. The growth of the tournament model in the 1930s, together with financial difficulties created by the Great Depression, largely ended the practice until after World War II.

The national policy debate circuit was not a formal system but consisted of a predictable set of tournaments, which squads that aspired to be successful at the NDT and that had budgets sufficient to extensively travel chose to attend, with a reasonable expectation that other aspiring squads would also attend. While some of these national tournaments required an invitation from the host, the more prevalent model was always the open tournament, the participants of which would include not only the nationally aspiring squads but also squads from the surrounding regional circuit and far-away teams choosing to attend to test their debating abilities against nationally competitive debaters. The characteristics of the circuit were magnified. Strategizing about particular opponents and judges was necessary for success. Styles, arguments, and judging preferences became more homogenous, and debaters wishing to break in needed to adapt to those preferences and helped disseminate the preferences to the various local circuits, not unlike bees pollinating plants.

The national circuit became, in a sense, the commonality constituting an important source of social capital during the technical era. The coaches of the national circuit programs were recognized as the leaders of the activity, or at least the trendsetters. Innovations in debate practice started at that level before spreading out across the country. Graduates of the national programs sometimes went on to coach in other programs, reinforcing the interdependence of the programs and the national circuit. The system was not closed, and programs moved in and out of the national circuit due to various factors: effective coaches, strong school support, and, most notably, talented debaters able to master the intricacies of national circuit debate. The decision by the NDT to give at-large bids to the tournament, with the teams selected by vote of the NDT committee, effectively reinforced the system. To receive a competitive at-large bid, a team presumably had to have a successful record in the most strenuous competition, which was at the national circuit tournaments.

The national circuit tournaments also introduced another innovation: power matching. Power matching was probably first introduced at the West Point national tournament. Rather than having a random matching system, teams were matched using systems based on their previous record in the tournament in an attempt to achieve the most accurate ranking of the teams going into the elimination rounds. Prior to the West Point tournament, there was not a particular priority in power matching, since there seemed to be less at stake for winning and losing. As the national circuit became more prominent and the zero-sum game of qualifying for and being successful at the National Debate Tournament increasingly influenced norms, power matching at tournaments became much more common.

Power matching did have a side effect: it provided opportunities for social interaction. Debaters could get to know one another more easily, not only because they would compete against each other at various tournaments throughout the season but also because there was time during the tournament for interaction while waiting for the next round, which was scheduled after a delay to allow power matching. Even as elimination rounds continued, there would be groups of contestants advancing and eliminated who formed bonds of friendship and camaraderie. The establishment of personal relationships between participants was one of the most significant social influences of the technical and post-technical eras. While easy to visualize in the post-technical era with the growing importance of social media, the social interactions between like-minded individuals participating in forensics during the technical era were a marked change from the public oratory era, when only coaches had the opportunity to establish long-lasting relationships. This is not to characterize this socialization as completely benign, as the competition norms were always present and mitigated the deep personal relationships characterized by genuine play, but the relationships between competitors from different programs were likely as important a source of socialization, as were the relationships formed by students in other realms of their university and school experience.

THE DOWNSIDE OF FORENSICS AS PLAY

Before concluding this chapter, we must address the circumstances under which the play metaphor led to undesirable consequences in the activity. Forensics as play invited the use of game theory as a guide to practice. There is nothing inherently wrong with game theory, and it is an important theoretical concept in various disciplines. Placed in the context of a competition-grounded activity such as forensics, however, game theory created the likelihood of competitors testing the rules and norms of the game. This may be human nature. There have been, throughout the history of forensics, any number of different conflicts grounded in both actual and perceived violations of particular rules and norms governing behavior generally and competition in particular. Three such conflicts are worthy of brief mention to establish our point: concerns about the ethics of rapid delivery in debate, the fairness and predictability of competitive judging, and whether the activity was biased against women and nonwhite competitors. We will discuss the first two concerns in this chapter and leave the question of sex and ethnicity to the following chapters.

Rapid delivery in debate was the lightning rod for conflict about the ethics, values, and practices of forensics during the century. Rapid delivery, often referred to as "spread delivery," became a shorthand reference for a variety of disagreements among forensics educators. Delivery at one level became the dispute over whether forensics was a communication-centered or information-centered activity. It represented the eternal dispute between style and invention as dominant rhetorical canons. It was the stand-in for disagreement about ethical standards for participants and the desirability of national competition norms for guiding practice. Delivery became the tipping point for both the emergence of stand-alone public speaking and interpretation contests and the wide splintering of the debate community in the mid- and late technical era. Outside observers invariably commented on what they perceived to be incomprehensible delivery rates in high school and college debates and made the unfavorable comparison between those contests and the "ideal" debate, usually without providing any description of the characteristics of the ideal. Delivery represented the case study for the massive difficulties in finding consensus about the educational values of forensics, as well as the inability of practitioners to engage one another in serious academic discussion of the underlying issues and their tendency instead to resort to invective and scorn.

The spread strategy was a by-product of the forces changing debate competition during the technical era. As debate became a more private than public good, style changed to reflect nonexistent audiences, the imperatives of information presentation in a future shock age, and the importance of gamesmanship as a behavioral motivator. Debaters talked fast because in a zero-sum game, the benefits outweighed the costs. The siren song of success in national competition was far more seductive than the clucking of critics who themselves chose the route of either leaving the debate activity or creating their own new organization whose purpose was invariably to "correct the flaw" created by rapid delivery. That strategy of separation was regularly employed (and continues to be). New debate forms and organizations such as the Cross-Examination Debate Association, International Public Debate Association and National Parliamentary Debate Association debate, and NFL Lincoln-Douglas all represented this strategy, but almost inevitably the debates, over time, came to represent the strategies and flaws of their predecessor. Each organization reverted to the default.

Forensics was hardly alone in witnessing the downside of play. Recruiting scandals in college athletics, drug scandals in professional and amateur sports, and the infamous sports gambling scandals represented the same phenomena in much more public venues. The devastating effects of rapid delivery on the forensics activity, however, seemed to outweigh the effects of these other issues on their respective sports. This is not due to some consensus about the ethics of rapid delivery or some belief that rapid speaking is harmful. Rather, the conflict reflected the deep-seated underlying disagreement about whether forensics was central to the rhetorical tradition of the communication discipline as well as the inherent gap between well-funded and nationally successful forensics programs and those with less resources and a different orientation. We discussed the nature of this divergence in chapters 5 and 6. The technical era was characterized by pervasive jealousies manifested in the competition-stoked matter of delivery in debate.

The second controversial perspective caused by the forensics-as-play viewpoint was the long-standing dispute about contest judging. This issue emerged concurrently with the growing popularity of contest speaking and debating in the public oratory era. Writers discussed whether decision debating itself was proper, whether judges should be trained or lay, whether there should be empirical standards for licensing judges, and, much later, whether the contestants themselves should have input regarding their judges in the form of mutual preference or strike systems in tournaments. This issue again is a cover for the deeper issue of what the role of forensics should be. Should the debaters and speakers adapt to the audience, or should the audience (judge) respect the choices made by the speakers? When the contest was considered as a game with rules, almost inevitably the pendulum shifted in the direction of encouraging the judges to adapt to the speakers, made all the easier by the tendency of those judges perceived to be outside the contest norm to leave that particular activity in favor of one the judges perceived to be more consistent with their personal and professional beliefs. Contests became dominated by self-selection bias in which homogeneity was preferred as a critical means of reinforcing the paradigm that the purpose of the contest was to identify the best contestants rather than primarily to help students become more skillful arguers and speakers.

CONCLUSION

This chapter analyzed the underlying sustainability of forensics relating to its function as an enjoyable and fun activity for competitors. The value of fun in education is well understood. However, as we have shown, in an effort to justify the legitimacy of forensics within the curricula of speech departments, the fun aspect of forensics had to be minimized. Students benefited from simulation, socialization, and community and conversation. Simulation enabled students to have fun while practicing their critical thinking and communication skills in the laboratory setting of a tournament. Socialization for students competing in forensics was inherently part of the competitive structures that were created and resulted in positive, lifelong relationships and memories. The building of social capital through communication and participation in different contexts within the forensics community was satisfying and contributed to relationships and practices that supported the continuation of particular forms of forensics, despite criticism from different forensics groups. While there were both positive and negative implications of possibly minimizing the fun of forensics in favor of justifying the activities on the basis of their educational value, our contention is simply that the reason forensics survived the extreme tensions it experienced during its evolution in the twentieth century was that, inherently, forensics was fun; those who participated in its activities enjoyed what they were doing, and that enjoyment kept them coming back for more. In the following chapters, we change our focus from the positive aspects of forensics as fun to the darker side of forensics that reflected its prejudices and elitist perspectives as they applied to different ethnic groups and women.

REFERENCES

Allen, R. R. (1963, February). The effects on interpersonal and concept compatibility of the encoding behavior and achievement of debate teams. *Central States Speech Journal, 14*, 23–26.

Beaird, T. M. (1937). Educational value in speech contests. *Rostrum, 12* (4), 4–5.

Beckman, V. (1956). An investigation and analysis of the contributions to critical thinking made by courses in argumentation and discussion in selected colleges. Unpublished dissertation. Minneapolis: University of Minnesota.

Blyton, G. (1970). The American Forensic Association: A history. *Journal of the American Forensic Association, 7* (1), 13–16.

Brembeck, W. L. (1947). The effects of a course in argumentation on critical thinking. Unpublished dissertation. Madison: University of Wisconsin.

Brockriede, W. E., and Ehninger, D. (1960). Toulmin on argument: An interpretation. *Quarterly Journal of Speech, 46*, 44–53.

Buehler, E. C. (1963). What Delta Sigma Rho has done for me. *Gavel of Delta Sigma Rho, 45* (4), 59–60.

Christopherson, M. G. (1960). The need for style in argument. *Communication Education, 9* (2), 116–20.

Cohen, H. (1994). *The history of speech communication: The emergence of a discipline, 1914–1945.* Annandale, VA: Speech Communication Association.

Constans, H. P. (1949). The role of intercollegiate debate tournaments in a post-war period. *Speech Activities, 5* (4), 151–53.

Cortright, R. L. (1933). Forensic values for the college. *Gavel of Delta Sigma Rho, 16* (1), 8–10.

Cowperthwaite, L. L. (1946). History of intercollegiate forensics at the State University of Iowa. Unpublished thesis. Ames: Iowa State University.

Debating: History of the Harvard-Princeton-Yale Triangulars, 1909–1959. (n.d.). Available at Harvard University Archives: HUD 11320.959.

Dewey, J. (1916). *Democracy and education: An introduction to the philosophy of education.* New York: Macmillan.

Engleberg, I. N. (1993). Frankfurters to forensics. *Communication Education, 42*, 307–9, 399.

Ewbank, H. L. (1951). Debating in the good old days. *Gavel of Delta Sigma Rho, 34* (1), 6–9.

Fernandez, T. L. (1959). 108 years of oratory. *Gavel of Delta Sigma Rho, 41* (4), 51.

Fest, T. B. (1956). Golden jubilee citations. *Gavel of Delta Sigma Rho, 38* (4), 99–105.

Fifty famous alumni of Pi Kappa Delta. (1963). *Forensic of Pi Kappa Delta, 48* (3), 27–55.

Foster, W. T. (1904). *Debating at Harvard University.* Cambridge, MA: Caustic-Claflin Company.

Freeley, A. J., and Steinberg, D. L. (2009). *Argumentation and debate* (12th ed.). Boston: Wadsworth Cengage.

Friedley, S. A. (1992). Forensics as a laboratory experience in interpersonal communication. *National Forensic Journal, 10* (1), 51–56.

Friedman, R. P. (1957). Why not debate persuasively? *Communication Quarterly, 5* (1), 32–34.

Glaser, E. M. (1941). *An experiment in the development of critical thinking.* New York: Columbia University Teachers College.

Gray, P. (2008). Freedom to learn. Retrieved from http://www.psychologyto day.com/blog/freedom-learn/200811/the-value-play-i-the-definition-play -provides-clues-its-purpose?page=4.

Gruner, C. R., Huseman, R. C., and Luck, J. L. (1971). Debating ability, critical thinking ability, and authoritarianism. *Speaker and Gavel, 8,* 63–65.

Hanks, L. D. (1948). A modern forensic program. *Debater's Magazine, 4* (2), 68–70.

Harvard vs. Yale—Debate. (1917). Available at Harvard University Archives: HUD 11320 917.2.

Hayes, A. R. (1952). The influence and impact of Edwin Dubois Shurter on speech education in Texas. Unpublished dissertation. Austin: University of Texas.

Highsaw, J. L. (1916). Interscholastic debates in relation to political opinion. *Quarterly Journal of Public Speaking, 2* (4), 365–83.

Huseman, R. C., Ware, G., and Gruner, C. R. (1972). Critical thinking, reflective thinking, and the ability to organize ideas: A multi-variate. *Journal of the American Forensic Association, 9* (Summer), 261–65.

Jackson, T. R. (1961). The effects of intercollegiate debating on critical thinking ability. Unpublished dissertation. Madison: University of Wisconsin.

Jacob, B. E. (1928). *NFL Bulletin, 3* (3), n.p.

Jones, C. H. (1954). Speech training helps preaching. *Gavel of Delta Sigma Rho, 37* (1), 17.

Kemp, G., Smith, M., DeKoven, B., and Segal, J. (2012). *Play, creativity and life-long learning.* Retrieved from http://helpguide.org/life/creative_play_fun_ games.htm.

Levin, A. N., and Goodfriend, H. B. (Eds.). (1914). *Harvard debating—1892– 1913.* Cambridge, MA: Caustic-Claflin Company.

Mayer, J. E. (1948). Personality development through debating. *Debater's Magazine, 4,* 3–4.

McBath, J. H. (1964). Debating on television. *Quarterly Journal of Speech, 50,* 146–52.

McBath, J. H. (Ed.). (1975). *Forensics as communication: The argumentative perspective.* Chicago: National Textbook.

McBath, J. H., and Cripe, N. C. (1965). Delivery: Rhetoric's rusty canon. *Journal of the American Forensic Association, 2* (1), 1–6.

The National Forensic League contests. (1946). *Debater's Magazine, 2* (3), 162–64.

National Institute for Play. (2010). Digital places. Retrieved from http://www .nifplay.org.

Nichols, E. R. (1936a). A historical sketch of intercollegiate debating: I. *Quarterly Journal of Speech, 22* (2), 213–20.

Nichols, E. R. (1936b). A historical sketch of intercollegiate debating: II. *Quarterly Journal of Speech, 22* (4), 591–603.

Nichols, E. R. (1937). A historical sketch of intercollegiate debating: III. *Quarterly Journal of Speech, 23* (2), 259–79.

Olson, D. O. (1948). An evaluation of debate. *Debater's Magazine, 4* (2), 64–68.

Paine, R. E., and Stanley, J. R. (2003). The yearning for pleasure: The significance of having fun in forensics. *National Forensic Journal, 21* (2), 36–59.

Perrill, H. B. (1935). Development of debating as revealed in early references [1848–1914]. *Gavel of Delta Sigma Rho, 17* (4), 57–61.

Portes, A. (1998). Social capital: Its origins and applications in modern sociology. *Annual Review of Sociology, 24,* 1–24.

Potter, D. (1944). *Debating in the colonial chartered colleges: An historical survey, 1642–1900.* New York: Bureau of Publications, Teachers College, Columbia University.

Potter, D. (1954). The literary society. In K. R. Wallace (Ed.), *History of speech education in America: Background studies* (pp. 238–58). New York: Appleton-Century-Crofts.

Putnam, R. D. (2000). *Bowling alone: The collapse and revival of American community.* New York: Simon and Schuster.

Quimby, B. (1952). It's not the championships. *Gavel of Delta Sigma Rho, 34* (2), 2–4.

Schrier, W. (1930). The Forum: University of North Dakota. *Gavel of Delta Sigma Rho, 12* (4), 17.

Secord, A. E., and Thomas, R. H. (1946). Speech in the extra-curricular program. *Debater's Magazine, 2* (1), 5–9.

Sillars, M. O. (1949). History and evaluation of intercollegiate forensics at the University of Redlands. Unpublished thesis. Redlands, CA: University of Redlands.

Smith, D. K. (1954). Origin and development of departments of speech. In K. R. Wallace (Ed.), *History of speech education in America: Background studies* (pp. 447–70). New York: Appleton-Century-Crofts.

Special Feature: Southwestern College, Winfield, Kansas. (1945). *Debater's Magazine, 1* (3), 92–97.

Stelzner, H. G. (1961). Tournament debate: Emasculated rhetoric. *Southern Speech Journal, 27,* 34–42.

Stone, A. P. (1914). Introduction (1893). Reprinted in A. N. Levin and H. H. Goodfriend (Eds.), *Harvard debating—1892–1913* (pp. 5–23). Cambridge, MA: Caustic-Claflin Company. Available at Harvard University Archives: HUD11320.914.

Swinney, J. P. (1968). The relative comprehension of contemporary tournament debate speeches. *Journal of the American Forensic Association, 5* (1), 16–20.

Thum, M. (2012). Confucius says: The top 10 wise Confucius quotes. Retrieved from http://www.myrkothom.com/confucius-says-the-top-10-quotes-by-con fucius.

Toulmin, S. E. (1958). *The uses of argument.* Cambridge: Cambridge University Press.

The USC testimonial dinner. (1947). *Debater's Magazine, 3* (1), 61.

Washington, D. (Director). (2007). *The great debaters* [Film]. Beverly Hills, CA: Weinstein Company.

9

❖ ❖

The "Other" in Forensics

The African American Experience

Throughout this book, we have identified systemic variables affecting the evolution of forensics in the United States during the twentieth century. For example, the inspiration of the Progressive movement, the changing nature and purpose of higher education, the challenges of shaping and standardizing an educational innovation marrying competition and critical thinking, and the economic and political conditions in the country and world affected how forensics activities were enacted.

We explored these variables through an examination of the written histories and materials available to us. However, as Martin and Nakayama (2010) noted, "Many historical events never make it into books" because they are part of what is described as "absent history" (p. 124). Absent history in this case must include the experiences of those termed as the "Other" by Riggins (1997). The Other functions outside the dominant coalition of social, economic, and political actors within a social system. From a critical perspective, Othering is consciously and unconsciously constructed by the dominant coalition and enacted toward the Other systemically through intent, words, and actions.

In the context of American forensics during the twentieth century, the dominant coalition of forensic honoraries, led by white men, functioned in educational institutions established and maintained by social norms and political and legal mandates. While some of the characteristics of these forensics leaders and the policies and practices of these organizations may be judged as immoral or unethical by current standards, the reasons for them may have been strong, and the impact of countering or confronting them at the time may have impacted negatively the future growth and acceptance of the activity. For example, creating a system that allowed people of a particular race or group to share equal participation not allowed by law or court decision may have resulted in the elimination of forensics activities totally. That said, how forensics evolved certainly reflected the social and political forces at work in twentieth-century America.

While the nature of the dominant coalition in forensics changed during the twentieth century as a result of social movements for discrimination and equal rights, American forensics did not escape the discrimination directed at members of particular minority groups and women. Thus, we have not attempted to create a comprehensive record of the practices that occurred; rather, our account is descriptive and impressionistic. We focus on two groups, African Americans and women, who faced particular obstacles and challenges as they sought to engage in competitive forensics activities. We examine the forensics experiences of African Americans in this chapter and reveal the challenges faced by women in chapter 10. As we include quoted materials drawn from historical documents, we retained the descriptive terminology used by the original authors (e.g., Negro, black).

THE EXCLUSION OF AFRICAN AMERICANS

As previously explained, early qualifications for membership in the forensic honoraries admitted those individuals who participated in the various forensics activities. For example, the Delta Sigma Rho (DSR) constitution made participation in intercollegiate contests "the sole condition necessary for membership" (Rarig and Greaves, 1954, p. 509). This excluded its founders but guaranteed that those admitted would be involved in forensics at a level that extended beyond the local literary and campus contests, making it accessible to only the elite male members of the team who were chosen to travel. Tau Kappa Alpha sought to establish itself as the Phi Beta Kappa of forensics, adding the academic qualification for members of being in the upper 35 percent of scholarship in their college class after two years of participation in intercollegiate debate and discussion or a speakers' bureau. With the creation of these criteria, only the elites among the forensics teams in a state could be admitted due to the limited competition opportunities afforded by the system of dual meets and triangular or quadrangular leagues.

Pi Kappa Delta (PKD) began using a more open system of qualification for membership, since its founders suggested that they wanted to provide opportunities for more students, coaches, instructors, and alumni to be involved. Article III, Section 1, "Eligibility," of the Constitution read, "The candidate shall be a regular collegiate student in good standing or a graduate of an institution of college rank and shall have won first honors in a recognized local oratorical contest, or shall have represented his [*sic*] college in a recognized intercollegiate oratorical contest, or debate, or shall be an instructor in public speaking or a coach of oratory or debate in a recognized college" (Constitution, 1920). However, in the minutes of the 1922 Biennial Convention, E. R. Nichols reported,

> We have received a letter asking for petition blanks from one of the colleges of the South conducted for the education of members of the African race. Our policy does not permit a chapter in such an institution. The committee recommends that some action be taken concerning this application at the convention, and recommends that the officers of Pi Kappa Delta be authorized to extend their services in an unofficial capacity in an effort to get the colleges of the Negro race to organize an honorary of their own. (Secretary's minutes, 1922, p. 5)

The minutes contained no mention of such an exclusionary policy. The "Report of the Committee on Constitutional Amendments" was designated with the following editorial insert: "For the report of this committee [comprised of G. W. Findley (chair), H. C. Libby, P. R. Brees, Leon E. Hickman, Douglas G. McPhee, Harry D. Wolf, and S. R. Toussaint], see the revised copy of the constitution which appears elsewhere in this issue" (Secretary's minutes, 1922, p. 12). The constitution was printed with this clarification: "as revised by the Fourth National Convention, held in Indianola, Iowa, March 28, 29, 30, 1922, and rewritten by the Committee on Constitutional Amendment" (Constitution, 1922, p. 16). Article III, Section 1, "Eligibility," was changed from the earlier version to read, "The candidate, who shall not be of the African race, shall be a regular college student . . . a graduate . . . an instructor . . . or a coach" (Constitution, 1922).

This insert made Pi Kappa Delta a segregated organization by constitution. However, the records are unclear as to how this came to be and the extent to which its members realized and/or participated in discriminatory practices (Bartanen, 2013). Beil (2008) suggested that the decision to segregate was made by "gentlemen's agreement," according to one of the Pi Kappa Delta founders, J. Thompson Baker of Southwestern College in Kansas, who wrote his account, published in a 1934 history of Pi Kappa Delta. At the 1920 convention, a heated debate about extending membership to Negroes resulted in a deadlock. The delegates finally agreed that they would not put the exclusion clause into the constitution but would leave it to the local chapters not to recommend an African American for membership. When applications for membership were sought by historically black institutions between 1920 and 1922, Nichols made the report suggesting a policy (that may have been the agreement). Following that report and off-the-record discussions, the modification to the constitution explicitly excluding the African race appeared and made official what had been agreed upon. The expansive growth of Pi Kappa Delta during this period may have made it difficult for a gentlemen's agreement to bind the membership. Well into the 1930s, Pi Kappa Delta remained segregated (Jarrett, 1935). It wasn't until sometime after World War II that Pi Kappa Delta removed the exclusion clause from its constitution and admitted African American students and their coaches into membership.

Delta Sigma Rho also was forced to confront the issue of admitting African American members. Bates College directly challenged the honoraries' discriminatory policies. The college had admitted African American students for many years and one, Arthur Dyer, was president of the Bates debate team and unsuccessfully sought membership in DSR (Bartanen, 2013; Branham, 1996). Bates protested the apparently unwritten DSR discriminatory membership standards but remained a DSR member. Shortly thereafter, Bates challenged the policy a second time over the unsuccessful application of Benjamin Mays for membership. (Mays would later become a legendary educator and a teacher of Martin Luther King Jr.) Bates students introduced motions at DSR conventions and lobbied other chapters, but the honorary did not take action until 1935, when the discriminatory practice was overturned and Mays, long after his graduation, was admitted as the first African American member (Branham, 1996). However, DSR continued some discriminatory practices, including denying historically black college/university (HBCU) institutions' applications for chapter membership into the 1950s.

Of course, the argument may be advanced that this reality of discrimination was a natural extension of the introverted nature of the forensics organizations, reflecting the societal, economic, and political discrimination occurring outside the educational context. The introverted-reserved organizations created affiliation criteria, limiting which schools could join and instituting membership restrictions to ensure the continuity of their particular value orientation within the forensics community. While the introverted-expansive organizations allowed for greater diversity in the schools that could affiliate institutionally, they had explicit membership criteria based on participation and experience. In addition, due to the nature of forensics programs, participants became part of an exclusive group when they became members of the team. Thus, by their very nature, forensics organizations appeared to be exclusive entities in which insiders and outsiders were identified.

While we must acknowledge this exclusive and negative aspect of forensics history, our purpose in this chapter is not to critique the system as much as it is to describe and acknowledge the absent histories of African Americans who participated in the American forensic innovation throughout the twentieth century. Their experiences matter, and the history of those who were involved in forensics can help others to "think in more complex ways about the past and the ways [the past] influences the present and future" (Martin and Nakayama, 2010, p. 124).

THE AFRICAN AMERICAN EDUCATIONAL EXPERIENCE

We cannot discuss the forensics experience of African Americans in the twentieth century without providing some context about the educational system available to them prior to that time. As the history of slavery and the fight for civil rights and justice in America are documented elsewhere, our discussion does not provide a chronology of events. Rather, we suggest that educational opportunities for African Americans reflected "the progressive stages of the Negros in the American social order . . . from chattel [pre–Civil War] to human being [Civil War], to freeman [Civil War to about 1895], to citizen [1896–1953], to elector [1954–present]" (Bowles and DeCosta, 1971, p. 11). In addition, we place these opportunities—particularly as they are related to forensics—within the context of changes that occurred in American higher education, particularly the restricted, classical training for the preparation of ministers and other professional fields; apprenticeship training; the training of teachers, particularly in normal schools and teachers colleges; and the expansion of broader curricula for undergraduate and graduate degrees throughout all of higher education.

Prior to the Civil War, the number of African Americans graduating from any American college was small. Bowles and DeCosta (1971) indicated that "only about 28 persons of acknowledged Negro descent were graduated with baccalaureate degrees by 1860" (p. 12). They offered reasons for the low graduation rates, including the absence of any kind of public education system in the South to prepare students for higher education, the low number of free African Americans prepared and able to enroll in baccalaureate programs outside the South, and restrictive admissions policies of colleges in the southern states: "Aside from Oberlin College, Berea College, and some other Midwestern colleges, relatively few American colleges admitted Negro students on a continuous basis" (Bowles and DeCosta, 1971, p. 13).

Bowles and DeCosta (1971) identified several factors in the years leading up to and immediately following the Civil War that influenced how higher education would evolve for African Americans in America: by 1865, the number of free and freed African Americans grew to approximately 5 million; as late as 1900, approximately 90 percent of the African Americans in the United States remained in the southern states; no system of public schools existed in the southern states (except in Kentucky and North Carolina); the thousands of elementary schools for African Americans established by religious groups under the protection of Union forces were subsequently destroyed by hostile white groups; and the federal Freedmen's Bureau was founded and made efforts to cooperate with religious and social groups interested in educating African American students.

Two avenues were open to African Americans interested in higher education: private and public institutions. Immediately following the Civil War, religious groups (e.g., Baptists, Methodists, Presbyterians, and Congregation-alists) founded private colleges to educate African Americans. According to Bowles and DeCosta (1971), from 1865 to 1890, hundreds of private, HBCUs were founded. Most of these included elementary and secondary instruction be-cause, prior to the Civil War, the education of slaves was illegal, and a system of public education in the South had not been developed. This was not unique to African American colleges at the time (U.S. Department of the Interior, 1896, p. 2121), as most colleges provided elementary and/or secondary levels of instruc-tion. Because the vast majority of African Americans had no formal education, the first institutions of higher education offered instruction at the level of the entrants, with the understanding that as literacy levels among African Americans increased, eventually the presence of these elementary and secondary programs would diminish.

The impetus for the creation of HBCUs in the South came as a result of the Morrill Act of 1890, when southern states were forced to set up land-grant colleges for African American students. These colleges followed the boarding school model, and because of the need for teachers at the primary and second-ary levels, they became normal schools focused on teacher education. With the founding of the HBCU land-grant institutions, public higher education was no longer denied to African Americans in the South.

However, two U.S. Supreme Court decisions influenced how educational op-portunities for African Americans in America evolved in the twentieth century: *Plessy v. Ferguson* in 1896 and *Brown v. Board of Education of Topeka, Shawnee County, Kansas* in 1954. The first decision created legal justification for the sepa-ration of the races in all facets of social life—in schools, churches, cemeteries, drinking fountains, and restaurants (Franklin, 1965). The latter disallowed the structures created to separate the races and mandated the equalization of opportu-nity for all citizens, particularly in the public educational systems of the country.

Plessy v. Ferguson enabled local authorities with the blessing of the federal government to adopt laws and practices that perpetuated the unequal status of blacks within their communities. Specifically, the decision "held that separate coach laws are not in conflict with the equal protection clause of the Fourteenth Amendment" (Mangum, 1940, p. 203). While pertaining to practices restricting access of African Americans to the railroad coach cars used by white passengers, this decision set the precedent for the creation of a "separate-but-equal" doctrine that changed how schools were created and maintained within school districts. Mangum (1940) described the impact on the development of public education for African Americans in the South: "All public schools must be separate and pupils of the White and Negro races are not permitted to attend the same school" (p. 79). The result was the creation of what Bowles and DeCosta (1971) de-scribed as "a separate and distinctive Negro school system" (p. 37), essentially dependent on the local white government structure for its support. Examples were common of little-to-no state funding for school buildings serving African American students and reduced per-pupil expenditures as compared with white students. Similarly, the African American system of education was completely separate from the white system. Bowles and DeCosta (1971) provided a detailed explanation of this phenomenon, basing their argument on the absence of common guidelines for white and nonwhite schools, teachers for white children and nonwhite children being educated at separate institutions, standards and requirements determined internally and separately, and no crossovers in administrators, teachers, or students. They concluded, "The White system was all White and the Negro system was all Negro" (Bowles and DeCosta, 1971, p. 37). This separation resulted in the African American system developing as a "distorted mirror image of the white system" because the African American school system had to "develop itself according to what it could see of [the white] system . . . without knowledge as to the internal workings of the system or guidance as to how to evolve concepts of operation based on its own problems and resources" (Bowles and DeCosta, 1971, p. 38). For over fifty years, the African American system of education continued to suffer as the separate-but-equal clause was upheld by the court system as constitutional.

The second court case, *Brown v. Board of Education*, was prompted by the position of advocates for the African American community that students coming out of nonwhite schools were not prepared to enter the white system because the two systems had evolved separately. Bowles and DeCosta (1971) described the nonwhite educational system as "of American education but not in it" (p. 43). The groundwork for *Brown v. Board of Education* was laid from 1930 to 1945, as the National Association for the Advancement of Colored People (NAACP) focused on the equal aspect of *Plessy v. Ferguson*, particularly as it referred to graduate and professional education. Despite numerous attempts, they failed to overturn *Plessy v. Ferguson* until the early 1950s, when advocates for abandoning the separate-but-equal doctrine were able to demonstrate the inherently unequal educational facilities in which African American students were being taught. This led to the 1954 conclusion of the Supreme Court that "in the field of public education, the doctrine of 'separate but equal' has no place" and "racial discrimination in public education at all levels would be held unconstitutional" (Bowles and DeCosta, 1971, p. 62).

The result of this ruling was the reclamation of federal jurisdiction over the public education of all students in the country. School systems were forced to integrate, and public funding for the education of all students, but particularly African Americans, improved. In 1957, HBCUs were admitted into the Southern Association of Colleges and Schools, which provided internal access for accreditation and application of evaluative criteria to academic programs for African

American students. These events did not change radically the educational experience for all African American students, but they did create the basis for equality that had not previously existed.

In summary, changes for African Americans in the social order of American society and the impact of *Plessy v. Ferguson* and *Brown v. Board of Education* influenced the development of educational opportunities for all students in the United States, but particularly for African American students. Separated from their white counterparts, nonwhite educational institutions produced African American teachers who taught African American students. They modeled their academic programs and activities based on what they observed. Thus, as we will observe, the forensics experience for African Americans in twentieth-century America in part reflected the traditions and practices of their white counterparts.

THE AFRICAN AMERICAN FORENSICS EXPERIENCE

To begin, understanding the evolution of the African American forensics experience is aided by the identification of two systemic factors: first, because the African American system was kept separate from the so-called white system due to the separate-but-equal doctrine previously described, African American educators developed their academic and extracurricular programs based on what they could observe of their white counterparts from outside that system; second, the inherent capacity of students to disseminate information about the American invention of forensics almost instantaneously through school newspapers, publications, and other informal means of communication meant that African American students were as likely to become familiar with and communicate about particular debate practices through their publications as their white counterparts.

Some previous research specifically has chronicled the forensics experiences of African American students (Amey, 1934; Johnston and Henderson, 1917; Little, 2002; Parker, 1940, 1955). For African American high school students, little is known about their forensics participation or practices, particularly at segregated schools. Due to the severe funding crises experienced by most segregated schools, an excess of funds to support forensics is unlikely. However, the National Forensic League (NFL) archives document African American students among the winners at the district and national tournaments they sponsored, suggesting that when African American students were enrolled at NFL-chartered schools, they were not excluded from competing and qualifying for national competition.

The basis for much of what is known about collegiate forensics for African American students comes from the campus newspapers and publications that emanated from the HBCUs themselves. A collection of primary sources and other materials drawn from the archives of historically black institutions by Allen Louden at Wake Forest University provided the firsthand accounts and descriptions included here. In the following sections, we integrate some of Louden's impressionistic accounts with our own to trace the development of debate and forensics at some of these HBCUs.

Literary Societies

As at the majority of the colleges and universities in the United States, the earliest type of extracurricular student organization established at nonwhite colleges was the literary society: "Practically all Negro colleges during the latter half of the nineteenth century had literary societies which offered opportunities for writing, speaking, and declaiming" (Boulware, 1947, p. 116). Table 9.1 identifies some areas of comparison between literary societies at white institutions and those at the HBCUs.

The literary societies founded at non-HBCUs were described in earlier chapters of this book. However, to summarize, they were student-driven entities that provided an intellectual challenge and social context for residential students to engage in activities outside the classroom. While men were dominant in the earliest societies due largely to the fact that more men were enrolled as students, there were some mixed societies that allowed female members, as well as all-female societies. While the purpose of the societies was to allow for personal growth and intellectual development, the intraschool competitions between the societies were popular with the campus and community audiences. Because of the reliance on classical topics and methods of speaking, the literary societies took on an elocutionary focus with an emphasis on the canons of style and delivery.

Table 9.1. Comparison of Characteristics of Non-HCBUs and HBCUs

Non-HBCUs	HBCUs
Student driven	Faculty and student driven
Male centered with opportunities for women	Male centered with opportunities for women
Intraschool competition	Intraschool competition
Audience centered	Audience centered
Reliance on classical topics and activities	Reliance on classical topics and activities

For the most part, the literary societies that formed at HBCUs were very similar to their white counterparts. However, some differences existed. For example, in 1868, a group of Fisk University faculty and students called an assembly for the expressed purpose of forming such a club. Faculty members were more involved with the literary societies at HBCUs as advisors and participants. The result—the Union Literary Society—was open to all preparatory students and was one of the longest continuously operating extracurricular organizations of its kind in the history of black higher education (Little, 2002). Literary societies emerged at other HBCUs and African American institutions: Tougaloo College's faculty and students founded the Willard and Cheeseman literary societies.

Male students were predominant as literary societies formed. At Atlanta University, male students organized the Ware Lyceum and the Eureka and Phi Kappa literary societies, while their female counterparts established the Phyllis Wheatley, Athene, and Douglass literary clubs. Later, undergraduate men from Atlanta, Morehouse, Clark, and Morris Brown founded the Intercollegiate Society. Elsewhere, there was hardly an African American school that did not have at least one literary society, usually named after some famous person or quality of freedom and material success or invoking memories of ancient Greece and Rome: Sodalian, Payne, Ciceronian, Garnet, Philosophian, Mason, Forum, Dunbar, Philomathean, Willing Workers, Atheneum, Wheatley, Pierian, Liberty, Excelsior, and Stowe.

In the early years, according to one account, women were allowed to attend the recitations and debates of the Ware and Phi Kappa societies (Hamilton, 1914). However, in 1884, the women were not permitted to come to the meetings. This left the young women devoid of their usual Saturday night amusement, so in the fall of 1884, the normal classes met in the girls' parlor and planned for themselves, eventually founding the Phyllis Wheatley Society. Its purpose was twofold: first, to provide the same stimulating literary activities among the girls, and second, to provide "wholesome amusement for them on Saturday nights" (Hamilton, 1914, p. 90). Their first program was on February 12, 1885, in celebration of Lincoln's birthday, with essays, debates, orations, readings, and music (including an original song honoring Lincoln). The women's society continued for decades after its founding.

The literary societies were campus focused, providing competition internally on a wide variety of issues. Some topics reflected the jingoistic and imperialistic spirit of late-nineteenth-century America: the annexation of territory acquired during the Spanish-American War, the protection of American missionaries in the South Sea Islands, granting territorial status to Alaska, and "annex[ing] the Sandwich Islands." A few subjects were of the more traditional sort: Was Henry VIII's reign "productive of more good than evil to England?" "Which is the most useful to man—a Horse or a Cow?" Was Phyllis Wheatley "the greatest of African poets?" Other questions concerned problems of national reconciliation, urbanization, industrialization, politics, and education: African American protest against Jim Crow "car laws" in the South, direct election of public officials, restrictions on foreign immigration, pensions for Union and Confederate Civil War veterans, changes in the American Tract Society, the use of English in teaching Native Americans, the natural sciences versus the classical languages, textbooks for nonwhite schools by African American authors, and "Does higher education meet the demands of the time?" (Little, 2002, p. 45).

The literary societies provided an opportunity for the students to examine a broad range of issues: the pulpit versus the bar, migration to Africa, Columbus versus Washington for praise, Benedict Arnold versus Aaron Burr for blame, coeducation, national temperance, and whether the United States should be permitted to arrest felons in Mexico. In later years, literary topics gained in popularity, as when they considered "if Brutus was sincere in his professions after Caesar's death" or the state of American literature. On occasion, students discussed theological issues, as revealed in the minutes of the Ciceronian Literary Society for November 7, 1890: "Resolved, that a man can fall from grace" (Little, 2002, p. 44).

Literary societies carried out a number of additional functions at the African American colleges and universities. Some, like Wilberforce's Sodilian and Tawawa literary societies, were responsible for founding and editing campus journals and literary magazines. These were often the vehicles by which features of forensics were communicated across the country. A few clubs established private libraries, much like Fisk's Beta Kappa Beta and Union literary societies, which in 1888 possessed book collections totaling 110 and 140 volumes, respectively. They even served as quasi-official social clubs, sponsoring instrumental and vocal music recitals, poetry readings, annual observances of important dates in African American history, hunts, field trips, intramural sports contests, and other types of recreational and cultural diversions for their members and the general community.

These literary societies were not without their shortcomings. Despite their efforts to sponsor as wide a variety of extracurricular activities as possible, students frequently complained about the lack of diversion when literary societies did not schedule programs. In addition, debating—the principal method employed by literary societies to nurture intellect and develop the power of reason among their members—sometimes degenerated into rhetorical exercises in which sheer persuasion superseded logic in importance. Finally, the restrictive membership requirements of some literary societies made them little more than exclusive clubs (Little, 2002, p. 46).

Intercollegiate Debate

As intraschool competition between literary societies expanded to interschool competition, debate as a distinct form of forensics emerged for African American institutions in much the same way as it did for predominantly white secondary and postsecondary institutions. The first recorded intercollegiate debates at an HBCU occurred on March 10, 1905, when Atlanta University hosted Fisk University. Bacote (1969) quoted a university publication (*BAU*, 1905), describing this meeting as the "pioneer debate in Southern institutions of this character" (p. 211).

Forensics in the Public Oratory Era

The identification of the public oratory era provides a starting point for comparing the evolution of competitive forensics at non-HBCU and HBCU institutions. Table 9.2 identifies how the two contexts compared.

Table 9.2. Comparison of Non-HBCUs and HBCUs during the Public Oratory Era of American Forensics

Period	Non-HBCUs	HBCUs
Public oratory	Male dominated, women in same-sex and mixed events	Male dominated, women in same-sex and mixed events
	Competition self-determined excluding HBCUs	Competition self-determined within HBCUs
	Shift from provincial to national focus	Provincial focus, limited by geography of HBCUs
	Debate norms and practices initiated	Debate norms and practices copied
	Creation of national forensic establishment by prominent male coaches/teachers	Programs directed by prominent male coaches/teachers, no national forensic hierarchy
	Formation of honorary organizations (DSR, TKA, PKD, PRP, NFL)	Development of HBCU alumni groups, Gamma Delta Sigma short-lived
	Public, audience centered	Public, audience centered
	Exposure to British debate challenges norms, introducing less competitive style	Exposure to international debate liberalizes norms by introducing interracial competition

Characteristics of Forensics at Non-HBCUs

The characteristics of the public oratory era of American forensics for the non-HBCUs are part of the official record previously described in earlier chapters of this book. However, in brief, during the public oratory era, white male debaters were the majority, with few women identified on early competitive teams, due in part to the need for additional chaperones when women traveled with male coaches and male students. Competition was self-determined by forensics teams, following the dual-meet, triangular, and quadrangular league system. Later, schools met at tournaments designed to save money and provide additional competitive opportunities for more students.

Coaches and instructors at white institutions initiated the debate norms and practices used by the students. For example, team structure, time limits, topics, methods of judging, alternative forms of debate (e.g., Oregon Plan), alternative formats (e.g., discussion, student congress), and all other aspects of the competitive debate experience emanated from the forensics establishment that had been formed by significant male coaches and teachers who created national forensics organizations with rules, customs, and practices that influenced how forensics evolved.

The public, audience-centered approach to forensics remained a dominant orientation due to the emphasis on citizenship training and the reliance of less urban communities on public programming to provide a cultural and educational environment. The arrival of international debaters from Oxford, England, challenged the norms of the establishment by introducing a less competitive style and a more extemporaneous and challenging form of presentation.

Characteristics of Forensics at HBCUs

Remarkably, the timeline for the evolution of debate at HBCUs reflected what was happening in the educational system of the majority. When intercollegiate debate began at HBCUs, male students dominated; a review of the yearbooks of several colleges reveals no women on the debate teams. Photos of the HBCU team members reflect the male dominance that was also evident on teams at predominantly white institutions. That is not to say that there were no female debaters at HBCUs. On the contrary, women were members of the teams, and when necessary, schools fielded all-female teams to debate other all-female teams in featured public debates. Eventually, mixed teams debated same-sex teams. However, this was not the norm.

Just as at non-HBCU institutions where selection of sites for competition was self-determined, for the first three decades of the twentieth century, African American debaters engaged in dual debates and triangular, quadrangular, and league activity, modeling the framework for competition common among non-HBCUs described by previous forensic historians. Some of the best known of the triangulars included Fisk University (Tennessee), Howard University (Washington, DC), and Atlanta University (Georgia); Morehouse College (Georgia), Knoxville College (Tennessee), and Talladega College (Alabama); and Wilberforce University (Ohio), Lincoln University (Missouri), and Virginia Union University (Johnston and Henderson, 1917).

The debates typically occurred in the spring, allowing for on-campus debates between classes (e.g., freshmen versus sophomores, juniors versus seniors) to occur in the fall and winter months. The earliest debates were student driven, but accounts from the period suggest that coaches or instructors played key roles in encouraging their students and chaperoning them. This may have been due to the nature of travel for African American minors during the period and the need for greater security en route to debate locations. As Beil (2008) noted, "African American teams faced one obstacle never encountered by their white counterparts. Almost every debater during this period either observed or was threatened with lynching."

The HBCUs retained a provincial focus for their debating due to several factors, including the location of their institutions and their exclusion from interracial debate by the forensic honoraries. These institutions also relied longer on more classical debate formats due to the continuation of the public debates and the rhetorical tendencies that were inherently part of the African American style of public oratory. The HBCUs were primarily located in the southern and eastern parts of the country. Thus, as competition outlets were established, schools tended to remain close to their home institutions when engaging in debate. Similarly, since HBCUs routinely were kept from debating at white institutions, their focus remained at the regional level, in contrast to the national network that formed among the majority of the nation's schools. There were some debates between white and HBCU debaters, but often as a result of some special circumstance or opportunity. For instance, Wiley College was one of the first HBCUs to have "colored students" debate "white students" in the South at Oklahoma City University on March 21, 1930, and Wiley College debated the University of Southern California on April 2, 1935, before two thousand people in Los Angeles (Tolson, 1935). This latter debate was the inspiration for the 2006 movie *The Great Debaters*. Tolson claimed that Wiley and Oklahoma City participated in the first interracial debate, but that claim is disputed by fragmentary records of LeMoyne College, which sponsored a very active debate program during that period.

The exclusion of HBCUs from the honoraries and from more frequent competition with non-HBCU institutions was the product not solely of institutional racism but of the influence of accreditation forces as well. College accreditation began in the 1890s as an effort to ensure public confidence that schools and colleges were providing the educational services they were advertising. In the absence of rules established by the federal government, as education was traditionally viewed as outside its purview, the accreditation process quickly gained favor and for most of the century precluded more direct federal oversight or intervention. Accredited institutions were afforded more prestige and confidence in an emerging activity such as forensics. This was particularly important when added to the fact that the speech discipline itself was new and had emerged in part from very loosely structured schools of oratory and declamation that probably lacked appropriate rigor when compared to the very well established disciplinary standards for other, more traditional disciplines. The forensic honoraries, established near the time of the introduction of accreditation, used accreditation standards to assess institutions as they applied for membership and to exclude institutions felt to not measure up. Tau Kappa Alpha was the most vigorous in this process, intending for its members to emulate the standards of Phi Beta Kappa, which was the most prestigious academic society in the nation.

HBCUs and other schools for African Americans were excluded from the accreditation process (Bartanen, 2013). Their relative impoverishment and inability to attract faculty whose qualifications equaled those at white institutions would have likely made it difficult for those institutions to meet the required accreditation standards in the early years of the century. But being an accredited institution was a prerequisite for institutional membership in the honoraries, providing a convenient fig leaf for the exclusion of unaccredited schools and colleges. As forensics was valued during the public oratory era as a means for burnishing an institution's image as being of high quality, there was no particular advantage for these colleges to compete against unaccredited institutions, let alone deal with the fallout if they should happen to lose to one of them in a round of competition! It is likely that these unaccredited institutions were invisible. With the exception of the occasional article in the *Forensic of Pi Kappa Delta*, the white college community likely never considered the possibility that HBCUs also engaged in and benefited from forensics.

Because the HBCUs were excluded from the white system of education, those inside the HBCUs had to model or imitate what they could observe as outsiders. Thus, as debate practices and norms were introduced, the students and forensic coaches at HBCUs learned about what was happening in forensics in much the same ways as white students and forensic coaches: through the college newsletters, yearbooks, and other publications.

The audience-oriented nature of forensics during the public oratory era made it possible for people to observe and learn through that experience. Just as with public debates between teams from non-HBCUs, the public debates among HBCU teams were popular, and large crowds attended. They were held in prominent locations (e.g., Galloway Auditorium at Wilberforce University, Rankin Chapel at

Howard University) and had an appointed presiding officer who typically was the college president or administrator. Programs and accounts from the early public debates reflected a high level of decorum, as flags, flowers, bouquets, banners, musical performances, and receptions were part of these events. As at non-HBCU events, high-level or respected members of the community served as judges, with the local team often enjoying the benefits of the home advantage.

The HBCU teams often debated the national topics selected by PKD (even though they were excluded from debating these topics at PKD-sponsored tournaments), including the following: "Resolved: That the federal government should own and operate the telegraph and telephone systems of the United States" (1914); "Resolved: That the United States should immediately take steps to make a material increase in its army and navy" (1915); and "Resolved: That the national government should require compulsory arbitration of disputes between capital and labor and constitutionality be waived" (1917). On occasion, a topic was related to the African American experience (e.g., "Resolved: That a separate public school system should be established for Negroes in northern cities having a large Negro population"). However, the HBCU forensic coaches and teachers wanted their students to be able to debate the national topics (ironically determined by an organization that excluded them from membership), and so avoided the special interest focus. Parker (1940) observed, "Negro college students should be led to broaden their minds by thinking, not alone in terms of the Negro group, but in terms of American citizens, and of an American democracy in which, more and more, we look forward to their increased participation" (p. 34).

The absence of a national forensics organization among the HBCUs limited their influence and kept their activities out of the scope of what forensic historians of the day were recording. Neither E. R. Nichols, who chronicled the first five decades of American forensics in the *Quarterly Journal of Speech*, nor David Potter, who provided great detail about debate in nineteenth-century America, mentioned the robust debate culture emerging at HBCUs. Similarly, no HBCU forensics program was featured in the *Debater's Magazine* or *Speech Activities* publications covering forensics during the 1940s and early 1950s (even though all mainstream forensics organizations had someone covering their activities for the "Campus News" and "Special Features" sections of the publications). What became known of the debate community among the HBCUs was pieced together by reviewing yearbooks (e.g., the *Mirror* and the *Bison* of Howard University); school publications (e.g., the *Scroll* and the *Crimson and Gray* of Atlanta University); student publications, bulletins, and programs from their public debates; campus newspapers (e.g., the *Lincoln News*); or publications of the NAACP (e.g., the *Crisis: A Record of the Darker Races*).

Scholarship about forensics at HBCUs was scarce, if published at all. The *Journal of Negro Education* published three articles (Boulware, 1947; Parker,

1940, 1955) addressing debate practices and speech training in the Negro college and offering insight into forensics practices and developments. Despite commentaries during the public oratory era about extending the benefits of forensics to all students or seeking to unite all of the forensics community under the American Forensic Association (AFA), acknowledgment of the forensics activities of the HBCUs was missing from the AFA's *Register* and the *Journal of the American Forensic Association*. The result of this lack of coverage was the perpetuation of a system that segregated knowledge from official records and publications about a segment of American forensics bringing the intellectual benefits of the activity to African American students at HBCUs. The absence of a national presence by the HBCUs created an information gap that was allowed to continue by the established forensics community, reflecting the broader socioeconomic and racial attitudes that pervaded American society.

The coaches and teachers at HBCUs were significant due to the impact they had on their school programs and the students who learned from them. However, only a few received recognition for their activities outside forensics (e.g., Melvin Tolson, coach of the Wiley College debate team during the 1930s) or for distinguishing themselves in some way (e.g., Dr. Thomas F. Freeman, longtime coach of Texas Southern University [TSU] in Houston, who began coaching in 1943 and traveled around the world with his TSU debate teams) (Wiltz, 2011/2012).

The HBCUs largely were introduced to interracial debate through the arrival of the British debaters from Oxford to America in 1922. Although not widely involved until the 1930s, the HBCUs invited and often were victorious over their British visitors ("Lincoln wins," 1927). As Johnson (1928) noted, "The fine showing of the Lincoln undergraduates in these international, interracial debates [in 1927] showed, as stated in the New York World, that colored young men trained in institutions like Lincoln University are a match for the seasoned debaters from across the seas in effectiveness of delivery, nimbleness of wit, and keenness of argument" (p. 13). As HBCU debaters experienced success against the British teams, they began to seek out other interracial opportunities for debate. LeMoyne College was particularly active in international debate, taking a world tour in 1939. Parker (1957) reported, "The trip extended over six months during which time the coach and the debaters covered more than 30,000 miles, engaged in 36 debates, participated in over 40 radio broadcasts, and addressed about 320 meetings. This epoch-making tour carried them through the United States, British Columbia, Hawaii, Australia, and New Zealand" (p. 68). While such debates were infrequent at first, by the start of World War II, particular HBCUs found ways to regularly schedule at least one interracial debate annually. With the rise of the tournament format, the opportunity for more African American students to participate in interracial debate increased.

Summary

A comparison of debate practices between the non-HBCU and HBCU institutions during the public oratory era revealed almost complete similarity in the primarily male composition of teams, the staging of competitions and public debates, the norms and practices used by debaters, and the audience-centered focus. The differences came as a result of the exclusion of the HBCUs from mainstream forensics competition, the more provincial focus for the HBCUs that resulted from geographic and segregation laws and norms, the absence of prominent national forensic leaders and honorary organizations for students from the HBCUs, the inability of the HBCUs to initiate debate practices that influenced the non-HBCU programs, and the liberalization that resulted from the introduction of interracial debating prompted by the arrival of the British debaters in America.

Forensics in the Technical Era

The technical era of forensics followed World War II as Americans and the speech discipline shifted from a rhetorical focus to a communication or social scientific orientation. As the established forensics community moved into the technical era, the influx of students of all ethnicities after the war dramatically increased the size of the student populations on most American campuses and created a new and different interest in forensics as we have previously noted. Table 9.3 provides a comparison of forensics activities at non-HBCUs and HBCUs during this period.

Characteristics of Forensics at the Non-HBCUs

Part of the influx consisted of returning soldiers who, eager to improve their socioeconomic status, sought college degrees expecting to move up in society. However, in addition to simply an increased number of students, the desire of the students for expanded opportunities for employment broadened the need for a curriculum that varied from the classical, traditional approaches used before the war and that provided a more social scientific emphasis. The increase of students brought diversity, resulting in the observance of a shift from the white/male student dominance of the prewar period to the inclusion of more nonwhites and women. As the civil rights movement gained traction, the political and legal systems forced the integration of schools and removed all structural barriers to the inclusion of African Americans in educational and forensics organizations. The attitudinal barriers stemming from the dominance of the rational world paradigm for determining success in forensics (e.g., reliance on deductive argumentative structure, large amounts of evidence, deference to vocal and physical authority, and establishment of a motivational link for persuasion) among mostly male

Table 9.3. Comparison of Non-HBCUs and HBCUs during the Technical Era of American Forensics

Era	Non-HBCUs	HBCUs
Technical	Post–World War II influx of soldiers and others seeking college degrees	Post–World War II influx of soldiers and others seeking expansion of career options
	Gain of top students from former HBCUs context to non-HBCUs	Loss of potential students seeking expanded educational opportunities at non-HBCUs
	Shift from white/male student dominance to inclusion of nonwhites/women	Male student dominance with opportunities for women to compete
	Mostly male coaches and judges	Mostly male coaches and judges
	Removal of systemic barriers to integrated forensics by civil rights legislation	Expansion by some HBCUs of interracial debate
	Increased focus on tournament debating	Increased focus on tournament debating
	Introduction of Urban Debate Leagues by forensics coaches at non-HBCUs to increase participation of minorities and inner-city high school students in non-HBCU forensics	Limited, if any, involvement in Urban Debate League movement
	Introduction of social scientific and rhetorical studies to critique forensics and seek explanations for lack of diversity and gender equality	No forensics research from HBCUs
	Introduction of Louisville Project and critical studies to affect the forensics establishment	HBCU forensics programs silent about Louisville Project

coaches and judges remained a barrier to success for women and ethnic groups seeking to advance to the highest levels of competition within the forensics tournament systems (Murphy, 1989). Once integration was mandated, efforts began to increase participation of African Americans and students from lower

socioeconomic groups in urban areas through the Urban Debate League movement. At the close of the technical period, social scientists and rhetoricians began to study and critique forensics to seek explanations for the lack of diversity
and gender equity that persisted in the activity. The Louisville Project emerged
as a culture-centered assessment of the activity (or, in debate terminology, a
kritik) and experienced push-back from the policy debate community.

Characteristics of Forensics at HBCUs

Within the HBCU system, the return of African American soldiers and the impact
of the influx of more students into the collegiate environment had the same effect on forensics. Their increased general interest in higher education reflected a
growing desire among members of the African American community to expand
their career options beyond the established teaching and ministerial professions.
Because HBCUs comprised mostly students of African American descent, and
because HBCUs primarily were located in the southern states, where the largest
concentration of African Americans resided, their debate teams naturally were
composed of black students. Thus, the HBCUs did not experience the shift,
with regard to the increase of nonwhites and women, that non-HBCU forensics
programs experienced. However, just as at the non-HBCUs, the HBCU forensics
community relied primarily on male coaches and judges to direct the programs
and render decisions at the tournaments.

As at many non-HBCUs and high schools following World War II, the nature
of the coaching ranks in HBCUs also changed, as did the expectations of what
was required to maintain a forensics program. Because forensics had been part of
nearly every high school and collegiate extracurricular program during the public
oratory era, administrators considered the presence of a debate and/or declamation team to be important and an integral part of their school offerings. The public
debates, interschool competition, and formal culture surrounding forensics had a
quaint, cultural, and traditional place in the education of every American student.
After World War II, the world had changed, and what was considered traditional
became old-fashioned. This posed some problems for administrators. Whereas in
the public oratory era, students engaged in the more rhetorical, public forms of
forensics, expressed through on-campus and limited competition with one or two
other nearby institutions (which could be coached by educated individuals with
good public speaking skills), with the rise of the technical era and with the availability of a national forensic calendar that, for example, listed 114 debate and
forensics tournaments across the country (Parker, 1955, p. 150), a more highly
trained coach with considerable time and ability to travel was required.

The lack of African American coaches with this kind of specialized training in
argumentation, extensive debate coaching experience, and interest, willingness,

or ability to travel across the country to tournaments resulted in many HBCU debate programs faltering. The following figures help to demonstrate what transpired at HBCUs as World War II ended and the technical era of education and forensics began. Parker (1955) noted that between 1944 and 1947, most HBCU debate institutions scheduled one or two debate contests per year. Because travel was restricted for financial reasons during the war years, these likely would have been dual meets between institutions. From 1949 to 1953, the number of debates increased from 107 in 1949 to 263 in 1953. However, "only 6 (five colleges and one university) or 21 per cent of the institutions [HBCU debate programs] participating in this study accounted for 802 or 62 per cent of the ten-year total of the 1,314 intercollegiate debate contests conducted" (Parker, 1955, pp. 151–52). By 1955, the most active HBCUs were Howard University, Alabama State College, Virginia Union University, Arkansas State College, North Carolina Agricultural and Technical College, Lincoln University, Southern University, Morgan State College, and Texas Southern University (Parker, 1955).

For those schools continuing active forensics programs, a schedule that included interracial debates reduced the interest in remaining segregated in their competition. Some HBCU debate teams excelled and, under the direction of expert coaches, advanced to the National Debate Tournament and the winners' circle at many invitational tournaments. Howard University was such a program, winning the district debate tournament in 1950 and advancing to the competition at the West Point National Debate Tournament. Those HBCUs without expert and able coaches found financial or other reasons to phase out their forensics programs. Among these reasons was a declining interest among many African American students in an extracurricular activity that simulated the real world; they preferred to engage the real-world environment of American society, in which the fight for equal rights under the law represented a worthier goal than winning a round of academic debate.

In the 1950s and 1960s, the rise of the civil rights movement challenged the dominant paradigm of racial inequality in America. As greater numbers of the dominant coalition of whites began to speak out against discrimination, and as the legal and political systems overturned discriminatory laws and established new standards and practices to provide greater opportunities to African Americans and other minorities, many organizations began a period of self-examination to correct past practices and create new opportunities in an integrated system. Such was the case in the forensics community.

While the shift was not as dramatic as some of the changes occurring in other aspects of education in America during this period (e.g., bussing students to force integration), records drawn from HBCU archives document more interracial debating, as well as increased tournament travel for more active programs. For some HBCUs, the civil rights movement may have syphoned off some of the more vocal and active African American students and coaches, leaving the school without the forensic leadership to sustain a debate or a forensics program during a time when resources were being diverted to strengthen curricula and bring HBCUs up to the standards established by accreditation boards across the South and other parts of the country.

Another reason for the decline in debate programs across the HBCUs after World War II may have stemmed from the impact of the characteristics associated with the technical era of debate, which one of the British debaters described as "simply too fast, too quote-dependent, and too overly competitive" (Gerber, 2009, p. 80). As the HBCU debaters entered an integrated, competition-driven forensics environment, they experienced a technical form of debate that was being adopted by many non-HBCUs. This new style contrasted with the more traditional, classical style of debate used by HBCU debaters and the nonnational circuit debate programs, often resulting in tournament round losses when the two segments of the debate community mixed and the judge pool consisted of critics trained in the technical practices.

In addition, as the public emphasis of debate became privatized, the rhetorical appeal of debate may have been lost for some African American students seeking to engage the larger white society in the public arena. The critic system of judging rewarded doing a better job of debating by set rules/standards in a round of competition rather than finding the right decision regarding a societal problem. This left African American students—wanting to focus on the latter—losing rounds of competition because their style of debate was not as conducive to what was becoming a more rapid-fire style of presenting as much evidence as possible in order for the opponent to drop a point or leave key arguments unanswered in the round (Gerber, 2009, p. 84).

Urban Debate Leagues

As the technical era changed the nature of debate from audience centered to individual centered, and as the gap widened between debate programs based on the level of financial support available to them, some programs built on the rhetorical traditions found themselves becoming less and less successful competitively. In addition, as a result of growing self-examination going on within the broader forensics community, some individuals at non-HBCUs began identifying the absence of women and particularly African Americans from the competitive environment. Well-intentioned efforts resulted in the formation of Public Debate Leagues and Urban Debate Leagues (UDLs) to bring the traditions of debate back to the students in the urban areas of the country where programs had declined or disappeared (National Association for Urban Debate Leagues, 2007). The NFL and Phillips Petroleum Company provided initial financial support for the expanding UDLs. Later, the Open Society would use the Atlanta model to spread UDLs across many urban areas.

UDLs were conceived as a national consortium of cities in which groups of high schools restarted competitive interscholastic policy debate where debate had been eliminated due to budget cuts (Preston, 2006). Melissa Wade at Emory University in Atlanta (Georgia) and George Ziegelmueller at Wayne State University in Detroit (Michigan) were among the first collegiate debate coaches to initiate debate programs in conjunction with local high schools in their large cities to restart debate for minority and low-income students. The series of UDL tournaments that started in Atlanta as a partnership between the Barkley Forum of Emory University and the Atlanta Public Schools in 1985 is "widely considered as the birthplace of the UDL" (Zorwick, Wade, and Heilmayr, 2009, p. 33). The initial goal of these programs was to create a noncompetitive environment for African American and other minority students who had not previously debated to learn debate fundamentals, in the hope that these newly trained debaters would continue their involvement as they moved into the more competitive high school and collegiate environments (Ziegelmueller, 1998). Although it has yet to be determined if the UDLs actually contributed to more diversity in collegiate forensics programs, a study conducted by Allen et al. (2004) found that most of the diversity in collegiate forensics programs was found at institutions in more urban areas.

UDLs were formed to add more diversity to the debate community in terms of both groups of people and styles of debate. In addition, Zorwick et al. (2009) suggested that UDLs became a way for the forensics community to reduce prejudice: they expanded the general knowledge of debates about a wide range of topics, involved authority figures from overarching UDL organizations (the National Debate Project, the National Association for Urban Debate Leagues, and the Associated Leaders of Urban Debate) to promote diversity and prejudice reduction as primary goals, provided training and materials for UDL programs about debate techniques and diversity, and offered summer debate camps for UDL students modeled after the elite camps associated with national circuit debaters. Preston (2006) noted that participants in UDLs found benefits from their involvement (e.g., enhanced critical thinking skills, reading skills, and vocabularies; improved grade point averages). Tucker (2003) added that these benefits enabled participants "to succeed in college classrooms, at workplaces, and around the democratic public sphere" (p. 5).

In 1996, the Open Society Institute partnered with the Barkley Forum at Emory University to begin seeding UDLs in other urban cities. By 2009, high schools in twenty-four cities were involved in UDL activities (87 percent minority, 79 percent low income). In all, the National Association for Urban Debate Leagues reported that as of 2008, over thirty-three thousand students from 311 high schools and fifty-one middle schools had participated in UDL programs (Zorwick, Wade, and Heilmayr, 2009).

While the intentions of the framers of the UDLs may have been to provide the benefits of debate to minority and low-income students (which they clearly may have accomplished), the nature of the debate experience was developed and taught through the perspective of the traditional, elite policy debate establishment. Policy debate was the activity of choice, and the style of debate promoted mirrored what was happening at the collegiate level (e.g., rapid delivery, large amounts of evidence, less formality). Some observers noted that rather than being centered in the lives and experiences of minority and low-income groups, UDLs became recruiting opportunities for non-HBCU debate programs in the debate community seeking to perpetuate the highly technical policy debate that was beginning to experience a decline among some forensics programs in academic programs questioning the worth of an activity that did not promote effective speaking skills.

The Activity Kritik

One of the practices introduced to competitive policy debate near the end of the twentieth century was the kritik, essentially a value-based argument directed against the affirmative proposal by the negative. Advocates suggested that this real-world argument added a higher level of argumentation to the debate. Brayton (2006) described this as "a decision calculus—a framework within which the judge must vote in a debate." Kritiks could be used on different levels (e.g., plan, resolution, philosophical). As an extension of the kritik, the Louisville Project led by Dr. Ede Warner emerged as a culture-centered response to increase particularly the voice of the African American competitor in the debate arena by challenging the debate process itself. Quoting Stokely Carmichael speaking at Morgan State University in 1967, Bailey (2005) wrote, "Perhaps that is the greatest problem that black students face . . . they are never asked to create, only to imitate." When we use the term "culture centered," we mean that the kritik came from those African Americans involved in debate who sought a new paradigm and introduced it as an appropriate way to address their views as "black radical intellectuals" about the debate activity itself. At the collegiate level, the Louisville Project began as a kritik to the debate community's established practices and has been since referred to as a "movement" (Bailey, 2005).

The first aspect of the project was to challenge the orthodoxy of debate. Bailey (2005) described the basis for this challenge: "Many of the Louisville debaters originally accepted the traditional model but eventually discarded it altogether. 'Traditional debate excludes blacks,' said Stephanie Mitchell, who was a traditional debater at her Chicago high school. Herded into Urban Debate Leagues, African American debaters rarely compete with their white counterparts and have distinctively separate and unequal experiences."

Once the challenge was made, an alternative model was advanced. In this instance, traditional forms of evidence were challenged, providing for the legitimacy of organic intellectuals who challenged the dominant structure using counterhegemonic discourse and social location using personal experiences as they related to the topic. To be sure, the established policy debate hierarchy did not embrace the activity kritik. Brayton (2006) echoed the sentiment of many when he wrote, "If I were to judge a team using an activity-level kritik—any activity-level kritik, not just this one—not only would they lose, they would get the lowest score possible and a scathing critique at the end of the round from me. . . . My answer to such kritiks is simple: there's the door."

Despite ongoing discussion, the Louisville Project brought to the forefront an issue that had not been introduced previously: forensics by design was created as a reflection of the established white educational elites and through its very form excluded and disadvantaged those who were the Other. The activity could not be fixed; it had to be changed.

Summary

As the development of a separate forensics culture evolved at HBCUs, African American students experienced through their own structures the values and practices of competitive debate created by white elite coaches and organizations. The forensics experiences of HBCU and non-HBCU students were similar during the public oratory era. However, during the technical era and corresponding with the civil rights movement, forensics for HBCUs changed. The removal of separate-but-equal status and a growing desire to be fully integrated into American society prompted many African American students to realize that their forensics experience may have been one of imitation.

The resistance some African American debaters experienced when they introduced their own version of policy debate at the collegiate level was taken as proof that there was an inherent prejudice systemically favoring the communication styles and formats developed by white men. The efforts by the policy debate community to restart debate in urban areas provided some students with exposure to the benefits of critical thinking and the skills needed for successful entry into collegiate debate. However, the promotion of traditional forms of debate in these urban areas may have been indicative of a system seeking to return to its former prominence, rather than to renew itself as a more inclusive activity for the future.

REFLECTIONS ON FORENSICS AND THE OTHER

The question remains: How could the forensics community in good conscience navigate the ethnic divide that pervaded American society throughout the twentieth century? With the promotion of civic engagement and effective communication as its core tenets, forensics should have found it natural to challenge the established values and practices that discriminated against the African American community prior to the passage of the civil rights legislation of the 1960s. However, the forensics community remained silent about the systemic discriminatory policies, enabling the practices to perpetuate the dominant paradigm within the forensics community until late in the century, and relied on systemic mechanisms such as the absence of accreditation as a basis for excluding HBCUs from membership in the honoraries.

There may be some reasons why the forensics community chose to navigate as it did. The first reason is economic. The extracurricular nature of forensics necessitated financial support. Administrators controlled the funds and responded to constituents who were elites, who held on to their power by reflecting the dominant paradigm. Challenging the paradigm risked losing the funding and support needed to build and sustain programs. Social influences provide a second reason. Forensics was perceived as an intellectual sport, and those who engaged in public debate and activities were very similar in their level of academic achievement and interests. The emergence of honor societies reflected the interest of these individuals in being recognized for their excellence and in being part of an elite group. Elites set themselves apart from others, making it unnatural for them to cross the divisions that separated segments of society (e.g., ethnic groups). During the first half of the twentieth century, the major influx of immigrants into the United States was without English as their first language. This meant that it was natural for those with excellent communication skills to view themselves as elites and to remain introvert-expansive toward others of like background and experience, yet introvert-restrictive regarding people who were different.

In addition, we may underestimate the power of the political and legal systems in perpetuating racist and discriminatory practices, providing the reason for the way forensics evolved. The American Civil War was only one generation removed from the public oratory era of forensics. Those whose families had fought and lost members due to the fight over slavery held deep feelings about the issue and expanding opportunities for African Americans. At the least, the *Plessy v. Ferguson* court decision creating separate-but-equal opportunities provided African American students with the chance to engage in forensics, and it provided white institutions with the opportunity to accept the separation as a part of the normal order of things.

Martin and Nakayama (2010) are helpful in explaining these dynamics through the majority identity search process. The first phase is unexamined identity, in which individuals recognize differences between themselves and others as a descriptive reality. This phase is followed by acceptance of the differences and is manifested by either avoiding contact with those who are different or adopting a stance toward them (usually based on superiority or in response to self-esteem needs). The next stage involves passive or active resistance to the perceptions and actions of the majority reflecting superiority, followed by a redefinition of what it means to be white or in the majority group. Finally, the integration phase allows for the new perspectives to become a part of the worldview of the majority, in which the minority is included in a broader cultural focus.

Applying this model to forensics makes sense. The forensics community began as a group of men who came together to create an activity that enabled them to compete intellectually and to develop effective communication skills that would help them in their chosen professions, which were societally identified as appropriate (e.g., doctors, lawyers, ministers). They acknowledged that not everyone was in their circumstances and accepted their superiority as their station in life. The avoidance of contact with the HBCUs was a form of their acceptance of societal distinctions, and the same white supremacy/male hegemony pervading society may have dominated the worldview of the forensics leadership, particularly prior to World War II. With the arrival of the British debaters, intercollegiate interracial debates provided the impetus for resistance to the superiority of the majority, and forensics began to liberalize. The remainder of the century saw the redefinition of what it meant to be majority and minority in the forensics environment. The end of the twentieth century saw the coming of the integration phase in forensics. However, the fractionalization that resulted during the final decades reflects the continued tension that existed in the forensics community between the established majority and those seeking an alternative view of what good forensics should be, however that is defined (e.g., educationally, competitively, or by level of formality).

CONCLUSION

Not every forensics memory is positive. This chapter identified some of the clouded moments of forensics, when the dominant coalition influenced the evolution of competitive speech and debate activity in ways that segregated and discriminated against the Other. Through our inclusion of materials that were formerly what Martin and Nakayama (2010) referred to as "absent history," we provide a basis for a more holistic understanding of the experiences of African Americans who participated in forensics. Throughout the twentieth century, by its structure and through its practices, forensics reduced the acceptance, legitimacy, and contributions of African American perspectives. Despite a call for the authentication of all voices in forensics (K. Bartanen, 1995), the end of the twentieth century found some forms of forensics to be unappealing to those nonwhites and students who previously had eagerly sought inclusion in the activities. As the twenty-first century of forensics unfolds, the lessons learned from these groups may provide direction for the next generation of forensics educators.

In the next chapter, we continue our examination of the Other through an examination of the positive and negative ways women were integrated into the forensics community. The openings for women to gain access and acceptance created by the world wars and the changing status of women in American political and legal systems reinforced by the passage of the Nineteenth Amendment to the Constitution reflect how societal influences impacted the evolution of forensics.

REFERENCES

Allen, M., Trejo, M., Bartanen, M., Schroeder, A., and Ulrich, T. (2004). Diversity in United States forensics: A report on research conducted for the American Forensic Association. *Argumentation and Advocacy, 40*, 173–84.

Amey, J. T. (1934). Debating at Clark in 1934. *The Mentor: A Journal of Negro College Life*, Atlanta, GA: Clark College.

Bacote, C. A. (1969). *The story of Atlanta University: A century of service, 1865–1965.* Atlanta, GA: Atlanta University.

Bailey, P. M. (2005, January 25). Louisville Project changes face of collegiate debate. Retrieved from http://www.louisvillecardinal.com/2005/01/louisville -project-changes-face-of-collegiate-debate.

Bartanen, K. (1995). Developing student voices in academic debate through a feminist perspective of learning, knowing, and arguing. *Contemporary Argumentation and Debate, 14*, 1–13.

Bartanen, M. D. (2013). "The worst of time" in Pi Kappa Delta: The history of discrimination against African-American students and colleges. In S. Millsap and D. West (Eds.), *The history of Pi Kappa Delta: Volume 2* (pp. 17–33). Ripon, WI: Pi Kappa Delta.

Beil, G. (2008). Wiley College's great debaters. Retrieved from http://www .humanitiestexas.org/news/articles/Wiley-Colleges-great-debaters.

Boulware, M. H. (1947). Speech training in the Negro college. *Journal of Negro Education, 16* (1), 115–20.

Bowles, F. H., and DeCosta, F. A. (1971). *Between two worlds: A profile of Negro higher education.* New York: McGraw-Hill.

Branham, R. (1996). *Stanton's elm: An illustrated history of debating at Bates College.* Lewiston, ME: Bates College Press.

Brayton, E. (2006, May 10). Dispatches from the creation wars: The Louisville Project. Retrieved from http://scienceblogs.com/dispatches/2006/05/10/the -louisville-project-1.

Brown v. Board of Education of Topeka, Shawnee County, Kansas. 347 U.S. 483.

Constitution of Pi Kappa Delta. (1920). *Forensic of Pi Kappa Delta, 6* (1), 27–36.

Constitution of Pi Kappa Delta. (1922). *Forensic of Pi Kappa Delta, 8* (1), 16–25.

Franklin, J. H. (1965). The two worlds of race: A historical view. *Daedalus, 94* (4), 899–920. Retrieved from http://www.jstor.org/stable/20026950.

Gerber, M. G. (2009). Toward public sphere intercollegiate policy debate: The path to participation. *Contemporary Argumentation and Debate, 30,* 80–93.

Hamilton, E. E. (1914). The history of the Phyllis Wheatley Society. *Scroll, 18* (6), 90–91.

Jarrett, H. (1935). Adventures in interracial debates. *Crisis, 40* (8), 240.

Johnson, W. H. (1928, February). Men of Lincoln: What they do in church and mission field, medical work, education, public life and service. *Lincoln University Herald, 32* (2), 1–17. Retrieved from http://www.lincoln.edu/library/specialcollections/herald/1928.pdf.

Johnston, V. D., and Henderson, E. G. (1917). Debating and athletics in colored colleges. *Crisis, 14,* 129–30.

Lincoln wins first interracial international debate. (1927). *Lincoln News,* 7. Photocopy in possession of the authors.

Little, M. H. (2002). The extra-curricular activities of black college students, 1868–1940. *Journal of African American History, 87,* 43–55.

Mangum, C. S., Jr. (1940). *The legal status of the Negro.* Chapel Hill: University of North Carolina Press.

Martin, J. N., and Nakayama, T. K. (2010). *Intercultural communication in contexts* (5th ed.). Boston: McGraw-Hill.

Murphy, J. M. (1989). Separate and unequal: Women in the public address events. *National Forensic Journal, 7,* 115–25.

National Association for Urban Debate Leagues. (2007). Urban debate history. Retrieved from http://www.urbandebate.org/debatehistory.shtml.

Parker, J. W. (1940). Current debate practices in thirty Negro colleges. *Journal of Negro Education, 9* (1), 32–38.

Parker, J. W. (1955). The status of debate in the Negro college. *Journal of Negro Education, 24* (2), 146–53.

Parker, J. W. (1957). Some observations on debate in the Negro college. *Forensic of Pi Kappa Delta, 52* (2), 67–71.

Preston, C. T., Jr. (2006). The interconnectedness between intercollegiate policy debate and the Urban Debate Leagues: From a distance, five years and change later. *Contemporary Argumentation and Debate, 27,* 157–72.

Rarig, F. M., and Greaves, H. S. (1954). National speech organizations and speech education. In K. R. Wallace (Ed.), *History of speech education in America: Background studies* (pp. 490–517). New York: Appleton-Century-Crofts.

Riggins, S. H. (1997). *The language and politics of exclusion: Others in discourse.* Thousand Oaks, CA: Sage.

Secretary's minutes of the Fourth Biennial Convention. (1922). *Forensic of Pi Kappa Delta, 8* (1), 1–13.

Tolson, M. B. (1935). Interracial debates. *Forensic of Pi Kappa Delta, 21,* 142–45.

Tucker, E. (2003). Building high schools to educate the new majority: Teachers see UDLs as an instrument to improve critical literacy skills. *Urban Debate Chronicle, 2* (1), 5.

U.S. Department of the Interior, Bureau of Education. (1896). *Report of the Commissioner of Education, 1890–91* (Vols. 1 and 2). Washington, DC: Author.

Wiltz, T. (2011/2012, December–January). A worthy professor. *AARP Magazine,* n.p.

Ziegelmueller, G. (1998). The Detroit experience. *Contemporary Argumentation and Debate, 19,* 85–88.

Zorwick, M. L. W., Wade, M. M., and Heilmayr, D. P. (2009). Urban debate and prejudice reduction: The contact hypothesis in action. *Contemporary Argumentation and Debate, 30,* 30–51.

10

❖ ❖

The "Other" Sex

Women and the Forensics Experience

In chapter 9, we began our discussion of how the forensics community Othered individuals and groups, preventing full participation. While African Americans experienced overt discrimination as they were excluded from the national forensic honoraries and thus forced to create their own parallel forensics system of competition, women also were excluded overtly and subtly. In this chapter, we reveal the dominant paradigm of forensics, created by men and for men, shaping how women were perceived and devalued as competitors and teammates. Then we briefly describe the educational context facing women in the twentieth century and how women experienced competition in the public oratory and technical eras.

THE DOMINANT PARADIGM

To begin, we must identify the dominant paradigm of forensics as white male hegemony. Men founded forensics. Rarig and Greaves (1954) documented what archival research verified: the first publicly popular intercollegiate debates were organized in 1892 by male students at Harvard and Yale; Delta Sigma Rho (DSR) was founded in 1906 by Henry E. Gordon (Iowa), E. E. McDermott (Minnesota), and Thomas C. Trueblood (Michigan); Tau Kappa Alpha began in 1908 through the efforts of Oswald Ryan (Butler University); Pi Kappa Delta (PKD) got its start in 1913 from John Shields (Ottawa University), Edgar A. Vaughn (Kansas State), and E. R. Nichols (Ripon College); and Phi Rho Pi (PRP) formed under the leadership of Roland Shackson (Grand Rapids Junior College, Michigan). At the high school level, Bruno E. Jacob (Ripon, Wisconsin), a member of PKD, founded the National Forensic League (NFL). As a discipline, seventeen men formed the National Association of Academic Teachers of Public Speaking (NAATPS) in 1914. While there may have been others, these men referred to themselves as founders and often communicated to their constituencies as such.

Further perpetuating their dominance, as their best forensics students graduated and went on to academic appointments elsewhere, they brought the perspectives of their own coaches and mentors to their new assignments. This inbred nature of forensics, stemming from some of the most successful programs, meant that the dominant paradigm continued. Murphy (1989) discussed this inbred tendency when describing programs, perceived to be powerhouses in the late twentieth century, continuing to rely on coaches trained at particular schools with established programs and forensics traditions. Continuing throughout the twentieth century, men held the prominent leadership positions in forensics organizations and were the impetus for new groups and movements that sought change in the forensics landscape—for example, the National Debate Tournament (NDT), the Cross-Examination Debate Association (CEDA), the National Forensic Association, and the Guild of Forensic Educators, to name a few.

The history of public and private education in America documents a white male paradigm that affected who matriculated to secondary and postsecondary schools, as well as how they functioned within and were rewarded by those institutions. White male students involved in high school and collegiate forensics comprised the vast majority. Yearbooks and professional photographs displaying the literary and debating societies show either groups of white men or white women or teams of mostly white men with a few white women. The presence of ethnic diversity is an anomaly. While high schools had more of a balance between boys and girls in their photos, the teams that traveled to compete in international, interstate, or interscholastic competitions were predominantly white men.

When the debates and declamation activities of literary societies became competitive and teams formed, the sports analogy found application. There were coaches, teams, speaking drills, practice debates, decision-based competitions, judges, and decisions with winners and losers. Even during World War II, when more female students were involved due to the absence of men serving in the armed forces, coaches sought students with particular male characteristics, as Smith (1943) suggested: "intellect, physical stamina, character, personality, speaking skill, cooperative attitude, a willingness to work, and a willingness to accept criticism" (p. 255).

These characteristics were all associated with male students, as women were perceived as weaker, of questionable character, having limited personality and a feminine, ineffective speaking style, and being uncooperative, unwilling to work, and unable to accept criticism. Cowperthwaite and Baird (1954) characterized the acceptance of women in debate, as follows: "Throughout the early years of intercollegiate forensic competition, the appearance of women upon the public platform continued to be viewed with disfavor" (p. 269). Students in forensics, it was commonly believed, needed to possess superior intellect with the capacity to handle the added research and preparation without it affecting their other academic pursuits. In addition, the actual work of debate was such that superior physical stamina was required to handle the long hours of preparation and the travel to practices and regularly scheduled debates. Women had to be prepared to manage the schedule at all times of the month. In the pre–Title IX era, men were more easily cast as meeting these characteristics than women.

For female students to compete, they either demonstrated considerable talent or adapted to the male paradigm used by the white European males who dominated the coaching and judging roles. Once accepted into the competitive environment, women felt additional pressure to maintain the male paradigm. A 1920 article in the *Forensic of Phi Delta Kappa* about equal suffrage for women, in addition to stating that PKD made no distinction in its membership between men and women, said that the passage of the Nineteenth Amendment placed additional responsibility on those women who were already members to "themselves exemplify an intelligent and active citizenship and . . . be leaders in bringing their emancipated sisters up to the standards which our Order sets before all those belonging to it" ("Equal Suffrage," 1920, p. 5).

In short, the dominant paradigm of forensics was male centered in every aspect. Men created forensics, forensics showcased the attributes typically associated with the male persona, and men sought to control how others were included within the inner circles of forensic leadership and competition. This dominance represented centuries of beliefs and practices about a woman's purpose and role in society. However, just as women found ways to challenge this dominance in other contexts, the male-dominated forensics community could not withstand the pressure to include women in all aspects of forensics, despite the fact that it took nearly the entire century to do so.

WOMEN AND THE FORENSICS COMMUNITY

While African Americans and women shared some common experiences as they engaged the education system in the United States, the basis for their engagement with the system was fundamentally different. While both groups were perceived as inferior by the white male establishment, African Americans entered the country as products of slavery, having been forced to come to America to fuel an economic system. Certainly, in the history of the world, people of African origin were not uniquely slaves. Thus, their struggle in America by nature was for emancipation from the system of slavery and subsequently acceptance by the dominant white society.

Women, however, engaged the education system as the perceived inferior sex based on centuries of Judeo-Christian Western practices that made women and children the property of their husbands and directed women to their perceived natural purpose of procreation and maintaining households. Their struggle was for the right to determine their futures based on individual freedom to control their bodies and their actions. While passage of the Nineteenth Amendment to the U.S. Constitution gave women the legal right to vote, the removal of this structural barrier limiting a woman's full involvement in America's political system did not dissolve the attitudinal barriers associated with including women in civic affairs (e.g., women were incapable of understanding the issues, women would be controlled by their husbands or male family members as they exercised their right to vote, and women would make decisions based on emotional rather than logical reasons).

We cannot leave a discussion of the Other in American forensics without including women and the attitudes that constrained their participation and levels of success. To begin, we briefly describe the context of education for women in the late nineteenth and early twentieth centuries. Then we provide a general description of the resistance and discrimination women faced as they entered the educational system and a timeline of involvement by women in forensics. This is followed by a description of some of the major barriers to full participation in forensics that women endured throughout the twentieth century.

Context for the Education of Women

We will not attempt to provide a comprehensive examination detailing the history of women in American education (see Burstyn, 1973; Faragher and Howe, 1988; Madigan, 2009; Woody, 1929). Three factors generally described educational opportunities for women in the nineteenth and early twentieth centuries: (1) girls and women were excluded from ongoing education beyond the basics (reading, writing, and arithmetic) for attitudinal reasons stemming from religious traditions and customs; (2) when educational opportunities were made available to women, a vocational emphasis was typical; and (3) educational opportunities were segregated to the extent that resources were available to sustain separate schools, and attitudes were strong enough to maintain established traditions favoring male students and faculties. Later in the twentieth century, Gelb and Palley (1982) suggested that the women's movement and federal legislation—for example, the GI Bill (1944), the National Defense Education Act (1958), Title VI of the Civil Rights Act (1965), and Title IX of the Education Amendments (1972)—served to increase the interest of women at all levels of education in seeking opportunities to "operationalize self-determination for women in political, economic and social roles" (p. 4). However, despite increased interest and activity, women continued to face the impacts of male hegemony stemming from years of established practices associated with privileging the communicative style and social practices of white males (Scott and Smith, 1969).

Exclusion of Girls and Women

Throughout history, in most cultures, women have faced the reality of being labeled by most established male hierarchies as intellectually inferior and physically weaker. Relegated to the domestic environment of the home with the expressed purpose of raising offspring and maintaining the household, a woman's place has been defined nearly universally across most cultures. As a result, the educational emphasis for girls and women in the United States, even into the late twentieth century, was on providing training in the skills needed to cook, clean, and care for children. Formal education beyond the basics was considered unnecessary and wasteful, and encouragement and training for women to participate fully in civic affairs was unheard of. A review of the American political system at the federal level reinforced the impact of this belief as the absence of prominent women in elected political office continued throughout the twentieth century.

Limited Educational Opportunities

In colonial America, all boys and girls were taught the basics at dame schools. Madigan (2009) defined dame schools as home instruction for small groups of children led by a woman, modeled after the English system. The boys were taught the skills needed to attend the town schools or academies, while the girls learned what was needed to function in their home environments. The expectation was that most of the girls would not go on for additional schooling. While some girls did attend the town schools, especially if their families had financial status, they typically attended at different times from the boys (e.g., either at different times of the day or seasonally, when boys were at work in the fields). Educational institutions beyond the dame and town schools were "private, segregated by sex, and exclusive to wealthy families" (Madigan, 2009, p. 11).

Segregated Colleges Developed to Teach Women

Only three private colleges admitted women prior to the Civil War: Antioch, Oberlin, and Hillsdale (Harwarth, Maline, and DeBra, 1997). As the American common public school system expanded, the availability of literature for women increased, the Industrial Revolution brought with it labor-saving devices increasing the amount of leisure time, and employment opportunities outside the home expanded (e.g., for domestic servants, agricultural laborers, seamstresses, milliners, teachers), women found themselves with greater amounts of freedom from the traditional tasks associated with maintaining a household (Harwarth, Maline, and DeBra, 1997).

The result of this freedom was an expanded interest in seeking ways to widen their educational opportunities. The emergence of women's movements in America fueled this increased interest as women sought ways to become engaged in civic activities. The options available for women included academies to provide moral, literary, and domestic education; Catholic church seminaries to train female teachers for girls' schools; women's colleges offering varied curricula (e.g., Georgia Female College, Mount Holyoke Seminary, Elmira Female College); private affiliates of male colleges that kept women carefully segregated from men; and public schools and colleges where coeducational opportunities were available but a two-track system was used to direct men into college prep work and women, African Americans, and minority groups into vocational programs like domestic science and home economics (Harwarth, Maline, and DeBra, 1997).

As women sought entry to the collegiate environment, some educational institutions with sufficient financial resources and endowments to sustain themselves established affiliated schools for women (e.g., Harvard and Yale). As the United States expanded westward and new colleges and universities grew, insufficient male enrollments and economic constraints made segregated schools impossible to maintain, and women were allowed to attend (Rosenberg, 1988). The passage of the Morrill Act of 1862 added support for the inclusion of women at land-grant institutions being established in every state (Rosenberg, 1988).

General Treatment of Women in Higher Education

Rosenberg (1988) described the resistance and discrimination women faced as they entered higher education. Because they already perceived women as invading their domain, male students were a primary source of resistance and discrimination. At the turn of the twentieth century, the male culture at colleges and universities was described as rowdy and brawling. The "freshman-sophomore feud" often resulted in physical fighting and strongly entrenched traditions that had no place for female involvement (Rosenberg, 1988). Because many male students perceived coeducation as forced upon them by administrators, they acted in ways that excluded women from as much of the collegiate environment as possible. For example, male students beat up any men seen talking to a female student, barred women from appearing in the yearbook, and excluded women from membership in student organizations. The absence of women in early yearbook photographs of debate teams or in any school activities outside the classroom suggested that these efforts to exclude women were in large part successful. Even in the classroom, segregation prevailed, with "women seated on one side of the room, men seated on the other" (Rosenberg, 1988).

Male students were not the only source of discrimination, as the faculty also resisted the inclusion of women at higher levels of education. Prior to the entry of women into colleges and universities, male faculty members attempted to show that women were physically incapable of higher education. When this failed to stop institutional leaders from denying access to women, some faculty continued to demonstrate their resistance through their treatment of women in the classroom. Rosenberg (1988) cited examples of male faculty members at several different institutions addressing mixed classes of men and women as "gentlemen" and calling on a female student as "Mr. so-and-so." The denial to women of conventional honors of academic achievement awards also reflected the resentment of some faculty members, who explained, as they failed to acknowledge the academic excellence of women, that "when it comes to finding a job, men needed the help of this honor [Phi Beta Kappa key] more than women did" (Rosenberg, 1988).

Despite the determination of the male college establishment to stop women from fully engaging in the opportunities afforded by higher education, women persisted and coeducation provided women "the satisfaction of knowing that they could meet the same educational challenges faced by their brothers" (Rosenberg, 1988). The serious, career-oriented focus of the first generation of female students to demonstrate their ability to excel at the collegiate level kept to a minimum the need to supervise their out-of-classroom activities. However, by 1900, as more and more women entered academia, some of these second-generation students were perceived to be less interested in finding a career than in finding a suitable spouse. This increased emphasis on the social aspects of collegiate life served to stimulate a concern about the mixing of sexes, and deans of women and rules for social conduct were adopted (Rosenberg, 1988). While some small Catholic and historically black colleges/universities (HCBUs) continued adherence to strict rules on and off campus, this stricter focus on supervision continued until policies relaxed at the public colleges and universities as a result of the sexual revolution of the 1920s.

Brief Chronology of Women's Entry into Forensics

While men dominated forensics throughout the twentieth century, women shared an interest in debate and declamation from the start. The literary societies provided an opportunity for women to practice debate and speaking skills, and as soon as women were allowed to enroll in colleges, they formed their own groups. The first ladies society was formed at Oberlin Collegiate Institute in 1839.

By the turn of the century, although women's colleges had been debating each other for some time (Keith, 2007), according to an account in the May 1921 issue of the *Iowa Alumnus* (Iowa City) reported by Cowperthwaite and Baird (1954), the first women's intercollegiate debate purportedly was on May 21, 1921, when the University of Indiana debated Iowa State University on the issue of Philippine independence (p. 269).

The forensic honoraries excluded women from membership until the start of World War I forced the suspension of men's literary societies on most college campuses and the honoraries realized their continued existence would be jeopardized unless they added female members (Nichols, 1936). PKD opened full membership to women in 1920, holding the first separate competitions for men and women in extemporaneous speaking and oratory at a national convention and tournament in 1922. In 1926, at the sixth national convention held in Estes Park, Colorado, separate debate divisions for men and women were added to the competition. The system by which men and women were able to compete was unique, in that for several years, the preliminary rounds for men and women were held at separate colleges and even in different towns. For example, in 1926, Colorado Agricultural College (Fort Collins) and Colorado Teachers College (Greeley) were used for preliminaries, with finals at Estes Park. In 1928, the men were at Otterbein (Westerville, Ohio) and the women at Baldwin-Wallace College (Berea, Ohio). The finals were held in Tiffin, Ohio. Beginning in 1930, in Wichita, Kansas, men and women competed in the same city (Nichols, 1936, p. 206). By the mid-1920s, Berry (1928) reported that women were participating in intercollegiate debate in ever-increasing numbers. This trend also was observed at HBCUs during this period.

Forensics provided women the opportunity to demonstrate their capacity to meet the same competitive challenges that were experienced by men. While there were separate spheres for men and women in forensics and women were generally treated as second-class citizens, any time enrollments dropped at colleges or universities during wartime, women were encouraged to fill the ranks and help maintain the viability of forensics teams.

One factor influencing the participation and success rate of women during this time was the unevenness in the numbers of female coaches. The status of women as instructors was not equal to that of men. There were fewer women, and they were often pigeonholed as instructors rather than tenure-track faculty. It would not be uncommon, for example, for the director of forensics to be a man, with many of the assistant coaches being women. Often these women also would be instructors in public speaking classes. Having good role models is well understood as a precursor to educational success. The role disparity between women and men in the professoriate likely held at least some women back from facing the challenges of entering a male-dominated activity.

While we have focused on the collegiate forensics experience thus far, at the high school level, girls and boys were competing on coed debate teams in some states from the beginning of the twentieth century. For example, Littlefield (1998) identified the first state champions from Leeds High School (North Dakota) in 1909–1910 as Laura Pace, Sidney Host, and Edna McRae (p. 56). Local high school yearbooks from the period show that mixed debate teams were common. In addition, girls were listed as state winners in declamation events throughout the public oratory era and often placed among the top students in the country, according to NFL top-ten records (Mayer, Bond, and Schreiver, 1950, pp. 72–74). Despite what might appear to be a level playing field, however, girls and women were not welcomed with open arms into the forensics community.

Barriers for Women in Forensics

Unlike African American students, who were separated by law from interaction with white students, white girls and women were not legally prohibited from schools that boys and men attended. However, the elite status afforded to male students involved in competitive forensics made the presence of female students nonetheless invasive. We now identify barriers that affected the ability of women to participate fully in forensics during the twentieth century. These barriers were not equally present at all times but rose to the surface as the activity evolved.

Separate Contests for Men and Women

As women sought to enter the competitive arena of debate and speaking contests, they were either subjected to a system in which they participated in separate categories from the men (e.g., men's debate, women's debate) or allowed into mixed categories, often determined by those responsible for establishing the governing rules or those overseeing the tournaments. The motivation for separating the sexes was justified for several reasons, including providing the ability for girls and women to be competitively successful, the need to judge women's styles differently, and the fear that women would win unfairly if they competed against men.

Some people argued that because girls and women were less intelligent, less effective as speakers, less able to handle criticism, and generally less than their male counterparts, they needed separate categories in order to be able to win. The basis for this perspective was the belief in the superiority of the male student, and the motivation was altruistic and patronizing. A second reason stemmed from the belief that male and female speaking styles were different, necessitating the creation of categories in which the unique style used by women could be more fairly adjudicated without the presence of the male style that was generally preferred by judges. This separate-but-unequal status continued in public speaking events like extemporaneous speaking into the 1960s at the collegiate level and into the 1980s at the high school level (Kramer, 1974).

The darker perspective was fueled by the fear among the male establishment that if men and women competed in the same categories, women would win unfairly. One female debater articulated her explanation of this male fear of losing unjustly to women:

> They [women] never win a debate, because they are logical, because they have a good case, or because they are better than the male opposition. According to the male debaters, there are four reasons for losing to a female: 1. The females refused to argue on the males' grounds, and the judge didn't realize this; 2. The females beguiled the males with their charm, perfume, smiles, and sweaters; 3. The females flirted with the judge; and 4. The females had such a bad case that the judge felt sorry for them and gave them the debate. If by chance you are a female debater with a male partner, then he is the object of sincere sympathy from all other male debaters. If by chance you and your partner do well together, then the comments go something like this: "My, he must be good, since he won all these debates with her as a partner." . . . There is always the chance that someday if we work hard, some male debater might pay us the supreme compliment of all by saying—You debate just like a man. (Cole, 1957, pp. 69–70)

This fear that women might win unfairly or come to dominate the male domain revealed itself in other related contexts. As increasing female enrollments in colleges and universities were observed, particularly in previously male-dominated institutions, restrictive enrollment caps and policies were introduced to prevent women from gaining a majority. Male school administrators believed these actions were justified in order to prevent the "feminization" of their institutions and also to attract the most promising male students, who might reject their institution because of too many female students, deciding instead to select a more elite school where men still held the majority and represented the institution in competitive contexts (Rosenberg, 1988).

The Misplaced Value of Women in Forensics

We must acknowledge that from the very beginning, the elite schools where literary debate societies first presented themselves were segregated, and because all of the students were male, the literary societies and debate teams reflected that dominance. Debate was an academic competition whereby the brightest and best speakers represented their societies against other groups on campus or, later, against neighboring rivals.

In this context, forensics was a reflection of the men who invented and sustained the activity. Thus, the first barrier facing women dealt with what role they would play in this competitive environment. Rather than being valued for what they brought to the competition, they were viewed as an enhancement to the social environment surrounding the activity, and their competitive contribution was minimized. Women were fun to have around, and the literary societies were recognized as a social opportunity for men and women to mix at residential colleges where male and female students were kept separate in the classroom.

Because of this factor, women were placed in a position in which if they wanted to engage in forensics, they would need to form their own literary societies to do so. Lillich (1956) provided an account of the first women's literary society in the United States that was started at Oberlin Collegiate Institute on July 21, 1835; the Young Ladies Association's purpose was "to stimulate the intellectual and moral improvement of its members" (p. 5).

Throughout the public oratory era, archival accounts of social activities associated with the forensic honoraries included photographs of women as part of the festivities. Perhaps the words of Pi Kappa Delta's past president Sylvester Toussaint (1963) at the fiftieth anniversary of the organization's founding reflected an all-too-prevalent thought about women's place in forensics: "The forward-looking nature of the society was evidenced in the admission of women to membership. . . . As I look out at the co-eds in this audience, I'm sure glad we *let you in*; what would a convention be without *girls*? Maybe that's why we did it in the first place—for we were the first to have open national conventions" (p. 15; our emphasis).

Toussaint's motive for using the phrasing "let you in" and "girls" must be inferred but clearly reflects the perspective held by the male leadership of the honoraries: the idea that the reason for admitting women may have been to make forensic conventions more enjoyable for the men. This further suggested that adding high-quality speakers and debaters to the competition may not have been in the forefront of people's thinking when women were welcomed as members.

The Perceived Limited Capacity of Women

Another attitudinal obstacle was the belief that women were not capable of debating effectively. Smith (1943) noted that coaches looked for particular characteristics associated with the male persona. Some educators thought it best that women, considered intellectually inferior, were kept from the platform. Cowperthwaite and Baird (1954) recounted what was reported in 1897: "Ladies in that capacity [on a debate team]" were thought to "do no credit to themselves or co-education by participating in intercollegiate debates" (p. 269). Some thought women unable to "argue" (Berry, 1928, p. 90) and incapable of debating.

Illegitimacy of Women as High-Level Competitors

We first must acknowledge that for the male forensics establishment, there was a difference between participation and membership in the forensic honoraries. Women could participate on debate teams at the beginner's level based on the disposition and practices of the debate coaches and institutions. If a coach didn't want to work with women, he didn't include them, as the following comment indicates: "tried women's teams once—never again" (Berry, 1928, p. 90). However, by the 1915–1925 period, women had become the mainstay of many programs, and men's, women's, and mixed teams competed.

Nichols (1937) observed that mixed teams were more common in high schools and junior colleges, following Pi Kappa Delta's established separate categories for men and women. In a survey of intercollegiate debate programs in the Midwest, Berry (1928) found that nine out of every ten colleges had women participating in intercollegiate debate, and forty-four of the fifty-six institutions responding had separate women's teams, with some eleven of those having a separate coach for the women.

Despite what appeared to be a growing presence of female contestants in forensics, the presence of women among the top debaters and speakers (as archival photographs of winning debate teams during the period suggested) was not as apparent. While no statistics exist to substantiate our claims during the public oratory era, several studies of forensics during the technical era substantiated the argument that the higher the level of competition, the lower the percentage of female contestants included among the winners (see Bartanen's 1995 review of literature exploring participation and success rates of men and women; Matz and Bruschke, 2006; Olson, 2001).

The Perceived Sexual Vulnerability of Women

The fourth barrier for women was overcoming what was thought to be their sexual vulnerability. The mind-set that women needed to be protected drew from societal beliefs that women were easily manipulated and could be taken advantage of by unscrupulous men. Having a female chaperone for the female debaters was an added expense, and it was unlikely that a female coach would be sent to supervise male students, further reflecting the practice of and need for hiring men to coach the debate team. As late as 1948, forensic publications were addressing questions such as this: Is it proper for teams of girls to make overnight debate trips alone, with a coach or other chaperone? Based upon the response provided, the different standards for men and women were evident: "In college debate . . . teams of men go around the world alone, and teams of girls cannot be found hundreds of miles from home without a chaperone or coach" (Musgrave, 1948, p. 89).

Publications provided reasons why, even after graduation, there was special value for "even the humble housewife" drawn from forensics participation—for example, deliberation skills were needed for a wife when conversing with her husband, knowledge of justice and fair play provided the basis for disciplining children, understanding preemptive arguments and consistent use of evidence would come in handy when negotiating with teenagers, and refutation skills would save the housewife from unscrupulous traveling salesmen (Fenner, 1955).

Perceived Role for Women in Policy-Making or Leadership Positions

Women were not perceived to be of value for their contributions following their forensic involvement. In a 1952 article by Nichols codifying American debate, there was no mention of women or their contributions to the activity. A decade later, at the golden anniversary of PKD, women were still absent from the list of presidents, secretary-treasurers, and journal editors. Not until 1965 was Georgia Bowman of William Jewell College in Liberty, Missouri, elected president, and it would be another twenty years before a second woman was elected to that office. Women did not hold prominence in any of the male-dominated forensic honoraries. When DSR celebrated its fiftieth anniversary, only one woman (Helen Catherine Newman, the first female librarian of the U.S. Supreme Court) was noted among its celebrated alumni; similarly, for PKD, two out of the "famous fifty" were women (Elisabeth Howard Elliott, a missionary in Ecuador, and Evelyn Hunter Whitcomb, a teacher and school administrator).

We noted earlier in this chapter one important reason for this gender disparity. Women were treated very differently in universities with regard to their positions within departments. They often were instructors rather than tenure-track professors, especially in the larger research universities. Their research and teaching were also found in subjects such as oral interpretation and theater and less commonly in argumentation and debate. World War II provided the impetus for more women to hold leadership positions. In the same way that the war opened opportunities for competitors, it also created a need for women to replace men to keep the various professional organizations running. While there was not an immediate shift in perceptions that would lead to women assuming an equal leadership role, it certainly was a step in overcoming such prejudice.

High school forensics experienced a similar dearth of women in leadership positions at the national level. The NFL had no women as national officers between 1925 and 1950, while twenty-six men served the organization as national president, vice president, secretary, or director, and six men edited the *Rostrum* (Mayer, Bond, and Schreiver, 1950, pp. 12–20). When the organization recognized individuals for significant service, ten men were identified during the first twenty-five years (Mayer, Bond, and Schreiver, 1950, pp. 64–65). As high school forensics moved into the technical era and beyond, women experienced a similar shutout, as only one woman—Carmendale Fernandes of California—was elected to serve as the national president of the NFL during the twentieth century.

An initial explanation for the absence of women as forensic leaders during the public oratory period may have been the fact that women did not enter the academy as faculty in significant numbers until the 1930s, when roughly 28 percent of the faculty was female (Rosenberg, 1988). This coincided with what likely were the mid-careers of most of the established male forensic hierarchy, who were not ready or willing to relinquish their control over the activity or the forensic honoraries.

As forensics moved into the post–World War II era and the technical emphasis of higher education spread into competitive debate, the former speech departments were evolving into communication departments with areas of specialization and an increased demand for scholarly output from the faculty. As this transition occurred, female faculty with children and families experienced great pressures due to the increased expectations for research adding to the demands of a competitive coaching schedule. A consequence of this transition was a reduction of women in the coaching and judging ranks, limiting the influence of women in the decision-making of the national forensics establishment and further contributing to the preference of male coaches and judges for the "comfortable, conservative discourse reflecting the rational world paradigm . . . preventing legitimate alternative strategies from achieving success" (Murphy, 1989, p. 122).

Women in the Technical Era

As forensics became more technical, norms associated with new forms of proof and delivery shaped debate and the individual events in profound ways. Standards evolved that challenged the established practices and placed competitors in a new environment in which success was determined on the basis of how well one adapted. By nature, the new norms were developed by the dominant groups within the community, which were predominantly men and favored the male contestant. Female contestants had two choices: either master the characteristically male-centered skills and experience success or rely on "alternative styles of communication based upon their subordinate status, their tasks, the division of labor between the sexes, and their talk among themselves" (Murphy, 1989, p. 120), become frustrated with their inability to achieve success in competitive contexts, and "grow discouraged about the activity" (p. 122).

Even when women mastered the norms and succeeded in the male-dominated environment, their presence was not welcome, as male critics attacked their success as the product of bitchiness and overaggressiveness. Murphy (1989) further suggested that adapting placed women in a less than satisfying situation:

In order to succeed, women must speak a foreign tongue. And these adaptations also extend to nonverbal attributes. Women are encouraged to speak more slowly, to lower the pitch of their voices, and, in many ways, to appear in the proper suit, imitating a man, in public address. Such changes create distinct discomfort on the part of many women, who are then also told that they need a more "natural" delivery style. Given such circumstances, women are unlikely to reach their potential in the activity. (p. 123)

The result of the constant push-back from the dominant male hegemony was a decline in participation by women in debate as the century came to a close. A review of gender inequity in debate by Matz and Bruschke (2006) revealed that "the percentage of female collegiate debate competitors is low compared to the population of females enrolled in universities and colleges," despite the fact that women were overtaking men by several percentage points in national enrollment trends (p. 29). Using the NDT and CEDA as examples, Southworth (2003) found that between 1947 and 2002, female participation never exceeded 24 percent at the NDT, and Stepp and Gardner (2001) concluded that female debaters never exceeded 41 percent of the participants in preliminary rounds. The reasons for these figures may vary, but the overall conclusion to be drawn supports the argument made by Kristine Bartanen (1995) that forensics reduces the acceptance of feminine perspectives, preferring the masculine style, and that until all voices are authenticated, the subordination of women in forensics will continue.

CONCLUSION

Much about women's role in forensics is characteristically similar to what women have faced throughout the history of Western civilization. In a world dominated by men, either women have been forced to take on the characteristics of men to achieve their goals or they have accepted the place assigned to them by the dominant order. For women in twentieth-century America, more choices were available than at any time in history as a result of the Nineteenth Amendment giving women the right to vote. However, challenges continued throughout the educational system as women sought their rightful place. We have discussed several obstacles that women faced in their struggle to compete. Some of these obstacles were still prevalent as the technical era came to an end.

In the final chapter, we return to our initial argument that forensics was socially constructed through the communication and practices of a group of students and forensics educators who found the competitive structures and outcomes enjoyable and satisfying. In addition, while it may be too soon to have enough historical distance to make a judgment, we suggest some aspects of the postmodern era that may have an impact on how forensics evolves through the remainder of the twenty-first century.

REFERENCES

Bartanen, K. (1995). Developing student voices in academic debate through a feminist perspective of learning, knowing, and arguing. *Contemporary Argumentation and Debate, 14,* 1–13.

Berry, M. F. (1928). A survey of intercollegiate debate in the Midwest debate conference. *Quarterly Journal of Speech, 14* (1), 86–94.

Burstyn, J. N. (1973). Women and education: A survey of recent historical research. *Educational Leadership.* Retrieved from http://www.ascd.org/ASCD/pdf/journals/ed_lead/el_197311_burstyn.pdf.

Cole, N. (1957). Trials and tribulations of a woman debater. *Gavel of Delta Sigma Rho, 39* (3), 69–70.

Cowperthwaite, L. L., and Baird, A. C. (1954). Intercollegiate debating. In K. R. Wallace (Ed.), *History of speech education in America: Background studies* (pp. 259–76). New York: Appleton-Century-Crofts.

Equal suffrage. (1920). *Forensic of Pi Kappa Delta, 6* (2), 5.

Faragher, J. M., and Howe, F. (1988). *Women in higher education: Essays from the Mount Holyoke College sesquicentennial symposia.* New York: W. W. Norton.

Fenner, F. (1955). The value of forensic training in domestic life. *Gavel of Delta Sigma Rho, 37* (3), 50, 67.

Gelb, J., and Palley, M. L. (1982). *Women and public policies.* Princeton, NJ: Princeton University Press.

Harwarth, I., Maline, M., and DeBra, E. (1997). *Women's colleges in the United States: History, issues, and challenges.* Darby, PA: Diane Publishing Company. Retrieved from http://www2.gov/offices/OERI/PLLI/webreprt.html.

Keith, W. M. (2007). *Democracy as discussion: Civic education and the American Forum Movement.* Lanham, MD: Rowman & Littlefield.

Kramer, C. (1974). Women's speech: Separate but unequal? *Quarterly Journal of Speech, 60,* 14–24.

Lillich, R. B. (1956). The first ladies literary society. *Gavel of Delta Sigma Rho, 39* (1), 5–7.

Littlefield, R. S. (1998). *Voices on the prairie: Bringing speech and theatre to North Dakota.* Fargo, ND: Institute for Regional Studies.

Madigan, J. C. (2009). The education of girls and women in the United States: A historical perspective. *Advances in Gender and Education, 1,* 11–13.

Matz, S. I., and Bruschke, J. (2006). Gender inequity in debate, legal and business professions. *Contemporary Argumentation and Debate, 27,* 29–47.

Mayer, J. E., Bond, T. C., and Schreiver, L. D. (1950). *The National Forensic League, 1925–1950.* Ripon, WI: The National Forensic League.

Murphy, J. M. (1989). Separate and unequal: Women in the public address events. *National Forensic Journal, 7*, 115–25.

Musgrave, G. M. (1948). Technically speaking. *Debater's Magazine, 4* (2), 89–90.

Nichols, E. R. (1936). A historical sketch of intercollegiate debating: II. *Quarterly Journal of Speech, 22* (4), 591–603.

Nichols, E. R. (1937). A historical sketch of intercollegiate debating: III. *Quarterly Journal of Speech, 23* (2), 259–79.

Nichols, E. R. (1952). Codifying American debating: Rules and customs. *Speech Activities, 8* (3).

Olson, C. D. (2001). Extemporaneous speaking and gender: Leveling the playing field. *Rostrum, 75* (8), 10, 12, 14, 48.

Rarig, F. M., and Greaves, H. S. (1954). National speech organizations and speech education. In K. R. Wallace (Ed.), *History of speech education in America: Background studies* (pp. 490–517). New York: Appleton-Century-Crofts.

Rosenberg, R. (1988). The limits of access: The history of coeducation in America. In J. Mack and F. Howe (Eds.), *Women in higher education: Essays from the Mount Holyoke College sesquicentennial symposia* (pp. 107–29). New York: Norton. Retrieved from http://beatl.barnard.columbia.edu/learn/documents/coeducation.htm.

Scott, R. L., and Smith, D. K. (1969). The rhetoric of confrontation. *Quarterly Journal of Speech, 55*, 1–9.

Smith, C. C. (1943). Practical procedures in coaching high school debate. *Quarterly Journal of Speech, 29* (2), 222–34.

Southworth, W. (2003). A history of the national debate tournament. Retrieved from http://commweb.fullerton.edu/jbruschke/web/ResultsArchives/archive index.aspx.

Stepp, P. L., and Gardner, B. (2001). Ten years of demographics: Who debates in America. *Argumentation and Advocacy, 38*, 69–82.

Toussaint, S. R. (1963). This is our heritage. *Forensic of Pi Kappa Delta, 48* (4), 13–16.

Woody, T. (1929). *A history of women's education in the United States.* New York: The Science Press.

11

❖ ❖

Reflections on a Century of Forensics in America

When we started this project nearly a decade ago to examine the evolution of forensics during the twentieth century, we recognized the need for a study that would do more than chronicle significant events or records of accomplishments. Forensics evolved as a uniquely American innovation, and the changes in the activity reflected the responses to various internal and external tensions buffeting the activity. Early practitioners constructed competitive forensics using their values and vision for the activity as both a method of citizenship training and a means of enjoyment. The activity evolved in response to social forces and events that necessitated new norms and practices to maintain the relevance of forensics in a rapidly changing world.

To conclude our analysis, we consider three issues in this chapter. First, we return to the theme introduced in the opening chapter—forensics is best understood from a social constructivist perspective. The evolution of forensics was not haphazard, nor was it always intentional. It was simultaneously proactive and reactive in its relationship to larger social and intellectual forces shaping the century. Forensics was also a case study in the dynamics of intellectual innovation, which can sometimes be messy and frustrating even as it possesses an inherent beauty coming from the whole being much greater than the sum of the parts.

Second, we consider whether, at the end of the twentieth century and beyond, forensics has actually evolved into a new postmodern era. We argue that its continued evolution reflects the same proactive and reactive social construction that greatly shaped forensics in the public oratory and technical eras. Finally, we revisit the importance of the epistemic and rhetorical properties of a century of forensics as the key pieces to explaining why—despite all the controversies about rules, norms, and values, the dissociation from the communication discipline, and the constantly changing educational landscape—forensics has been and will continue to be a critical educational force in the United States and abroad in the twenty-first century.

THE SOCIAL CONSTRUCTION OF FORENSICS

In chapter 1, we suggested that just as social systems construct reality or truth in a way that enables them to develop and adapt to their changing environments (Berger and Luckmann, 1966), so, too, did forensics follow that pattern during the twentieth century in America. From early on, we revealed our perspective that forensics was an uneasy fusion of contradictory premises. There is a familiar aphorism that describes a camel as a horse designed by a committee. It would not be inaccurate to compare forensics to the committee-designed camel.

We observed that the evolution of forensics was the product of what Allan Nevins labeled "consciousness of unity" created by both planned effort and aimless drifting, which have always been present. Forensics was not an accident. It emerged as an intentional effort by students to make themselves better citizens, to improve American life and politics, and to have some fun along the way. The students and teachers who introduced competitive debate and public speaking acted out of an impulse to challenge orthodoxy and create a new learning model, not by reading about it in a book but by engaging in practice even as they were trying to figure out what the rules should be! They reacted to changing conditions, they created communities of the like-minded to guide practice, and they even bickered like siblings in a large family. They constantly constructed, tore down, and reconstructed forensics systems and practices.

Many internal and external forces influenced the emergence of a forensics community and its subsequent construction, tearing down, and reconstruction over a century of activity. Those forces revealed the appropriateness of using forensics to demonstrate how the social constructivist paradigm works. We briefly return to four elements of constructivism (Spiering, 2008) and their application to interpreting forensics history.

Critical Stance toward the Existing Order

The first principle involved the questioning of established order and systems to identify ways to improve or strengthen the social construction of reality. In the case of forensics, from the beginning, literary societies emerged because students found the classroom context too confining for intellectual engagement. Students questioned the existing educational settings in search of an active learning environment free from the restrictive lecture and memorization utilized by faculty training in homiletics, elocution, and the practices of Delsarte.

When literary societies declined and debating clubs formed, students continued as the driving force behind the activity. Eventually, faculty and coaches were included, but initially forensics was the result of students seeking hands-on learning opportunities that were fun and more than what the established academic environment could provide. As time passed, the critical assessment regarding whether forensics was curricular, cocurricular, or extracurricular continued to stimulate the questioning of established norms and practices.

On a broader level, the formation of multiple forensic honoraries reflected the critical stances taken by individuals regarding the philosophy and structure of recognition for those participating in forensics. Each honorary had its own requirements for membership, and each organization developed its own constitution and practices. When Pi Kappa Delta (PKD) initiated the tournament format and tournaments became a focus for forensics activities, those who sought to downplay the competitive aspects of forensics mobilized their resistance through many initiatives designed to offer competitive alternatives to promote a more educational view of the activity. Later, when the American Forensic Association (AFA) formed as the organization to oversee all forensics activities, those new leaders of the AFA who came from their respective honoraries carried with them previously held beliefs that influenced their actions. Those who did not agree with the vision of the AFA leaders questioned their legitimacy, and a fracturing of the forensics community resulted.

Academically, the critical appraisal of forensics as it evolved was clearly represented in forensics scholarship throughout the century. Forensics scholarship addressed the constant tensions between those favoring the competitive aspects of the activity versus those seeking more educational outcomes. There were many sources of tension. Early scholarship vigorously examined matters such as switching sides and following a decision versus no-decision outcome. Other scholars discussed whether using expert versus lay judges was more appropriate. Practitioners speculated regarding the factors appropriate in making a debate decision and inquired philosophically about why a particular perspective was justified. Their investigations were also practical, contributing an understanding of basic concerns such as speech organization or delivery. Writers proposed alternative forensics practices and discussed tournament management procedures. This scholarly tradition reflected a critical focus among those inside the forensics community on affecting and perfecting the activities.

For those outside the forensics community, the shift of focus from universal audience to particular audience to what we have described as preferred audience also reflected a questioning of established ways of thinking. The public oratory era relied on the canon of style and universal appeals that were audience focused.

The benefit of the activity was to create a public good in the form of trained citizens who could engage in the American democracy. After World War II, the activity changed due to a questioning of the relevance of the oratorical style in favor of one that reflected the technical and scientific trends pervading American society. Competition necessitated that arguments be crafted and performances be delivered in ways consistent with particular technical rules upon which participants and coaches mostly were in agreement. The critic-judges represented a shift from the public focus to a private focus, and the audiences were essentially removed from the environment of competitive forensics. As national competition created a split within the forensics community, those participating on the national circuit questioned the value of the parochial norms and came to prefer and expect a particular kind of critical judgment and decision nexus. This evolution provided the basis for considerable critical appraisal from outside and within the forensics community.

The challenges to forensics stemming from the exclusion or minimization of particular groups (women, minorities) was another source of critical questioning, as some forensics educators later in the century began challenging the white male hegemony and judging preferences that shaped participation and success rates for women, African Americans, and other minority groups. Some critical appraisal was evident through scholarship. However, for the most part, the forensics community did not acknowledge or engage the historically black college/university (HBCU) forensics community, and women continued to experience discrimination and harassment overtly and covertly from judges, coaches, and other competitors throughout the twentieth century. Finally, as we described in chapter 6, the uneasy relationship between academic departments and forensics continually produced critical examination as active coaches and teachers sought ways to legitimize their place in the communication discipline and provide ways to train students in critical thinking and the development of effective speaking skills.

In summary, social constructivism as a paradigm relies on the critical appraisal of taken-for-granted ways of viewing reality in order to strengthen the construction of reality—in this case, the educational system and its related opportunities for learning and expression. The evolution of forensics during the twentieth century provided an example of how this introspective, critical stance afforded both those who participated in forensics and those who observed forensics the opportunity to challenge the assumptions on which the activity was based. In addition, this critical stance enabled questions to be raised, structures to be challenged, and practices to be enhanced.

Influence of History and Culture

As social constructivists function within the reality they create, they acknowledge that ways of thinking are influenced by history and culture and that reality reflects those factors. Thus, as the social construction of forensics as an American educational innovation occurred, the contextual elements of history and culture were inescapable in shaping what evolved. These contextual elements included both historical events and social/cultural movements.

The major historical events occurring during the late nineteenth and twentieth centuries that we have identified as factors shaping forensics include the passage of federal legislation (e.g., Morrill Acts of 1862 and 1890) providing public and higher educational opportunities to larger portions of the population (women and minorities); the *Plessy v. Ferguson* decision justifying what was later declared separate-but-equal status for African Americans and overturned by *Brown v. Board of Education of Topeka, Shawnee County, Kansas*; the passage of the Nineteenth Amendment to the Constitution extending suffrage to women; the world wars and the Cold War; and the passage of civil rights legislation giving African Americans and other minorities equal protection and opportunity under the law. These historic events provided the historical backdrop for the evolution of forensics.

The passage of federal legislation and the rendering of Supreme Court decisions were influential in shaping the context for the evolution of forensics because these historical events affected who could participate and where that participation could occur. Because of these laws and decisions, the way the forensics community classified African Americans and women changed. Eventually, the white male hegemony that permeated every aspect of forensics was challenged, and how those who enjoyed that dominance dealt with the entry of new groups of participants had a marked effect on the organizations and their practices.

The world wars represented another set of historical occurrences that affected how forensics evolved. One major rallying cry for a nation in wartime was the promotion of democracy. Debate and public speaking represented an active citizenry and a healthy country. Thus, as the male students marched off to war, the forensic honoraries recognized the need, in order to remain viable, to open up opportunities for women to participate and compete. The influx of women resulted in the offering of separate categories for women (particularly in extemporaneous events) until late in the century. The wars also changed the perspectives of those who returned from battle and reentered the educational systems. As previously explained, with the onset of the Cold War, the emphasis on science and technology in all aspects of society found its way into the forensics arena, changing how debaters spoke, the forms of proof that were acceptable, and standard practices that were best evaluated by the expert critic-judge. In addition, the Red Scare and the threat of Communism worked to unify the forensics community as it rallied in support of debaters having the opportunity to debate both sides of the 1954–1955 policy resolution calling for the establishment of diplomatic relations with the Communist government of China.

The economic impacts of the Great Depression and an expanding transportation network across the United States drew the attention of all American educational institutions and caused a reevaluation of resource allocations for forensics. As a result, the forensics community constructed its own solutions, one of which was the tournament format, as a way to reduce costs and provide more debate opportunities for growing programs. The costs of supporting a forensics program were greater when more students participated and teams had to travel greater distances to find competition. Thus, economic constraints associated with the economic position of the country influenced what became one of the main features of forensics, the tournament, particularly in the technical era.

In addition to historical events, movements and other sociocultural events were influential in shaping the education system and ultimately how the forensics activities were constructed. To begin, the tenets of the Progressive Era influenced the proliferation of grassroots, local organizations and provided examples of how communities could take responsibility for transforming society. Local groups were stimulated to launch their own organizations promoting the common good once they recognized they had the power to create them. The forensic honoraries and even the emerging academic associations reflected their inherent capacity to make a difference in their communities and discipline. The policy orientation of these Progressive advocates promoted civic engagement and democracy, both of which benefited from an educated public trained in critical thinking, debate, and effective public speaking.

The increased educational opportunities afforded women and African Americans in the late nineteenth century also contributed to an increase in the number of these groups attending community schools and continuing on to college. As the twentieth century began, the separate HBCU debate community clearly determined how African American debaters and non-HBCU debaters would interact. The influence of the dominant white male hegemonic forensic culture was evident in the HBCU forensic culture as African American male students dominated and the formality of the public oratory period influenced how the HBCU forensics community constructed its separate activities. The efforts of a few HBCU coaches and teams to debate non-HBCU teams did provide some opportunity for interracial debates. However, these debaters were few and received little coverage in the mainstream forensic publications, contributing to the construction of an absent history.

When the civil rights movement successfully culminated with the passage of federal legislation in 1964 and 1965, the established forensics community made attempts to be more inclusive of minorities in the forensic honoraries. However, the presence of systemic barriers continued to restrict membership and success rates for women and minority groups. This contributed to the development of Urban Debate Leagues and other corrective approaches.

In short, as the major historical events and movements of the twentieth century occurred, they influenced how the forensics community responded and shaped its activities. The most evident effects of history and culture on the construction of forensics involved who had access to the activity and where that access could take place. Throughout the twentieth century, whom the established forensics community allowed to participate and how shaped the construction of forensics.

The Act of Communication

An essential element of social construction is analysis of the means by which the construction occurs—that is, the act of communication. In this area, there were multiple ways that communication among the participants and members of the forensics community occurred: forensics participants built social capital in multiple communication settings, like-minded individuals found interacting in social settings to be enjoyable, forensics was unique because it facilitated communication across levels of experience and interest, the forensics community created infrastructure to facilitate the interaction, and the local and national publications kept all members of the forensics community in touch with each other on personal and professional levels.

First, because we characterized forensics as an educational movement bringing people together in various communication settings (interpersonal, team, small group, mediated, public), the opportunities for communication were endless. A principal reason for the communication stemmed from the fact that like-minded people came together and built social capital by sharing experiences through their interaction. A social fabric was created because relationships were established and maintained. Even the parallel HBCU forensics culture mirrored the non-HBCU culture in its bringing together of individuals who sought similar academic and intellectual challenges.

Another factor that enhanced the actual communication that occurred among members of the forensics community was the fact that forensics stimulated interaction that was fun. There was always a social side to forensics, whether in the form of social exchanges between literary societies, celebrations as part of public debates or speaking events, banquets and parties at conventions and tournaments, or down time waiting between debate rounds while power matching was being completed. While success and winning were part of the equation, being able to talk to friends who shared the forensics experience was viewed as equally important. For some, this communication as a means of maintaining relationships with friends was more important than winning the tournament or competition.

The communication that occurred in forensics circles took place among many different levels or groups of individuals, producing interaction between the participants (students, teachers, coaches, judges, alumni, communities, administration). To clarify, a unique dimension of the communication that occurred was its ability to cross of the boundaries that might otherwise limit communication. For example, students interacted with each other, their own teachers and coaches, other teachers and coaches, judges, alumni from their institutions or others, administrators, and members of the communities they represented. This ability to communicate across levels was unique to forensics. In contrast, as a member of an athletic team, it would be rare for a player to interact with more than a few members of the opposing teams, their coaches, the referees, the athletic directors or school administrators of their opposition, or members of the public who attended the event. For members of the forensics community, the ability to interact with relative ease across levels created lifelong relationships and created the channels by which information could be shared by all.

As competitive forensics grew in popularity, due to the fluid nature of the communication previously discussed, voluntary grassroots associations (both introverted and extroverted) formed to organize and coordinate the communication infrastructure. These associations began at the squad level at individual institutions, expanded to intersquad activity, and provided the impetus for leagues, state associations, and national organizations. This forensics infrastructure sustained the communication by providing a framework within which members of the forensics community could come together to compete, conduct association business, and enjoy each other's company.

Finally, communication took various forms. In addition to the interpersonal communication that occurred between participants, coaches, and judges at tournaments or meetings/conventions, the yearbooks, school newspapers, and publications supported by the forensic honoraries and significant leaders, such as E. R. Nichols, enabled forensics participants to know personal information, team information, association information, and scholarly information as it was happening in the activity. In summary, the social construction of forensics as a competition-based activity with an infrastructure designed to bring people together on different levels and in various contexts was unique and dependent upon communication.

The Mix of Knowledge and Social Interaction

Finally, in order for social constructivism to occur, there must be an interaction between knowledge and communication in order for participants to collectively formulate beliefs and values that will be followed and a language that will identify the participants and establish a common view of the reality created. As we have shown, there were many ways that knowledge and social interaction occurred within the reality that the forensics community constructed: a unique language of forensics, an established set of forensics practices and management procedures, the ability to counter and refute external attacks to the community, the demonstration of critical thinking needed to engage in theoretical argumentation, the opportunity and ability to continually repeat the activity for enjoyment, the commitment to fuel the democracy with engaged citizens, an interest in bridging secondary and collegiate levels, the need for HBCUs to imitate non-HBCUs in order to participate, the ability to develop grassroots organizations to recognize student accomplishments and mastery of the socially constructed system, and the creation of an opportunity for forensics educators to use their knowledge of their field to craft scholarship that colleagues would perceive as legitimate.

The forensics community created a language that was mastered by its members to communicate within and outside the competitive environment. The language of forensics was learned and passed between schools, across secondary and collegiate boundaries, and within and outside academic units. The language was constructed to be audience focused in the public oratory era (catering to the universal audience) and later modified to be critic focused in the technical era (focusing on specific criteria required by a preferred audience). The language of debate and individual events became more specialized as the activity evolved, even to the point that those who considered themselves within the communication discipline but outside the forensics activity assigned the negative term "jargon" to the lexicon of forensics. The significance of this specialized language of forensics was never more apparent than when a judge was flowing the argumentation during a particularly competitive elimination round of debate at a tournament.

Similarly, the practices used by forensics participants and judges that were acceptable or preferred at various points throughout the twentieth century were demonstrated through the interaction that occurred in competition and modeled by the participants as they continued their forensics participation. The introduction of the tournament format provided an excellent example of how knowledge of the process was communicated by competing in the tournament or helping with the management of the tournament. Coaches who wanted to host a tournament often served on the tabulation staffs at several tournaments in order to learn how the different tasks associated with managing a tournament were performed. Usually, experienced coaches mentored new coaches and helped them with their first tournaments to maintain a level of quality that would bring schools back to subsequent tournaments. In addition, the experimental character of forensics (particularly in the public oratory era for debate and in the technical era for individual events) was observable and able to be tried by the participants. With the knowledge of forensics practices and the opportunity to interact by competing or managing, the forensics community established a commitment to consistency. This constructed consistency was advantageous because the forensics community knew what to expect when attending a tournament, no matter where it was held or who was in charge.

Knowledge of the benefits of the activity also was advantageous for the community when challenged by external forces (e.g., Theodore Roosevelt, who considered switching sides to be unethical, and the North Central Association of Colleges and Schools, which proposed that competitive forensics at the high school level had no value and should be eliminated). The community came together in both instances and constructed refutation arguments that prevailed and saved forensics from elimination.

On a theoretical level, the nature of argumentation was such that explanation necessitated interaction about what was known and unknown, acceptable and unacceptable, within the context of the debate. The selection of the resolution, the topicality of the case, the link to a claim, the uniqueness of a position—just to name a few—all required interaction to determine their relevance to the debate. The critical thinking required to engage in forensics demonstrated the interaction of knowledge and practice at the highest level.

A unique consequence of the interaction that occurred when an individual's knowledge of forensics enabled that participant to engage in transformative-integrative play was fun. The repetitive nature of forensic competition allowed participants, coaches, and judges to repeat the activity over and over again. The excitement, satisfaction, or thrill of participation resulted because of the participants' ability to use the language and preferred practices to successfully interact with opponents and persuade the judge that they had done the better job of debating or presenting their speech. The desire to do it again was compelling.

Since forensics often was justified because it developed skills that would enable its participants to become engaged citizens, the principles of democracy and civic engagement were reinforced through the convention of forensics speaking. As technology became more readily available to the general American public, the forensics community constructed ways to use the media (radio and television) to transmit debates to the American public. This was an attempt to demonstrate the relevance of forensics training for engaged citizens.

Knowledge and social interaction also were evident as forensics developed in parallel fashion at the secondary and collegiate levels. The interaction between high school and collegiate forensics demonstrated how the knowledge and practices of participants at one level influenced norms and standard practices used at the other level. For some at the high school level, the practices of collegiate debate were considered detrimental to the future of high school debate. Specifically, the national circuit style and the so-called elite community of the college National Debate Tournament (NDT) became a constructed reality that high schools with sufficient resources found attractive. As teams at both the college and secondary levels adopted highly technical and specialized forms of NDT debate, those schools that did not participate on the national circuit often felt that they were considered as second-class citizens when the two groups mixed. On another level, the African American students and women who engaged in debate were similarly degraded and unsuccessful in competitive situations if they did not conform to the NDT style of debate.

Certainly, the parallel development of the HBCU and non-HBCU forensics communities was a classic example of how knowledge of particular forensics practices from one context influenced the knowledge and practices of forensics practices constructed in another, separate context. The criticism of debate by members of the African American community because it did not allow for the creation of unique forms of argument but only reinforced the imitation of tradi-tional forms of argument resulted in the activity kritik. The Louisville Project was the manifestation of what some members of the African American community considered an appropriate way for them to demonstrate their knowledge of what the activity should be in order to include African American perspectives and experience.

On an organizational level, the knowledge of the adult education movement, the Progressive movement, and the rise of an engaged citizenry enabled those interested in forensics to move forward with their own grassroots organizations. The principles of democracy that inspired the use of a constitution to govern were followed as organizing documents were constructed, and the knowledge held by participants of the Masonic principles provided a way for participants to demonstrate their mastery of the principles and practices that constituted the forensics activities.

Lastly, through the scholarly outlets available to college faculty to publish their research, knowledge of forensics was constructed and presented in ways that would enhance their legitimacy within academic departments that were begin-ning to challenge the practices forensics embraced during the technical era. As the communication discipline became more specialized, forensics educators ex-panded their research to explore dimensions beyond the philosophical and practi-cal focus that earlier had characterized their work. Studies of interpersonal and organizational aspects of forensics surfaced as forensics educators constructed their research to conform to the expectations of their colleagues who were disin-terested in the applied area of forensics as a legitimate field of study.

In summary, by using communication, members of the forensics community gained knowledge of the language of forensics. Through the use of this language, along with accepted practices that were acquired through competition and interac-tion, members of the forensics community constructed their reality. Their under-standing of the value of forensics enabled them to refute external attacks. As they became more sophisticated in their understanding of forensics, particularly as forensics became more specialized, they changed their approach to become more technical and engaged in repetitive competitive situations because of the thrill of competition and the fun they experienced. Forensics educators understood the relationship between forensics and democracy, utilizing the latter as justification for the continuation of the activity. The uneasy relationship between secondary and collegiate forensics occurred because the knowledge of collegiate practices by high school participants often changed the nature of competition at the secondary level, resulting in push-back from those who preferred a less technical and specialized form of debate. The imitation of non-HBCU forensics by the HBCUs provided a classic example of how knowledge and social interaction were essential for the construction of a parallel forensics community for African American debaters. In the end, knowledge of organizations and established fields of study within communication affected the way forensics educators managed their business and conducted their scholarly research. Clearly, the social construction of forensics was evident through the connection between communication and the social interaction of the forensics activities themselves.

A POSTMODERN PERIOD?

As forensics evolved, its participants adopted new practices and perspectives that characterized the activity in particular ways. For example, the public oratory and technical eras were distinct in their orientation to whether the focus should be on the public versus the private good. Similarly, World War II became a marker that changed the very nature of educational systems in the United States, further separating the public oratory and technical eras. While there was certainly not a great awakening in which forensics educators and participants suddenly realized that the activity was different, it surely had to be clear that the assumptions, processes, and values of the public oratory era would inevitably need to be adapted to the reality of a world with nuclear weapons, growing anti-intellectualism, and very high demands placed on educational systems, especially colleges, to train students for technical careers, without totally abandoning the emphasis on citizenship training. The question now becomes whether forensics has transitioned from the technical era to what we would tentatively and speculatively label as the postmodern era.

There are signs that the change has begun even if the demarcation between eras is not as clear as a world war in shifting our viewpoint about the purpose and practice of forensics. It is also important to reiterate a crucial point of understanding that when a new era begins, it largely subsumes and alters what came prior. The technical era did not abandon all aspects of public oratory but modified some (e.g., the role of delivery in debate) and added others (e.g., an exploding number and popularity of individual speaking events).

Beginning in the 1990s and continuing in the following two decades, forensics activity exhibited signs that the technical era was losing steam and the activity was entering yet another period that contained parts of both the public oratory and the technical eras but had its own guiding principles. We will not try to create an elaborate justification for labeling the new era as postmodern. The term itself, implying multiple viewpoints, the rejection of singularity, and the value of personal experience, seems like a close enough fit to what seems to be happening. It is also the case that hindsight is 20/20, and it may be some time before the true nature of the era comes into focus and a more lucid view of the nature of forensics during this time will be possible.

Three trends that began in the 1990s suggest that the postmodern era has begun: multiple frameworks, a concentration on the here and now, and the impact of new technologies.

Multiple Frameworks

One characteristic of the postmodern era seems to be a shift from the forensics community functioning on the basis of contingency theory to accepting the tenets of paradox theory. By way of explanation, we have argued that throughout most of the twentieth century, preserving forensics as a competitive educational outlet for students meant finding agreement or unity among competing contingencies or alternatives. The result of this desire for unity was the creation of multiple tensions, described by Smith and Lewis (2011) as collaborative-control, individual-collective, flexibility-efficiency, exploration-exploitation, and profit-social responsibility. The tensions we described in previous chapters have elements associated with each of these respectively (e.g., selection of national debate topic, private versus public good, standardization of tournament format, alternative forms of promoting the skills of active citizenship, and the relationship between the high school and collegiate communities). As forensics educators grappled with these tensions, they maintained the perspective that, in the end, unity was dependent upon arriving at consensus about which contingency was chosen.

In contrast, in the post-technical era, a shift occurred that can be described as reflective of paradox theory. Smith and Lewis (2011) described this approach to resolving tensions as "an alternative approach . . . exploring how organizations can attend to competing demands simultaneously. Although choosing among competing tensions might aid short-term performance, a paradox perspective argues that long-term sustainability requires continuous efforts to meet multiple divergent demands" (p. 381).

Extending this explanation, the felt need for unity among those in leadership positions within the various forensics organizations resulted in their making choices that helped forensics to move past each sticking point, preserving unity for the short-term or until the next tension demanded resolution. What appears to be the case in the post-technical era is the apparent willingness of forensics educators and participants to accept simultaneously multiple frameworks as equally acceptable ways to engage in forensics activities. No longer bound by the need for unity of practice, forensics educators and competitors accepted the paradoxes associated with learning, belonging, organizing, and performing in order to sustain forensics for the long term. Our explanation of this shift follows.

The paradoxes of learning "buil[t] upon, as well as destroyed the past to create the future," reflecting "the nature and pace of engaging new ideas, including tensions between radical and incremental innovation or episodic and continuous change" (Smith and Lewis, 2011, p. 383). In the post-technical era, multiple frameworks allowed for this paradox to exist as new competitive events, techniques, and approaches to forensics have been invited as a way to keep participants involved and satisfied with the activity. Unity is no longer the desired outcome; rather, sustainability of the activity serves as the overarching objective.

The complexity and diversity associated with forensics affects the paradoxes of belonging. As Smith and Lewis (2011) noted, these resulted from tensions "between the individual and the collective, as individuals and groups [sought] both homogeneity and distinction" (p. 383). This paradox is evident in the forensics of the post-technical era, as individuals no longer swore fealty to one national organization, but selected among national venues—for instance, the National Individual Events Tournament, the National Forensic Association (NFA), or national tournaments sponsored by honoraries—or multiple frameworks for involvement. The freedom to associate with whichever collective best represented the interests and needs of the individual superseded loyalty to one forensics entity.

Despite the desire of national forensics organizations to provide workable structures for their members, organizing paradoxes also present themselves in the post-technical era, involving issues of "collaboration and competition, empowerment and direction, or routine and change" (Smith and Lewis, 2011, p. 384). The freedom for forensics educators to create multiple organizations and competition structures reflecting their perspectives required that the external environment allow for such structures to coexist. The postmodern era provides for multiple organizational systems that provide both structure and flexibility, where opportunities to collaborate may be found, with no structure preventing their interaction.

Finally, "performing paradoxes stem from the plurality of stakeholders and result in competing strategies and goals" (Smith and Lewis, 2011, p. 384). Stakeholders in forensics include both internal and external groups: students, competitors, judges, coaches, teachers, mentors, advocates, tenure committees, administrators, parents, and employers, to name some of the most obvious. These stakeholder groups are not mutually exclusive, as a college student simultaneously may serve as a competitor, judge high school debate, coach at a middle school, be a parent, and serve as a forensics advocate. Thus, the strategies and goals for different stakeholders require an overarching paradigm allowing for the coexistence of these roles simultaneously, as well as enabling participants to select those strategies that best meet their goals and objectives.

A closer examination of the public oratory and technical eras further reinforces this shift from contingency to paradox theory. During the public oratory era, the main organizing frameworks were debate as the dominant competitive form, the honoraries as the arbiters of rules and norms, and the local tournament as the focus of activity. In the technical era, policy-grounded debate and individual events were the dominant forms, a finite number of national organizations—such as the AFA, NFA, NDT, PKD, the Cross-Examination Debate Association (CEDA), Phi Rho Pi, Delta Sigma Rho–Tau Kappa Alpha, the National Forensic League, and the National Catholic Forensic League—shared responsibility for setting rules and enforcing norms within their own spheres of influence, and the national tournaments became the focus of the activity. In the postmodern era, the number and types of competitive forms have expanded almost exponentially; the number of national organizations continues to grow while their individual influence holds steady or is in decline, and the competitive focus has shifted toward local, national, international, and even digital means.

The number of competitive forms has expanded, creating the likelihood that while the number of schools and individuals participating in some form of forensics has remained largely stable, the number competing in any particular form is smaller. This is admittedly an assertion without necessarily having evidence in support. During the public oratory era the number of participants and tournaments on the collegiate level was closely tracked. The *Gavel of Delta Sigma Rho* and the *Forensic of Pi Kappa Delta* published such information as space allowed. In addition, as late as the 1980s there were publications tracking collegiate forensics. Seth Hawkins and Jack Howe founded *Intercollegiate Speech Tournament Results* as an annual publication that for many years listed tournaments, winners, and tournament size. Howe brought that methodology to CEDA, which, as noted earlier, was one of the sources of attraction for member schools, as they were able to compare themselves to the success of others. There is no comprehensive source of that collegiate information today. But it is clear that the number of types of competition has greatly expanded. Current debate forms include the traditional policy debate formats, Lincoln-Douglas format, parliamentary style, British parliamentary style (Worlds style), public forum debate, and extemporaneous debate (International Public Debate Association). The number of individual events and competitive forms has increased significantly at both the high school and the college levels.

The number of governing bodies for forensics also expanded at the likely decline in influence of any single organization. The AFA, created early in the technical era with the intention, for at least some of its founders, of being the umbrella organization, has largely left governance to the various organizations and their members. Articles about forensics pedagogy and practices are rarely published in the organization's journal, and there has been little progress or interest in refining professional standards, promoting growth in graduate education for forensics practitioners, or addressing persistent ethical concerns. While some schools and individuals are members of multiple organizations, each of those organizations has a core of deeply committed members who wield significant influence on organizational affairs.

Finally, the competitive focus has again shifted toward a combination of emphasis on local tournaments (public oratory era) and national tournaments (technical era), with growing interest in international competition, digital competition, and local competition to promote debate among underserved populations. International tournaments, many using the Worlds-style debate format, are extremely popular and well attended as they are rotated among all parts of the world. The number of Internet-housed debate tournaments, while still small in number, seems poised for explosion. The continued concern with fossil fuel consumption, persistent constraints on funding for high school and college debate travel, and the gravitation of participants toward integrating the Internet and social media into their daily lives and learning habits all suggest that the number and type of online competitive outlets will increase. There has also been a growing interest in promoting forensics among underserved populations, which has resulted in reviving local tournaments, especially at the high school level, as a competitive outlet for students, especially in urban areas, to learn and practice debate training. The National Urban Debate League has grown significantly and is highly regarded in many cities and educational circles.

In short, the presence of multiple frameworks reflects an emerging characteristic that marks the entry of forensics into the postmodern era. Instead of unity as an overarching value in a zero-sum environment, allowance for paradoxes to coexist within the community to sustain its viability has become the more dominant perspective. The tensions resulting from the existence of paradoxes will continue to challenge forensics. However, as Smith and Lewis have suggested, for long-term sustainability, this may contribute to the continued presence of forensics as an educational competitive activity.

A Decline in the Number of Career Professionals

A second characteristic of the postmodern era of forensics may be the changing nature of what it means to be a forensics educator and the corresponding decline in the number of career professionals. While we recognize that forensics began in the public oratory era as organized and managed by students, the advancement of forensics within the field of speech and later into the technical era came as a result of faculty members and coaches who were committed to forensics for life. The archives are replete with stories about individuals who started forensics programs at their high schools or institutions of higher education and were responsible for their management until career retirement. Being a forensics professional was viewed as a vocation as much as a profession. As forensics moved into the technical era, professional training for teachers and coaches was a common component of the forensics education programs, even if forensics as a whole was considered to be a marginal element in the communication discipline at the graduate level. The need for teachers and coaches at the high school level provided some additional incentive for college departments of speech to continue their forensics education courses.

It was not until the social science shift in the technical era that less emphasis was placed on communication education, producing a decline in the number of teachers at both college and high school levels. Fewer individuals made forensics a long-term career choice, some faculty focused their energy on research and scholarly activity instead of coaching, and colleges allowed student-run programs to be a part of their array of extracurricular programs. At the high school level, as the curricular needs shifted to an emphasis on science and technology, fewer speech electives were offered, depleting full-time teaching positions for communication majors seeking jobs. By the end of the technical period, without communication positions with extracurricular forensics coaching, communication education programs saw a decline in enrollment figures, and high schools were forced to turn to recent alumni and part-time coaches to perform the bulk of coaching and judging. As we enter the postmodern era, the activity has, in a sense, come full circle.

Obviously, committed forensics career professionals have not disappeared. But the idea that someone such as E. R. Nichols would spend nearly sixty years as a competitor and coach seems remote. This trend is surely not self-inflicted as much as, like in earlier times, the tides that shape education as an industry also dictate career choices and, more critically, career rewards. Forensics education seems more suited to a format like a medical residency, in which coaches spend time in the activity to, in a sense, pay it forward before moving to other pursuits in continuing the sense that forensics is a young person's game. However, an unexpected consequence of the decline in number of long-time forensics professionals may be witnessed through the scholarship being produced during this new era, often revisiting topics with limited acknowledgment or understanding of the context from which those issues evolved through previous eras.

At the high school level, continuing pressure on outcomes assessment and college preparation through means such as Advanced Placement and International Baccalaureate programs and standardized testing puts pressure on schools to maintain those programs, on teachers to balance that priority with traditionally low professional incomes, and on students to find the time to commit to an activity whose technical demands to achieve success are very high. The postmodern era of forensics is thusly characterized as a time when institutional memory of and long-term association with the activity is unlikely.

Impact of New Technologies

The third defining characteristic of the postmodern period is the growing influence of technology. While the advent of radio and television during the public oratory and early technical eras provided additional platforms for forensics competitors to engage in their activities, at no time has the impact of technology been more evident than in its effect on the content of the messages being developed and presented. The impact of new technologies on leveling the playing field for individuals and teams has never been more apparent. With a connection to the Internet, access to information no longer privileges the wealthy or larger schools.

To the modern competitor, the notion of the card catalog is likely as exotic as the Egyptian pyramids. In contrast, for today's forensics competitor, the Internet and computer have made gathering information on debate or speech topics both easy and virtually limitless in scope and size. Many competitive forms have become even more technical, and expectations have evolved as to what constitutes evidence for claims. This has created a backlash for many, mirroring the intellectual disputes about the canon of delivery in debate in the 1960s. For example, some competitive forms prohibit connecting to online sources during the debate round because not all teams have access to the same equipment. Other competitive forms use Wi-Fi and other technologies to promote interaction between partners and opposing teams during the debate itself.

As noted earlier, online competition, while in its infancy, will further transform competition. While digital-based forms have significant advantages in overcoming the problems of travel and time, those advantages come at the expense of decreased interpersonal interaction. This threatens the socialization functions of forensics tournaments discussed earlier. Again, this is not unique to forensics, as educators and social critics alike decry the social isolation associated with increased time spent on social media and other digital forms. However, as long as participants enjoy competition in their digital environments, who is to say how these online practices may evolve and thrive?

The integration of new technologies into the invention process and interaction between teams and individuals will have a profound effect on forensics in ways that can only be speculated upon in the present context. However, this changing dynamic may have as much of an impact on higher education and forensics in the twenty-first century as a major war or the launching of a satellite had in the century before.

Summary

Just as the technical era drew from the practices of the public oratory era as it moved through its convergence and divergence periods, so has the postmodern era drawn from the technical era (e.g., success measured by individual achievement, forensics as an extracurricular activity). However, three characteristics appear to have the potential to mark the postmodern era of forensics as unique to the eras preceding it: the emergence of multiple frameworks due to a shift from practices to promote unity in favor of practices that allow for paradoxes to exist (Smith and Lewis, 2011), the decline in the number of career forensics professionals, and the influence of new technologies on invention and interaction. While the future always is uncertain, these defining characteristics will shape the evolution of forensics.

THE EPISTEMIC NATURE OF FORENSICS

In chapter 1, we identified five assumptions or themes that would shape our discussion of how forensics evolved during the twentieth century: forensics moved through distinct eras that could be identified and characterized; forensics had a dynamic and uneasy relationship with higher education and the communication discipline; collegiate forensics had a parallel but not symbiotic relationship with high school forensics; the construction of forensics was influenced more by changes in higher education than was previously realized; and forensics was viewed as a resilient and enduring educational form characterized by fun, personal growth, and the creation of significant personal and interpersonal relationships. Given the complexities of these variables, questions remain: (1) How did forensics as an educational movement survive the twentieth century? (2) Why does forensics continue to exist in the educational systems of the twenty-first century?

Clearly, the birth and subsequent growth of forensics testifies to the belief that the activity inspired student passion and public support regardless of any understanding or appreciation individuals outside the activity may have had for what actually was occurring. However, for the participants, the knowledge gained through involvement—at whatever level and to whatever extent—drew them into the activity, kept them involved, and left them changed and better able to meet the challenges they faced in other aspects of their personal and professional lives.

We have suggested elsewhere that forensics is epistemic, based upon the premise that participation creates knowledge that is unique to and about the activity, and that knowledge provides truth or certainty about human interaction in the broader context for those who engage in its competitive activities (Littlefield, 2006). Our broad review of forensics in the twentieth century suggested that regardless of whether particular forensics practices were educational, participants gained an understanding of and appreciation for human interaction that could not otherwise have been attained.

The experience of forensics provided its worth to participants because it imparted knowledge. This learned knowledge was perceived in a number of ways; forensics was viewed as creative, created in context, based upon certainty, involving coping and strategizing, and being processual, argument driven, and culturally adaptive. Forensics was considered an art; there was never perfection as participants strove to be creative in every competitive setting. Forensics was contextual; participants had to cope with the dynamics of each environment from preparation through competition and critique. Forensics was certain; the desire for someone or some team to win in every round of competition ultimately prevailed and became the centerpiece of the tournament concept. Forensics was strategic; there were factors beyond the control of those who participated, and learning how to deal with those uncontrollable elements provided knowledge for future uncontrollable situations. Forensics was processual; while the goal may have been to win, knowledge of the process of winning brought participants back time and time again. Forensics was argumentative; every position requiring a choice was based on the knowledge of how to construct an argument. Finally, forensics was culturally adaptive; participants gained the knowledge of how to function successfully in any culture or community by understanding nonverbal communication, chronemics, worldviews, language usage, norms and practices, and organizational constraints as constructed by the forensics community.

While controversy surrounded the tension between forensics as education versus forensics as competition throughout the twentieth century, this tension was an artificial misapplication used to justify changes in forensics brought about by those who sought to minimize or maximize the competitive elements. The knowledge afforded to forensics participants provided a certainty of truth that could not be duplicated in any other academic environment. Because of this, forensics survived and continues to provide inherent value for participants in the twenty-first century.

As forensics moves through its second decade of the twenty-first century, we who have studied and pondered the construction and evolution of these activities marvel at its resiliency. As forensics educators build and retire from programs that rise and fall, students continue to be drawn to the challenges and opportunities forensics provides. In the end, the knowledge gained by students and the relationships they build continue to sustain forensics. How future generations will construct forensics we cannot know. But we do know they will build and shape it together.

REFERENCES

Berger, P. L., and Luckmann, T. (1966). *The social construction of reality: A treatise in the sociology of knowledge.* New York: Doubleday.

Littlefield, R. S. (2006). Beyond education vs. competition: On viewing forensics as epistemic. *Forensic of Pi Kappa Delta, 91* (2), 3–15.

Smith, W. K., and Lewis, M. W. (2011). Toward a theory of paradox: A dynamic equilibrium model of organizing. *Academy of Management Review, 36* (2), 381–403.

Spiering, K. (2008). The impact of faculty perceptions on international students' adaptation to the United States. Unpublished dissertation. Fargo: North Dakota State University.

Index

311